THE
FUTURE
OF HUMAN
RESOURCE
MANAGEMENT

64 THOUGHT LEADERS
EXPLORE THE CRITICAL HR ISSUES
OF TODAY AND
TOMORROW

EDITED BY

**MICHAEL
LOSEY**

**SUE
MEISINGER**

**DAVE
ULRICH**

SOCIETY FOR
HUMAN
RESOURCE
MANAGEMENT

Society for Human Resource Management
Alexandria, Virginia
USA

WILEY
John Wiley & Sons, Inc.

CONTRIBUTORS

Geoff Armstrong is Director General of the Chartered Institute of Personnel and Development, the professional body with 120,000 members across the United Kingdom and Ireland. He also serves as the elected president of the World Federation of Personnel Management Associations, which works to raise standards of HR management globally through five continental federations representing more than 70 national associations and 450,000 HR professionals.

He has worked internationally at board level in the automobile, engineering and banking industries, as well as serving on a range of government committees and working parties.

Bruce J. Avolio is the Clifton Chair in Leadership at the College of Business Administration at the University of Nebraska-Lincoln (UNL). Avolio is also director of the Gallup Leadership Institute, codirector of the UNL and Gallup MBA/MA program in executive leadership, and director of the PhD program with a specialization in leadership at the College of Business Administration at UNL. His current research interests are in the authentic processes underlying leadership development.

Kathleen S. Barclay was elected General Motors vice president in charge of global human resources in 1998. In addition to her 22 years with GM, Barclay performed HR roles for the Southland Corporation and the Allen-Bradley Company. Barclay was named a fellow with the National Academy of Human Resources in 2000. She is a member of the National Academy of Human Resources board of directors, the Cowdrick Group, the Michigan Virtual University board, and the Detroit Women's Economic Club.

Richard W. (Dick) Beatty, SPHR, is professor of human resource management at Rutgers University and a core faculty member at the University of Michigan's Executive Education Center. He has published several books and more than 100 articles and is associate editor of the journal *Human Resource Management.* He was president of the Society for Human Resource Management Foundation and received the society's book award. He is coauthor of *The Workforce Scorecard: Human Capital and Strategy Execution,* to be published by Harvard Business School Press in 2005.

Richard A. Beaumont, founder and managing director of the RAB Group LLC, was formerly president, CEO, and chairman of ORC Worldwide, and is now chairman emeritus. In more than 40 years of leadership in the field, he served as a consultant to major corporations, various branches of the federal government, and state and local governments.

He also was deputy undersecretary of the U.S. Navy and senior vice president and member of the board of directors of Amerada Hess Corporation. Early in his career, he was assistant director of research for the Hawaii Employers Council and director of administrative services for the American Management Association. He is an emeritus member of the board of the Colgate Darden Graduate School of Business of the University of Virginia.

An author, editor, and researcher of materials on management organization and industrial relations, he is an editor of *Industrial Relations to Human Resources and Beyond* (M. E. Sharpe,

2003). He was a member of the Formation Group of the National Academy of Human Resources, to which he was elected a fellow in 1993.

He holds a bachelor's degree from the University of California and a master's degree from the University of Hawaii.

Brian E. Becker is Professor of Human Resources, and Chairman of the Department of Organization and Human Resources, in the School of Management at the State University of New York at Buffalo. His current research and consulting interests focus on the relationship between human resources systems, strategy implementation, and firm performance. He is coauthor, along with Mark Huselid and Dave Ulrich, of *The HR Scorecard* (Harvard Business School Press, 2001). Along with Mark Huselid and Richard Beatty, he is coauthor of the forthcoming book, *The Workforce Scorecard: Managing Human Capital to Execute Strategy* (Harvard Business School Press).

John W. Boudreau is professor and research director at the Marshall School of Business and Center for Effective Organizations at the University of Southern California, is recognized worldwide for breakthrough research and consulting that bridges human capital, talent, and sustainable competitive advantage. A fellow of the National Academy of Human Resources, he has authored over 50 books and articles that have been translated into multiple languages, won research awards from the Academy of Management, and been featured in the *Wall Street Journal, Fortune,* and *Business Week.*

Peter Cappelli is the George W. Taylor Professor of Management at The Wharton School and Director of Wharton's Center for Human Resources. He is also a Research Associate at the National Bureau of Economic Research in Cambridge, Massachusetts, and currently serves as Senior Advisor to the Government of Bahrain for Employment Policy. He has been a Guest Scholar at the Brookings Institution, a German Marshall Fund Fellow, and a faculty member at MIT, the University of Illinois, and the University of California at Berkeley. Professor Cappelli's more recent research examined changes in employment relations in the United States; his publications include *Change at Work* (Oxford University Press, 1997) and *The New Deal at Work: Managing the Market-Driven Workforce* (Harvard Business School Press, 1999.)

Wayne F. Cascio is US Bank Term Professor of Management at the University of Colorado at Denver. He is past chair of the HR division of the Academy of Management and past president of the Society for Industrial and Organizational Psychology. An elected fellow of the Academy of Management, he received the Distinguished Career award from the Academy's HR division in 2000 and an honorary doctorate from the University of Geneva (Switzerland) in 2004. Currently, he serves on the boards of directors of CPP, Inc., Society for Human Resource Management Foundation, and the Academy of Management.

J. T. (Ted) Childs Jr. is IBM's vice president, global workforce diversity, with worldwide responsibility for workforce diversity programs and policies. He is a graduate of West Virginia State College and a member of the board of directors and a past president of the university's Foundation. He is also a member of the Executive Leadership Council and the Conference Board's Work Force Diversity Council. Childs has served on various councils including the New York State Governor's Advisory Council on Child Care, the White House Conference on Aging, and the U.S. Treasury Secretary's Working Group on Child Care.

James G. Clawson taught for three years at the Harvard Business School before joining the Darden Graduate School of Business at the University of Virginia in 1981. He has consulted with a number of corporations and organizations on issues of organizational design, management development, career management, managing change, leadership development, and human resource management. Dr. Clawson designed and led several of the University of Virginia's Darden School executive education programs. His most recent books are *Level Three Leadership: Getting Below the Surface, Second Edition* and *Practical Problems in Organizations: Cases in Leadership, Organization Behavior, and Human Resources.*

Jean-François Coget is an assistant professor of management at HEC School of Management, Paris. He earned his PhD from the Anderson School at UCLA. His research aims at understanding intuitive sense-making and leadership under stress. It integrates previously unconnected fields in psychology such as cognition, memory, emotion processes, regulation, and decision making. His goal is to further a much needed paradigm shift in psychology and management in which rational and nonrational processes will be integrated.

Debra J. Cohen, SPHR, is the chief knowledge officer for the Society for Human Resource Management and is responsible for the Society's Information Center and Research Department. She has oversight responsibility for the HR Certification Institute (HRCI) and the SHRM Foundation. Prior to joining SHRM, Cohen spent 15 years as an academician, most recently at George Washington University. She has published over 30 articles in journals such as *Personnel Psychology, Human Resource Development Quarterly, Journal of Management,* and *Human Resource Management Journal.*

Samuel A. Culbert is professor of management at UCLA's Anderson Graduate School of Management and an experienced organization and executive consultant. His views are outspoken, bold, and well respected, and he has received a McKinsey award for best *Harvard Business Review* article and an AAP award for best business and management book. His writings include "The Organization Trap," "The Invisible War: Pursuing Self-Interests at Work," "Radical Management," "Mind-Set Management," and "Don't Kill the Bosses!" The latter, his most recent, emphasizes the importance of two-sided accountability in the workplace.

Steve Darien is a Principal in the Cabot Advisory Group, providing organizations with strategic HR management advice on a variety of critical issues including organizational design, succession planning, board relationships, employee communications, strategic planning, and HR technology. As head of Human Resources for Merck & Co., Inc., he was responsible for all areas of human resources management including: employment and placement, labor relations, employee communications, compensation and benefits, executive succession, training and development, human resources information systems, affirmative action, technology assessment, and productivity improvement.

Robert D. Dewar is associate professor of management and organizations at the Kellogg School of Management. He is a member of the American Academy of Management and has served on the editorial boards of the *Academy of Management Journal* and the *Administrative Science Quarterly.* From 1980 to 1988, Dewar served as chairman of the organizational behavior department at the Kellogg School of Management. His areas of expertise include the implementation of strategy through design of organizational systems and delivering customer service. Dewar frequently consults with major corporations.

Ellen A. Drost is an international management and research development consultant. Until recently, Drost was on the faculty at American University. She has authored numerous articles, papers, cases, and chapters on international HR management, cross-cultural leadership, international training and development, and business practices in Mexico. She has consulted to several multinational corporations, benchmarked Mexican manufacturing and service organizations, and conducted executive education programs in Mexico and Taiwan. Drost is on the board of

Community-Based Learning Solutions, a nonprofit organization that focuses on environmental and service learning.

Lee Dyer is professor of human resource studies at the ILR School, Cornell University. His teaching and research interests currently focus on agile enterprises. He has been an active contributor to the HR field since receiving his PhD at the University of Wisconsin-Madison in 1971. He was inducted into the National Academy of Human Resources in 1993 and awarded the Herbert G. Heneman Jr. Career Achievement Award by the HR division of the Academy of Management in 2003 and the Michael R. Losey Human Resource Research Award by SHRM in 2004.

Bruce Ellig, SPHR, is an author, consultant, and speaker in the area of human resources. He had worked as the corporate vice president of employee resources at Pfizer, Inc. Mr. Ellig has been associated with the Society for Human Resource Management for several years in various capacities, including chair of the board of Directors in 1966. He is a past president of the New York Personnel Management Association and currently a fellow of the National Academy of Human Resources. He holds a BBA and an MBA from the University of Wisconsin.

Jeff Ericksen is a PhD candidate at the ILR School, Cornell University. His dissertation focuses on the relationships among HR management principles, HR scalability, and firm performance in small businesses.

Ursula F. Fairbairn is executive vice president of Human Resources and Quality of American Express Company with global responsibility for HR business unit support, recruiting and staffing, all compensation, benefits, diversity, employee and executive development, employee relations, organizational and succession planning, health services, and HR technologies/operations. She also serves as the executive resource for the board of directors' Compensation & Benefits Committee. Prior to joining American Express, Mrs. Fairbairn was senior vice president of Human Resources at Union Pacific Corporation, where she had similar corporate-wide responsibilities from 1990 to 1996.

Jac Fitz-enz is acknowledged as the "father" of human capital strategy and benchmarking. Twenty-five years ago he carried out the original research on human resources measurement and followed that by producing the first national human capital metrics report in 1985. Before retiring as founder and chairman of Saratoga Institute in 2002 he led the development of the world's most comprehensive human capital benchmark database. He has trained more than 80,000 managers in 40 countries. Dr. Fitz-enz has published over 170 articles, reports and book chapters and is the only two-time recipient of the SHRM Book of the Year Award.

Eric G. Flamholtz is professor of management in the Anderson School of Management at UCLA, where he has taught and done research in the areas of accounting, HR management, and entrepreneurial management. He is also president of Management Systems Consulting Corporation, which he cofounded in 1978 and where he focuses on organizational development and HR management.

He received his PhD degree from the University of Michigan in organizational behavior and HR management. His most recent books (coauthored) include *Changing the Game: Managing Organizational Transformations of the First, Second, and Third Kinds* (Oxford University Press, 1998) and *Growing Pains: Transitioning from Entrepreneurship to Professional Management* (Jossey-Bass Publishers, 2000).

Mirian M. Graddick-Weir is executive vice-president of HR at AT&T. She is responsible for the design, planning, and administration of all HR functions including compensation, benefits, recruiting, and training for AT&T's 54,000 employees. In 2003, the Society of Psychologists in Management named Graddick-Weir the Distinguished Psychologist in Management award recipient. In 2001, she was named a fellow to the National Academy of Human Resources. In 2000, she was named HR Executive of the Year by *HR Executive* magazine.

Lynda Gratton is professor of management practice at London Business School. She directs the school's strategic HR program to which participants from over 30 countries come. Her books include *Living Strategy* (FT Prentice Hall, 2000) and *The Democratic Enterprise* (FT Prentice Hall, 2004). She is currently preparing a book provisionally called *Integrating the Enterprise*.

Patricia J. Harned is president of the Ethics Resource Center (ERC), a nonprofit organization dedicated to the development, implementation, and assessment of ethics programs across business, nonprofit, and educational sectors. Harned received her PhD from the University of Pittsburgh and has authored several works including *Creating a Workable Company Code* (ERC, 2003), *Common Sense & Everyday Ethics* (ERC, 2003), *Partnering Character Education and Conflict Resolution* (Kappa Delta Pi Record, 1999), and *The Critical Nature of Professional Development for the Young Professional, New Directions for Student Services* (Jossey-Bass, 1999). Harned serves on the editorial board of *Public Integrity*.

Frances Hesselbein is the chairman of the board of governors of the Leader to Leader Institute, formerly the Drucker Foundation. Mrs. Hesselbein was awarded the Presidential Medal of Freedom, the United States of America's highest civilian honor, in 1998. In 2002, Mrs. Hesselbein was the first recipient of the Dwight D. Eisenhower National Security Series Award for her service with the U.S. Army. She is the author of *Hesselbein on Leadership*, published in August of 2002. *Be, Know, Do: Leadership the Army Way*, introduced by General Eric K. Shinseki and Frances Hesselbein, was published in February of 2004.

Gordon Hewitt is distinguished visiting professor of international business and corporate strategy at Michigan Business School. His interests focus on creating new strategic and organizational capability to compete in dynamic and complex markets. He has conducted major strategy and educational programs for firms such as Sony, IBM, AstraZeneca, UBS, and Microsoft. In his native Scotland, Gordon is on the International Advisory Board of Scottish Enterprise and chairman of court at Abertay University, Dundee.

Paul Hirsch is the James Allen Professor of Strategy and Organization and chair of the Management and Organization Department at Northwestern University's Kellogg School of Management. Hirsch first called attention to the issues of downsizing and restructuring in his book *Pack Your Own Parachute* (Addison Wesley, 1988) and continues to study the issues of organizational learning and change. He teaches in the Executive Programs of the Kellogg School, coedits the *Journal of Management Inquiry*, and received the "Distinguished Scholar" award from the Academy of Management's Division of Organization and Management Theory.

John Hofmeister has served as HR Director for Royal Dutch/Shell Group of Companies since 1997. Prior to Shell, Hofmeister served as VP International Human Resources, based in Hong Kong, for AlliedSignal, Inc. (now Honeywell) and was also the VP Human Resources for AlliedSignal Aerospace, which he joined in 1992. From 1988 John worked at Nortel's Switching Business as HR Director and later became VP Human Resources for Nortel's U.S. businesses. He is a Fellow of the National Academy of Human Resources and is currently chairman of the Advisory Committee of the Centre for Advanced Human Resources Studies at Cornell University.

Mark A. Huselid is professor of HR management in the School of Management and Labor Relations (SMLR) at Rutgers University. Huselid has published and consulted widely on the linkages among workforce management and measurement systems, strategy execution, and firm performance. His book *The HR Scorecard: Linking People, Strategy, and Performance* (with Brian Becker and Dave Ulrich) was published in 2001 by the HBS Press. His new book (with Brian Becker and Dick Beatty), *The Workforce Scorecard: Managing Human Capital to Execute Strategy,* will be published by the HBS Press in 2005.

William Joyce is professor of strategy and organization at the Tuck School of Business at Dartmouth College.

Edward E. Lawler III is distinguished professor of business and director of the Center for Effective Organizations in the Marshall School of Business at the University of Southern California. He has been honored as a top contributor to the fields of organizational development, HR management, organizational behavior, and compensation. He is the author of over 300 articles and 35 books. His most recent books include *Rewarding Excellence, Corporate Boards: New Strategies for Adding Value at the Top, Organizing for High Performance, Treat People Right, Creating a Strategic Human Resources Organization,* and *Human Resources Business Process Outsourcing* (Jossey Bass, 2004).

David Lewin is the Neil Jacoby Professor of Management, Human Resources and Organizational Behavior at the UCLA Anderson School of Management where he is also senior associate dean for the MBA program. A specialist in HR management and industrial relations, he has published 17 books and more than 150 articles in scholarly and professional journals. Among his recent books are *International Perspectives and Challenges in Human Resource Management* and *Human Resource Management: An Economic Approach* (Howard W. Sims & Co, 1994). Lewin is a fellow of the National Academy of Human Resources.

Michael R. Losey, SPHR, is the past president and CEO of the Society for Human Resource Management (SHRM). Before being named to the Society's top position in 1990, Losey served 30 years in HR management and executive-level positions with two Fortune corporations. Losey has been active in international human resources and is a past president of the North American Human Resource Management Association (NAHRMA) and the World Federation of Personnel Management Association (WFPMA). Mr. Losey has also served on the SHRM board of directors and the National Academy of Human Resources, which he helped established. President of MikeLosey.com, Mr. Losey has authored more than 60 articles, coedited *Tomorrow's HR Management* (John Wiley & Sons, 1997), and speaks frequently on HR issues. He is Emeritus Advisor to Monster Worldwide and serves on the advisory boards of Business and Legal Reports and Holmes Corporation.

Susan R. Meisinger, SPHR, is president and chief executive officer of the Society for Human Resource Management (SHRM), the world's largest association devoted to human resource management. Meisinger, who has served as president and CEO since March of 2002, previously held the position of executive vice president and chief operating officer of SHRM from 1999 to 2002. She also served as senior vice president from 1997 to 1999 and as vice president of Government and Public Affairs from 1987 to 1997. Prior to joining the Society, Meisinger served as deputy under secretary for the Employment Standards Administration (ESA) in the U.S. Department of Labor. Currently, Meisinger is a member of the board of directors for SHRM as well as the Human Resource Certification Institute (HRCI), an affiliate of SHRM, and the Ethics Resource Center, a nonprofit devoted to fostering ethical practices in individuals and organizations.

Grant Miles is associate professor of management in the College of Business Administration at the University of North Texas. He received his PhD from The Pennsylvania State University. His research interests are focused primarily on organizational adaptation and the role of knowledge, learning, and collaboration in the adaptive process. His research has been published in both academic and practitioner journals including the *Academy of Management Journal, Strategic Management Journal,* and *California Management Review.*

Raymond E. Miles is professor emeritus and the former dean of the Haas School of Business at the University of California, Berkeley. He has written five books and over 50 articles and chapters drawing on his research on managerial leadership, organizational strategy and structure, multifirm network organizations, and the investments essential to the development of collaborative capability within and across organizations. He has consulted with numerous firms and agencies in the United States and abroad, and he has been a board member of two NYSE-listed corporations.

Douglas S. Newburg is on the faculty of the Department of Surgery at the University of Virginia Medical School. Dr. Newburg was recently named to the Academy of Distinguished Medical Educators at the University of Virginia. As a consultant, Dr. Newburg has shared his work with executives from dozens of major corporations. He has also worked with athletes and coaches at the collegiate, professional, and Olympic levels. He has authored or coauthored articles and chapters in several business publications as well *Olympic Coach* magazine. Dr. Newburg has a PhD in sport psychology from the University of Virginia.

Nitin Nohria is Richard P. Chapman Professor of Business Administration at the Harvard Business School. His teaching and research centers on leadership, corporate accountability, and organizational change. Coauthor of 10 books, his most recent include *What Really Works: The 4+2 Formula for Sustained Business Success, Changing Fortunes: Remaking the Industrial Corporation* (Harper Business, 2003) and *Driven: How Human Nature Shapes Our Choices*(Jossey Bass, 2002). He is also the author of over 75 journal articles, book chapters, and teaching cases.

Coleman Peterson is president/CEO of Hollis Enterprises, LLC, formed in May 2004 following Peterson's retirement as the executive vice president of people for Wal-Mart Stores, Inc. At Wal-Mart, Peterson had the distinction of being chief HR officer of the world's largest private workforce—Wal-Mart's 1.5 million "associates" worldwide. Wal-Mart is a $256 billion a year retailer and was named as the 2003 and 2004 "America's #1 Most Admired Company" by *Fortune* magazine. It is presently the number one *Fortune* 500 Company.

Jeffrey Pfeffer is the Thomas D. Dee II Professor of Organizational Behavior at the Graduate School of Business, Stanford University. He is the author or coauthor of 10 books, including *The Human Equation: Building Profits by Putting People First* and *The Knowing-Doing Gap: How Smart Companies Turn Knowledge Into Action* (Harvard Business Press, 2000). Pfeffer serves on the boards of directors of Actify, Audible Magic, SonoSite, and Unicru. He has presented seminars in 27 countries as well as for numerous organizations in the United States.

Vladimir Pucik is professor of international HR and strategy at IMD. Born in Prague, he received his PhD from Columbia University. Before IMD, he held academic positions at Cornell University and the University of Michigan. His research interests focus on global HR strategies and people issues in international acquisitions and strategic alliances. Pucik teaches regularly in executive development programs in Europe, the United States, and Asia and has consulted and conducted workshops for major corporations worldwide.

Peter M. Ramstad is executive vice president for strategy and finance at Personnel Decisions International (PDI). In addition to his leadership role at PDI, Ramstad has done extensive research in HR strategy and measurement. He is a frequent faculty member for executive education events and speaker at professional conferences. He holds research conferences with faculty from leading institutions to study how people create value and how that value can be measured.

Hayagreeva Rao is the Richard L. Thomas Distinguished Professor of Leadership and Organizational Change at Northwestern University. Rao has published widely in the fields of management and sociology and studies the social and cultural causes of organizational change. He serves as the associate editor of *Administrative Science Quarterly* and teaches courses on organizational change and managing people for competitive advantage to MBA and executive audiences. He has consulted with and conducted executive workshops with executives for organizations such as the American Cancer Society, British Petroleum, Coca-Cola, Group Suez, Honeywell, IBM, Mass-Mutual, and Seyfarth and Shaw.

Bruce Roberson is the executive vice president of marketing and sales at Safety-Kleen in Texas. Previously, he was a partner for 11 years at McKinsey & Company in Dallas.

Russ Roberts is a consultant, professor, and board member. He helps clients turn around declining or stagnant performance, accelerate profitable growth, and navigate revolutionary market and organizational change. He assists his clients in clarifying and carrying out their business strategies, building effective organizations, and developing the capabilities and cultures essential to achieving their goals. Roberts is also an adjunct professor at the Kellogg School of Management at Northwestern University, where he teaches consulting frameworks and practice.

Libby Sartain, SPHR, HR and chief people officer at Yahoo! Inc., is responsible for leading Yahoo! Inc.'s global HR efforts and managing and developing the HR team. Prior to joining Yahoo! in August 2001, Sartain was vice president of people at Southwest Airlines, where she led all HR functions including employment, training, benefits, and compensation. Sartain also served as chairman of the Society for Human Resource Management in 2001 and was named fellow of the National Academy of Human Resources in 1998.

Craig Eric Schneier is executive vice president of HR at Biogen Idec in Cambridge, Massachusetts, the world's third largest biotechnology company. Prior to joining Biogen Idec, Schneier was president of his own management consulting firm in Princeton, New Jersey, where he provided consulting services to over 70 of the *Fortune* 100 companies, such as GE, JPMorganChase, General Motors, and Merck, as well as several of the largest European and Asian firms.

Patricia Seemann is CEO of Sphere Advisors (www.sphereadvisors.com), where she specializes in advising CEOs on how to deal with issues concerning power, trust, and politics. Her background is in large-scale organizational collaboration and the integration of intangibles. She has served in numerous executive positions, most recently on the management board of Zurich Financial Services as the head of group communications. She is also the founder and CEO of her own consulting firm, Group21, which specializes in advising CEOs and senior executives on intellectual capital.

Norm Smallwood is founder, along with Dave Ulrich, and president of Results-Based Leadership (RBL), a collective of broadly experienced management educators and consultants whose clients include Ford, Glaxo-Smithkline, Hallmark, Harley-Davidson, Intercontinental Hotel Group, Intel, and Nike. He is a coauthor with Dave Ulrich of three books: *Results-Based Leadership, Why the Bottom Line Isn't* (Harvard Business Press, 1999) and *The Change Champion's Field Guide: Strategies and Tools for Leading Change in Your Organization* (Best Practices Publications, 2003). Norm sits on the faculty at the University of Michigan Business School's Executive Education Center.

Scott A. Snell is Professor of Human Resource Studies and Director of Executive Education in the School of Industrial and Labor Relations at Cornell University. He received a BA in Psychology from Miami University, as well as MBA and PhD degrees in Business Administration from Michigan State University. Prior to joining the faculty at Cornell, Dr. Snell was on the faculty of business at Penn State University. Professor Snell has worked with companies such as AT&T, GE, IBM, Merck, and Shell to address the alignment of human resource systems with strategic initiatives such as globalization, technological change, and knowledge management.

Charles C. Snow is the Mellon Foundation Professor of Business Administration and chair of the department of management and organization in the Smeal College of Business at Pennsylvania State University. His research interests are in the areas of competitive strategy, new forms of organizing, and industry evolution. He has taught management subjects to students and managers throughout the world.

Lea Soupata, senior vice president for UPS, manages an HR organization that serves nearly 357,000 employees worldwide. She has been a member of the UPS management committee since 1995 and a member of the UPS board of directors since 1998. Committed to maintaining UPS's reputation as an employer of choice, Soupata oversees the company's strategy in training, developing, and retaining a diverse and highly skilled workforce. Soupata serves as chair of the UPS Foundation, the company's charitable arm, and has been active in a number of community services programs, including United Way.

Mary B. Teagarden is professor of global strategy at Thunderbird, The Garvin School of International Management. Her pioneering cross-cultural management fieldwork on knowledge transfer and strategic HR management has appeared in over 60 articles, chapters, and cases. She has served on the editorial boards of seven journals and as Center for International Business Education and Research (CIBER) fellow and research director. She has provided consulting and executive development services to more than 30 *Fortune* 500 companies and governmental agencies in Mexico, Malaysia, Colombia, Albania, and the People's Republic of China.

Thomas Thivierge is currently the director of global succession planning for General Motors. He has worked for GM for 19 years. Prior to his current assignment, he held positions as the director of talent acquisition for GM's North American Operations and as the director of HR for GM's operations in Québec, Canada. He received a BA in history from Yale University and an MBA from Michigan State University, majoring in HR.

Fons Trompenaars is the world authority on Managing Cultural Diversity for profitability. As Managing Director of Trompenaars Hampden-Turner Intercultural Management Consulting (previously known as the Centre for International Business Studies), he works with major global corporations to benefit from the vast opportunities presented by cultural differences. Dr. Trompenaars has worked for the Royal Dutch Shell Group handling operations in nine different countries during his 15 years of research. He now develops programs for cross-cultural management that empower organizations throughout the business world. A highly acclaimed author of seven books and many articles, Dr. Trompenaars' books include *Riding the Waves of Culture* and *21 Leaders for the 21st Century*.

Anne S. Tsui is Motorola Professor of International Management at Arizona State University. Prior to that, she was at the Hong Kong University of Science and Technology (1995 to 2003), the University of California, Irvine (1988 to 1995), and Duke University (1981 to 1988). She was the fourteenth editor of the *Academy of Management Journal,* founding president of the International Association for Chinese Management Research (www.iacmr.org), and founding editor of *Management and Organization Review* (MOR), a journal dedicated to publishing China-related management and organization research.

Dave Ulrich has been named by *Business Week* as the top guru in management education. He has written or coauthored over 100 articles and 12 books, including *Results-Based Leadership* (Harvard Business Press, 1999), *Why the Bottom Line Isn't!* (John Wiley & Sons, 2003), and *The HR Value Proposition* (Harvard Business Press, 2005), and is a Professor at the University of Michigan School of Business Administration. Ulrich serves on Herman Miller board and has consulted with over half of the *Fortune* 200.

Mary Ann Von Glinow is director of the Center for International Business Education and Research (CIBER) at Florida International University. Von Glinow is vice president of the Academy of International Business and department editor of *JIBS*. She has authored over 100 journal articles and 11 books. Her most recent include *Organizational Learning Capability* (Oxford University Press, 1998), a popular textbook. Von Glinow was the 1994/1995 president of the Academy of Management and is a fellow of that association, as well as the Pan Pacific Business Association.

Peter Woollimas is a partner with Trompenaars Hampden-Turner Intercultural Management Consulting and is also Professor of International Business at the Ashcroft International Business School, Anglia University, United Kingdom, having formerly been Professor of Management at the East London Business School in the United Kingdom. He has worked extensively as an academic and practitioner management consultant throughout the world with many leading organizations and management gurus and is visiting professor at several international institutions.

Patrick M. Wright is professor of HR management and director of the Center for Advanced Human Resource Studies (CAHRS) in the School of Industrial and Labor Relations, Cornell University. Wright teaches, conducts research, and consults in the area of strategic HR management. He has published over 60 research articles and book chapters, serves on seven editorial boards, and serves on the boards of directors for both the Society for Human Resource Management Foundation and World at Work. He has done executive development and consulting work for over 50 corporations.

Joshua B. Wu is an obstetrics doctoral student in the department of management, W. P. Carey School of Business, Arizona State University. His current research interests include self- and collective-efficacy, employment relationship, performance feedback, and coping with job loss. His teaching interests include organizational behavior and cross-cultural management. Prior to joining the doctoral program, Wu was an HR consultant at TMP Worldwide and Hewitt Associates.

Arthur Yeung is Philips Chair Professor of HRM at China Europe International Business School and a professor at the University of Michigan Business School. Before his return to academia, he served as CLO and subsequently chief HR officer of Acer, a leading global PC firm. Yeung's research focuses on strategic HR management, organizational transformation, and leadership development. He serves as associate editor of *HRM Journal* and advisory board member of *HBR (China) Journal*. In addition to sitting on the board of a publicly listed firm, he is advisor to several leading Asian firms in Taiwan and Mainland China.

CONTENTS

Section II
INVEST IN THE NEXT GENERATION OF HUMAN RESOURCE PROFESSIONALISM 55

Section III
LEARN TO MASTER AND PLAY NEW ROLES   93

Section V
RETHINK ORGANIZATIONS AS CAPABILITIES, NOT STRUCTURES   195

Section VI
SEE HR AS A DECISION SCIENCE AND BRING DISCIPLINE TO IT   257

INTRODUCTION

THE FUTURE OF
HUMAN RESOURCES

MICHAEL R. LOSEY, SUE MEISINGER, AND DAVE ULRICH

We set out to prepare this book because of our individual and collective passion about the human resources profession. One would be hard pressed to find three people more committed to the HR profession. We each bring a unique perspective to this profession. With more than forty years' experience in the profession, Mike has held HR leadership roles in large corporations and also served as the president and chief executive officer (CEO) of the Society for Human Resource Management (SHRM), the world's largest HR association. Sue's legal background has enabled her to influence public policy and the legislative environment that HR operates in; she now serves as SHRM's president and CEO. Dave has written extensively about the theory and role of human resources in helping organizations compete through their capabilities and helping individuals perform through their abilities. Collectively, we believe that HR matters. We know that HR professionals can make the difference between success and failure in an organization, and that they affect the lives of the people they work with.

We also know that the profession is in transition, with changing demands, increased opportunities, and requirements for new and greater competencies. In the face of so much change, we decided to update the 1997 book, *Tomorrow's HR Management,* and to explore future directions for the profession.

We are pleased that we could work once again with our publisher John Wiley & Sons, this time with Emily Conway, who assisted us almost daily. But most of all, we are indebted to the diverse and talented authors who were willing to share their perspectives on future opportunities, challenges, trends, and requirements for the profession.

HUMAN RESOURCE MANAGEMENT AS A PROFESSION

In 1996, Thomas Stewart, the current editor of the *Harvard Business Journal,* wrote an article for *Fortune* magazine suggesting that HR was bureaucratic and ineffective, and added little to organizational success. Thus it should be "blown up!" (Stewart, 1996).

Much has transpired since that article was published. At a recent SHRM conference, Mr. Stewart led a program for the top HR professionals from *Fortune*'s "100 Best Companies to Work For." This is not to suggest he has completely changed his mind about the impact, role, and effectiveness of human resources. It is more likely that both Mr. Stewart and HR managers have concluded that the profession is here to stay and can become more effective than it has been in the past.

Defining HR requirements is not an easy task given the dynamic rate of change in the workplace. Since the early twentieth century, much has been accomplished in identifying an HR body of knowledge that can be taught, learned, and tested. More remains to be done before we can realize the potential of the profession.

This book is targeted to help achieve that goal.

ANTICIPATING THE FUTURE— KEY TO HR SUCCESS

It is essential for HR leaders to accurately anticipate the future and how such changes may affect their accountability. Without the capacity to recognize and accurately plan for changes in the business landscape, coping strategies cannot be proactive—they can only be reactive—and at a much higher cost.

Given the accelerated changes occurring in today's workplace, any HR leader desiring to make a strategic contribution must look to the future with more foresight and accuracy than ever before.

This is not an easy task. In this book, one author may suggest a specific policy or practice, whereas another may suggest exactly the opposite approach. But who might be correct is not at issue. The issue is that HR leaders, consultants, and academics must examine the present and present challenges for the future in a dedicated and orderly way. Only then can we do a better job than we have done in the past.

This was our challenge to sixty-four HR leaders when we asked them to help us create this book. To ensure originality and to make some order among these sometimes very different articles and their perspectives, we used the following approach.

Imagine giving a group of very thoughtful and smart people the assignment to write something profound about life's enduring questions: What is truth? What is the purpose of life? What is the ultimate source of meaning? Each response would draw on unique experiences and offer different insights.

Essentially, this is what we have done. We contacted thought leaders in the HR profession—academics, consultants, and corporate HR managers. We asked them a generic question, "What is the future of HR?" And their responses reflect the biases and insights of each author.

Then we faced the task of organizing the material, of seeing patterns in the individual contributions, and of connecting the ideas. Our methodology for identifying related chapters was simple. As we read the essays, we looked for common themes and issues. When asked about the future, some chose to respond by focusing on the HR professionals (their roles and how to develop them); others focused on the outcomes of doing HR work (such as managing culture change or being engaged in the public policy debate).

As we reviewed these essays, our organizing logic following a simple paradigm. Look at an HR textbook today. The chapters are probably clustered around the functions or activities of HR: staffing, compensation, training, benefits, labor relations, communications, and so on. We believe that a book on the Future of HR should have a new and different set of chapter headings. These chapter headings reflect the future challenges for HR, not just by investing in an HR practice or activity, but in using that practice to create an outcome of value. With this lens, we were able to categorize these individually written papers as chapters within the various psarts. As seen in Table I.1, each chapter adds deeper meaning to the phrase, "In the future, an effective HR professional must . . ."

Each section has independent chapters, so the prescriptions may differ. But, we can envision future HR textbooks having similar organizing logic. The Parts in this book reflect where HR management is headed: They focus on outcomes, not actions, and results, not activities.

We hope these essays generate more debate than solutions and that they frame future scenarios to which HR professionals must respond. We hope they alert HR professionals to their potential of what they can become and the requirements to do so. We hope they confirm what seasoned HR professionals have come to know, and capture the imagination of the next generation of HR professionals. We hope we have provided a road map for the

Table I.1
Future HR Requirements and Why

In the Future, an Effective HR Professional Must:	*Logic*
Part I Understand and manage people	No one suggests changing the name from "human" resources. People—finding them, motivating them, keeping them, and exiting them when necessary— are still central to what we know and do. We have to think about employees and how to nurture and develop them.
Part II Invest in the next generation of HR professionalism	HR professionals must continue to learn and grow, within the profession and within the firms.
Part III Learn to master and play new roles	HR roles determine what HR professionals know and do. There are emerging roles that HR professionals must master given the world we work in.
Part IV Discern, create, and adapt culture to business conditions	Organizations have a personality known as its culture. This culture shapes what people come into the company and how people react when in the company. Culture is like a firm brand, or identity. It is what HR professionals deliver.
Part V Rethink the organization as capabilities, not structures	Organization is not a structure, but a set of capabilities. These chapters introduce this concept (4 chapters) and then talks about the duality inherent in focusing on capability (3 chapters).
Part VI See HR as a decision science and bring discipline to it	HR is not a random set of events, but a disciplined set of choices. Making those choices clear and explicit helps bring HR from an art to a science. These chapters show how the rigors of HR research change what we do and how we think about HR.
Part VII Create mutually collaborative ventures	Collaboration and cooperation become hallmarks for the future organization. This means that HR must help the whole be greater than the parts and help different units work together.
Part VIII Respond to social expectations and public policy	Organizations and HR actions in organizations are increasingly under scrutiny. Media attention for corporate malfeasance requires that HR step forward to monitor and govern work.
Part IX Live globally, act locally	Globalization is inevitable. It affects everything we do and HR professionals are not immune. These chapters focus on the choices for making global and (not vs) local decisions.

profession and how we can constantly reinvent ourselves that allows us to better contribute to the people we serve, the organizations we shape, and the societies in which we operate.

As editors, we are indebted to the more than sixty HR executives, consultants, and scholars from around the world for their generous contributions to this book. We marvel that so many accepted our invitation and shared their insights. We are not alone in caring about the profession. In addition, we are once again grateful that each author has agreed to donate the royalties from this book to advance the interests of the human resources profession. The editors have directed that all royalties are to be donated to the SHRM Foundation. Finally, we are equally indebted to the Society for Human Resource Management and its 200,000 members for its professional and tangible support in making this book possible. We should note that SHRM is a copublisher with John Wiley & Sons.

REFERENCE

Stewart, T. (1996). Taking on the Last Bureaucracy, *Fortune,* January 15, 105–108.

SECTION I
UNDERSTANDING AND MANAGING PEOPLE

Most of the emphasis in this book is proactive and directed to the future. We wanted to avoid what happens when we do not adequately search for clues of change. Within every management function, the failure to accurately anticipate the future causes incomplete planning or errors in execution that can seriously harm the organization. For instance, if engineering designs something incorrectly, it is back to the drawing board for corrections—and life goes on.

If manufacturing cannot meet cost, delivery, or quality requirements, they will quickly correct the problem—and life goes on.

If marketing and sales fail to meet objectives, they will soon create a new program to meet those objectives—and life goes on.

If finance misses earnings projections, or accounting has debited something that should have been a credit, entries are reversed—and life goes on.

If human resource managers do not accurately anticipate the future and do not plan appropriately—we affect more than mere designs, machines, sales, and numbers—we touch people's lives. Almost never can we undo our mistakes.

There are many examples of failures by administratively focused HR professionals to accurately anticipate the future. And of these examples, none was more serious and delayed progress more than the failure to see and fully gauge the impact of the civil rights movement:

- In 1941, A. Philip Randolph, president of the Brotherhood of Sleeping Car Porters, convinced President Franklin D. Roosevelt to sign an executive order that called for an end to discrimination in

1

defense plant jobs. Many view this action as marking the start of "fair employment practices" and affirmative action. But how many in HR—practitioners, consultants, or academics—paused to consider what this action would mean not only for those who so unfairly bore the brunt of discriminatory practices but for the future requirements of their profession? Not many.

- In 1948, additional efforts by Randolph encouraged another president, Harry S. Truman, to issue an order integrating the U.S. military as well as all federal civil service jobs. Again, how many HR leaders saw this change within the largest employer in the nation as a precursor to what would almost assuredly become, for social as well as legislative requirements, a major issue in the workplace? Again, not many.
- The 1954 U.S. Supreme Court decision in *Brown v. the Topeka, Kan , Board of Education* was yet another major leading indicator of probable changes in the workforce. If black and white children went to school together, would they not also expect to work together?
- A 24-hour filibuster led by the late Senator Strom Thurmond of South Carolina narrowly defeated the 1957 Civil Rights Act. But this proposed legislation outlined many unattended civil rights abuses and was a preview of the Civil Rights Act of 1964. Once again, most HR and other business leaders did not see the need for meaningful, voluntary, and affirmative change.

This example illustrates how any failure to accurately anticipate the demands of demographic, social, economic, ethnic, and global changes can cost organizations dearly. Worse, such delinquencies touch many lives and can do great harm to ordinary people. This is a burden that no profession should bear, and that no one associated with the profession should ever permit.

The chapters in Section 1 deal with major issues that can touch people's lives as well as the employer's interest.

For instance, Anne Tsui and Joshua Wu's article addresses the "new employment relationship." Can improved employee commitment be obtained by trading job security (loyalty) for a challenging job with a fixed compensation package and the possibility of gaining new skills? Or does the traditional mutual loyalty approach produce the most productive, loyal and committed employees as well as the best company performance?

James Clawson and Douglas Newburg (Chapter 2) discuss the degree of a person's engagement at work or what they call "managing energy." Some research suggests that most companies have only moderately engaged workers and that great potential exists in managing people differently.

Cole Peterson, Wal-Mart retired senior vice president, outlines how the world's largest employer gets, keeps, and grows people (Chapter 4). He emphasizes how to use simple strategies that incorporate the organization's culture and overall operating philosophy.

Also included in this section are two articles on the same subject but with different conclusions. Peter Cappelli offers facts and a conclusion that there will not be a United States long-term labor shortage. Mike Losey suggests exactly the opposite.

We intentionally invited these two individuals to report their opinions on this subject. We did this to highlight that when we search for clues to the future it is not important when experts differ in their appraisals. The key benefit is knowing that such a difference of opinion exists.

Rather than rendering a planning process undecided or inconclusive we know now what to watch and what to continue to test. Of course, only one theory will ultimately prevail. But the alert strategic HR planner will be looking for the confirmation of one strategy over the other. This will allow them to check what assumptions and projections are coming true. And the benefit is they will see the final result and will be able to react much sooner than if they did not know the alternate theories existed.

CHAPTER 1

WILL THERE REALLY BE A LABOR SHORTAGE?

PETER CAPPELLI

Recent studies warn that the U.S. economy will experience widespread job vacancies that cannot be filled because of a shortfall of workers. It is true that employers will face new and more difficult challenges in recruiting and hiring than previous generations faced, but the challenges have to do with changes in the employment relationship, not a shortfall of workers caused by demographic changes. These developments have important and positive implications for older workers. More generally, the solutions to these recruiting and hiring challenges focus back on employers and their own human resource strategies.

RECENT DEMOGRAPHIC DEVELOPMENTS

The dominant demographic event of the past century, the baby boom's entry into the labor market, preceded what became a long period of economic stagnation and slow growth in the economy. It was hard for many workers to find jobs in this period, and unemployment rates remained relatively high. Chronic unemployment of young workers in particular was common as was widespread overqualification of workers for jobs. Evidence suggests that the rapid expansion of the workforce associated with the entry of the baby boom workers depressed their wages and lifetime earning opportunities.

This chapter is drawn from a larger study, "Will There *Really* Be a Labor Shortage?" in *Organizational Dynamics,* vol.3, 2003.

In contrast, the years from 1998 to the recession year of 2001 saw very tight labor markets; finding workers was a challenge and wages began to rise sharply. The studies that envision a future labor shortage assert that this period represents the beginning of a fundamental shift in labor markets, in some ways the reverse of the slack labor markets during the 1970s. They foresee circumstances that will be even more difficult for employers than the tight labor markets from 1998 to 2001.

Behind the predictions of a coming labor shortage is a demographic event called the "baby bust" generation. This cohort is just behind the baby boomers and is roughly 16 percent smaller. Those predicting a coming labor shortage assert that this smaller cohort will be unable to staff all the jobs currently filled by the much larger baby boom cohort. A frequent assumption is that this baby bust cohort is now just entering the labor force, but in fact, they entered about a decade ago. Table 1.1 illustrates the population distribution of the United States in 1980, 1990, 2000, and the projections for 2010. The average age of the baby-bust cohort in 2004 was 31 years and represented 71 percent of the workforce.

LABOR SUPPLY TRENDS

Taking the labor shortage arguments seriously begins with an assessment of the role of the baby bust cohort in the overall supply of labor. Just behind it in the population is another, larger cohort that some refer to as the "echo" of the baby boom, the children of boomers. This larger cohort is just now coming into the labor force. The baby bust cohort therefore did not cause the population or even the labor force of the United States to stop growing. The echo cohort and immigration enabled the labor force to grow roughly 1 percent per year throughout the 1990s; and government projections suggest that, through 2014, growth will actually increase at a slightly faster rate than occurred during the 1990s. The rate of increase will then begin to slow, although the labor force will still be growing over the following decades.[1] illustrate the labor force, as opposed to the population. One can see that the projected labor force in 2010 is older but not smaller.

But the biggest demographic development in the future will continue to be the baby boom and the increasing number of older individuals as the

Table 1.1
Civilian Labor Force by Sex, Age, Race, and Hispanic Origin, 1980, 1990, 2000, and Projected 2010 (Numbers in Thousands)

Group	Level 1980	Level 1990	Level 2000	Level 2010	Change 1980–1990	Change 1990–2000	Change 2000–2010	Percent Change 1980–1990	Percent Change 1990–2000	Percent Change 2000–2010	Percent Distribution 1980	Percent Distribution 1990	Percent Distribution 2000	Percent Distribution 2010	Annual Growth Rate (percent) 1980–1990	Annual Growth Rate (percent) 1990–2000	Annual Growth Rate (percent) 2000–2010
Total, 16 years and older	106,940	125,840	140,863	157,721	18,900	15,023	16,858	17.7	11.9	12.0	100.0	100.0	100.0	100.0	1.6	1.1	1.1
16 to 24	25,300	22,492	22,715	26,081	-2,808	223	3,366	-11.1	1.0	14.8	23.7	17.9	16.1	16.5	-1.2	.1	1.4
24 to 54	66,600	88,322	99,974	104,994	21,722	11,652	5,020	32.6	13.2	5.0	62.3	70.2	71.0	66.6	2.9	1.2	.5
55 and older	15,039	15,026	18,175	26,646	-13	3,149	8,471	-0.1	21.0	46.6	14.1	11.9	12.9	16.9	.0	1.9	.9
Men	61,453	69,011	75,247	82,221	7,558	6,236	6,974	12.3	9.0	9.3	57.5	54.8	53.4	52.1	1.2	.9	.9
Women	45,487	56,829	65,616	75,500	11,342	8,787	9,884	24.9	15.5	15.1	42.5	45.2	46.6	47.9	2.3	1.4	1.4
White	93,600	107,447	117,574	128,043	13,847	10,127	10,470	14.8	9.4	8.9	87.5	85.4	83.5	81.2	1.4	.9	.9
Black	10,865	13,740	16,603	20,041	2,875	2,863	3,439	26.5	20.8	20.7	10.2	10.9	11.8	12.7	2.4	1.9	1.9
Asian and other[a]	2,476	4,653	6,687	9,636	2,177	2,034	2,950	87.9	43.7	44.1	2.3	3.7	4.7	6.1	6.5	3.7	3.7
Hispanic origin	6,146	10,720	15,368	20,947	4,574	4,648	5,579	74.4	43.4	36.3	5.7	8.5	10.9	13.3	5.7	3.7	3.1
Other than Hispanic origin	100,794	115,120	125,495	136,774	14,326	10,375	11,279	14.2	9.0	9.0	94.3	91.5	89.1	86.7	1.3	.9	.9
White non-Hispanic	87,633	97,818	102,963	109,118	10,185	5,144	6,155	11.6	5.3	6.0	81.9	77.7	73.1	69.2	1.1	.5	.6

[a] The "Asian and other" group includes (1) Asians and Pacific Islanders and (2) American Indians and Alaska Natives. The historical data are derived by subtracting Black and White from the total; projections are made directly, not by subtraction.

Source: Howard Fullerton Jr. and Mitra Toossi, "Labor Force Projections to 2010: Steady Growth and Changing Composition," *Monthly Labor Review,* November 2001, 124(11), p. 21 (AN 5785627).

baby boomers age. Those over age 65 account for roughly 13 percent of the population at present, a figure that will grow to 20 percent by 2050. The baby boomers are expected to live longer and be more active than any previous cohorts, which raises interesting and important questions for society, such as how we will pay for their retirements. It also raises important questions about the future supply of labor, the topic here. Life expectancy is roughly 15 years higher now than when the retirement age of 65 was established in the United States through the Social Security program, and all indications are that it will continue to rise. Many of the studies that foresee labor shortages in the future assume that retirement patterns will be unchanged, and that people will retire at the same age even as life expectancy and the ability to work longer go up. Surely this is unrealistic if for no other reason than financial resources for retirement may not allow it. There are many indications that the baby boom generation expects to keep working longer. Even a small increase in the retirement age (to 67 by 2027) of baby boomers will increase labor supply substantially because this cohort is so large.[2]

The first conclusion, therefore, is that the population and the potential labor force will still be growing at typical rates for the foreseeable future. If older workers decide or can be persuaded to work longer, the labor force may grow even faster, and since older workers are already experienced and trained, the average quality of the labor force may improve over time.

A second point is that the size of the entry-level cohort of workers may be less relevant now. In the 1960s, large employers primarily hired from the population of school-leavers and then promoted from within. Now, they increasingly hire laterally, filling positions at all levels from the outside. Further, even though the entry-level cohorts may be smaller in the future than they were in the baby boom, the overall number of college graduates in the period since the baby bust cohort left high school has risen, and U.S. Department of Education projections suggest slow but steady growth in all degrees through the foreseeable future. If any group within the baby bust cohort is noticeably smaller, therefore, it is likely to be those with high school or less education, a group that is not particularly in demand.

LABOR SUPPLY AND ECONOMIC GROWTH

Does the labor force have to grow for the economy to grow? No, because productivity growth can allow each worker to contribute more to the economy. Productivity rises when employers invest in equipment and systems that help workers do their job or when workers receive more training and skills that improve their performance. A comparison of the U.S. economy now with its status at the end of World War II shows that it is roughly eight times larger, but the workforce is only twice as large. Each employee is roughly four times as productive now compared with employees in the late 1940s. If there had been no productivity growth, the U.S. economy would need four times as many workers as we currently have to sustain its current level. Productivity growth has been fastest when labor markets are tight, because wages are rising then. So if the labor market should tighten for a sustained period, efforts to increase labor productivity should help offset that tightness.

The more sophisticated labor shortage arguments put forth by experts agree that the growth rate of the economy as a whole depends on productivity growth—output per worker. They argue, however, that it also depends on growth in the number of workers: Output per worker multiplied by the number of workers equals total output in the economy. And so, the argument goes, if the growth rate of the labor force is falling, other influences being equal, then the growth rate of the economy has to fall as well. But this argument applies only if the economy is operating at absolutely full employment, and it almost never is.

If labor markets become tight and wages rise, human resource managers have an increasingly simple alternative to offer, and that is to *off-shore* the work by sending it to contractors or even their own operations in countries where labor is less expensive. Indeed, many observers believe that the opportunities to off-shore work have essentially expanded the available labor force for U.S. employers to such an extent that the logical consequence is a sharply declining labor market for workers. Offshoring is a far easier option than expanding immigration as the former can be done unilaterally, whereas the latter requires government intervention.

Some proponents of a coming labor shortage argument use evidence from the 2001 recession and the fact that the number of unemployed and

available workers following 2001 was at the lowest level among modern recessions. They contend this indicates that a labor shortage is imminent when
the economy rebounds and that we have moved into a new era of tight
labor markets. But all recessions are not the same. Recessions are defined
by relative, not absolute, measures—a decline in the economy, not an absolute level of economic activity. And the 2001 recession, which followed
the longest economic expansion in modern times, was among the shortest
and weakest.

Finally, there is an argument that increasing the labor supply would help
the economy by holding down wage growth, which would encourage hiring. The complication is that stagnant real wages also hold back consumer
demand. Although adding workers faster than productivity growth might
help expand Gross National Product, standards of living would fall, and it
is not obvious that such a goal would be desirable.

Surveys indicating that employers have job openings that they have not
filled are sometimes used to suggest that there is a labor shortage. These surveys do not indicate what wages and benefits the employers are offering,
however. From the perspective of an individual employer, it is a real problem for them if they cannot find workers with the skills they feel they need
at the wage they can afford to pay, even if that wage is below the market
level. But it is not a labor shortage or even necessarily a problem for public policy if employers cannot pay the market price for what they need.

AN OVERALL ASSESSMENT OF THE LABOR SITUATION

For the economy as a whole, then, there will be no decline in labor supply.
Indeed, it will continue to grow, and the growth will likely increase (e.g.,
through delayed retirements) if labor markets tighten and wages and job
opportunities improve. There is absolutely nothing about the changing demographics of the U.S. labor market that guarantees tight labor markets. As
long as there is unemployment, it is next to impossible to argue that the
labor force is holding back economic growth or that expanding the labor
force would help to create new jobs. To see that demographics are not destiny and that labor supply does not dictate the state of the economy, it is useful to look at the experience of Europe where many countries have sharply

falling birth rates and true declines in labor supply. Yet virtually all these countries still suffer from high unemployment.

What causes tight labor markets is sustained periods of economic growth that exceed productivity increases. That growth then begins to draw down the additional pool of workers who will be added to the labor force every year. (It is worth remembering that the 1999/2001 tight labor markets resulted from the longest sustained period of economic growth in U.S. history.)

Does it matter if the arguments about long-term shortages of labor are wrong, especially for individual employers? If there is a long-term shortage of workers, then human resource managers will find that any policies designed to get work done—offshoring, substituting capital for labor to automate lower-skill jobs, raising wages and other terms and conditions of employment to attract more applicants, and so on—become perfectly sensible. If there is no long-term shortage, then these options do not necessarily make sense, and other approaches make more sense.

What Is Different Now

Although the demographic picture in the 1990s was not that different, many human resources managers have a gut feeling that the labor market situation they experienced then was a sea change. Part of the explanation may be just that few managers now have memories long enough to recall that tight markets were the norm in the 1950s and especially the 1960s. The period between 1998 and 2001 offered up new challenges in addition to tight labor markets, however, and it is these new challenges to which employers are reacting. The first is increased employee turnover, which forces human resource departments to be in a continuous hiring mode. The second is the pressure to hire new skills and expertise from the outside for jobs at all levels of the organization in order to restructure quickly. This is in contrast to previous generations where recruiting was almost entirely limited to entry-level positions filled by newly minted college graduates.

At the same level of labor market tightness, then, contemporary employers face considerably greater recruiting and hiring challenges compared with earlier periods. The underlying problem for most employers was in not recognizing this change in the underlying employment relationship.

Hiring could not meet their labor force challenges, hence the conclusion was easy to reach that the problem was beyond their control and must be due to an overall shortage of workers. But the problem was that many human resource departments relied solely on recruiting to respond to these developments, when in fact, retention management should have been at least as important a mechanism for addressing this new environment. Performance management also became crucial. Recruiting and selection to find the best workers became a potential source of competitive advantage, although few employers adjusted fast enough to do anything strategic in this area.

The economy had turned down by the time many human resource departments began to develop more sophisticated recruiting and selection systems, retention management programs, and performance management competencies. By the middle of 2001, retention problems virtually evaporated for most employers as new jobs dried up. Hiring demands fell drastically when voluntary turnover declined and even faster once company growth slowed. (Note that the demographic picture was basically the same in the boom year of 1999 as in 2001, a bust year.)

When the economy rebounds, problems will resurface, and they will be the same ones that employers faced before. And if employers rely solely on hiring to address them, they will have the same sense that there are not enough workers to go around. Instead, human resource departments need to invest in a range of responses beginning with performance management to identify which workers are crucial to retain. Even in the height of the 1999 boom, most employers conceded that their problem was retaining their *best* workers, not workers per se.

Companies have to get better at recruiting as well, but simply attracting more applicants is unlikely to be cost effective because of the effort required to sort through to find the best ones. Employers need to invest in programs that help them target appropriate recruits and identify where their recruiting investments are most effective.

IMPLICATIONS FOR OLDER WORKERS

Overall, then, what can we conclude about the future from this quick summary of the past? From the 1970s until the late 1990s, most employers enjoyed an abundant supply of labor that made it possible to offset and overlook the gradual decay of their human resource competencies and practices. Employers did not have to be good at recruiting or selection when overqualified applicants were queuing up at their door. They did not have to worry about retention policies when no one was quitting. They did not have to develop employees when corporate hierarchies were shrinking and any talent that was needed could easily be hired from outside. And when companies were downsizing and restructuring, human resource capabilities were the first thing cut. When labor markets tightened, surplus labor was no longer available to camouflage the problems caused by not having these competencies. The recruiting function, which had eroded into the role of simply taking and filling job requisitions, could not solve all the problems caused by the breakdown of these other systems.

It would be as much a mistake to believe that the slack labor markets of the 2001 recession have eliminated the challenges facing employers as it would be to believe that we are facing an inevitable shortage of workers. No one knows whether future labor markets will be tight or slack—it depends almost entirely on growth and productivity prospects for the economy. It is fair to say, however, that the persistent worker surpluses associated with the baby boom that made it possible for employers to ignore virtually all human resource challenges through the mid-1990s may not be back any time soon. As the interest in performance management has increased, it has become easier for employers to recognize how valuable the best employees are. One consequence of this is an understanding that there are never enough "good" employees. To respond to this challenge, employers will have to develop competencies in recruiting and selection, performance management, retention policies, and other practices that support finding and keeping quality workers even if labor markets remain slack.

An important new competency that should be part of the future for human resources is managing the older workforce. In many organizations, the human capital "pipeline" began with inexpensive, inexperienced workers, who then advanced through the ranks with seniority-based pay to become experienced and expensive workers. Efforts to restructure costs, therefore, often meant—at least implicitly—getting rid of older workers and replacing them with younger ones. When employers thought about retaining older workers, they saw problems because the pay for those workers—tied to seniority—was high.

The days of lifetime employment and seniority-based systems are largely over now as companies move toward models of contingent work, independent contracting, and more free-market arrangements. At the same time, a very large group of experienced, often highly skilled, workers are leaving their current employers, and increasing numbers of them would like to be doing *something* in the labor market even if it does not resemble what they did before. As the baby boom ages, this pool of retirement age individuals looking for alternative working arrangements will grow every year. A tremendous opportunity awaits companies that can adopt policies and practices to accommodate the interests of this enormous group of reentrants. It requires going somewhat further down the path to flexibility than many employers may find suitable: Older workers do not necessarily want to work the long schedules of their younger counterparts, and they may not be as willing to manifest the commitment and "rah-rah" spirit that some organizations require even of their contractors. But these workers also offer skills and competence and are often willing to work for much less money than their younger, career-minded counterparts. It is a big challenge for human resource managers to develop these alternative policies and possibly an even bigger challenge to persuade the rest of the organization of the need to do so. Employers that cannot adapt to embrace this new workforce will miss a significant source of competitive advantage.

NOTES

1. Howard Fullerton Jr. and Mitra Toossi, "Labor Force Projections to 2010: Steady Growth and Changing Composition," *Monthly Labor Review,* November 2001, 124(11) pp. 21–28.
2. See Alan L. Gustman and Thoman L. Steinmeier, "Retirement Effects of Proposals by the President's Commission to Strengthen Social Security" Cambridge, MA: NBER Working Paper w10030, October 2003, for projections about retirement trends.

CHAPTER 2

THE MOTIVATOR'S DILEMMA

JAMES G. CLAWSON AND DOUGLAS S. NEWBURG

Setting goals is the first step in turning the invisible into the visible.
—*Anthony Robbins*

Goals too clearly defined can become blinkers.
—*Mary Catherine Bateson*

The major challenge facing leaders and human resource management professionals over the next 20 years will be managing energy. In fact, our favorite definition of leadership has become "leadership is about managing energy, first in yourself and then in those around you." The challenge of energy management, though, is not just an individual endeavor; it extends to organizations—big time.

Many, if not most people, seldom bring their best efforts to work; they seem to save them for evenings and weekends. If you ask managers, "Of all the people you have met in your career, what percentage of them are fully engaged at work?" most say, "Less than 10 percent." One does not need nationwide polls or leadership seminar participants' opinions to observe this phenomenon; virtually every working establishment is full of people going through the motions. We define *energy* as the percentage of a person's engagement at work, physically, mentally, spiritually, emotionally, and socially. People who are 90 percent engaged are high energy, while people who are 40 percent engaged are low energy.

This is not to say that employees are not working; they are, and they are doing their jobs "good enough." But in a competitive global business environment, good enough is no longer enough. Oddly, nonprofit organizations like churches, rescue squads, sport leagues, and charitable organizations can get people to engage fully. We are aware of a well-paid lawyer who took a leave of absence and a 75 percent cut in pay to do public service. We know an academic who put his professional activities on hold for three years while he went off to lead a missionary effort for his church. We know of secretaries who give up their nights and weekends to receive training and serve as rescue squad volunteers without pay. There are millions of people who drag themselves through the workday, yet suddenly find pools of energy in the evenings and on weekends. What we see, everywhere we go, is a vast majority of people going through the motions at work, doing good enough; it is a formula for mediocrity. This leads us to a problem that we have come to think of as the *Motivator's Dilemma:* How can managers tap that latent energy in their employees?

Throughout the Industrial Era, the primary leadership approach to the problem of energy management was goal setting. The establishment of measures, the subsequent setting of goals, and then the management required for achievement have formed the unexamined mantra of business leaders everywhere. The very measurement of success in developed industrial society as a function of goal achievement has become so pervasive that we take goal orientation for granted. "What's measured improves" has become the contagious meme of business management. Business leaders everywhere set annual goals, quarterly goals, and monthly goals and strive diligently to manage toward achieving them—neither too low nor too high so as to avoid surprises.

THE DARK SIDE OF GOALS

But there is a huge problem here: At some point, external goals actually reduce motivation. This phenomenon creates a dilemma in which goals and goal orientation become de-energizing instead of energizing. Consider the following event. A colleague and one of the authors were teaching a week-long executive education seminar to a group of 50 upper middle level managers in a global firm. On Thursday afternoon, the number two officer in the company flew in on the company jet to talk to the troops. The two instructors were sitting on the back row eager to hear what he would say. In essence, he leaned against the chalkboard and said, "It's June 30. The stock price is 95. If the stock price doesn't get to 125 by December 31, the CEO

and I don't get our annual bonuses, so you need to get your rears in gear!"
The room was stunned; that giant sucking sound was the sound of their
energy flowing out of the room into the hallway. The executive left and
flew back to company headquarters, and the two instructors went to din-
ner with the participants. They were utterly demoralized. This executive
was doing what he thought was the right thing. He made a special trip to
"motivate" his employees. He was well meaning and yet his approach was
utterly de-energizing. How often does this happen? How can HR professionals tell when it is about to happen? That is the Motivator's Dilemma.

THE SHIFT FROM INSIDE-OUT TO OUTSIDE-IN

Healthy children between the ages of one and six develop a natural curiosity about the world. Before long though, kids are sent to school, and
there they learn a hundred times a day things that they are supposed to
know and do. In the words of Robert MacCammon:

> We all start out knowing magic. We are born with whirlwinds, forest fires
> and comets inside of us. We are all born able to sing to birds and read the
> clouds, and see our destiny in grains of sand. But then we get the magic
> educated right out of our souls. We get it churched out, spanked out,
> washed out, and combed out. We get put on the straight and narrow and
> told to be responsible. Told to act our age. Told to grow up, for God's sake.
> And you know why we were told that? Because the people doing the telling
> were afraid of our youth and because the magic we knew made them
> ashamed and sad about what they had allowed to wither in themselves.

Adults have tacitly agreed that there are numerous things that kids need
to learn to succeed in life. And competition is heating up, so the kids have
to learn more and more sooner and sooner just to keep up. Somewhere
along in there, learning for most, but not for all, shifts from an inside-out
natural fun thing to an outside-in, arbitrary, obligatory thing. Alfie Kohn
has documented this process extensively. Learning soon becomes for most
an obligation that they turn their backs on as soon as school is over.

The loss of energy in school and one's own learning is one thing; it is
quite another when the person leaves school and goes to work. New employees are confronted immediately with goals and targets—10 percent this
year, and 11 percent the next year. We repeatedly hear corporate employees

talk listlessly about their imposed annual goals, and their voices often have no energy or enthusiasm in them. If anything, they feel beaten down by the inexorable march of the stretch goal.

THE RELATIONSHIP BETWEEN FEELINGS AND PERFORMANCE

Well, you may say, professionals do what they have to do and do not let their feelings get in the way. Perhaps, but let us ask you this question, "Does how you feel affect your performance?" If you said yes, like 99.9 percent of all the people whom we have asked, then the next question is, "How many times in your career has your manager/supervisor asked you how you want to feel today?" If your answer is "Never," then your experience is again like 99.9 percent of the people to whom we have put *that* question. These two queries represent an emerging focal point of Doug Newburg's research over the past 15 years on the phenomenon of resonance. Most managers and leaders *assume* that professionals will do what they have to do and not let their feelings get in the way. And that is the problem. Feelings affect our performance, plain and simple. *Descartes' Error* was not recognizing that fundamental fact when he established the scientific method and rational analytical thinking.

There is a basic difference between choice and obligation. When we *choose* to do something, we have more energy for it. When we *have* to do something, our energy is likely to flag even if we set our own goals. Consider Dave Scott, six-time winner of the Hawaii Ironman Triathlon. He says, "During a race, I never wear a wristwatch, and my bike doesn't have a speedometer. They're distractions. All I work on is finding a rhythm that feels strong and sticking to it." Scott's message seems clear. When he is paying attention to his split times, those goals become outside-in obligations and he feels he *has* to meet them to do what he wants to do, but ironically, this drains his energy. When he discards the external measures and focuses on an inner rhythm—a feeling—that he thinks is sustainable and just focuses on that, he blows the competition away. When we choose to do a thing, our energy level is likely to be higher. If we do a thing because we have to or because we feel obligated, our energy curve tends to flatten and even decline.

UNDERSTANDING THE MOTIVATOR'S DILEMMA

The Motivator's Dilemma is the challenge of knowing when the effect of external goals becomes de-energizing instead of energizing. When managers observe latent energy in people, they are tempted to set goals for them, but the very fact of setting the goal shifts a person's focus from *experience* (inside-out feelings) to *performance* (outside-in measurable results) and that signals a shift from choice to obligation. How can leaders and managers know when their attempts to motivate by external measures and goal setting have tipped over from motivating to demotivating? It is a difficult dilemma to manage especially because the desire to improve just a little bit here and little bit there is both natural and rational.

Our insight on this phenomenon was stimulated by many others including Doug Newburg's research on resonance, Csikszentmihalyi's work on flow, Gallwey's work on measurements and the "inner games," the whole quality of work life movement, research on intrinsic and extrinsic motivation including Kohn's work mentioned earlier, and Christensen and Raynor's book, *The Innovator's Solution: Creating and Sustaining Successful Growth.* In fact, the Motivator's Dilemma is, we think, directly analogous to the Innovator's Dilemma.

In the Motivator's Dilemma (Figure 2.1), the vertical axis is the proportion of employees' energy used by an organization. Over time, one

Figure 2.1
The Motivator's Dilemma

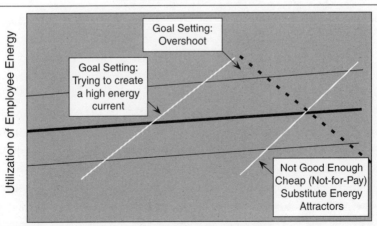

would hope this would be gradually rising. And there is a distribution of results of energy that employees bring to an organization. New employees usually begin work with high hopes. Then they find themselves subjected to increasingly difficult goals. Soon, without fanfare or even awareness, their motivation for the work shifts from choice to obligation. Then, the daily habitual thought is about what they have to do instead of what they want to do. Pressured by competition, management continues to set ever higher goals, even big hairy audacious goals. And the natural, rational conclusion is that they eventually reach "overshoot," the condition where the goals are so far beyond what people can do that they give up altogether. Before long, employees have come to believe—even to assume—that work is not fun and they save their best for other things.

A few organizations have understood the Motivator's Dilemma and managed it well. Southwest Airlines, SAS in Cary, North Carolina, and the Pike's Place Fish Market in Seattle, Washington, are examples of large, midsize, and small organizations that understand the Motivator's Dilemma and are organized to manage employee energy well. Yet most organizations persist in pushing the outside-in model of goal orientation in their attempts to manage employee energy despite growing evidence that an outside-in, exclusively goal-oriented structure sucks energy out of people instead of pumping it into them.

CONCLUSION

What should HR professionals do about this? We are not saying organizations should give up on goals altogether. It is like Christensen's argument in response to the question, "Is an industry profitable?" The informed response would be, "In which part of the cycle described by the Innovator's Dilemma?" The same is true of goals. If we ask, "Aren't goals motivating?" the answer is "In what part of the cycle?" If we administer reasonable goals shortly after employees have developed energy for a thing, goals might indeed improve performance. The dilemma, though, is in identifying the point at which the goals become ends that drain energy. Make sure your goals flow from the inside-out energy of your people and build on it instead of killing it. To manage energy, value both the *inside-out and the outside-in,* and do not let your goals overwhelm the inside-out motivation of your people—or else the energy of the organization will decline.

In this short chapter, we are asserting several objectives for the management of human resources over the next 50 years:

- Goal setting has been the primary means of management for the past 200 years, but goals have a pernicious tendency to drain energy.
- Most organizations unintentionally have replaced employees' natural energy with obligatory outside-in goals that dampen the energy of the organizational culture.
- Goals can be motivating if they match a person's passions; however, over-administered goals can drain energy rather than build it.
- The Motivator's Dilemma is knowing how to recognize when outside-in goal orientation becomes so strong that it suppresses inside-out choice driven motivation and tips over into a de-energizing force.
- Whereas you can get good enough, going-through-the-motions behavior from employees working in an outside-in, goal oriented system, you cannot get world-class performance until you are able to tap into the inside-out energy of individual choices.
- The difference between *good enough* and *world class* lies in the difference between obligation and choice. People who have developed the mental habit of thinking, "What do I *have to do* today?" at the beginning of each day have habituated themselves to mediocrity.
- Organizations that can honestly and truthfully balance the use of goals with intrinsic motivators demonstrate daily their ability to outpace their competition. There are many examples of such companies today, but they remain in the minority despite their obvious and well-documented advantages.
- Looking ahead, the biggest challenge facing human resource management professionals and leaders will be managing energy, first in themselves and then in the people around them.
- Organizations will improve their ability to manage the energy of their employees when they begin to apply the principles of the Experience Economy[1] not only to customers, but also to employees.

Leaders and human resource management professionals over the next generation will wrestle with the Motivator's Dilemma in their attempts to energize their employees. In the end, unless they understand and are willing to utilize the principles of world-class performance, they will be settling for good enough from their people.

NOTE

1. The "experience economy" is a term introduced by Joe Pine and Jim Gilmore in their book by the same title in which they point out that the high-margin businesses today are where customers pay for an ethereal experience that is gone as soon as it's over. While in the past we paid for commodities (agricultural era), goods (industrial era), and then services (early information age), the margins on all of these have evaporated. Yet people increasingly will pay huge margins for soccer games, rock concerts, and other kinds of "quality" experiences. Employers will have to recognize this and offer the same to their employees. Fortune's listing of the best companies to work for is a symptom of this growing trend.

REFERENCE

Pine, Joe, and Jim Gilmore. *The Experience Economy*. (Boston, MA: HBS Press, 1999).

CHAPTER 3

ANTICIPATING CHANGE: WILL THERE BE A LABOR SHORTAGE?

MICHAEL R. LOSEY

The issue of the future availability of labor needs to be fully examined and discussed. Some suggest the predicted labor shortage in the United States will not materialize. Others see current events as confirmation that there will be a labor shortage. Even worse are those who are indifferent or have not even thought about the likelihood of a shortfall.

Because the price of not carefully looking at such issues is increasing, this chapter presents the following information for consideration.

NET ADDITIONS TO THE WORKFORCE

Projections that the net additions to the workforce will drop to levels not reached for more a century can only be dismissed at great risk.[1] The book *Workforce 2000* (Johnston and Packer, 1987)[2] and *Workforce 2020* (Judy and D'Amico, 1997)[3] both illustrate how the net additions to the U.S. workforce will decrease dramatically, at least through 2020.

During the past 100 years, as noted in Figure 3.1, the United States experienced a 3 percent net addition to workforce only twice. Once was at the beginning of the twentieth century when immigration was essentially unlimited. That contributor to labor force growth was drastically and permanently reduced early in that century when the United States began to implement much more restrictive immigration policies. World War I also restricted immigration greatly.

The second major net gain in the workforce took place when the well-known post-World War II baby boomers entered the workforce in the 1970s and 1980s.

Figure 3.1
Net Additions to the Workforce

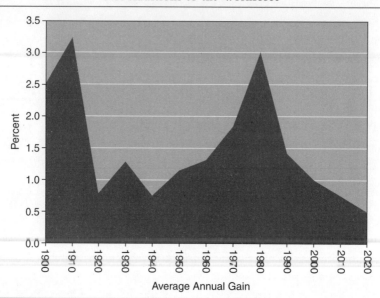

Source: *Workforce 2000* and *Workforce 2020.*

The historic low in net additions to the workforce happened about 70 years ago, during the Great Depression of the 1930s. A contributor to this low point was a rare occurrence: More people left the United States than entered as immigrants during this period.

As emphasized in a 2004 study commissioned by the U.S. Department of Labor and conducted by the Rand Corporation, the workforce grew from 83 million in 1970 to 107 million in 1980, 126 million in 1990, and 141 million in 2000. These figures correspond to annual growth rates of 2.6 percent in the 1970s, 1.6 percent during the 1980s, and only 1.1 percent in the 1990s.[4]

Furthermore, according to the statistics in that study, the Bureau of Labor Statistics (BLS) projects a continuing annual growth rate of only 1.1 percent until 2010. After 2010, the workforce growth is projected to slow even further. Between 2010 and 2020, the annual growth rate is projected to be just 0.4 percent, the lowest in more than a century.

It is important to recognize that these statistics are very predictable given our knowledge of birth, immigration, retirement, and death rates in the

United States. So we can use these rates to accurately estimate the impact on the workforce. It is also important to note that since the terrorist attacks of September 11, 2001, U.S. immigration laws have been more aggressively administered. In addition, immigration opportunities for skilled positions have been drastically reduced.[5]

RELATIVE LEVELS OF UNEMPLOYMENT (1982 TO 2004)

The recession of 2002 to 2003 may have caused many, especially HR professionals, to misjudge the future of the U.S. labor market. There seems to be a popular belief now that the labor shortage employers experienced but a few years ago is over. But very much the opposite may be happening. A closer review of recent unemployment statistics may be additional evidence that a systemic long-term labor shortage is still with us.

As illustrated in Figure 3.2, unemployment levels for the last three recessions have shown a downward trend.

Figure 3.2
U.S. Unemployment Percentage Past Three Recessions: 1980–2003

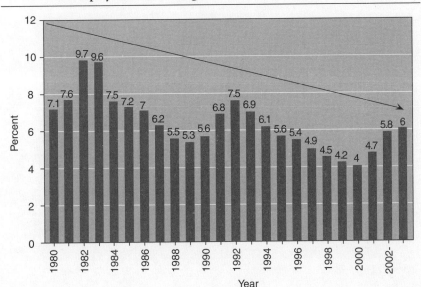

Note: August 2004 = 5.4 percent. *Source:* U.S. Bureau of Labor Statistics.

Some suggest the latest recession was simply less severe than the recessions in the early 1980s and 1990s. But the more likely reason the unemployment rate is less is that the net rate of people entering the workforce is decreasing. Therefore, the compounding effect is not as great as that experienced in the 1982 recession. At that time, the economy not only experienced a downturn but had to absorb new workers entering the labor market at a historically high rate of 3 percent. This compounding contributed to the 9.7 percent unemployment rate in 1982, 62 percent higher than the most recent recession's unemployment level of 6 percent.

The unemployment rate during the 1992 recession was 7.5 percent or 23 percent less than the 1982 recession. By 1992, however, the net additions to the workforce was already less than 50 percent of what it was during the 1982 recession—thus lessening the compounding effect of layoffs plus large numbers of new entrants.

Figure 3.3 illustrates that the average unemployment rate has been 6.3 percent since 1980.

Figure 3.3
U.S. 2002–2003 Recession Percentage Unemployment versus
Average Employment since 1980

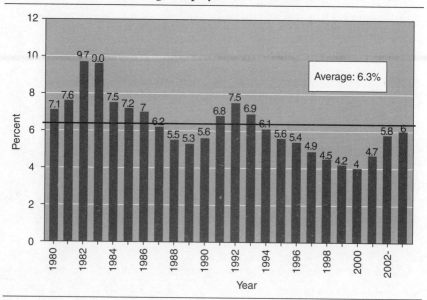

Source: U.S. Bureau of Labor Statistics.

Figure 3.4
U.S. Total Labor Force versus Total Unemployed: Last Three Recessions

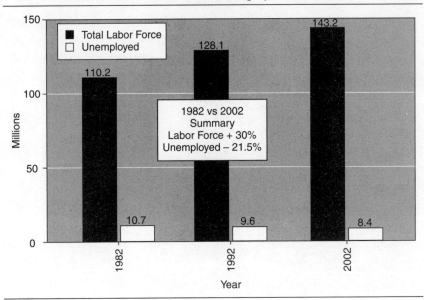

Source: U.S. Bureau of Labor Statistics.

What many people do not seem to realize, is that the unemployment rate for the last recession, at 6 percent, was less than the average unemployment rate for the past 20-plus years.

But even more telling is the actual number of unemployed during the past three recessions. As noted in Figure 3.4, the workforce has increased 30 percent since 1982, but the actual number of unemployed has decreased 21.5 percent.

Stated another way, the United States has added approximately 33 million people to the workforce since 1982, but at the height of the most recent recession still had 2.3 million fewer people unemployed than were unemployed in 1982.

THE "REAL UNEMPLOYMENT RATE"

During the most recent recession and as the economy seemed to be determining which way to go, a *USA Today* headline (February 10, 2004) proclaimed "Job Seekers Just Quit Looking." The article suggested that a January 2004 reduction in the unemployment rate was primarily influenced

Figure 3.5
Last Three Recessions: Labor Force Participation Rate

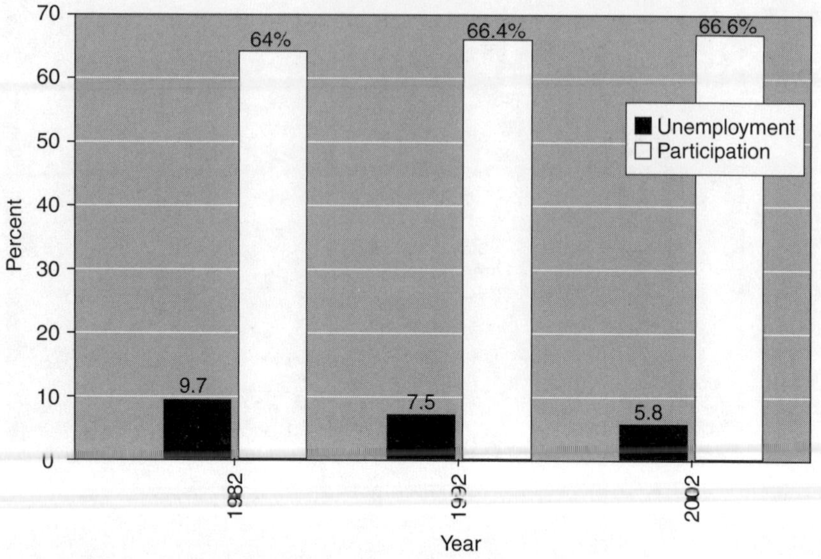

Source: U.S. Bureau of Labor Statistics.

by people simply becoming discouraged and dropping out of the labor market. Not by people getting jobs.

This can be a contributor to a reduction in the unemployment rate, but this is nothing new. As Figure 3.5 illustrates, the labor force participation rate for the most recent recession was higher, not lower, than the earlier recessions. So the headline-grabbing claim that the most recent recession was different in a fundamental way is really not true. It is misleading to the public as well as those in human resources. The truth is that this recession was much like the earlier ones. The only major differences are that the most recent recession was mitigated somewhat by the lower net additions to the workforce, and a greater percentage of service and white collar employees were laid off than in previous recessions.[6]

EMPLOYMENT POPULATION RATIOS

Others also suggest that the workforce has the capacity to expand by simply increasing the number of workers through higher rates of participation especially among women, disabled persons, and seniors.

Figure 3.6
Employment as a Percent of the Civilian Labor Force

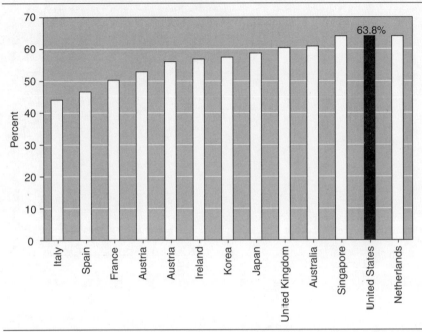

Source: U.S. Department of Labor, BLS. 2001 (latest available).

This is true, but what happens when a nation like the United States has, from a relative standpoint, one of the highest employment population ratios in the world already, especially for women?[7] See Figure 3.6 above and Figure 3.7 on page 30.

As noted in Figure 3.7 and the most recent statistics available, among 12 developed countries, the United States and Denmark, at 57 percent, had the highest women's employment-population ratios.

OLDER WORKERS WORKING LONGER?

Others suggest any shortfall in workers will simply be made up by enough older people who will continue to participate fully in the workforce.

But as highlighted in a recent Society for Human Resource Management (SHRM) study, this assumes that such older workers will be healthy enough to be able to continue working productively. This may not be a

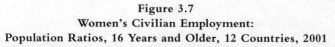

Figure 3.7
Women's Civilian Employment:
Population Ratios, 16 Years and Older, 12 Countries, 2001

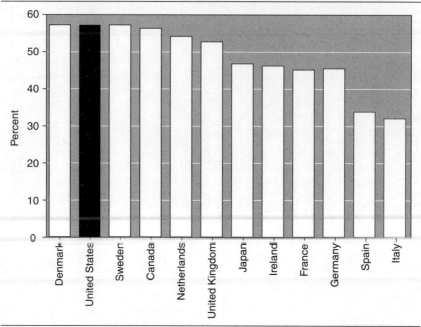

Source: U.S. Department of Labor, BLS. 2001 (latest available).

valid assumption. According to the World Health Organization (WHO), and as highlighted in Figure 3.8, the United States has the lowest healthy life expectancy among industrialized nations (2001).

Previously, life expectancy estimates were based on the overall length of life based on mortality data only. Now the WHO has calculated health life expectancy for babies born in 1999. This new approach is the Disability Adjusted Life Expectancy (DALE) that summarizes the expected number of years to be lived in good health.

As shown in Figure 3.8, Japan has the longest healthy life expectancy of 74.5 years followed by other industrialized nations. The United States ranks 24 on this list and at 69.3 years is the only major country to have an estimated healthy life expectancy of less than 70 years of age.[8]

Figure 3.8
Disability Adjusted Life Expectancy (DALE)

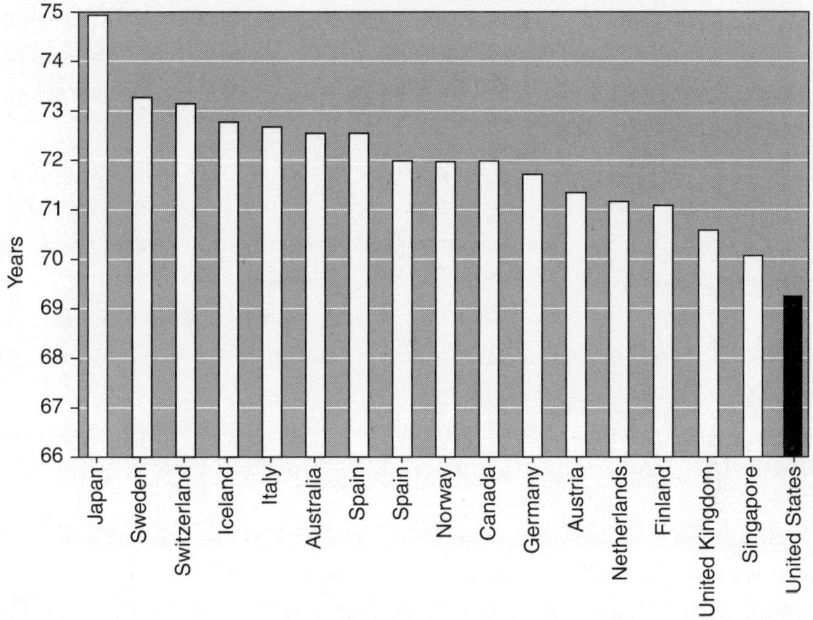

Source: World Health Organization as of 2000.

Those who desire or need to continue working well beyond 65 may not be able to do so as a result of chronic health conditions. Even those in good health may have family caringresponsibilities that keep them from working.

Also, research-based organizations such as SHRM have highlighted that the United States will still have relatively high life expectancy rates. So, in addition to poor health limiting the number of older workers in the workforce, many will nevertheless still live longer than in most other countries. Thus, the problem of having large numbers of individuals who will be relying on government retirement and health care programs is compounded.[9]

MORE THAN A LABOR SHORTAGE—A SKILL SHORTAGE?

Even if it is assumed that enough (quantitative) people will be available and there will not be a serious supply problem, the even greater likelihood of a skill (qualitative) shortage remains, especially in those occupations that are growing faster than others (Table 3.1).

Although these BLS projections are now several years old, it will be interesting to see how close they come to being accurate in 2008.[10] At a minimum, we can probably assume that jobs with the most job growth will also have higher earnings growth and less unemployment.

Complicating this growth will be a potential shortage of scientific and technical workers. People in these jobs are customarily well educated at the bachelor's degree level and higher.

There are signs that many young people simply are not taking the tough courses that equip them to pursue post-secondary education in these fields.

Also, some suggest that for too long now we have relied on other nations to supply the majority of our scientists and engineers. We simply produce too few of them ourselves.

Finally, as Dick Judy highlights in much of his work, the demographic groups in our society that are growing relatively rapidly (Hispanics, in par-

Table 3.1
The 10 Fastest Growing U.S. Occupations 1998–2008
(in Thousands of Jobs)

Occupation	Employment 1998	2008	Change Number	Percentage
Computer engineers	299	622	323	108
Computer support specialists	429	869	439	102
Systems analysts	617	1,194	577	94
Database administrators	87	155	67	77
Desktop publishing specialists	26	44	19	73
Paralegals and legal assistants	136	220	84	62
Personal care and home health aids	746	1,179	433	58
Medical assistants	252	398	146	58
Social and human services assistants	268	410	141	53
Physician's assistants	66	98	32	48

Source: Bureau of Labor Statistics.

ticular) and African Americans frequently lag in acquiring the educational foundation at the K-12 level. This hinders them in pursuing studies in technology, engineering, and science. Left unattended at industry and local school levels, this situation could become even worse.

Arnold Packer, author of the original *Workforce 2000* book summed up this contradiction in supply and demand to me recently by suggesting, "It is very possible that we shall experience a labor shortage and a labor surplus at the same time."

WHAT TO DO ABOUT IT

Many recruiting and employment departments were decimated during the most recent recession and will need rebuilding.

A lower level of hiring has contributed not only to less recruitment but also to less use of the new tools of the trade. This is especially true with online recruiting and related technologies and services. While recruiting departments took a recession-related nap, a fast-growing industry made up of companies such as Monster, CareerBuilder, and Hot Jobs continued to develop new programs and services. Recruiting and employment functions will need to be restaffed and provided with new and sharpened tools.

The difficulty of getting such departments back up to speed will be complicated by a probable increase in employee turnover. Thus, growth-oriented recruitment will have to compete with merely replacing those who are quitting to capture opportunities in an improved economy.

A 2003 survey by SHRM and the *Wall Street Journal*'s, CareerJournal .com indicated that there is a great risk that the HR professional will understate the likelihood of increased turnover.[11] As indicated by Figure 3.9, the opinion of HR pros about the possibility of increases in voluntary employee turnover when the recovery comes differed greatly from the opinions of potential job seekers. Employees surveyed by CareerJournal.com were five times more likely to suggest employee turnover would increase than was the typical HR professional surveyed by SHRM.

This disconnect must be recognized and corrected. Competing in a tighter labor market cannot be done solely by better recruiting. It must be a combination of recruiting and retention.

Figure 3.9
Likelihood of Increase in Voluntary Turnover: Once Economy Improves

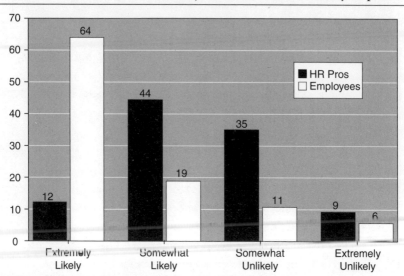

Source: SHRM/Career Journal.com Job Recovery Survey (2003).

Also, if the labor market tightens, continuing domestic and global competitive pressures will not permit HR professionals to simply "throw money off the balcony" to overcome recruitment and retention issues. More money for higher starting salaries as well as for offsetting the compensation compression effect on existing employees will not be a absolute solution or a recommendation most cost-conscious CEOs will quickly approve. Nor is it likely that better or new employee benefits will be a cost-effective remedy.

Instead, a better understanding of why employees walk away from an organization is needed and must be addressed. Some evidence suggests most of the reasons that terminating employees offer for quitting (although not the most frequent reason) are noneconomic issues.

According to the SHRM/Career Journal survey (multiple responses permitted), the major reasons employees quit are as follows:

1. Compensation and benefits (53 percent)
2. Career development (35 percent)

3. New experience (32 percent)
4. Job security (21 percent)
5. Career change (21 percent)

followed by the management indictments of:

6. Poor management (20 percent)
7. Boredom (18 percent)
8. Conflict with values (18 percent)

So what is the message here? Of course, all employers run a risk in the employment marketplace if they are not prepared to provide competitive and equitably administered pay, benefits, and other conditions of employment. But most people want much more out of a job than high pay and comprehensive benefits. Employees want a career and reasonable job security. They want an employer who thinks about them and their individual development, possible new experiences, and equitable consideration for advancement. Most important, they want to work for an organization and person they respect.

Should we not, therefore, work more on those employee-centered issues, especially since many of them "come for free" through improved HR practices and improved first-line supervision? Examples include good employee relations, career development, job enrichment and rotation, and reasonable opportunities for advancement. Then try to buttress those efforts with a work environment characterized by its challenge, appropriate values, and reasonable security, including the ability to speak up and be heard without fear of retribution.

SUMMARY

There is evidence that the labor and skill shortages are still here and are merely hidden or mitigated by the downturn of a business cycle that our economic system puts us through from time to time.

Such statistics cannot be easily dismissed. When the economy improves, the U.S. labor and skill shortage may also return, possibly worse than before. Now is the time to prepare and establish a competitive advantage through good HR planning and practice.

But this chapter is more than a brief thesis on whether there will be a long-term labor shortage. HR professionals cannot be distracted by current highly visible events and commentary. They cannot delegate their accountability for anticipating the future. If they do, they risk being held captive by the present; will fail to see the future, and may disadvantage their personal performance and success of their organization.

NOTES

1. The net additions to the workforce represent the net difference between new entrants, primarily students (born 16 to 18 years ago and thus very predictable) and immigrants of working age less the number of people exiting the workforce because of death, permanent disability, or permanent retirement.
2. *Workforce 2000: Work and Workers for the Twenty-First Century,* William B. Johnston and Arnold H. Packer, Hudson Institute, Indianapolis, Indiana, 1987.
3. *Workforce 2020: Work and Workers in the 21st Century,* Richard W. Judy and Carol D'Amico, Hudson Institute, Indianapolis, Indiana, 1997.
4. *The 21st Century at Work; Forces Shaping the Future Workforce and Workplace in the United States,* Lynn A. Karoly, Constantijn W. A. Panis, Prepared for the U.S. Department of Labor by Rand Corporation, Santa Monica, California, 2004.
5. In 2003, the H1-B skilled workers visa limit was reduced to only 65,000 annually from the prior year's level of 195,000, a two-thirds reduction in skilled workers available via immigration.
6. From 1984 through 2003, actual U.S. employment has increased from 105 million to 137.7 million. However employment of white-collar and service workers increased by a total of 34.0 million workers or 47.6 percent, while blue-collar employment actually decreased 1.2 million workers or 4.4 percent. This major shift to a white-collar and service workforce left organizations with no option except to reduce staff and related costs more aggressively in these areas also.
7. Many other nations, such as the United Kingdom, Germany, France, Canada, and Japan, have demographic profiles similar to the United States. Continuing workforce growth, however, characterizes the workforces of Mexico, India, China, South Africa, and Brazil.
8. As noted by the World Health Organization, several causes are given for the relatively low U.S. ranking among wealthy nations, such as poor health his-

tory of Native Americans, rural African Americans, and the inner city poor. HIV causes a higher proportion of death and disability among U.S. young and middle-aged than in most other advanced countries. Cancer related to tobacco use is also high as well as the incidence of coronary heart disease. Homicides are also higher when compared with other nations.

9. *SHRM 2004–2005 Workplace Forecast: A Strategic Outlook,* Jennifer Schramm and Mary Elizabeth Burke, Society for Human Resource Management, June 2004.

10. For the most current list of BLS Fastest-Growing jobs, see http://www .bls.gov/emp/emptab3.htm.

11. *SHRM/Career Journal.com Job Recovery Survey,* Society for Human Resource Management and the *Wall Street Journal*'s web site CareerJournal .com, September 2003. See http://www.shrm.org/hrresources/surveys _published/Job%20Opportunities%20Survey.pdf.

CHAPTER 4

GET, KEEP, GROW

COLEMAN PETERSON

The keys to tomorrow often lie in the past . . .

When I joined Wal-Mart in the spring of 1994, I thought that the Human Resources area (People Division) faced a daunting task of getting its arms around a company of 485,549 associates doing $50 billion in revenue. I was somewhat encouraged by the fact that it had taken Wal-Mart at least 30 years to get to this point, so I was confident that I would have time to adjust before the *real* growth began. Little did I know that 10 years later, we would be running a business of $250 billion in volume with 1.5 million associates.

On reflection, I would have welcomed a well-designed plan to meet those requirements. Anticipating the future, especially in dynamic, growing organizations, is not easy, sometimes almost impossibly complex.

But, just as Sam Walton had a simple but highly effective strategy for success, I am pleased that our People Division recognized that simplicity is better than complexity and that less is more. This is especially important as the authors of this book, and this chapter, attempt to consider the future of HR.

Sam's business philosophy was based on a strategy of making the customer number one. He believed that by serving the customer's needs first, his business would also serve its associates, shareholders, communities, and other stakeholders. Our goal at Wal-Mart's People Division was to incorporate Mr. Sam's culture and philosophy into a human resource management strategy while keeping it simple and highly effective.

Today, 10 years later, when asked about my role as the executive vice-president of Wal-Mart's People Division, I simply explain that we are—

and will continue to be—in the business of *getting, keeping,* and *growing* good people.

In truth, this is what human resource professionals are paid to do. If we implement these basic competencies well, our organizations will be better businesses. I do not intend to minimize the importance of roles like compliance, diversity, compensation, and benefits. What I submit is that if the basic exercise of getting, keeping, and growing a company's talent is well done, the other HR functions will reflect this excellence.

GETTING GOOD PEOPLE

It all begins here. Someone once asked Sam Walton what special training programs he instituted to have such upbeat, customer-focused associates. Sam reportedly thought for a moment with a quizzical look on his face and then asked, "Why not hire friendly upbeat people?" Much of our personnel energy and resources are, in fact, devoted to fixing or improving the *initial hiring decision.* We invest significantly in improving and upgrading technical skill or in improving or correcting workplace behaviors. A great example at Wal-Mart is addressing the classic retail challenge of employee turnover.

As we analyzed our situation, we noted that our turnover had increased steadily from a baseline in 1994 (the year I joined Wal-Mart and began measuring) to 1999 when we established stronger retention strategies. During this time, our internal and external environment had begun to change. Internally we were expanding from a purely general merchandise business of small hometown stores of 40,000 square feet to 180,000 square-foot "supercenters" that offer groceries as well as general merchandise. Many of these new operations were also 24/7; that is open 24 hours a day, seven days a week. What a significant shock to a store's operating system!

Additionally, in 1994, there were still many states with "blue laws." That is, their retail operations were not open on Sundays. As this has changed state by state, the dynamics of running a nonstop operation accelerated us to another level.

A final consideration was the "war for talent." The economy had gotten a second wind and unemployment dropped from 6.6 percent to 4.3 percent from 1994 to 1999. Employment appeared to be plentiful, and many job holders opted for frequent job changes.

At Wal-Mart, we embarked on a strategy to reduce our rising turnover. Part One of the strategy was *Get*. As we looked at our recruiting strategies, we realized that the starting point for turnover is *when* we hire and *who* we hire. Many of us do a great job of hiring our own turnover, and examples abound.

An associate leaves within the first 90 days because of a conflict in schedule or a preference to work in another area. Were these things discussed before the job offer was made? Or there appears to be attendance or punctuality problems that cause us to focus more on corrective discipline than training job skills and customer-related skills. Then we ask, Was there something in the person's background that I should have known? What did I miss?

Very early in my career, after having done college recruiting for some time, I took a class in selection and testing as a part of my graduate school curriculum. As the professor was orienting us on the first day of class, he stated, "Remember that the face-to-face interview is probably the most invalid selection process that exists!" Of course, I was stunned by this obviously erroneous statement because I felt that my ability to "size up" a candidate across the table was foolproof. I learned later that there is much to know about hiring decisions and how to ensure that your selections are adding to the strength of the team.

The good professor's point was that there were (and are) many behavioral instruments and validation processes that can help us maximize the desirable behaviors that we seek. It is for this reason that we increased our focus and training around picking good people, which encompassed everything from selection training classes to computer-based training on interviewing techniques. These efforts contributed significantly to our eventual results. Time and effort employed on the front end play a large part in the energy applied in the two remaining key areas—*Keeping* and *Growing* good people.

KEEPING GOOD PEOPLE

There has been much research about why people leave their company or organization. Even so, I know that I could ask any number of seasoned HR executives this question and they would rattle off the top three or four reasons without reaching for their latest survey. They are:

- Poor supervision
- Lack of job opportunities
- Pay

We could argue about the order of these; however, we all know that employees do not leave good companies, they leave bad bosses. The sense of connectivity with an organization and what future it holds for the individual is key. Don Soderquist, former senior vice-chairman of Wal-Mart, frequently quoted Fred Smith of Federal Express regarding what associates looked for in their organization. He maintained that a company that could answer these three questions was well on its way to establishing a long-term relationship with its employees:

1. Do you care about me?
2. What do I need to do to get ahead?
3. Where can I go to get justice?

(Note: I believe that Smith offered two other questions; however, I have always focused on these three because they especially resonated with me.)

Whether we are onboarding an entry-level hourly employee or a highly compensated technology manager, the need for thoughtful strategies around introducing new people to the organization is extremely important. It begins with *how* we bring them on board, *who* they meet early on, and *what* we tell them is important "around here."

Harvard professor, Rosabeth Moss Kanter, in her book *Corporate Culture,* defined corporate culture succinctly as, "how we do things around here." The course of a person's career is often imprinted in the first several months of that career. (Our own Wal-Mart study had indicated that in entry-level hourly positions, we lost 67 percent of the first-year turnover in the first 90 days!)

The need to understand the business you have joined, whether it is retail or manufacturing or telecommunications is critical. So it is imperative to afford newcomers the opportunity of getting exposure to the mainstream product or activity of the business. Above all; however, new hires need to meet the coaches—the leaders who run the operation. The connection between those who work in the store or plant or department and those who make the decisions cannot be overvalued.

One of my favorite exercises when I would visit our store, club, or distribution center locations around the world was to strike up a conversation with associates who were working. I would casually ask them how they were doing, how they liked their job, and so on. I would eventually get around to inquiring about supervision, with one favorite question, "What is the name of your store or club or distribution center manager?" The answer to this question offered tremendous insight into the access and familiarity with the facility manager. Did the associates know the manager's name? Did they recite the name with familiarity? Well-run organizations have a clear footprint of the leader.

Again, our retention strategies called for mandatory participation of the location manager in new employee orientation meetings. We wanted our associates to know their leaders from the very outset. I believe that an employee's feelings about "where they can go to get justice" correlates highly with the comfort level and trust that they have with their supervisors.

GROWING GOOD PEOPLE

Very few of us work for purely philanthropic reasons. As a result, we are always interested in what we need to do to get ahead.

We live in an impatient, "microwave" society, where anything that takes longer than a minute to process can create frustration. As HR professionals, we know that career development is a function of *time* and *experience*. The roots of true development are sunk deep in the experimental: *the doing*. It is ripe with good and bad decisions, varying business situations, quantitative, qualitative, and intuitive judgment. There is no substitute for time.

If this is so, how do we get the people in our organizations to feel good about their opportunities and where they are going? Two critical factors are:

1. How we tell the story about the opportunities that exist
2. Clarifying the process that gives an even playing field to all who
   have interest in those opportunities

We began our management career selection (job posting) process around the desire to respond to these needs. This effort contributed to reduced turnover as well as improved diversity and selections. We have continued to expand the selection process to more and more jobs over the years; the policy has served us well. Of course, the most credible impact to the organization is to hear about the single-parent telephone operator from a California Wal-Mart store who eventually became the vice-president of Recruitment and Placement for the entire organization. Real stories have real impact.

Associates want to be able to *see* opportunity. Even in Wal-Mart, an organization with an 9.0 percent annual population growth, there have been people who believed they had no opportunity. Overall, however, the fact that 70 percent of all management people at Wal-Mart began as hourly workers has always been strong proof that true opportunity exists.

SUMMARY

The basics of getting, keeping, and growing people are the cornerstones of human resource activities. This focus helped us reduce total turnover from 70 percent in 1999 (when the industry average was 63 percent) to 44 percent in 2003 versus a current industry average of 65 percent.

On days when my HR problems appear to be overwhelming, I dissect them into these three "buckets" for identification and solution. Those companies that GET good people, KEEP good people, and GROW good people will be around to celebrate their successes.

CHAPTER 5

THE NEW EMPLOYMENT RELATIONSHIP VERSUS THE MUTUAL INVESTMENT APPROACH: IMPLICATIONS FOR HUMAN RESOURCE MANAGEMENT

ANNE S. TSUI AND JOSHUA B. WU

The eve of the twenty-first century witnessed the dawn of a new employment relationship in corporate America. Consider these numbers: Between 1984 and 1986, nearly 600,000 middle and upper-level executives were laid off in the United States (Bluestone and Harrison, 1988). Between 1987 and 1991, over 85 percent of the *Fortune* 1000 companies eliminated 5 million white-collar jobs in total (Casio, 1993). In the first three years of the new millennium, corporate America cut another 2.7 million jobs (Nussbaum, 2004). Such workforce reduction was unprecedented in American history. With increasing globalization and hypercompetitive markets, most employers have resorted to headcount management to gain flexibility, remain competitive, and ensure survival. This dramatic corporate downsizing occurred in most industries and at all ranks, resulting in the breaking of the old traditional deal: a lifelong job with mutual loyalty between the employer and the employee. Replacing this is the *new employment relationship* (Stewart, 1998). Instead of loyalty (job security), an employer offers an employee a challenging job and a fixed compensation package, along with the promise of opportunities to learn valuable skills (Roehling, Cavanaugh, Moynihan, and Boswell, 2000). The employee, in turn, instead of loyalty, pays back the employer through job performance without a strong commitment to the organization. The bond between an employer and an employee is no longer a long-term relationship involving loyalty and commitment, but a contract-like economic exchange.

The purpose of this chapter is to take a closer look at this new employment relationship in the context of the more traditional forms of employer-employee relationship also found in many organizations. Based on recent research that compares different approaches, we argue that the economic value of the new employment relationship may not be as attractive as it might have been perceived to be. In fact, the data show that the traditional mutual loyalty approach produces the most productive, loyal, and committed employees along with strong company performance and corresponding profits or margins. We encourage future human resource executives to consider the *mutual investment employment relationship* as a competitive tool and to design human resource systems to realize the competitive advantages from this mutual loyalty and investment.

THE CHARACTERISTICS OF THE NEW EMPLOYMENT RELATIONSHIP

Employment relationship (ER) has been systematically studied by management scholars for many decades. Integrating many models, we have proposed a framework (see Figure 5.1 on p. 46) that juxtaposes two key considerations in the ER (Tsui, Pearce, Porter, and Tripoli, 1997; Tsui and Wang, 2002). One consideration is the contributions that an employer may expect from the employees including work performance, commitment, suggestions for organizational improvement, and so on. The other consideration is the rewards (defined broadly) or inducements that an employer offers to the employees in exchange for their contributions. We use the terms *expected contributions* and *offered inducements* to refer to these two major considerations (see Figure 5.1). The nature of the new employment relationship can be understood in the context of this framework.

The new employment relationship is, in essence, a quasi-spot contract (cell 1 of Figure 5.1); it is defined by a relatively narrow set of inducements

Figure 5.1
The General Typology of Employment Relationships Based on the
Inducement-Contribution Framework

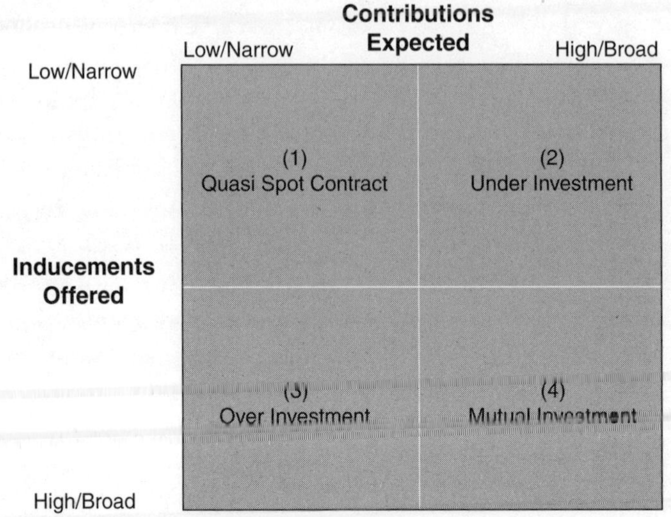

	Contributions Expected	
	Low/Narrow	High/Broad
Low/Narrow	(1) Quasi Spot Contract	(2) Under Investment
High/Broad	(3) Over Investment	(4) Mutual Investment

Inducements Offered

offered by an employer and a narrow set of contributions expected from an employee. It represents a pure economic exchange relationship, focusing on the short term and on a relatively well-defined set of duties. Many well-regarded employers, under competitive pressure, are shifting to temporary, part-time employees or contractors to avoid paying benefits (e.g., Wal-Mart). All of this breaks the traditional employer-employee contract and the bond between the two. Employers adopting this ER are interested primarily in a high level of employee task performance, without requiring commitment from the employees to the organization's overall success. In return, once employees meet the predetermined output expectations, they obtain the promised rewards without a promise of long-term job security from the employers. Though this type of exchange is usually found in relationships with contractors in unskilled, skilled, or even professional jobs, its application recently has extended to senior executives. Temporary executives, interim executives, or so-called corporate samurai are becoming popular in today's labor market (Lancaster, 1998; Thottam, 2004). Rather than "having a job," this new employment relationship form focuses on "doing a job" (Covey, 1996). Firms use the quasi-spot contract approach to gain flexibility in the employment and deployment of people resources.

Another form of the new employment relationship is the under investment approach depicted in cell 2 of Figure 5.1. Under investment occurs when a firm offers a narrow set of inducements but in return expects a broad set of contributions from employees. This ER is imbalanced to the advantage of employers because they can get more (from employees) out of less (from themselves). The economic downturn and the slow recovery have increased market competition, which pushes employers to increase productivity with limited resources. This demanding situation increases employees' workload while holding inducements constant. Fifteen people now do the work of 20 at the same pay scale! Without noticeable economic recovery, employees have to sustain such imbalance in the employment exchange for lack of alternatives. Some labor economists have observed, "Not only are companies making people work harder, but some people want to . . . they are trying to protect their job security" (Conlin, 2002). General Electric (GE), propelled by both the recession of the early 1980s and the desire to restructure the business, adopted the under investment approach by laying off thousands of employees, including layers of middle managers, while asking for a high level of commitment from their remaining employees. This imbalance is a form of disequilibrium that cannot be sustained in the long term. Many firms eventually migrate to one of the two balanced ERs, the quasi-spot contract or the mutual investment, which is explained in detail later in this chapter. GE today has moved away from the under investment approach. Many firms that experience performance pressure inevitably need to under invest in their employees, at least in the short term.

Do quasi-spot contracts and under investment deliver on their promise of flexibility and firm performance? The answer is not so clear-cut. In appearance, firms may realize flexibility in scaling up and down as dictated by market demands. Also, in terms of the short-term balance sheet, firms may create an attractive bottom line by adjusting employment levels. However, empirical evidence using systematic research on employee contributions to a firm and the firm's long-term strength raises some doubt on the wisdom of firms choosing these new employment relationship approaches.

Convincing evidence was provided by a study of 10 companies in five competitive industries, covering over 85 jobs and involving nearly 1,000 employees in a stratified sample (Tsui et al., 1997). The study results revealed that organizations adopting the quasi-spot contract and the under investment approaches reported several unfavorable employee outcomes. These negative outcomes include lower performance as rated by the supervisors, reduced employee engagement in citizenship behavior (behavior beyond the call of duty such as helping coworkers), expression of a tendency to leave the company if there were alternative employment opportunities, and less psychological commitment toward the organization. The employees also perceived a lower level of fairness, had less trust in their coworkers, and reported more frequent absences. Thus, while firms may gain some flexibility in employment, they may lose in terms of high performance and commitment from employees.

Another recent study (Wang et al., 2003) compared the performance (return to asset) of firms using different ER approaches in over 120 firms in China (including both domestic and foreign firms). The results showed that both the traditional Chinese firms and the multinational corporations had lower firm performance when they used either the quasi-spot contract or the under investment ER. On the other hand, organization performance was the best when firms adopted the mutual investment ER approach.

THE MUTUAL INVESTMENT APPROACH—OLDER BUT WISER

The goal of mutual investment (cell 4 in Figure 5.1) is to solicit a broader range of behaviors and stronger commitment from employees by making a high level of investments (high inducements) in the employees and requiring a high level of contributions in return. The firm focuses on developing a long-term and open-ended relationship with its employees. Under this ER approach, employees are expected to contribute broadly to their organization instead of focusing only on performing their own jobs. A classic example is Southwest Airlines. Flight attendants and pilots, as a team, help clean aircrafts and check passengers in together to get flights out efficiently, resulting in the shortest flight turnaround time within the aviation industry. Despite the negative impact of 9/11, Southwest Airlines remains a cost-efficient company and was the most profitable U.S. airline in fiscal year 2003 (Serwer, 2004). In return for the broad contributions, Southwest Airlines makes long-term investments in employees in extensive training, profit sharing, promotion from within, and job security. The relationship between the employer and the employees is social rather than economic in nature.

Another example of the mutual investment approach is the SAS Institute, the largest privately owned software company in the world. It ranked third in *Fortune*'s first survey of the best companies to work for (January 1998) and has remained in the top 10 since then (Levering and Moskowitz, 2004). According to an SAS executive, "The Institute is founded on a philosophy of forming lasting relationships with our customers, our business partners, and our employees. These critical relationships, combined with our leading-edge software and services, together form the basic elements of our success" (cited in O'Reilly and Pfeffer, 2000, p. 104). Throughout the years, SAS has maintained loyalty to employees in an industry famous for high mobility and rapid turnover. It is a place "where loyalty matters more than money" (O'Reilly and Pfeffer, 2000, p. 99). SAS treats people with dignity and is concerned about their total well-being. In return, employees contribute broadly to their teams and demonstrate creativity and conscientiousness at work. The institute's average turnover rate has been less than 4 percent, whereas the industry-wide attrition rate is greater than 15 percent. SAS is a real-life example of how the benefits of the traditional mutual investment ER surpass that of the new employment relationship. United Parcel Service (UPS) is another firm that promotes from within and whose employees take pride in the organization. Even though it is unionized, UPS offers substantial tuition assistance to its employees along with other benefits. In fact, most of the companies on *Fortune*'s list of "best companies" adopt the mutual investment ER with their employees. These companies are characterized by genuine and substantive caring behavior toward their employees along with an extremely high level of performance expectations—a description of cell 4 in Figure 5.1.

The underlying rationale for the effectiveness of mutual investment is twofold. First, when employees experience long-term investment from employers, they reciprocate with loyalty to the organizations and contribute much more than simply performing their jobs. This assumption of reciprocity is reflected in Southwest Airlines' mission statement: "Employees will be provided the same concern, respect, and caring attitude within the organization that they are expected to share externally with every South-west Customer" (O'Reilly and Pfeffer, 2000, p. 33). Second, the mutual investment approach sets higher performance goals and expectations for employees. Empirical research confirms that difficult and challenging goals lead to higher performance (Locke and Latham, 1990). Mutual investment is the older and wiser approach, contrary to the common wisdom in most companies now facing competitive pressure.

USING THE MUTUAL INVESTMENT APPROACH—THE ROLE OF HUMAN RESOURCE MANAGEMENT

In this section, we illustrate how to use four human resource practices in implementing the mutual investment ER. Instead of providing a complete checklist, our goal is to offer a few ideas that are both effective and easy to implement. Psychological research has shown that money is not a moti-vating factor for employees (assuming that basic needs are being met) and that other factors such as job satisfaction, respect, advancement, work en-vironment, and so on, are much more important in influencing employee attraction, motivation, and retention. In general, the mutual investment ER approach focuses on social and career investment more than on mon-etary benefits.

Recruitment and Selection

To establish a mutual investment ER from the outset, employers need to communicate their endorsement of the value of long-term loyalty and com-mitment to job applicants and state that they are looking for the same from employees. Based on this value foundation, employers should convey what they can offer and what they expect from employees. Especially, applicants should be well informed about the company's expectations of broad con-tributions from employees. Recruiters often exaggerate inducements (both tangible and intangible) to attract talents but tend to be vague or general about performance expectations. Peer recruiting or work team interview-ing can be a useful tool in communicating accurate expectations. By talk-ing with their prospective colleagues, applicants will gain a more realistic and accurate picture of what mutual commitment and trust mean in the organization, how to contribute broadly, and what to expect in terms of a long-term career within the firm. At Microsoft, interviewers include not only HR professionals, functional managers, and peers, but even people outside the traditional hiring group, who are well grounded in Microsoft's culture. The value of these "as appropriate" interviewers is to make sure that the newcomers fit the organization's culture (in our case, the mutual investment approach) and are not just filling out a vacant position. Other industry leaders such as Amazon.com, IBM, and Motorola also use peer interviewing extensively. This is the whole basis for the Demming Principle (Team Approach), which involves major players in the decision-making process because they will be working with new employees and are looking for fit. This approach builds commitment with both current and new employees. It also clarifies employers' high expectations for contributions from the new employees and a long-term oriented employment relationship.

Training and Development

To signal long-term investment, the focus of training and development is not on improving skills to perform the current job but on preparing employees for future responsibilities. Job rotation and participation in cross-functional or cross-divisional project teams are effective methods to build an organization-wide perspective and to promote organizational interests. Promotion from within and succession planning are the core elements of a company's broader development plans for its human resources. Finally, for employees to make broad contributions, teamwork training is essential so that they can learn the skills of effective collaboration. At General Electric, IBM, Hewlett-Packard, and Procter & Gamble, among many others, management development and succession planning are high priorities of the executive office. In these organizations, the most effective manager is the one who trains his or her own replacement and has that person in place ready to go. Promotion in part depends on whether a manager has a trained replacement ready to take over.

Performance Criteria and Evaluation

The mutual investment approach focuses employees' attention on their teams and the organization. Excellence in doing one's own job is only a small part of a total performance assessment. Performance evaluation criteria and processes should be related to broad contributions. In addition to individual evaluation, performance appraisal by peers and based on team performance is a common feature of the evaluation process. The broad-based contributions can be captured in a 360-degree feedback system. Employees' superiors, peers, subordinates, and even customers rate their performance. With an emphasis on developmental purposes, 360-degree feedback has been widely used by industry leaders such as AT&T, Du Pont, Honeywell, Intel, Texaco, UPS, and Xerox, among many others. The 360-degree feedback system is usually adopted by employers emphasizing a high level of broad-based contributions from their employees, one of the key requirements in a mutual investment ER.

Compensation and Benefits

The key to using compensation and benefits in building a mutual investment ER is not focusing merely on increasing the absolute amount of pay or benefits but communicating preferred behaviors and accentuating long-term investment in employees. To encourage long-term relationships between its sales force and customers, SAS rewards account representatives with a fixed salary instead of variable sales commissions. Lincoln Electric, a company known for its individual incentive system, has a team- and organization-based profit-sharing scheme as well as a no-layoff policy. Family-friendly benefits are another major form of broad investment in employees. In Synovus (one of *Fortune*'s 100 Best Companies for seven consecutive years since 1997), the "Right Choice" program enables employees to take time off to spend quality time with their children. Since 1996, Eli Lilly has appeared four times in the *Working Mother* magazine's top 10 list of the best companies in America for working mothers. The important point is that compensation and benefits practices in the mutual investment approach encourage and facilitate mutual commitment instead of serving merely as an economic bond.

SUMMARY

The purposes of this chapter are to encourage a return to the traditional mutual loyalty approach as a productive way to manage the employer-employee relationship, and to point out the unintended negative effects of the new employment relationship. The backbone of the mutual investment ER is generalized reciprocal loyalty, trust, and a focus on a long-term relationship. It emphasizes a high level of *both* offered inducements and expected contributions. Future human resource executives can shape a mutual investment ER by using human resource practices that accentuate both dimensions. The mutual investment ER is a strong tool that will improve an organization's ability to compete in the dynamic global environment through building a committed workforce eager to contribute to the company's success.

REFERENCES

Bluestone, B., and B. Harrison. (1988). The Growth of Low-Wage Employment: 1963–1986. *American Economic Review, 78,* 124–128.

Casio, W. F. (1993). Downsizing: What Do We Know? What Have We Learned? *Academy of Management Executive, 7,* 95–104.

Conlin, M. (2002, May 13). The Big Squeeze on Workers. *BusinessWeek, 3782,* 96–97.

Covey, S. R. (1996, January). The New Contract. *Executive Excellence, 13,* 1.

Lancaster, H. (1998, November 17). Some Veteran Bosses Find More Excitement in Doing Temp Work. *Wall Street Journal* (Eastern edition), p. B.1.

Levering, R., and M. Moskowitz. (2004, January 12). The 100 Best Companies to Work For. *Fortune, 149 (1),* 56–78.

Locke, E. A., and G. P. Latham. (1990). *A Theory of Goal Setting and Task Performance.* Englewood Cliffs, NJ: Prentice Hall.

Nussbaum, B. (2004, March 22). Where Are the Jobs? *BusinessWeek, 3875,* 36–37.

O'Reilly, C. A., III, and J. Pfeffer. (2000). *Hidden Value.* Boston, MA: Harvard Business School Press.

Roehling, M. V., M. A. Cavanaugh, L. M. Moynihan, and W. R. Boswell. (2000). The Nature of the New Employment Relationship: A Content Analysis of the Practitioner and Academic Literatures. *Human Resource Management, 39,* 305–320.

Serwer, A. (2004, March 8). Southwest Airlines: The Hottest Thing in the Sky. *Fortune, 149 (5),* 86–90.

Stewart, T. A. (1998, March 16). Gray Flannel Suit? *Fortune, 137 (5),* 76–82.

Thottam, J. (2004, April 26). When Execs Go to Temp. *Time, 163 (17),* 40–41.

Tsui, A. S., J. L. Pearce, L. W. Porter, and A. M. Tripoli. (1997). Alternative Approaches to the Employee-Organization Relationship: Does Investment in Employees Pay Off? *Academy of Management Journal, 40,* 1089–1121.

Tsui, A. S., and D. Wang. (2002). Employment Relationships from the Employer's Perspective: Current Research and Future Directions. In C. L. Cooper and I. T. Robertson (Eds.), *International Review of Industrial and Organizational Psychology* (Vol. 17, pp. 77–114). Chichester: Wiley.

Wang, D., A. S. Tsui, Y. Zhang, and L. Ma. (2003). Employment Relationships and Firm Performance: Evidence from an Emerging Economy. *Journal of Organizational Behavior, 24,* 511–535.

SECTION II

INVEST IN THE NEXT GENERATION OF HUMAN RESOURCE PROFESSIONALISM

The business world around us continues to change and to raise the bar for HR professionals. The knowledge and competencies required to be an effective HR professional keep growing more complex. Constant change is the only constant in business and in HR professionalism.

Change places a responsibility on HR professionals to pursue learning and professional development throughout their career to maximize their contributions for the organizations and employees they serve. What worked yesterday will not likely work today and is even less likely to work tomorrow.

In Section II, we learn how General Motors (GM) and AT&T are shaping the work of HR, and then examine some of the future educational and developmental opportunities for those in the profession.

Barclay and Thivierge (Chapter 6) share how GM has redefined the HR career path model based on the emerging role of the HR professional. Recognizing that ambiguity and constant change are here to stay, GM has identified the training and experience that will matter for new HR professionals, and has focused on recruiting into HR only those with educational or experiential expertise.

Cohen (Chapter 7) suggests components that should be included in the education and development of HR professionals to prepare them for the future in terms of what will be expected from employees, organizations, and the business community.

Graddick-Weir (Chapter 8) describes how AT&T developed its HR professionals in the wake of a large-scale outsourcing effort. After describing lessons learned from the outsourcing initiative, Graddick-Weir describes the ongoing work of HR and the competencies required going forward.

Meisinger (Chapter 9) and Armstrong (Chapter 10) are leaders of HR professional societies on opposite sides of the Atlantic. Yet their individual chapters highlight a shared view of the future HR professional. As milestones for the HR professional journey, Meisinger suggests Four Cs: Competent, Curious, Courageous, and Caring. Both authors stress the need to grasp the body of knowledge on which effective HR strategy is based, and the need to leverage HR expertise and business knowledge to make organizations more competitive and effective.

Common themes run through these chapters. They all emphasize the ever-increasing knowledge, skills, and abilities required to be in the HR profession and stress that continuous learning and a comfort with ongoing change are essential. Most importantly, all the authors highlight that the profession offers challenges and great opportunities and that it is an exciting time to be in HR.

CHAPTER 6

THE FUTURE HUMAN RESOURCE PROFESSIONAL'S CAREER MODEL

KATHLEEN BARCLAY AND THOMAS THIVIERGE

If you are about to graduate from an excellent undergraduate business school program with a specialization in HR, you are probably thinking, "Where do I go from here?" Should I go straight to an MBA program, since general business acumen is an essential HR skill? Or, should I try to get a job in a line position where I can gain a better understanding of the business?

Perhaps you have considered joining a large company that can provide you with the quality and breadth of specialized experiences that will develop two other key HR competencies—functional expertise and talent management. Or, you could work for a smaller firm, where you could gain more experience earlier in your career in the areas of change leadership and employee problem resolution and advocacy. And, where can you best get experience with the latest technology that is changing the delivery of HR services?

Just when you think that you have identified an answer to these important questions, you cannot help but wonder about the future of the HR function. Can you just skip the basic HR work that is increasingly being performed by outsourced service providers and go straight to being a strategic HR partner? Perhaps you should just get an MBA and wait until the future is more clearly defined. These are all natural reactions to the dramatically changing role of the HR function. For an aspiring HR professional, dealing with the ambiguity and the constant change is the only constant!

Over the past few years, I have been hearing these questions when I visit with students either in the classroom or when I host them here in Detroit.

Many of my HR executives—and many of my peers at other great companies—share my passion for the need to widely communicate the changing expectations of the HR profession and to provide some career development guidance to aspiring HR professionals.

Our operating line executives who have relationships with our key recruiting schools have also been including perspectives on the strategic role of HR in the business whenever they meet with students. The operational leader is often the best communicator of the skills that an HR professional needs to demonstrate. Therefore, this HR transformation message is also being conveyed to the next generation of operational leaders—the future customers for our strategic HR services.

For our existing workforce at General Motors (GM), we are trying to reduce this "expectations ambiguity" by redefining the HR career path model based on the emerging role of the HR professional. The following success profile is based not only on the research of academic thought leaders, but also on the input of my most senior HR professionals who have been living this transformation every day. We also interviewed our senior leaders in the company and asked them the following question: What capabilities should your HR professionals demonstrate to meet your business objectives?

As a result of this discovery process, we determined that our future HR employees—and our existing HR professionals—need to develop business acumen, functional expertise, talent management skills, change leadership, and partnership/relationship skills, while also learning how to use and implement technology. Our customers expect all these abilities to be put to use while performing both the employee advocacy and the strategic HR partnership roles.

Making this skill transformation has not been an easy task—and the job is not done. At GM, we have over 2,500 HR professionals supporting 341,000 employees in 58 countries around the world. Our annual HR budget is $900 million to support our $180 billon company. While our HR expenditures as a percentage of revenue have remained constant, our 2,500-employee infrastructure is 30 percent lower than it was just four years ago. More HR work is being performed in partnership with outsourcing service providers all around the world.

Another skill transformation challenge is that we must develop business acumen and drive common processes in the many industries and disciplines that reside under our one company—automotive, financial services such as insurance, commercial or mortgage lending and auto financing, marketing and advertising, satellite telecommunications, legal, government relations, real estate, and e-commerce. Complexity often results in process and skill variation. Therefore, how has GM focused on developing this future HR professional in this complex and challenging environment?

Since development is primarily through experiences, but also supported by training, what are the experiences and training that matter for the new HR professional? We have separated HR into three (3) distinct experience categories: talent management HR, manufacturing and labor relations, and operations HR. We have also implemented a three- (3) stage training process for all HR professionals. Tables 6.1 and 6.2 depict the primary HR skills that will be developed with this experience and training approach.

This approach is intended to help our current employees successfully make this transition. Most have enthusiastically embraced the challenge and are providing world-class HR processes and services to their customers. Not every current HR employee can clear the higher bar that has been established. Many simply do not have the experiences that could have

Table 6.1
The Experiences That Matter

Experience Area	Primary Skills Developed
Talent management (includes compensation, staffing, performance management, succession planning, change management, learning, and development)	Developing human capital, strategic line leader partnerships, and functional expertise (primarily a specific specialization area as well as customer service, leading change, and problem solving)
Labor relations (includes contract negotiation and administration, manufacturing supervision, and safety)	Employee advocacy, business acumen (primarily manufacturing), Union partnerships and functional expertise (primarily negotiating, conflict resolution, and lean thinking/TQM)
Operations (includes HR information technology, HR planning, health care/pension, policy, employment/payroll training, and contract services administration)	Third-party vendor partnerships, technology applications, and functional expertise (primarily data analysis/modeling, process knowledge, negotiating, and project management)

Table 6.2
The Training That Matters

Training Area	Primary Skills Developed
Vision Root Map Exercise (outlines the HR transformation vision, from transactional to strategic, two–three hours)	Trained every HR professional, and most key line customers, relative to HR's transformation vision. Exercise provided an interactive walk from the past to the future, with a focus on the barriers and enablers.
Skills for Success—Phases I/II/III (e-learning training in the core competencies required for success as an HR professional, 40 hours for phases I/II and approx. 120 hours over 8 weeks for phase III, with e-learning and group/individual project learning)	Curriculum provided by a university, first two phases taken over a two-year period for all HR employees (covers areas such as financial acumen, consulting skills, strategic partnerships, change leadership). Phase III is an MBA level course offered to higher performing/high potential HR talent, with a primary emphasis on global collaboration and consulting skills.
Mastery Level Training (includes intensive certification training in these core areas, with an average of three days' training per expertise area)	Skill-building training, with certification criteria post-training, in areas such as talent management, leading change, value stream mapping, coaching, performance intervention, and providing candid, constructive feedback.

prepared them for this new role. Therefore, when training and coaching fail, the only remaining choice is to help the individual to transition to another company or career option.

At GM, we believe that optimizing employee performance is the reason that HR exists. That old cliché "practice what you preach" applies here. To be a credible HR partner for line leaders, HR must be willing to address its own lower performers. We all know that the only sustainable competitive advantage in the future is the firm's human capital. The best HR talent must be assigned to this important human capital management task.

What about the next generation of HR professionals? Because of this shift, GM's hiring model has also begun to shift. In the past, GM would primarily source talent among interns and college graduates with BA degrees. Then, by providing assignments throughout the organization, GM would teach them all the functional basics and grow the best talent into managerial and executive positions.

This HR generalist, developmental approach of the past will not serve GM well in the future. Therefore, we are trying to adjust our hiring profile. First, most new college graduates will be sourced from MBA or Industrial Relations programs, with individuals who have both relevant job experience and a specialization in either human resources or labor relations. If other large employers adopt the same approach, most business schools will need to adjust their curriculum. Currently, both finance and marketing concentrations continue to dominate the MBA curriculum while HR concentration options are rarely offered. In addition, some undergraduate specialization programs, such as Safety, will also be excellent sources for functional expertise talent.

Our second-best source will be experienced HR professionals working for firms that are providing third-party services to major companies like GM. In the future, with their cash balance pension and health care accounts in hand, these early career individuals with operations HR experience will be in the best position to move from a service provider to a third-party service manager role for companies like GM. It may become common for companies with strong supplier partnership relationships to encourage the development of their employees by moving them back and forth between HR service providers and the main customer firm. This may be the only way that successful HR professionals can obtain both the operations and strategic partnership experiences that matter.

Our third-best source for talent will be from our own line employees who have successfully worked in functional areas that depend on the same skill set as HR. Current examples are finance and information technology (for talent management and operations roles) and manufacturing (for labor relations and safety roles). This cross-functional partnership model means that many finance, manufacturing, and information technology (IT) functional experts will also view an HR assignment as a critical experience in their developmental plan.

New college graduates might consider the following perspective: First, hold off on earning that master's degree until you have had some initial career success in either internship or full-time positions. Simply be successful in every job that you perform, whether you are working for a small, midsize, or large company or whether you work in HR or some other functional area. Such success usually means that you get results, that you are smart and know the business, and that you can work well with others.

With a track record of success, you are in a much better position to obtain the experiences that matter. These are experiences that can really affect business results. They are not only good for the business but they are also good for your development. It is a proven fact that we tend to learn and grow the most when we are in new, high-pressure situations.

HR is a high-pressure function, with a significant impact on the bottom-line performance of the company. In the past, we used to view company success in three primary areas: operation efficiency, financial performance, and customer satisfaction. The workforce was a secondary consideration and linking its capability to operational, financial, and customer satisfaction business results required an intuitive leap of faith.

Now, most operational leaders recognize that a workforce's ability to execute the business objectives is really the core element that will determine their company's success. Every HR process and practice must directly link to, support, and measure an employee's ability to achieve the company's business objectives. HR is all about building workforce capability and optimizing the performance of every employee. With the experiences and the training that matter the most, the HR professional function will meet this challenge. It really is a great time to join the HR function.

CHAPTER 7

HUMAN RESOURCE EDUCATION: A CAREER-LONG COMMITMENT

DEBRA J. COHEN

Like most business professionals, human resource (HR) professionals need a strong educational background to be successful. That education, however, needs to be quite varied. CEOs and senior business leaders have increasingly high expectations of their HR staff and HR functions. Studying the traditional aspects of HR is important—but equally important is learning from experience in HR as well as in business. Beyond HR basics is the critical need to understand broad business concepts and applications. So where does this education come from and how are these somewhat divergent needs blended?

To know what knowledge and education will be needed, we must first understand the issues that HR professionals will be facing in the future. Recruitment, selection, productivity, development, retention, and other key HR activities will always be initiatives in which HR gets involved and where deep knowledge and experience are necessary. As a result, knowledge of HR delivery, logistics, compliance, and strategy will be essential. But in the past decade, HR professionals have been increasingly called on to integrate a bottom-line orientation to their thinking, broaden their perspectives, anticipate changes, and develop innovative solutions to business problems. Today and in the future, HR professionals need to know how organizations work, how business operates, and what is unique about their own industry.

Take into account, for a moment, some of the workplace trends that organizations will face in the coming years. In a recent Society for Human Resource Management (SHRM) study, the top 10 overall trends were identified as follows (Schramm, 2004):

1. Rise in health care costs
2. Focus on domestic safety and security
3. Use of technology to communicate with employees
4. Growing complexity of legal compliance
5. Use of technology to perform transactional HR
6. Focus on global security
7. Preparing for the next wave of retirement/labor shortages
8. Development and use of e-learning
9. Exporting of U.S. manufacturing (and service) jobs overseas
10. Changing definition of family (e.g., children living with grand-parents; same-gender couples; unmarried cohabitation)

From a knowledge perspective, therefore, HR professionals must develop strategic and integrative skills that will allow them to draw all these issues together and effectively handle them. They must be educated to think independently and act independently—yet with the ability to apply current management thinking (Langbert, 2000).

Focusing on these issues requires a broad suite of knowledge skills and abilities. For example, to grapple with the issues of rising health care costs, HR professionals need an understanding of finance, economics, negotiation, demographics, and communication. Knowledge of information systems, privacy issues, and marketing will be critical for effective use of technology to communicate with employees or perform transactional HR functions. The growing complexity of legal compliance means that HR professionals not only need to understand the intricacies of the myriad laws covering HR, but also the interactions and possible contradictions of such laws. With all these complex issues exerting influence, it may be unrealistic to expect that the deeper intellectual skills required will be achieved easily or through a single mechanism. Continuous and continuing education are necessary. But more than this, educational interventions must include everything from legal issues to strategic thinking.

CURRENT HR EDUCATION ISSUES

Van Eynde and Tucker (1997) reported that HR executives were concerned that students of HR were learning primarily about the trees in the forest without really understanding the relationship of the trees within the forest. It may be that today in HR, both the forest and the trees are being recognized, but the interrelationships are still in need of understanding and development. HR professionals come from many backgrounds. There is no set educational path to become an HR professional. Unlike other disciplines such as accounting, engineering, or pharmacy, where one must achieve specific courses and education requirements, HR professionals can enter the field from many different disciplines. In a study by SHRM, only about one-third of surveyed HR professionals had a degree in HR, industrial relations, or psychology (Kluttz and Cohen, 2003).

Consider the options that an aspiring HR professional has in academia. At the undergraduate level, there are very few specialized degrees in HR. Most HR programs at this level are housed within a broader degree program, such as a major or a concentration in HR that might be offered in a business school. At best, these students will receive between four and seven courses in HR (Cohen, in press). And while they may be exposed to important business and social concepts, they will still lack the business experience that can help them assimilate and apply these concepts. Many students do not take internships or receive extensive experience. Interestingly, HR academics were split 50/50 on whether internships should be mandatory for an undergraduate degree, whereas the majority of students, HR, and senior HR professionals (65 percent, 63 percent, and 62 percent, respectively) thought that internships should be mandatory (Kluttz and Cohen, 2003).

Complicating matters for students is the difficulty of finding, and limited availability of, internships. Frequently, they are nonpaid experiences or do not provide the depth or range of experiences necessary. If internships are not required as part of an undergraduate degree program, which is typically the case (according to SHRM research), then students who attempt to enter the HR field may be discouraged or disappointed by unrealistic expectations, and organizations may likewise be disappointed or discouraged by what they see in candidates. If HR professionals are to advance not only in their career but in what and how they contribute to an organization, then they must be grounded in HR fundamentals, as well as in understanding how these principles are applied in organizations and, in turn, the implications of organizational goals and strategies for HR. Therefore, education for HR professionals must be a *continuous process*. Learning must be accomplished through both formal education and continuing professional development.

Demographic data covering the SHRM membership suggests that many HR professionals pursue advanced degrees. A major question though is what type of degree is best for HR professionals as they strive to contribute at a higher level in organizations? And, should a specific type of degree be required as a baseline? Broadly, there are options. Individuals can choose to pursue a "tagged" or specialized degree in HR, or they can seek an MBA that may or may not offer a concentration in HR. About 80 specialized degree programs exist today in HR (Heneman, 1999). Conversely, there are hundreds of MBA and other related master's programs in a wide variety of formats (e.g., full time, part time, online). Specialized HR programs are usually deep in HR content yet comparatively light on broader business issues. MBA programs typically are very well rounded in business issues but comparatively light in depth in any single subject area, even if there is an option to specialize in a particular discipline.

The purpose of this chapter is not to provide advice as to whether it is better to get an MBA or a tagged degree in HR. There are too many variations in these programs in course content, credit hours, and structure to make a generalized statement. However, the purpose is to suggest what educational and developmental components future HR professionals should seek in preparing to serve employees, organizations, and the business community. Courses, whether taken for credit at degree-granting universities or through formal professional development programs, are essentially time-limited (Thacker, 2002). Students may learn the concepts that are important in courses and may benefit from case studies or hearing about competitive practices, but time, experiential, and pedagogical constraints may prevent them from learning the application skills that go along with the concepts. As a result, part of an HR professional's education must include opportunities to learn through experience, observation, and mentoring.

RECOMMENDATIONS

Specific topics and issues can be identified that are important on a range of levels and degrees within most generalist HR functions. These can be delineated in several ways. Consider the five competencies identified in the

Table 7.1
HR Knowledge Template

	HR Knowledge and Delivery	HR Technology	Personal Credibility	Business Knowledge	Strategic Contribution
Entry					
Mid-Career					
Senior Professional					
Executive					

HR Competency Toolkit by SHRM and the University of Michigan (Brockbank and Ulrich, 2003): strategic contribution, HR delivery, business knowledge, personal credibility, and HR technology. These five domains can help HR professionals identify areas in which they need to obtain experience and education. The factors identified within each competency domain provide greater insights as well. The body of knowledge outline put forth by the Human Resource Certification Institute (HRCI) also delineates the detailed knowledge necessary to become certified in the HR profession. This outline can also serve as a guide for more in-depth development. In addition to excellent tools such as these, the best recommendation for HR education is for HR professionals to take a proactive stance in identifying and articulating their personal education needs and then to make a commitment to pursue this education. Table 7.1 shows one way to practice this proactive approach.

To use this grid effectively, each of the competencies, as put forth in the HR competency model, should be completed for each of the four broad career milestones. The grid should be completed individually by identifying the HR knowledge, business knowledge, and management skills that will be necessary for performing a current job well and for positioning oneself for the next level. This is a self-evaluation exercise at the core, but must also be completed with input from others. It is important to keep in mind that this exercise cannot take place in a vacuum. Several essential components must also be considered. First, the context of one's position and career aspirations must be articulated. Consider the following questions: What is the size of your organization? What is the nature of the industry? What is the culture of your organization? What are the expectations of senior management? Are there geographic considerations to take into account? Is the organization (and HR) engaged in global activities? Is it a unionized environment? What is your current position, and to what position do you aspire in this organization and in your career? Relevant contextual questions should be added.

Second, to truly create a blueprint for your HR education and success, input must be obtained from external sources. Ask for input from peers at your same or similar level, both in HR and in other functional areas. Consult HR professionals both inside and outside your organization, as well as senior managers and executives in other disciplines, particularly those in senior or executive ranks. Identifying role models and mentors may also be helpful in focusing on educational needs. The grid suggested here can be used broadly (e.g., identifying degree programs such as a BBA, an MBA, or a JD) and may also be used to get more granular in identifying courses

Table 7.2
HR Knowledge Template

	HR Knowledge and Delivery	HR Technology	Personal Credibility	Business Knowledge	Strategic Contribution
Entry	Recruitment	Internet recruiting	Personal communication	Labor knowledge	Understand organization goals
Mid-Career	Staffing metrics	e-HR	Effective relationships	Value chain knowledge	Change management
Senior Professional	Strategic staffing	HR tracking and measurement	Establish trust and credibility	Organization structure	Culture management
Executive	Bottom-line orientation	Overall organizational IT strategy	High integrity	Value proposition knowledge	Strategic decision-making

or specific experiences that will be necessary. Table 7.2 shows some of the knowledge areas that might be inserted in the grid for someone who is planning a career in HR. For those who enter HR via a more circuitous route than as a planned career, the need to identify knowledge gaps is even more critical.

Barber (1999) notes that an increasing amount of information is available to help guide our thinking about the specific skills needed by HR professionals. The resources used to help build an education plan, both human and archival, need to be dynamic and must be forward-thinking. Once a plan has been identified, it must continually be examined for currency and relevancy. As the needs of the organization or business shift, HR must be able to adapt its thinking and programs to account for the changes.

SUMMARY

HR professionals need an education and background that will prepare them to be analytical and strategic, thoughtful communicators, skilled negotiators, savvy business professionals, astute change agents, and expert HR generalists or specialists. To echo the words of Kaufman (1999), "There remains a significant gap between the skills and competencies provided to students in most HR/IR programs and those desired by business executives." To accomplish the necessary background, this gap must be closed.

One size does *not* fit all when it comes to HR education and knowledge. Even coming from the same degree program or taking the same professional development courses will not result in the same education or the same ability to apply the knowledge in the workplace. To be a successful HR professional requires continuous learning, an understanding of both HR and business acumen, and the ability to communicate effectively within the organization that people issues are business issues. In an age when human capital is being recognized both inside and outside the realm of the HR function as a company's most valuable asset, HR professionals must continuously hone their skills and prepare for the business and organizational challenges that have yet to be defined.

REFERENCES

Barber, Alison E. (1999). Implications for the Design of Human Resource Management—Education, Training, and Certification. *Human Resource Management, 38*(2), 177–181.

Barksdale, Kevin. (1998). Why We Should Update HR Education. *Journal of Management Education, 22*(4), 526–530.

Brockbank, Wayne, and Dave Ulrich. (2003, October). *HR Competency Toolkit.* Alexandria, VA: Society for Human Resource Management.

Brockbank, Wayne, Dave Ulrich, and W. Richard Beatty. (1999). HR Professional Development: Creating the Future Creators at the University of Michigan Business School. *Human Resource Management, 38*(2), 111–117.

Cohen, Debra J. (in press). Strategic Partnerships between Academia and Practice: The Case for Nurturing Undergraduate HR Education. In Vida Scarpello, *Thoughts on Human Resource Management Education in the United States.* New York: McGraw-Hill Publishers.

Heneman, Robert L. (1999). Emphasizing Analytical Skills in HR Graduate Education: The Ohio State University Mlhr Program. *Human Resource Management, 38*(2), 131–134.

Kaufman, Bruce E. (1999). Evolution and Current Status of University HR Programs. *Human Resource Management, 38*(2), 103–110.

Kluttz, Letty, and Debra Cohen. (2003, November). *SHRM Undergraduate HR Curriculum Study.* Retrieved from the Society for Human Resource Management's web site www.shrm.org/surveys/SHRM%20Undergraduate%20HR%20Curriculum%20Study.asp.

Langbert, Mitchell. (2000). Professors, Managers, and Human Resource Education. *Human Resource Management, 39*(1), 65–78.

Schramm, Jennifer. (2004, June). *SHRM Workplace Forecast: A Strategic Outlook 2004–2005.* Alexandria, VA: Society for Human Resource Management.

Thacker, Rebecca A. (2002). Revising the HR Curriculum: An Academic/Practitioner Partnership. *Education & Training, 44*(1), 31–39.

Tyson, Shaun. (1999). How HR Knowledge Contributes to Organizational Performance. *Human Resource Management Journal, 9*(3), 42–52.

Van Eynde, F. Donald, and Stephen L. Tucker. (1997). A Quality Human Resource Curriculum: Recommendations from Leading Senior HR Executives. *Human Resource Management, 36*(4), 397–408.

CHAPTER 8

LIFE AFTER OUTSOURCING: LESSONS LEARNED AND THE ROLE OF HUMAN RESOURCES AS A STRATEGIC BUSINESS PARTNER

MIRIAN M. GRADDICK-WEIR

Human resources outsourcing (HRO) is one of the fastest growing business process outsourcing segments. The growth rate between 1999 and 2004 was 32 percent, and the current market opportunity is over $60 billion—with a 30 percent future growth rate (Dataquest, Inc.). Many companies are outsourcing discrete services such as benefits enrollment, or blended services (entire processes such as the employment process). A few are adopting the full HRO model which consists of outsourcing a broad range of HR functions. The reasons for outsourcing are well documented; organizations hope to achieve significant cost savings, greater efficiency, increased value creation, and better leverage of capital investments in HR systems; create career opportunities for HR employees; and enable HR to focus on more strategic activities.

THE AT&T EXPERIENCE

AT&T negotiated a seven-year outsourcing engagement across a broad range of HR functions in 2002. Strategy and policy for all HR functions, the HR partner role, and functions that are deemed strategic were not a part of the outsourcing deal. Thus far, we have achieved the cost reduction targets, maintained service levels, and jointly managed several successful large-scale projects (e.g., the rollout of a new market-based compensation system); meanwhile, customer satisfaction results continue to improve. In this chapter—with two years' experience behind us and collaboration with other firms who have outsourced significant functions—we describe the lessons learned on this journey. The purpose is to summarize the key lessons learned from the outsourcing experience and to discuss the new strategic role for HR in today's competitive and rapidly challenging business environment.

WHAT WE HAVE LEARNED

Although we have learned much about outsourcing, there continue to be more lessons to learn. The following sections describe our most significant discoveries.

1. Operational Excellence in Employee Transactions

Transaction processing related to employees is critical to any organization. Line managers are basically agnostic to where these services are performed as long as they are accurate and user-friendly. In negotiating any outsourcing deal, HR must never forget that it is ultimately accountable for the quality, accuracy, and speed of employee-related services. If these services are not done correctly, HR will not become a value-added strategic partner. While obtaining significant cost reductions is important to any deal, it is equally important to select a partner with whom you have the greatest alignment around maintaining operational excellence both during and after the transition.

2. Relationships Matter

Many of us have learned that it is impossible to get all the terms and conditions right when you first close the deal. Therefore, you need people on both sides who value the partnership and who are fully committed to its ongoing success. When aspects of the contract need to be revisited, each party must be willing to offer creative, win-win solutions to resolve issues. Individuals who harbor ill feelings about the deal, or who never wanted it to happen in the first place, should not be assigned to manage the ongoing relationship. Select a partner who does not view the engagement simply as a legal and contractual relationship, but who values the partnership and is always committed to honoring the spirit of the deal.

3. Moving People into the Deal Has Advantages and Inherent Risks

Moving skilled people into the deal can enhance your ability to have a seamless transition during the cutover, which is key to making it transparent to line managers. Initial troubleshooting, communication, and understanding of the business are greatly improved. Also, if the outsourcer successfully grows its outsourcing business, people have greater career opportunities to develop their skills by transitioning to other projects over time. The inherent risk of moving the people with the deal is that you do not always get a fresh perspective when evaluating potential process improvements. It is crucial to jointly consider how functions are staffed to ensure an infusion of breakthrough ideas and not just incremental improvements.

4. Contract Management Is Key to Controlling Ongoing Costs and Managing the Overall Relationship

It is important to manage ongoing costs, ensure service levels are met, and have a single place where issues and problems can be escalated and resolved quickly. It is critical to set up a strong governance model and contract management team within HR. This team should ensure that any new requests are appropriate for inclusion, monitor compliance with the terms and conditions of the deal (including service levels), and serve as a point of escalation. We have been extremely disciplined about filtering any new work through this organization to ensure costs do not creep up and mitigate the initial savings. The size of this group depends on the deal; however, it must be adequately sized at the beginning of the transaction to handle the workload. The group can always be adjusted downward over time.

We have summarized the three keys to success as follows:

1. *Tenets:* Both sides must have a common vision, guiding principles that define the spirit of the deal, cultural compatibility, and trust.
2. *Teamwork:* Strong partnering and collaboration are essential at many levels.

3. *Tenacity:* It is necessary to overcome the many obstacles that surface along the way and to navigate through change, complexity, and uncertainty.

HR's Role as a Value-Added Strategic Partner

Life after outsourcing depends in part on life before outsourcing and whether HR has the capability to truly be a strategic player at the table. Having a successful outsourcing engagement is necessary, but certainly not sufficient. Many articles have focused on whether human resources would survive in an environment where new technologies replace many core functions and outsourcing vendors compete for HR roles once done within an organization (Society of Human Resources Management, 2002). If one were to poll a group of senior HR leaders and business unit leaders, I am confident you would get unanimous agreement that critical and value-added HR work exists and that there will always be a place inside the business for talented people to manage the work. HR leaders face the following critical workplace challenges:

- *Talent management:* Finding effective ways to attract, develop, and retain key talent in today's challenging marketplace. This includes proactively managing leadership development and succession planning, understanding emerging skill requirements and the impacts of workforce demographics and technology, and creating a high-performing culture where people at all levels are engaged and energized.
- *Workforce strategy:* Determining what work is core to the business and should be done inside the company versus what work is most effectively performed through partnerships, alliances, outsourcing, and so on (Moore, 2000). Making the right choices requires partnering with line managers and facilitating the development of an overall workforce strategy aligned with the business priorities.
- *Changing demographics:* Addressing the potential skill shortages resulting from a graying workforce, managing a more diverse workforce with cultural and language differences, and dealing with the cross-generational differences in expectations, attitudes, and learning styles.
- *Cost containment and governance issues:* Managing the rising costs of health care, dealing with the implications of increased regulatory

scrutiny such as Sarbanes-Oxley and the significant scrutiny on executive compensation.

The key question is whether we are selecting, training, and developing
HR leaders who are capable of stepping up to a broader range of skills necessary to be an effective player at the business table. During the past cou-
ple of years, several top HR positions have been filled with line managers
rather than with individuals with significant HR experience. It is unclear
whether this is becoming a trend or why it is occurring. One hypothesis is
that companies are placing a stronger focus on building general management skills and are therefore rotating line managers across a broad range of
functions, including HR. Another hypothesis is that as more HR work is
outsourced to expert practitioners, the emphasis in the senior positions becomes having the ability to connect the function with the business strategy
and results. In this scenario, having operational experience is viewed as a
significant asset. While these are merely observations at this point, this certainly bears monitoring. It is critical to understand the evolving role of HR
and the key experiences necessary for success.

Building HR Competency

HR is a profession with standards that certify proficiency across a range
of competencies. The Society of Human Resources Management (SHRM)
has recently sanctioned a certification assessment. In addition, it is possible to obtain specialized graduate degrees in Human Resources and In-
dustrial/Organizational psychology. Although the formal training to
ensure functional excellence is key, it is imperative that HR Leaders acquire the broad range of competencies necessary for success. Becker,
Huselid, and Ulrich (2001) summarized three large-scale HR competency
studies and found six critical domains. Table 8.1 captures these competencies and my view of what is particularly critical in today's fiercely competitive marketplace.

Given the increasing trend toward HR outsourcing, I would add yet another vital HR competency: managing virtual resources. This involves
managing a virtual network of resources across traditional and nontradi-
tional organizational boundaries while ensuring results are achieved when
you do not directly control the resources.

Table 8.1
Building HR Competency

HR Competencies	Becker, Huselid, Ulrich Findings	Application in a Highly Competitive Market
Knowledge of the business	Understanding the financial, strategic, technological, and organizational capabilities.	Having a relentless focus on financials, understanding customer needs, and demonstrating strong business acumen.
Delivery of HR practice	Ability to deliver state-of-the art, innovative HR practices. Mastering the theory of HR and adapting the theory to unique situations.	Demonstrating flexibility and nimbleness by quickly adapting innovative policies and practices to meet changing business requirements.
Management of change	Ability to diagnose problems, build relationships, set a vision, solve problems, and implement goals.	Increasing the velocity of implementing large-scale change interventions aligned with evolving business strategies.
Management of culture	HR as "keepers of the culture"—champions cultural transformation and reinforces desired behaviors.	Preserving core values while driving the adoption of new policies, practices, and cultural attributes to respond to changing marketplace dynamics.
Personal credibility	Living the values, establishing relationships built on trust, and having a point of view.	Demonstrating the ability to win in a competitive environment while maintaining integrity, candor, credibility, trustworthiness, and courage.
Strategic HR performance management	Orchestrating the firm's strategy implementation through balanced performance measurement systems.	Developing metrics to quantify the impact of HR initiatives and people strategies on delivering tangible results that contribute to the bottom line.

Developing HR Leaders to Achieve Success

It is critical to have the right combination of developmental strategies in place to build and maintain these HR competencies. These strategies include external hiring, training, and development and staffing. Several years ago, AT&T reignited its college hiring program and began hiring a small group of HR professionals with advanced degrees each year to infuse new ideas and ensure adequate succession over time. In the area of development, we launched a two-day HR partner-training program before our full-scale outsourcing to help strengthen and expand the skills of our HR partners. The senior leaders in HR also participate in a company-wide Client Executive Program where individuals are responsible for managing executive relationships with our large customer accounts. Providing HR executives an opportunity to interface directly with external customers is an excellent way to strengthen knowledge of the business and customer needs. It is also valuable to have HR leaders participate in key projects with line managers such as product launches, building new businesses, improving customer satisfaction, and so on. Finally, strategically staffing individuals into key assignments can optimize success. Job rotations from corporate roles into HR partner roles are invaluable and ensure that people have a chance to manage in different assignments (turnarounds, building a new business, global, etc.). Developing strong business acumen will also require a subset of HR leaders to have line experiences in areas such as marketing, finance, sales, and strategy.

SUMMARY

There is a growing trend to outsource administrative and transaction oriented HR work. Done well, it affords HR the opportunity to be a contributor at the business table and proactively lead critical workplace initiatives. It is imperative that we invest in ourselves to ensure we have the broader range of skills and experiences necessary to affect the bottom line. The bar has been raised. The opportunities are abundant.

REFERENCES

"The Future of the HR Profession: Eight Leading Consulting Firms Share their Visions of the Future of the Human Resources" (The Society for Human Resource Management, 2002). Online at http://www.shrm.org/press/futureofhr.asp.

Moore, Geoffrey A., *Crossing the Chasm* (Chasm: HarperBusiness, 1991).

Ulrich, Dave, Michael R. Losey, and Gerry Lake, *Tomorrow's HR Management* (New York: John Wiley & Sons, 1997).

CHAPTER 9

THE FOUR CS OF THE HR PROFESSION: BEING COMPETENT, CURIOUS, COURAGEOUS, AND CARING ABOUT PEOPLE

SUSAN R. MEISINGER

"**P**eople are our most important asset."

At some point, every HR professional has heard someone in his or her organization make this pronouncement. Sometimes it's in an organization with leadership that behaves as if it believes it. Sometimes, it isn't. The good news is that today the mantra, "People are our most important asset," is not just rhetoric. For most leaders, it's the reality.

In a recent Conference Board survey, CEOs ranked "engaging employees in the company's vision/values/goals," "developing and retaining potential leaders," and "talent identification and growth" as 3rd, 5th, and 10th, respectively, among the factors important to their companies' current success.[1] A 2003 Mercer survey of almost 200 CFOs showed that 92 percent believe human capital management has a great effect on customer satisfaction, 82 percent believe the effective management of human capital has a positive impact on profitability, and 72 percent believe human capital practices impact innovation and new product development.[2]

That's good news for the future of the HR profession. The world is seemingly ready to accept everything the profession has to offer. But is everyone in the profession ready to deliver? Are HR professionals ready to embrace this future?

As part of its mission to advance the profession, the Society for Human Resource Management (SHRM) has conducted informal research to better understand how the profession is perceived by other non-HR executives. The results are mixed. Some leaders see a "performance gap" between the potential of HR executives and HR executives' execution at a strategic level.[3] So, what will the successful professionals of the future look like? Successful HR professionals today, and in the future, have to be Competent, Curious, Courageous, and Care about people.

COMPETENT

While some may think that the need for competence goes without saying, I think it needs to be said—repeatedly. HR professionals must be competent not only in their field but also as business professionals. HR professionals aren't *entitled* to a seat at the strategic table because everyone else should understand the value of good HR management. We must *earn* the seat by demonstrating individual competency in delivering value.

A detailed body of knowledge outline, developed through literature review, research, and surveys of HR practitioners, has been regularly updated and published by the Human Resource Certification Institute (HRCI). The outline delineates the detailed knowledge necessary to become certified in the HR discipline.

But there's more. The Society for Human Resource Management (SHRM), the University of Michigan Business School, and the Global Consulting Alliance (GCA) developed the *HR Competency Toolkit* based on five competency domains for the profession.[4] These domains were identified by examining the characteristics of HR in high-performing organizations. These five domains, with examples, are:

1. *Strategic contribution:* Brockbank, Wilhelm, and Ulrich's research shows that this is the arena in which HR can make the largest contribution, and it's the one that is often the most challenging for those HR professionals who have focused on compliance-related activities for much of their careers. Indeed, in a 2002 survey of HR professionals conducted by SHRM and the Balanced Scorecard Collaborative, only 34 percent of the respondents indicated that their executives viewed HR as a strategic partner.[5]

   Making a strategic contribution means identifying problems, establishing strategy, and proposing alternatives. It means anticipating changes and putting systems in place to quickly respond and adapt to the changes.

For example, The Home Depot has a business strategy that includes growth in the number of new stores. Dennis Donovan, executive VP of HR, set about putting systems in place for meeting the staffing needs that this strategy would create in the future. To deliver pools of qualified applicants to meet current and future staffing needs, he created partnerships with the U.S. Department of Labor and state one-stop shopping employment offices, the AARP, and the Department of Defense. The Home Depot has a rich applicant pool as a result, tapping into the unemployed, older workers and soldiers who have recently completed their service with the military.

2. *Business knowledge:* HR professionals need to not only understand and speak the language of business but also contribute to the conversation around the strategy table.

When Mary Cheddie joined Orvis as VP for HR, she spent time learning the retail sales catalog business and gained an understanding of the drivers of profitability. She learned that the decisions made by buyers were key to the success of a catalog. So she examined the strategy used to source and recruit for these positions. Discovering that the strategy wasn't delivering the value it could, she changed it. She began recruiting buyers with more years of experience. While this strategy increased staffing costs, she was able to demonstrate that the new strategy increased profitability because more experienced buyers made more successful purchasing decisions.

3. *HR delivery:* HR professionals must deliver HR services seamlessly before we can ever hope to make strategic contributions in an organization. If jobs aren't filled, people aren't paid, and benefits aren't delivered seamlessly, it's irrelevant how strategically inclined we may be.

This requirement may mean delivering HR in ways never delivered before. For example, Vinny Stabile, VP of people with JetBlue, and his team implemented profit sharing for employees in their first year of employment, schedule-sharing for flight attendants, and 100 percent telecommuting for reservationists. As a result, one analyst called JetBlue's culture "a big recruiting magnet." HR is excelling at delivering the talent that's making the company successful.

4. *Personal credibility:* HR professionals need to get results, have solid interpersonal skills, and communicate effectively.

One way that Randy Harris, senior VP of HR for Nextel, was able to demonstrate personal credibility was by assuming additional line responsibilities and getting results. At Nextel, HR doesn't only develop the training materials and then train customer support staff. Nextel University, which is led by HR, has the lead responsibility in developing the product information provided to the customer and is responsible for customer support activities. Consistent information is communicated to both employees and customers, allowing employees to be more effective in dealing with customers. HR has gained credibility by leveraging its efforts on behalf of employees to the benefit of the customer. And HR has delivered results, with improved customer satisfaction.

5. *HR technology:* HR professionals need to be comfortable and knowledgeable about technology and the potential it offers to free us to focus on the strategic.

Consider what Arte Nathan was able to do as VP for HR for the Bellagio hotel. Confronted with the challenge of completely staffing a hotel when it first opened in 1998, he turned to technology. He developed an entirely paperless application process, capturing 75,000 applications in less than five months, hiring almost 10,000 people. This data then became the foundation for providing managers with electronic access to personnel files. Reliance on technology allowed HR to focus on the strategy of picking the right people—employees who would provide great customer service—which in turn helped make the Bellagio one of the top hotels in Las Vegas.

For some HR professionals, gaining these competencies will be an on-the-job undertaking because they have no background—academic or otherwise—when they enter the field. The challenge will seem as difficult as changing a jet engine while the jet is in flight.

A study of the educational achievements of SHRM members confirms this difficulty. While members are highly educated, only about a third have a degree in HR, industrial relations, or psychology, and a third have degrees in business. Another third were designated as "other."[6] And unlike many other fields of study with consistent courses of study across colleges and universities, there's great variation in the course work that leads to a degree in HR.

SHRM is working to address the wide variations in academic programs by developing a suggested curriculum for undergraduate and graduate study in HR. But for the foreseeable future, some HR practitioners will require education and skill development after they've entered the field. For example, an HR professional with a degree in psychology probably didn't focus on the study of finance—a gap that has to be filled to understand a business. Similarly, if an HR professional has a business degree but no courses in HR, he or she probably won't know what constitutes "hours of work" for purposes of calculating overtime. That knowledge is necessary to be competent in HR delivery.

Certification certainly helps to fill this gap, but HR professionals have an ongoing obligation to conduct self-assessments to determine where they should focus their own professional development efforts. What are the competencies required for their current role, and what do they already have? What are the knowledge requirements, and what do they know? What has changed in the business world around them, and how equipped are they to deal with it?

CURIOUS

HR professionals should be curious—curious about things going on within our organizations, curious about developments in the industries in which we work, and curious about what's happening in the world around us. It's difficult to operate at a strategic level if we don't understand what's going on in our organization, we don't know how well the organization is competing in its industry, and we don't know how it's all being impacted from a global perspective.

Internally, HR professionals should ask CEOs what keeps them awake at night. If the HR function isn't focused on the same issues, we won't be adding as much value as we could.

HR professionals should ask questions of colleagues to learn as much as possible about strategies, challenges, and opportunities. Unless we're aware of what they face, we won't be able to create people strategies to help.

HR professionals should be curious about the industries in which we operate and curious about how other HR professionals in the same industries grapple with common issues. We should be curious about how HR professionals operate in other industries and try to identify common issues and learn how the issues are addressed. By asking questions of HR colleagues, we can learn what else we could do, or what we shouldn't do, in our own organizations.

HR professionals need to be curious about emerging trends in the world around us, learning what those trends are, and considering how those trends may impact our organization in the future. For example, what will the impact of China's rapid economic growth mean to our business, and how can we prepare? What are the future staffing implications created by an aging workforce beyond potential skill shortages? Will the values—and expectations—of younger workers differ significantly from older workers, and will they change the corporate culture?

COURAGEOUS

Prior to retirement from his role as CEO of SHRM, Mike Losey, my coeditor, had a screensaver that said, "HR—Not a Job for Wimps!!!" Another HR professional told me, "If I don't think something I'm doing may put my job at risk at least a few times each year, I don't feel like I'm doing my job." When I moderated a panel of CEOs to discuss what they wanted from HR, one answered simply, "I want someone with guts!"

They're all describing another key characteristic of successful HR professionals: courage.

Recent corporate scandals have underscored the fact that not all organizations are committed to being law-abiding and doing the right thing. And a 2003 survey of HR professionals conducted by SHRM and the Ethics Resource Center found that only 53 percent had never felt pressured by other employees or managers to compromise their organization's standards of ethical business conduct to achieve business objectives.[7]

HR professionals must have the courage to do the right thing when we're under great pressure to do something else.

Certainly, courage to do the right things can come with the values learned in our childhood. But courage also comes with the self-confidence gained from being competent to do the job. An HR professional who understands business strategy is more likely to have the courage to challenge a colleague when the strategy is being ignored. An HR professional who can read financial statements is more likely to have the courage to object when financial statements don't accurately reflect the truth. An HR professional with a reputation as an honest coach and a consistent communicator is much more able to stand up to a colleague when the colleague is acting inappropriately. An HR professional who knows employment law is much more likely to have the courage to insist that laws not be bent or, worse, ignored. And if being courageous results in the loss of a promotion or even a job, competent HR professionals know they'll have other job opportunities.

Having the courage to model ethical behavior, and expecting it from others, is good for business. It creates an honest workplace, which leads to greater employee loyalty, higher productivity, and better organizational performance.

CARE ABOUT PEOPLE

Just as we've all heard someone say, "People are our most important asset," we've also talked to someone who has considered entering the profession because he or she "likes working with people." We groan inwardly because we know that the job is about much more than being a "people person." We know that for even the most competent HR professionals, some people can drive you nuts.

Valuing people and the contribution people can make to an organization *is* a key characteristic of good HR professionals and always will be. And we shouldn't apologize for it or try to minimize it in an effort to be viewed as "strategic."

HR professionals who care about people will automatically make strategic decisions and recommendations that are based on a full understanding of how it will impact people. The decisions or recommendations will be better as a result. HR professionals who care about people will expend the effort to eliminate or minimize the downside impact on people that may come from tough business strategies and decisions. HR professionals who care about people will provide exceptional HR delivery because they want to ensure that employees are treated fairly and with respect.

Caring about people and doing the right thing on behalf of employees are parts of being a business partner because it's good for business. It increases retention, increases the level of employee engagement, and helps build a corporate culture that will help advance the business strategy. And yes, it's the right thing to do.

HR professionals who are competent, curious, courageous, and care about people add real value to the organizations they serve and to the working lives of people employed there. And I think it's a pretty great way to spend a career.

NOTES

1. E. V. Rudis, "The CEO Challenge 2003," Conference Board, 2003. Retrieved March 1, 2004, from www.conference-board.org.
2. "Capital Management: The CFO's Perspective," Mercer survey, 2003. Retrieved March 1, 2004, from www.mercerhr.com.
3. "A Review of Executives' Opinions Regarding HR and Its Contributions," March, 2004, Society for Human Resource Management.
4. Dave Ulrich and Wayne Brockbank, Society for Human Resource Management, *HR Competency Toolkit: Competencies for the New HR Guidebook and HR Competency Self-Assessment,* University of Michigan and Globl Consulting Alliance, 2003, from http://shrmstore.shrm.org/shrm/product.asp?pf%5Fid=52%2E17503&dept%5Fid=5.
5. *Balanced Scorecard Collaborative Aligning HR with Organization Strategy Survey,* Society for Human Resource Management, 2002, p. 14.
6. Debra Cohen and Letty Kluttz, *SHRM Undergraduate HR Curriculum Study,* Society for Human Resource Management, 2003, p. 26.
7. Joshua Joseph and Evren Essen, *Ethics Resource Center 2003 Business Ethics Survey,* Society for Human Resource Management, 2003, p. 5.

CHAPTER 10

DIFFERENTIATION THROUGH PEOPLE—HOW CAN HR MOVE BEYOND BUSINESS PARTNER?

GEOFF ARMSTRONG

Human resource professionals around the world are rightly displaying a new confidence. We are emerging from a period of questioning and self-doubt to face the central challenge of a knowledge based, service intensive global economy.

How do companies and other employing organizations, whether in the public, private, or voluntary sector—generate and regenerate differentiated, competitive advantage? The places we were taught to look for much of the manufacturing-dominated twentieth century—technology, scale, standardization, protected markets, cheaper money—don't do it any more. In the people field, command and control, detailed compliance with standard procedures, scientific management, collective agreements as the main regulator of relations between manager and managed, labor as a commodity, and human resources as a cost to be minimized just don't lead to delighted customers.

Every organization has to use its resources as efficiently as it can. Continuous improvement in products, processes, and productivity is vital to success. Sensible procedures have to be in place for compliance, risk management, and accountability. But customers make their buying decisions on how they value what they are offered, not on how it suits the supplier to get it to them. Delighting customers comes from the discretionary behavior of the people working for the organization at every level, most of them a long way from head office and its ability to dictate conformance.

In turn, discretionary behavior, willing contribution, innovation, continuous learning and sharing, and use of initiative to anticipate changing needs and marshal the resources to meet them have to be organizational capabilities that are led and managed. They don't come about by accident.

HR LEADERS

This is where the HR professional has to earn his or her salt. Our profession has the lead responsibility, working closely with our line and other colleagues, to design the policies and practices that elicit the discretionary behavior that leads to sustainable success. We lead on finding, growing, deploying, motivating, and rewarding talent. We lead on training and developing the people who make it happen, including those with responsibility for others. We lead on creating cultures, learning environments, psychological contracts, systems, processes, and the feedback loops that measure how successfully the job is being done. We are at the pivotal point between understanding what success looks like in the eyes of the customer and translating that back into the organization in the form of employment relationships and working practices that give the organization the edge.

Increasingly, people are the business. When technologies, products, and systems are easily copied and leapfrogged, it is the people to whom we must turn for sustainably superior performance. And it is to the adaptive organization—one that is quick, flexible, and proactive in anticipation of, as well as responsive to, changing customer needs—to which we need to apply our creative efforts if we are to build sustainable, regeneratable strategies and practices for success.

How then can our profession contribute the most value? How can we design and deliver people strategies that support the achievement of business strategies? Beyond that, how can we turn people management and development into a differentiating advantage, a core competence that drives superior performance? How can HR move from being seen as just an implementer of decisions already taken by the *real* business leaders to being a source of capability and capacity that enables ever more ambitious strategies to be accomplished?

The answers lie in:

- Providing the evidence, in hard business performance terms, that progressive approaches to people management are worth doing.

- Demonstrating that the systematic design, application, and evaluation of strategies and practices for people are things real managers in the real world can do: HR is not a menu of fads, fashions, and prejudices only loosely connected to the business.
- Making explicit the body of knowledge on which effective HR strategy is based as a systematically learnable, constantly renewable management discipline.
- Demonstrating that the HR profession has up-to-date mastery of that body of knowledge and is sufficiently proficient in business management that it can craft the right people strategies both to support and take forward the strategic intent of the organization.

While there are no HR panaceas that work in all business contexts, the evidence shows that higher levels of performance result from better job satisfaction, commitment, and flexibility, which can be created by:

- Positive psychological contracts based on trust and respect, supported by progressive people management practices that are designed for purpose and monitored in implementation
- Opportunities for employees to share extensive information about their organization and to participate and be heard in decision making
- Well-designed, flexible jobs that stimulate people to contribute and grow
- Development of talent through careful selection, induction, and continuous learning
- Positive leadership at all levels working to a common purpose and values
- Getting value from diversity as a means of achieving business goals
- Organizational climate that recognizes and rewards the behavior required for success
- Self-managing teams and decentralized decision making
- Effective implementation and evaluation of people management practices

IDENTIFYING KEY PEOPLE DRIVERS

These issues are the meat and drink of our profession. We should focus on identifying the key people drivers for our organizations. What are the components that make most sense for our organizations in terms of building human capital and then enabling it to work in ways that make the winning difference? What are the relevant measures so that we know how we are doing? How do we best share that knowledge so that the organization can continuously refine its people strategies? How do we know that our investment in people is going to the right strategic priorities, and does the return justify the investment?

How can we report our progress and plans to the growing band of external stakeholders we need to convince in terms that enable them to assess our prospects of driving future value and to do it in ways that are ethically acceptable? How best can we measure the state of the internal psychological contract so that our business strategies are based on a realistic assessment of the extent to which we can rely on the willing contribution of people at all levels? How can we know if the people working for the organization want it to succeed and have the necessary ability, motivation, and opportunity to make it do so? How can we develop, articulate, and live out values that cause people to want to work with us and to contribute their discretionary commitment to make our organization sustainably more successful than our competitors?

These are not soft challenges. Neither do the answers we choose mean that we aspire to turn people management and development into a bookkeeping discipline, devoid of dynamism and judgment. People are not inanimate resources, conditioned to respond in predictable ways regardless of the context in which they work.

But it is essential that we develop the skills, tools, and measures to make the people dimensions of enterprise something that all managers can come to grips with, connect with the overall strategy of the business, and monitor in ways that have equal legitimacy with their more familiar financial and physical measures.

To develop those skills, tools, and measures, the HR professional must:

- Be clear about where the business is trying to go and what strategies and practices for people will take it there.
- Think and act like business managers first and functional specialists second.
- Be proficient across the range of management disciplines.
- Be comfortable with measurement and confident that we can put in place appropriate combinations of practices that lead both to superior

performance today and to the organizational capacity to aim for more ambitious future strategies.

UNIVERSAL ISSUES

As I talk to colleagues in the World Federation of Personnel Management Associations,[1] I am struck by how universal these issues are. Whether working in advanced economies operating high up the value chain or in developing economies seeking rapid progress toward global competitiveness, many of the same issues feature on the HR professional's agenda. Talent management, skill shortages, constant change, continuous learning, industrial restructuring, political and other stakeholder pressures, employee commitment, and its reciprocal need for employee-sensitive practices are not confined to national boundaries or particular organizations. We all read the same books, share access to research, and use the same tools, models, and scorecards in our quest to give our organizations the competitive edge that alone secures customer satisfaction and repeat business.

HR truly is emerging as a global profession. But unlike some others that are doing so mainly under regulatory pressure, HR is globalizing because organizations everywhere need, for solid competitive reasons, to learn from others' experience what works in creating advantage and in keeping ahead of the game.

This is an exciting time to be in HR. Never have the opportunities been greater for business leaders with the insight and skill to build people-centered strategies into what makes their organizations stand out from the crowd. Never have the career opportunities been greater for people professionals to make their mark at the heart of business and to move into the topmost positions. If people and the ways they are led, managed, developed, and motivated are the main, hard-to-imitate differentiators between success and failure, business-savvy people professionals are on the fast track to the top—but only if we are good enough, bold enough, and can demonstrate that what we do makes that winning difference.

PROFESSIONAL ASSOCIATIONS

All of these opportunities make new and stretching demands of the member associations to which HR professionals around the world look for help.

Although there is no universal pattern for what a professional body should do, there is a growing consensus, at least in aspiration, around a number of key issues.

Most associations aspire to set professional standards that express what it takes to be an effective HR professional, linked to an accreditation process that objectively certifies that those standards have been met. Most offer services such as magazines, conferences, training courses, and web sites. Some conduct research and seek to influence public policy on employment matters. Many offer networks, often geographical or subject based, so that members can share learning with one another. Some have policies on the ethical standards expected of their members.

In the United Kingdom and Ireland, the Chartered Institute of Personnel and Development (CIPD),[2] founded in 1913 and therefore the longest-established of associations, and, with over 120,000 members at various levels of professional qualification, one of the largest, has been grappling with these challenges over many years.

Without claiming to have all the answers, CIPD has followed a strategy of seeking to anticipate what its members will be called on to do and to put in place a comprehensive range of services to support them at every stage of their career. More widely, CIPD has set out to be a thought and practice leader across the whole field of people management and development, for application by its members, and by their line and other functional managerial colleagues. The institute never forgets that HR professionals can succeed only to the extent that they equip their organization and the managers in it with the skills and motivation to lead and manage people effectively. It is not just about HR processes, transactions, or policies isolated from the mainstream of organizational performance, although neither does the institute hesitate to take a view on important values, ethical issues, or public policy issues.

CIPD's professional standards for chartered membership are recognized at the postgraduate level, equivalent to other, more traditional chartered professions such as accountancy. But integral to those standards is that members must both know and understand the body of knowledge and be able to apply it in an appropriately tailored way in a variety of practical employment contexts. One-third of the total qualification is in business management because CIPD sees that area as a vital component of professional competence and credibility.

In addition to meeting the standards, chartered members must show that they have three years' experience at a relevant level in the profession and that they adopt a systematic approach to their own continuous learning. Professionalism is a career-long standard, not a hurdle to be left behind once qualified. Members also commit to an explicit ethical code of professional conduct and to be accountable to the institute for compliance with it.

CIPD members report that the model works for them, and they are constantly coming up with good ideas for further improvement. They see the need for professional learning networks that are external to their current employment. And they are prepared to undertake the learning and certification processes because they see those processes as adding to the value of their contribution to the strategy and performance of the many different organizations with which they work. And that is the way that HR can move beyond business partner and truly turn people into the winning difference.

NOTES

1. See World Federation of Personnel Management Associations (WFPMA) at http://www.wfpma.com.
2. See CIPD at http://www.cipd.co.uk.

SECTION III

LEARN TO MASTER AND PLAY NEW ROLES

Roles define expectations, actions, and perceptions of a person or group. In sports, role players perform their individual tasks so that the team accomplishes its goal. In theater, actors play roles to communicate the intent of the playwright. In relationships, roles are often performed to meet expectations and ensure stability.

HR professionals accept and play roles in their organizations. These roles offer metaphors for and characterize the work of HR. Traditionally, HR professionals have been employee advocates who ensure the organization has people to meet organization requirements and technical specialists who craft acceptable HR practices. In recent years, HR professionals have been business or strategic partners who help deliver business results.

The authors in this section propose emerging and new roles for HR. These authors have an established mix of professional experience and conceptual insights. They each have decades of HR experience and wisdom on which to base their projects. The roles they propose build on what has been, align with changing business conditions, and offer new metaphors for HR professionals.

In Chapter 11, Avolio proposes a *chief integrative leader* role where HR professionals pull together resources to meet business requirements. This integrator works with diverse cultures, conceptualizes how to deploy social networks, understands intangible value, and links people across time and space.

Cascio describes in Chapter 12 how HR professionals at SYSCO have become *drivers* of business success. As drivers, they have established processes to get the most from employees and to drive a profit chain from management practices to employee satisfaction to customer satisfaction to long-term profitability.

Childs in Chapter 13 reviews IBM's diversity role and suggests that diversity leaders manage traditional issues of race, gender, and age and emerging issues of multiculturalism, religious preference, and full inclusion. He reviews programs and initiatives that have sponsored and sustained IBM's legacy of commitment to diversity.

Darien suggests in Chapter 14 that HR professionals become *productivity czars.* He points out that productivity issues are of central concern to senior managers and that HR professionals are uniquely positioned to understand and advocate productivity gains. Productivity analyses put HR issues into line manager terms that resonate with them and thus have more impact.

Ellig puts forward three roles in Chapter 15. Business partners design HR practices that help managers meet their goals. Employee champions ensure a code of conduct and a value proposition for employees. Respected advisors give honest opinions as they coach senior managers about their personal and organization behaviors required for success.

Roberts and Hirsch in Chapter 16 advocate for a *chief organization effectiveness officer,* who enables leaders, builds cultures, strengthens performance, fosters innovation, and builds customer loyalty. This new role requires new accountabilities for the HR professional focused on the organization as well as people.

Lawler suggests in Chapter 17 that HR professionals play the roles of *business partner* (supports execution of business results), *strategic partner* (helps execute strategy), and *organization effectiveness expert* (helps make change happen).

Collectively, these emerging roles build on the past and suggest that employees continue to be treated with dignity and that HR practices be designed appropriately. But, these roles shape a future for HR professionals. While not abdicating people, they focus on organizations and processes. HR professionals in the future will need to play multiple roles, focused on people, practices, and organizations. "Human" resources may be expanded to "organization" resources. Abstract ideas such as culture and organization capability will need to be refined and defined so that people live and operate in an effective organizational setting. Organizations have many of the attributes of people, with a personality, history, and reputation. HR professionals must understand how to manage organizations to play new roles.

CHAPTER 11

THE CHIEF INTEGRATIVE LEADER: MOVING TO THE NEXT ECONOMY'S HR LEADER

BRUCE J. AVOLIO

Over the past four years, there have been few conversations that I've participated in or observed where there were more than two HR professionals in attendance that the phrase "getting a seat at the table" didn't come up in one form or another. I've tried to visualize what that table should look like, who will be at it, and what this all means for future leaders in HR. I have come to the conclusion that HR leaders might consider securing a seat at the next table, not the current one they envision.

CURRENT STATE

Let me begin with a basic question: Has the field of human resources now run its course? My answer is: Probably not, because there are too many stakeholders that feed from this profession's trough. Perhaps the more fundamental question is whether the HR profession is still needed. I conclude that the focus on HR is clearly needed at least into the foreseeable future.

Like most professional fields, the pipeline containing the future pool of candidates moves like crude oil through Alaska in January. My general concern is not about where the field is heading, but rather about the talent currently in the pipeline and being attracted into it, representing the next generation of "top" HR leaders.

Six Waves of People Issues in Organizations

Over the past 100 years, the field of people issues in organizations has gone through what I would call six distinct waves (Table 11.1).

In my estimation, we are now in the fifth wave probably slowed by a global recession, terrorism, ethics scandals, and the changing focus of our economies from IT to the biologically based economy now emerging. I am concerned about the pipeline of talent that we've created to deal with people issues in our organizations. Our learning institutions focus on training HR leaders for the first three waves, creating a pipeline of HR practitioners developed and reinforced for exercising transactional leadership and compliance (Avolio, 1999). Many HR practitioners have not been prepared to address the levels of complexity required to strategically lead complex

Table 11.1
The Six Waves of HR

Wave 1: Orchestrated the origins of the "organization" and facilitated getting people efficiently positioned with machines to produce large volumes of products.

Wave 2: Focused on identifying the "individual" and picking the right one for the right job, sending that person off into a rather long predictable career path.

Wave 3: Characterized by a dramatic rise in legislation, new laws, and employment guidelines. The population of workers was segmented into so many different categories that offices were created to keep track of them.

Wave 4: Integrated the workforce that was now very segmented around a common mission, vision, and values. The age of the organizational brand and diversity integration was born.

Wave 5: Signaled a shift from the organization of "one" to an organization of "many" who made their own choices and demanded individualized development programs. Terms such as ownership, intraprenuer, managing your own portfolio, being a personal agent of change, making decisions at the point of contact with customers, every employee matters, and an "Army of one" came into use.

Wave 6: Now emerging on the horizon is the period of strategic integration for organizations who are figuring out how to pull all of the pieces together in a globalized context, between geographically distributed units, within strategic alliances, while bringing diverse units of employees in alignment with diverse segments in customer markets.

people, in complex systems, working in a very complex world. Future HR leaders will need to be the force for integration or what I call the *chief integrative leader* (CIL).

The challenges we now face require a radically different brand of HR leadership. We must start by changing the brand at the front end so the crude coming into the pipeline offers the very best talent at the other end.

Our Current Attraction

The people we attract to the field of HR are the most compassionate, considerate, and concerned individuals that I have worked with in my career. Indeed, in a recent study of the 100 top HR leaders around the globe, the top strength defined by the Gallup Organization for this group was labeled *relators* (The Gallup Organization, 2004).

We simply may not have the right people in the pipeline for the transformative challenges confronting future organizations. To change what comes into the pipeline will take years, not months. Why? The field of HR is branded as the best able to handle "interpersonal facilitation." HR leaders are not typically seen as being able to lead complex projects such as mergers and acquisitions (M&As), even though most of the failures with these events are attributable to "people issues" (Schmidt, 2002).

How do you change the brand of an entire field? To what brand does HR need to change to successfully lead organizations through the sixth wave?

HR IS NOT ALONE IN THIS CHALLENGE

HR needs a course correction unlike any other it has experienced over the past 100 years. For example, looking to other fields requiring transformative change, the state of strategic leadership in healthcare organizations is probably at its worst point in history. You have to marvel at the advances in medical science contrasted with the poor healthcare delivery in the United States. How can we have the very best science, the very best technology, and the smartest consumers and yet be in such deep trouble in terms of delivery? We have people in the healthcare leadership pipeline who, no doubt, are great technicians but who do not have the talent to lead complex, integrated healthcare systems.

We must take a serious look at our pipeline and the type of leadership required for the sixth wave. We then need to go back to the front end to attract the right talent. Simply calling for HR leaders to be strategic won't work.

Five reasons that we need a radically different individual in the HR pipeline and field are:

1. People resources in organizations can no longer be monitored within any one function. If that were the case, why did we create the chief learning officer?

2. HR professionals are typically brought in for reconciliation, compromise, and conformance. We've selected them for those purposes, and we all know that many corporations use HR as a place to "soften" high-potential executives.

3. Many HR professionals do not understand the business they support. Warren Buffett, in a recent address to my class at the University of Nebraska, said that if you are a leader in business and don't understand accounting, you will spend your career bluffing your way through meetings. The fields of behavioral accounting and finance will blow past HR when it comes to calculating human and social capital.

4. M&As fail at a 60 percent and higher rate (Schmidt, 2002). In a Society for Human Resource Management (SHRM) Foundation/Towers Perrin survey of 450 senior HR executives worldwide, the authors found only 17 percent played a strategic leadership role in their organization's mergers or acquisitions. Similarly, the introduction of complex advanced information technology into organizations fails at a 70 percent rate. These complex changes fail largely due to people issues. Where's HR? (Schmidt, 2002; Avolio and Kahai, 2003).

5. With few exceptions, the field of HR education and training still produces practitioners not fully suited for the leadership challenges confronting sixth-wave organizations. "People issues" now span far too many domains to have them functionalized in any reasonable way.

6. Most significant problems in organizations keeping leaders up at night relate to *problems of integration* and alignment, for example:

- Trying to move into new markets, but the operations, distributions, and sales functions are not strategically aligned.
- Two years after the M&A was financially completed, the combined organization has failed to integrate different cultures.
- Some organizations operate every day across five continents and can't integrate their work.
- People and new information technology systems don't talk to each other.

Repeatedly, the core problem is not the absence of great vision, technology, people, new markets, or even brand. The core problem is the inability to integrate and reintegrate over time, which hobbles the growth curves of our best organizations. Most organizations simply do not grow well, which means they fail to integrate (Coffman and Gonzalez, 2002).

To create the CIL for organizations, our attention must shift to the front of the pipeline regarding the people selected, developed, and managed without necessarily neglecting those midway through and "processed." These new professionals will need to know enough about the domains that intersect around people issues to be their champion. Yet, they will also need to become the *masters of integration*.

THE STARTING POINT OF A NEW TIPPING POINT

There is much work to be done. We need to look to those who are at the forefront of transforming HR into a force for strategic integration. For example, I recently met someone who very closely fits the description of the CIL, a top-level manager at SYSCO. Perhaps not surprisingly, he does not refer to himself as an HR leader.

In a recently completed study funded by the SHRM Foundation working in conjunction with the Gallup Organization, the authors concluded that many of the 100 top-nominated HR leaders in the world described themselves as being more of a manager than an integrative strategic leader. Many of these 100 leaders specifically stated in structured interviews that they do not "like to take the lead" in situations such as meetings. Other key points included:

- These HR officers did not see themselves as offering futuristic thinking, ideas, or vision even though many did feel they were strategic problem solvers.
- Many viewed themselves more the guardians of policies and procedures versus the champion of values and vision.

Such leaders wait to be invited to the table versus creating the next table that is required to lead sixth-wave organizations. We need futuristic thinkers who can integrate diverse, rapidly evolving organizations. As we look at "refined" leadership at the top, we do not see a sufficient number of transformational agents being produced in the field of HR. This is a significant problem for the field of HR and its long-term viability in that someone will eventually fill this void.

WHERE DO WE START?

People are attracted, selected, and stay with professions that fit their self-image. How do we change the HR image in people's minds? This is a huge undertaking for any organization or profession. And it appears that HR will be attacked on at least several fronts.

On one front, the learning brigade will continue to whittle away at the HR role. I see much of this work going to corporate university leadership. If we get the "intangibles metrics" right, the valuing of people will likely go to accounting or finance. So, what will be left for HR? Perhaps handling the selection of talent, compensation, performance management, and/or benefits will remain, but in each of these areas, internal HR units are seriously under attack by consulting agencies.

For now, the starting and ending point for HR should be to focus on integration. As we continue to slice up organizations, there will be an increasing need for more deliberate integration strategies. Consider that organizations will be more globally dispersed, more culturally diverse, more specialized, and increasingly more connected by agile, mobile information technology. Keeping all of the parts integrated will be a massive undertaking.

It's time to ready the pipeline for the CIL. How might this translate into a future brand for the HR?

Here are some areas that could characterize the capabilities of future leaders:

- Ability to work with diverse cultures to achieve common points of integration.
- Ability to conceptualize and deploy different configurations of social networks to create the ones that optimize sustainable performance. For example, how can the leaders configure an organization's people networks to ensure that knowledge gets to the point where it is needed? That is, if I know something that someone else needs to know to do a task, does he or she know that I know it?
- Ability to accurately estimate the combined and integrated value of intangible and tangible assets. What will an organization be worth if it buys tangible assets such as a factory containing 600 employees, which it then combines with its existing R&D operation?
- Ability to understand how to best link people across time, distance, and cultures via advanced information technology. Having assets does not mean they are optimally deployed. Linking people with task and technology across market segments is an integrative challenge for our CIL.
- Ability to envision where key points of integration will need to emerge and how to lead an organization to those points. How can we get the right people in the right place at the right time with the right resources focusing on the right objectives?

Are we attracting and developing the right people needed to drive strategic integration? A perusal of the latest graduate and undergraduate guide to HR programs published by the SHRM Foundation (2004) shows that very few programs are focusing on developing these core capabilities. A fundamental correction in both the educational and certification process is required to ready the field for its sixth wave.

Each generation has served the growth of what constitutes and becomes *an organization*. And there comes a time when that generation must change the way the next organization is developed. The time for profound change in how we attract, select, and develop HR professionals is now upon us . . . again.

REFERENCES

Avolio, B. J. (1999). *Full Leadership Development: Building the Vital Forces in Organizations.* Thousand Oaks, CA: Sage.

Avolio, B. J., and S. S. Kahai. (2003). Adding the "E" to E-leadership. *Organizational Dynamics, 31,* 325–338.

Butler, T., and J. Waldroop. (2004, June). Understanding People People. *Harvard Business Review,* 80–86.

Coffman, C., and Gonzalez-Molina, G. (2002). *Follow This Path: How the World's Greatest Organizations Drive Growth by Unleashing Human Potential.* New York: AOL Time Warner.

The Gallup Organization. (2004). *Preliminary Report on 100 HR Leaders.* Unpublished technical report.

Schmidt, J. A. (2002). *Making Mergers Work: The Strategic Importance of People.* Alexandria, Virginia: A Towers Perrin/SHRM Foundation Publication.

SHRM Foundation. (2004) *Graduate Programs in Human Resource Management.* Washington, DC: SHRM Foundation.

SHRM Foundation/Towers Perrin Survey Report cited in J. A. Schmidt. (2001). *Making Mergers Work: The Strategic Importance of People,* p. 6. Alexandria, Virginia: A Towers Perrin/SHRM Foundation Publication.

CHAPTER 12

FROM BUSINESS PARTNER TO DRIVING BUSINESS SUCCESS: THE NEXT STEP IN THE EVOLUTION OF HR MANAGEMENT

WAYNE F. CASCIO

A common metaphor in business these days is "raising the bar." General Electric Corporation (GE) popularized this idea when it referred to "stretch goals." "Stretch is reaching for more than you thought possible. A stretch mentality isn't easy to get, and by no means does GE have it throughout the company" (Welch and Byrne, 2001, pp. 385–386). How about developing a stretch mentality throughout an entire profession? Perhaps the greatest challenge in human resource management today is to get the thousands of professionals in this field to strive, grow, and reach for more than they thought possible.

The field has evolved over time from the *file maintenance* stage up through the mid-1960s, to the *government accountability* stage soon after the Civil Rights Act of 1964 was passed. During this stage of development of the field, managers outside the field of HR management began to take notice because top management let it be known that ineptitude in this area simply would not be tolerated. Staying out of court became a top priority. In the 1980s, a combination of economic and political factors (high interest rates, worldwide recession, shrinking U.S. productivity growth), along with social trends (more women, minorities, older workers, and highly educated workers in the workforce), led to the demand for greater accountability in dollar terms for all of the functional areas of the business. HR was not exempted from this demand for accountability. Thus HR evolved to a third growth stage, termed *organizational accountability*.

The massive restructuring of organizations in the 1990s saw the first large-scale outsourcing of transactional HR activities (payroll, benefits administration, some types of training). At the same time, the growth of intranets enabled e-HR and employee self-service with respect to a wide variety of HR activities. In fact, in the late 1990s *Fortune* magazine published a story about "blowing up the HR function." In many organizations, HR was not seen as adding strategic value. Both academics and practitioners preached the need to be a strategic business leader for HR to survive. In a DVD sponsored by the Society for Human Resource Management (SHRM) Foundation, *HR Role Models,* we set out to learn what that means from the perspective of CEOs and top HR leaders in their own organizations. We did not write a script. We simply listened to what the leaders said. Then we pieced their comments together into four short videos: *HR Role Models, HR in Sync, HR in High Tech (Large Companies),* and *HR in High Tech (Small Companies).* Their comments and insights reflect a fourth stage of development of the HR field, namely, *strategic business partner.* The idea was, and is, that if transactional activities are being eliminated, the survival of in-house HR talent depends on a demonstrated ability to add value to the business.

To add value to an organization, according to what our HR business leaders told us in *HR Role Models,* a number of key competencies are necessary. These competencies include proficiency in areas such as the following:

- *Your organization's business model:* how it competes for business in the product or service markets in which it operates. It also includes understanding the constraints that managers face, as well as the needs of internal and external customers. Do this by getting into the field and working with managers and employees responsible for operations and by serving on a management team with other executives to gain experience and exposure.
- *Basic business literacy:* corporate finance, marketing, accounting, information technology, and general management.
- *Functional areas within HR:* legal requirements, recruitment, staffing, training and development, performance management, compensation and benefits, labor and employee relations, occupational safety and health.

- *Listening skills:* as well as the courage to raise difficult issues with senior executives based on what you have learned by listening.
- *Skills as a strategic business partner:* creating an overall talent or people mind-set; creating an HR strategy that aligns people, processes, and systems; developing human capital metrics that are aligned with the strategy of the company; the ability to assess talent during the due-diligence phase of a proposed merger or acquisition; ensuring that ethical standards are practiced.

Peg Wynn, vice president of worldwide human resources for Xilinx Corporation, neatly summarized the overall payoff from having these proficiencies: "Influence in leadership is all about understanding the business well enough so that what you DO recommend adds value to the bottom line of the organization." That's what being a great business partner means. Tony Rucci, senior vice president for administration at Cardinal Health Systems, provided a vision for HR professionals to aspire to: "You need to look at the business through the eyes of the CEO."

Strategic business partnership is an important role for HR professionals to play, for it demonstrably adds value to any organization, but in and of itself, it is not sufficient. Interviews with senior managers at SYSCO Corporation for a second SHRM Foundation video, *HR in Alignment,* provided a glimpse into the emerging future role for HR professionals. That role encompasses strategic business partnership but, in addition, requires HR professionals to understand and identify the key drivers of individual, team, and organizational success that are consistent, or aligned with, the strategy of an organization. The drivers become the basis for human capital metrics to assess work-unit or organizational performance. The mere existence of metrics is not enough, however. The challenge is to link the human capital metrics to the behavior of customers and to important financial outcomes of the business and to build a coherent management system around the entire process. In a nutshell, the future role of HR encompasses three broad areas: to ensure compliance, to gain commitment, and to build capability.

To understand this new role and how it is being enacted now, consider SYSCO Corporation of Houston, Texas. SYSCO is the number one food service marketer and distributor in North America. Its revenues exceed

$26 billion, it employs almost 48,000 people, and it serves 420,000 customers with approximately 300,000 different products. What makes SYSCO special is that it excels in innovation as well as in the execution of a well-developed strategy.

Ken Carrig, SYSCO's senior vice president and chief administrative officer, is responsible for ensuring that SYSCO's HR strategy is aligned with its overall business strategy. With respect to SYSCO's business strategy, Ken emphasized that the key thing that SYSCO tries to do is to differentiate itself in the marketplace by providing value in its products and services to the customer. SYSCO isn't looking to be the low-cost provider. It does try to play a corporate-office role for its customers so that they can use SYSCO as a resource if they're buying land or if they're making investments. SYSCO not only provides them with groceries for their customers but also tries to be a business partner with them to help them be more profitable.

In managing people, HR at SYSCO focuses on ensuring that five core processes are in place. We might call these the five Cs:

1. Common understanding (of SYSCO's mission, values, and goals).
2. Clear expectations (between employees and their managers, using the performance-management process).
3. Compliance (operating within federal and state laws or country-specific laws).
4. Commitment (Employees are inspired about coming to work, they're satisfied, and their needs are met. At SYSCO, about 75 percent of the employees say they are satisfied or very satisfied to be there.)
5. Capability (Every employee has the skills and technology he or she needs to contribute as an individual, as well as a team member, to the organization.)

According to Ken Carrig (2004): "I see HR as a key partner in all of the processes. We tend to work together to build the framework and provide the guidelines. And then we market those to the line managers to take those, execute those, even better than what we've developed, put their customization to them." Having processes in place is certainly important, but execution and measurement are no less important. Consider the measures SYSCO uses to assess the contribution of HR to the execution of these key processes.

A key step SYSCO took about five years ago was to recognize that it had to have a better understanding of how its operating units were working. To do that, the company identified four key metrics—customer, operations, human capital, and financial. On the human capital side, executives assess three key dimensions. The first dimension is work climate or satisfaction level. This is an important metric because if a company has employees that are committed and satisfied, they should be, but are not always, more productive and they help build greater organizational capability. The second human capital dimension that SYSCO looks at is how many employees an operating company uses per 100,000 cases that it sells. The third dimension that SYSCO addresses is: Are we retaining those people in warehouse, sales, finance administration, and in each function as well as in the aggregate? SYSCO does the same thing in the financial, operations, and customer areas. The result is a bundle or a pattern of metrics that enables the company to see how well it is doing overall and to predict to some degree how well it is going to do in the future.

Top executives at SYSCO meet on a quarterly basis to review the metrics. Specifically, they review the indices around work climate (leadership support, front-line supervisor, rewards, quality of life, engagement, diversity, and customer focus), around employees per 100,000 cases, and around the retention. The purpose is to see if those numbers are, in fact, consistent with the operating expenses and the pretax earnings of each operating company (of which there are 147), as well as with those of the corporation as a whole. SYSCO has found a strong correlation ($R^2 = .46$) among work-climate scores, productivity, retention, and operating pretax earnings. The relationship is lagged about six months, such that employee satisfaction drives customer satisfaction, which drives long-term profitability and growth. In short, SYSCO has been able to determine not only what practices and processes are helping to drive the human capital indices but also how those, in fact, influence the financial metrics over time. This led SYSCO to develop the business model shown in Figure 12.1 (Carrig, 2002).

This is management by measurement. To illustrate the effect of effective HR management on the bottom line and on the company's stock price, consider the financial impact of employee retention at SYSCO. Because 75

Figure 12.1
Value Profit Chain: A Revised Model

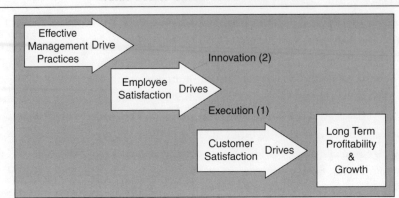

percent of SYSCO's operating costs are people-related expenses, that implies about $3 billion of expenses. SYSCO has about 10,000 marketing associates. Consider the financial impact when it can improve the retention rate from 70 percent to 80 percent. At a turnover cost of $50,000 per marketing associate, that turns out to be more than $70 million of savings per year. Since 1998, SYSCO has moved its marketing associates' retention rate from 70 percent to 82 percent. Next, consider delivery associates, who are very critical to SYSCO's success because they know the customers; they're the ones that the customers rely on to get the groceries to them on time and in good condition. To get groceries to customers on time, the company needs to have the same person going to the same customer on a regular basis. SYSCO was able to move the retention rate of its delivery associates from about 65 percent in 1998 to 85 percent in 2004 (a 31 percent improvement). HR professionals cost out the training and hiring loss for delivery associates to be about $35,000. That's almost another $50 million in savings. For SYSCO investors, because every $5 million represents a penny per share, that's about 10 cents per share based on improved retention of delivery associates.

Indeed, industry observers are taking notice. For example, In *Fortune* magazine's 2003 list of America's Most Admired Companies, SYSCO ranked number five for its quality of management.

The evolution of the HR role at SYSCO is exciting and revolutionary. Over time, it has moved from file maintenance, to compliance, to organizational accountability, to business partner, to driver of business success. With the development and implementation of its key metrics (customer, financial, operational, and human capital) and the demonstration of strong relationships between key metrics and measures of financial outcomes, senior executives cannot even imagine running the business without paying careful attention to HR processes and HR management and to its strong cadre of HR professionals. Shouldn't that be the way all companies view the role of HR?

REFERENCES

Carrig, K. (2002). A revised value-profit chain model. Unpublished manuscript, SYSCO Corporation, Houston, Texas.

Carrig, K. (2004, April 12). Personal interview, SYSCO Corporation, Houston, Texas.

Welch, J., and J. A. Byrne. (2001, September 17). Jack and the people factory, *Fortune*, pp. 75–86.

CHAPTER 13

WORKFORCE DIVERSITY: A GLOBAL HR TOPIC THAT HAS ARRIVED

J. T. (TED) CHILDS JR.

Today, workforce diversity is a global topic—a global workplace topic and a global marketplace topic. Any business that intends to be successful in this global arena must have a borderless view and an unyielding commitment to ensuring that workforce diversity is part of their day-to-day business conduct.

Success must also be measured as it pertains to a company's composition and its program content. A company's management team must ask itself, "Do we look like our customers, at all levels of our business? Do our programs reflect an understanding of the demand for talent in a competitive, worldwide marketplace? Is our business culture one that fosters inclusiveness and tolerance in each country where we do business?" And, most important, "Are we using workforce diversity issues to improve marketplace performance and grow shareholder value?"

To be successful, global companies must continue to look toward the future, not the past. And CEOs, senior line and HR management, and diversity leaders play a key role in that process. If we are to address the complex issues in the twenty-first century, such as the continuing core issues of race and gender, the growing issues of child- and eldercare, the emerging issues of multiculturalism, tolerance of religious practices, and the full inclusion of people with disabilities in the workplace, then diversity professionals must lead. They must lead because businesses cannot get there by themselves. Let me emphasize, however, that workforce diversity cannot be delegated. This must be a partnership. While the HR team plays the key staff role, total delegation from the top without active involvement is a recipe for failure.

IT'S ABOUT LEADERSHIP

There's a great deal of debate about the qualities needed for a successful diversity executive. "What attributes must a diversity executive have to be effective in corporations today?" is a question asked by experts and senior line executives. Others ask, "How can a diversity executive work in the corporate boardroom, but stay in touch with the various constituency groups and their needs and still remain credible and effective?"

These are good questions, and there are many good answers that address them. During my 37-year IBM career, I've thought about these questions often and about the answers even more. Over and over again, I come to the same conclusion: It's about passion and leadership.

Do we exhibit leadership both in our personal approach to diversity and the policies we embrace for our company, and do we care about the outcome of the debates we engage in —do we hate to lose?

To answer these questions, I draw my response from two people that I have learned from and admire greatly. The first example comes from professional sports. The second example comes from business. Both are legends. I'm talking about Jackie Robinson of the Brooklyn Dodgers and Tom Watson Jr., of IBM.

"Life is not a spectator sport," said Robinson, who broke the baseball "color barrier" in 1947. "If you're going to spend your whole life in the grandstand just watching what goes on, in my opinion you're wasting your life."

And Robinson lived as he believed. While in the Army from 1942 to 1945, before baseball, Robinson challenged segregation at Camp (Fort) Hood. As he went through military channels stating his cause to superior officers, Robinson's protest led to desegregation at the camp. He also once faced and defeated court-martial proceedings after refusing to move to the back of an Army bus when the driver gave the order. Robinson's protest, a legitimate one since Army regulations prohibited discrimination on government vehicles, eventually led to all charges being dismissed.

Robinson lays out a valuable lesson for diversity executives today. Our work is not for spectators, but for those who thrive on change. It's not for change alone, but change that is a catalyst for improvement—creating fairness when it doesn't exist, moving organizations from separate but equal points of view to inclusiveness, and migrating people from conflict to collaboration.

Diversity leaders can also learn from the leadership of Tom Watson Jr. When it involved IBM, he also sought to live by his values as he led the business. In his book, *A Business and Its Beliefs,* Watson said, "If an organization is to meet the challenges of a changing world, it must be prepared to change everything about itself except its basic beliefs as it moves through corporate life. The only sacred cow in an organization should be its basic philosophy of doing business."

He identified three basic beliefs to serve as the cornerstone of IBM's approach to business:

1. Respect for the individual
2. Service to the customer
3. Excellence must be a way of life

Watson led by these beliefs, reflecting his view of the values required to lead a great company during the time in which he lived and worked. And he walked the talk. In a personal meeting with Watson in 1990, I asked him why he wrote what I believe is America's first equal opportunity policy letter in 1953—one year before the Brown U.S. Supreme Court decision integrating America's schools and 11 years before the Civil Rights Act. The letter communicated his commitment to fairness and inclusion. He replied that during negotiations with the governors of two southern states regarding the building of IBM plants, he told them that there would be no "separate but equal" racial policies at IBM. To ensure the governors took him seriously, he wrote a letter to his management team in 1953 and made the letter public. As a result, he said, both governors responded by choosing payroll and tax dollars over bad social policy—they chose progress.

The cornerstone in the partnership between senior line management and diversity leadership must be their passion about the people working for their company and their customers. Leaders must help all people involved with their business understand that workforce diversity can be the bridge between the workplace and the marketplace. Passion is contagious and, when combined with leadership, the equation is very effective.

To achieve this convergence of passions, the most important quality for the diversity leader is the ability to motivate others to be part of the leadership on this subject and see it as part of their personal, day-to-day performance. A diversity leader must be able to draw others into the debate and be the catalyst who can convince others that helping to change the content and character of the workplace makes the team stronger and a better performer in the marketplace.

WHY IS DIVERSITY LEADERSHIP IMPORTANT?

The answer to why diversity leadership is important is simple: Our work is not done. First, we have not solved the problems of gender and race. Women represent more than 50 percent of the world's population, but they're not 50 percent of our workforce and certainly have not achieved parity on our management and executive teams. They are, however, increasingly becoming members of our executive teams and owners of their own businesses. We must view them in a more important and inclusive context—as workforce talent and customers.

The issue of race has been a pivotal item in the United States since its founding. Today, driven by immigration patterns, the growing presence of people of color as citizens, business owners, and customers puts this issue on the social, business, and political agendas of many countries.

Second, the gay and lesbian workplace issue achieved legitimacy as a discussion topic in the past decade. The driving force was the debate around whether to offer domestic partner benefits. Although approximately 145 *Fortune* 500 companies offer domestic partner benefits today, many other companies don't.

While the domestic partner benefits issue is still a legitimate topic of discussion, we need to move forward within the gay, lesbian, bisexual, transgender (GLBT) discussions to address issues of leadership. Do we have equivalent programs to attract, develop, and retain GLBT talent as we have done for women and people of color?

Are we being evenhanded? Are we just saying, "Well, gay and lesbian people work here, so we need to solve this benefits thing"? Or, do we see them as a part of our core business environment—employees, leaders, and customers? We must ask the same inclusion questions about our disabled community. Is our approach to "disability" anchored in sympathy or based on respect for the individual and a high regard for "ability?"

Third, a key emerging issue is the concept of being global, whether we're in the United States, Europe, the Asia-Pacific region, Latin America, or Africa. When we look at our businesses, what do we see? Do we see a business that is limited to conducting its day-to-day operations in our country, or do we have a perspective about our company that crosses borders? What are our expectations about our business's conduct in other countries? Do we have a commitment to ensure fairness in the treatment of women, people with disabilities, gays and lesbians, and ethnic minorities—no matter where we do business?

Are we taking steps to understand the workforce diversity legislation in each country where we do business? Is our company in compliance with the expectations of the legislation in each country where we do business?

A HERITAGE OF LEADERSHIP

IBM is committed to building a workforce as broad and diversified as the customer base it serves in 165 countries. Reflective of this customer base, we have a broad definition of diversity. In addition to race, gender, and physical disabilities, diversity includes human differences such as culture, lifestyle, age, religion, economic status, sexual orientation, gender identity and expression, marital status, thought, and geography.

We consider diversity a business imperative as fundamental as delivering superior technologies in the marketplace. And to ensure that talented people can contribute at the highest possible level, our company insists on a workplace that is free of discrimination and harassment and full of opportunity for all people.

At IBM, diversity is composed of the following three areas: equal opportunity, affirmative action, and work/life. The common denominator is access to the workplace—access through an environment free of harassment in a workplace that provides the tools to eliminate disadvantage and a workplace that understands that work/life balance makes it possible for employees to come to work and be productive.

From its inception more than a century ago, IBM has embraced workforce diversity as a fundamental value. IBM's commitment to workforce diversity can be traced back to 1899, when we hired our first women and Black employees—20 years before women's suffrage, 10 years before the founding of the NAACP, and 36 years after the signing of the Emancipation Proclamation.

Part of that heritage is the fact that eight IBM chairmen have acknowledged the importance of workforce diversity to our business, to our culture, to the marketplace, and finally, as a cornerstone of our IBM values.

Under the leadership of IBM chairman and CEO Sam Palmisano, IBM's values have been redefined and drive everything we do:

- Dedication to every client's success
- Innovation that matters—for our company and for the world
- Trust and personal responsibility in all relationships

IBM's leaders, in every generation, believed that diversity was right for the company no matter what the prevailing issues of the day mandated. That kind of leadership didn't just happen. It sprang from our shared beliefs and values and from the efforts of our visionary founders to infuse every aspect of our business conduct with the deeply held convictions of IBMers. And that type of leadership begins with the CEO and the leadership team.

When Palmisano, IBM's eighth CEO, took over the helm of IBM in 2002, he not only had the responsibility for heading up one of the world's leading global technology companies but also was entrusted with ensuring that IBM continued its commitment to diversity.

This was no trivial matter because all of Palmisano's predecessors had personalized their commitment to building an inclusive IBM community where talent was the common denominator. After more than a century of small victories, IBM's record in diversity is unassailable—one that is unmatched by any other company in its industry. The forward-thinking vision of the company's CEOs has put IBM on the forefront of promoting diversity, challenging institutional barriers that preclude a more inclusive community.

What is the future of diversity at IBM and where is it heading? According to Palmisano, the lesson that IBM draws from a century of leadership in diversity is to stay true to the company's shared values. The marketplace demands it, and it's what we believe—and have always believed—is the right thing to do.

GLOBAL DIVERSITY WINNING PLAYS

Today at IBM, we're attacking diversity issues through innovation and actions that we call *winning plays*. These winning plays are distinctive and allow us to execute globally and compete locally, for example:

- Building on what was America's premier corporate commitment to basic child-care and dependent care initiatives in the 1980s and 1990s to creating IBM's $50 million Global Work/Life Fund Strategy in 2000/2006. We remain the only company to have such a strategy, which includes 74 child-care center relationships around the globe.
- Creating eight executive task forces in 1995 (Asian, Black, Hispanic, Native American, Gay/Lesbian [currently named Gay/Lesbian/Bisexual/Transgender], People with Disabilities, Men, and Women) to each look at IBM through the lens of their group and answer these four questions: What is required for your group to feel welcomed and valued here? What can IBM, in partnership with your group, do to maximize your productivity? What decisions can IBM make to influence the buying decisions of your group? What outside organizations that represent the interests of your group should IBM have a relationship with?
- Growing our investment in our supplier diversity program from $370 million in 1995 to $1.3 billion in 2003 in the United States and $263 million outside the United States.
- Helping to address the Digital Divide through programs such as our signature initiatives including Reinventing Education, Native American, Black Family, and La Familia Technology Weeks, to offering Exploring Interests in Technology and Engineering (EXITE Camps) for middle-school girls.

- Showcasing our assistive technology at the California State University Northridge (CSUN) Conference and subsequently in six Global Accessibility Centers.
- Incorporating the eight constituencies mentioned earlier into our advertising and marketing campaigns—which speaks to advocacy.

The business of workforce diversity is constantly evolving and presents us with new and different challenges, especially as businesses become more global.

One major winning play we are developing at IBM is a global workforce strategy that will span 2004 through 2010. This strategy will address the growing equal opportunity legislation taking shape around the world, play a positive role in shaping the debate about global sourcing, and respond to the growing variety of multicultural/ethnic minority issues becoming a dominant factor in the labor market.

When we look at the landscape, we are confident we will maintain a path of innovation and leadership. Every year, we demonstrate our willingness to solve new challenges. In Canada, for example, we developed separate washing facilities for our Muslim employees who need to cleanse their feet before they pray—over 100 employees use the solution daily. In Brazil, as a result of our EXITE camp, we had a 16-year-old girl open a bakery business.

For IBM, maintaining the integration of our global diversity initiatives within the mainstream of the corporation is crucial to our future success in the information technology industry.

Diversity is becoming a key factor in helping to define leadership in today's marketplace. Workforce diversity is about effectively reaching customers and markets. As a company we are clearer than ever before about our values and our commitment to diversity.

We have some very tough and challenging diversity issues today. The world is smaller today than it was when I was a boy growing up in Springfield, Massachusetts. But one thought has guided me during my lifetime: My mother continues to tell me to always set high goals. She says, "Never reach for the mountaintop. If you fall, you may fall to the bottom of the mountain. Always reach for the stars; if you miss, you may land on the mountaintop." We still have several mountaintops worth pursuing.

If reaching the stars will help our companies have the most diverse, talented workforce we can assemble in our respective marketplaces, then it is a goal our shareholders, customers, and employees deserve we pursue.

REFERENCE

Watson, Tom, Jr. (2003). *A Business and Its Beliefs: The Ideas That Helped Build IBM.* New York: McGraw Hill.

CHAPTER 14

"NOT JUST ANY SEAT AT THE TABLE"

STEVE DARIEN

The desire to "have a seat at the table" has become a mantra for HR executives. Too often, however, our own shortcomings have kept us from warming that seat. Those who have failed to get to the table may have indulged in too much navel gazing, gotten too caught up in HR processes and tactics, and focused almost exclusively on the transactional, day-to-day activities of HR and not enough on the business's big picture.

If you have a seat at the table with your management peers, congratulations. You've likely demonstrated the intellectual and business acumen that your colleagues, and your boss, admire.

But how secure is your grasp on that seat, and how is your presence perceived?

I ask the question because one of the things I see is that we in HR have been losing our edge as a vital unit of the corporation. I want to explore this trend and offer suggestions so that we not only keep our place but also occupy *not just any seat at the table.*

FIRST, A LITTLE HISTORY

In the 1950s, HR executives concerned themselves with union relations or keeping their facilities union free. Working in what was then known as *industrial relations,* we managed collective bargaining negotiations, labor disputes, and union-free campaigns.

By the 1960s, as union power diminished, so did the power of HR. Our clout was revived by government enforcement of equal employment opportunity (EEO) and affirmative action (AA) goals, which required diligent monitoring by HR to keep companies in compliance. CEOs knew they had to get this right or they'd be in hot water. There were significant sanctions for organizations that didn't comply, so HR regained its power.

By the 1990s, EEO/AA matters were under control. As we entered the twenty-first century, HR again seemed somewhat adrift, relegated to handling a narrow band of administrative tasks. With no mandate other than reducing headcount and holding the line on pay and benefit costs, our influence was again weakened. I know this might seem like a harsh generalization, and it certainly doesn't apply to everyone. I wish it were a gross exaggeration. Unfortunately, it's not.

Furthermore, frequent turnover among HR people has hobbled the credibility and prestige of our function. HR, like a number of other staff functions, is vulnerable when corporations feel pressed to reduce corporate headcount or when new CEOs decide they aren't getting what they want from HR (in many cases, CEOs don't know what they want) and install an executive with whom they feel more "comfortable." Often these staffers are less qualified than the people they replace, and HR's credibility suffers from their inexperience.

HR executives who find themselves constantly in a reactive, rather than proactive, mode won't have a lot of fun even if they've been given a seat at the management table. As HR leaders, we need to have a broadly acknowledged capability that is distinctive and regarded as crucial to the company's optimal performance. For this to happen, we have to stake out the responsibility for business success that we can really own, a key staff responsibility our colleagues will recognize and endorse. In today's business climate, the opportunity is there for HR *to claim responsibility for the productivity of the corporation through the maximization of human intelligence, interaction, and skill.* Human productivity, whether in manufacturing, engineering, marketing and sales, R&D, or administration, is what ultimately drives all external measures of a corporation's success: share price, return on stockholder equity, growth rates, and so on. There's a seat at the table for a *productivity czar*—and we should be in it.

PRODUCTIVITY CZAR?

Yes, us. I'm not talking about a pie-in-the-sky, fad program like so many that HR departments have endorsed and then abandoned: job enrichment, job enlargement, self-directed teams, managerial grids, to name a few. Over the years, these have been touted as the solutions to all sorts of problems. We've learned, sometimes painfully, that there's no silver bullet that solves every problem and that what solves problems in one company doesn't necessarily solve them in another.

You also may have used programs you found to be successful, but you had a hard time proving that investments in those programs (regarded as costs by the accountants) translated into increased profitability for the company.

There's good news here. The developing HR analytics models promise, for the first time, to help us understand and quantify the impact of management decisions, including human capital consequences, on the P&L. I propose that measurement of and accountability for stimulating management decisions on productivity be the new raison d'être of HR.

Gene Tange, a director in the National Performance Analytics practice of Deloitte (formerly Deloitte & Touche), has written persuasively of the power of these diagnostic tools:

> Originally, "analytics" and "metrics" (basic one-to-one data point comparisons) were considered synonymous. Today, however, analytics have evolved through the addition of competitive databases and complex formulas that combine disparate data (primarily HR and financial data) to bring new insight and solutions to basic business challenges. This new capability has developed from a stand-alone HR tool to an integral component of a broader corporate performance framework. This affords real-time, strategic and tactical decision making with much greater accuracy and with a much better understanding of the human component on business outcomes—namely, productivity and profitability. (2004, p. 44)

Tange offers a case study: A manufacturer with $20 billion in revenue and more than 100,000 employees was facing stiff competition and financial difficulties. The company had excellent relations with an extremely loyal and long-serving workforce, something its management had long considered a plus. But when analytics were introduced, it became clear that low turnover/high loyalty pointed to a productivity level 20 percent below industry averages. The company also had higher compensation costs because too many employees were in supervisory and management roles, and the rewards for longevity were becoming increasingly costly to the company. The annual financial impact was calculated as a $900 billion drag on productivity, plus $300 million in extra costs for a too-large, top-heavy staff and their benefits (Tange, 2004).

I see HR as the logical staff group responsible for providing the type of analysis in Tange's example. Working with line chiefs throughout their organizations, we could develop remedies to problems such as the one described earlier and help implement them. We should be asking: *Are we getting the right products? The right sales penetration? The right production rates?* and monitoring and measuring the whole process by which people contribute to the enterprise. The responses can involve organization, training, knowledge transfer, compensation, communication, corporate intelligence, recruiting, retention, and a whole host of areas where HR has expertise. The agreed-on spectrum of activities designed to improve company performance is something we in HR should define and then be prepared to have our performance measured by its success.

OBTAINING ENDORSEMENT FOR THE NEW HR MISSION FROM THE CEO

There's no point in being at the table (or even at the company) if the CEO doesn't think we belong there. Taking our proposal to lead productivity improvement to the CEO for approval will put us at a critical juncture in our careers with the organization. Some CEOs will buy it; others won't. If yours doesn't, there's not much you can do but move on in search of a company headed by a more enlightened CEO who understands why this proposal is important.

The CEO is ultimately responsible for the organization's productivity, and line executives need to make sure that the right things happen to increase productivity. But we can be the key to success. By offering to make HR the focal point for standards, practices, and productivity measurement—something the CEO hasn't time for and division heads, with their necessarily tighter focus, can't accomplish on behalf of the whole organization—we are adding a tool to management's arsenal. More traditional measurement instruments, such as P&Ls and other data captured by generally accepted accounting principles (GAAP) on the finance side of the business, serve their purposes well but do not provide the information needed to know how to leverage human productivity. As HR leader, we have the bird's-eye view of the organization, and that makes us uniquely qualified to work on the cultivation of its talent base and measurement of its output.

If the CEO is skeptical, we can point out that data show that the lion's share of the average market value of companies is shifting from the tangible asset category of the balance sheet to the intangible. A large portion of those intangible assets is human capital. Economist Juergen Daum (2002) has observed:

> The importance of intangible assets, the immaterial value of companies such as relationships with business partners, brand awareness and new business ideas, but also know-how, corporate culture, and the ability to innovate, has greatly increased in the last two decades. One clear indication of the trend is that the portion of a company's total market value that exceeds its book value has increased from 40 percent in the early 1980s to over 80 percent at the end of the 1990s.

New York University accounting and finance professor Baruch Lev, an expert on intangible assets, said in an interview with Daum, "The absence of reliable information about intangible assets represents a major economic and social problem today" (p. 1), because it forces managers into guesswork and investors into the dark about the value of innovation and enterprise and how much they should risk on it.

"Managers should develop the capability to assess the expected return on investment in R&D, employee training, information technology, brand enhancement, online activities and other intangibles and compare these returns with those of physical investment in an effort to achieve optimal allocation of corporate resources," Lev says. It's vital to do so, he adds, because intangibles are "the major driver of corporate value and growth" (p. 2).

We should boldly outline an agenda that includes working closely with corporate accounting to capture the data about human capital enterprise that, until now, have been slipping through its fingers. Tange's work in HR analytics and Daum's and Lev's arguments for valuing intangibles as assets are providing us with concepts and opportunities that can help us to understand productivity, channel it, increase it, and calculate a value for it. And we in HR should be leading the process, just as we did in the 1960s and 1970s when companies were required to implement affirmative action goals and devise ways to foster change and measure their success in reaching goals. Although just one example, it shows there is plenty of precedent for us to take on a companywide task that seems huge and unwieldy and organize it into manageable elements that can be measured and meaningfully interpreted for the betterment of the organization, its customers, and its shareholders.

Our function is uniquely equipped to make the process more organic and less vertical by reaching across the company as well as up and down. I hope your CEO sees and respects that agility and gives you the go-ahead you'll be asking for.

CONVINCING THE LINE EXECUTIVES THAT THIS WILL WORK

The next hurdle is persuading line executives that our productivity programs will help, rather than hassle, them. We'll have to convince them that we're not usurping their oversight or autonomy or adding tasks to their already packed agendas. This is where, in a manner of speaking, the rubber meets the road.

To be credible, we must be fluent in the vernacular of the business and familiar with the operational imperatives and constraints these people deal with day after day. We need to understand, from the ground up, what the line executive is grappling with. My colleague, Cabot president and COO Pam Farr (2001), has said:

> An effective HR leader has to be able to synthesize the factors that will most directly affect the HR management strategy, functions and processes, *within the business context.* This is not to say that HR professionals with technical depth in traditional HR specialties aren't needed, but that the HR leaders who supervise specialists in recruiting, compensation, benefits, labor/employee relations, organizational development and training can link their efforts to the business at hand. (p. 26)

That means beta testing HR analytics with your own HR department before you roll them out companywide. We need to be able to take compelling results from that process into the field to "market" our productivity plans to division heads. The analytics for a staff function will look somewhat different from the analytics for line functions, but the principles will be easier to convey if we have data from a department inside our own organization as well as examples from others. It's a start. This approach can help make abstract concepts seem more concrete and may help us obtain buy-in for a companywide productivity program.

If you haven't spent much time with line executives, you'll need to make that a larger part of your agenda as an HR leader. The transactional functions of HR—getting people hired, managing benefit costs, diversity initiatives—remain important and need to be done by capable staff. We, however, need to be working across the organizational chart to sell and implement the programs that will show changes in productivity and how they're contributing to the bottom line.

Yes, Productivity Czar! Us! Now!

REFERENCES

Daum, Juergen. "Interview with Baruch Lev: Accounting, Reporting and Intangible Assets," *The New Economy Analyst Report,* March 6, 2002 (a shortened version of an interview with Lev from the book *Intangible Assets and Value Creation* by Juergen Daum, Hoboken, NJ: John Wiley & Sons, 2002). Retrieved 2004.

Daum, Juergen. Introductory statement, www.juergendaum.com. Retrieved May 27, 2004.

Farr, Pam. "The Future of HR." Unpublished manuscript, 2001.

Tange, Gene. "The Human Factor," *Human Resource Executive,* March 2, 2004, pp. 44–46.

CHAPTER 15

What Distinguishes the Outstanding HR Executives from the Others

BRUCE ELLIG

For decades the chant has been heard from "wannabes" that "HR needs to be at the management table (even better, at the board table) as a full business partner." The good news is that more and more organizations are recognizing that there is a need for a business partner with HR responsibilities at the management table. The bad news is that not many HR people are successful once they get there, and even more will never get to the table. Thus, the question is: "What distinguishes the outstanding HR executives from the others?" The answer is that outstanding HR executives are not simply business partners; they must also be respected advisors by both management and employees. Most get to the top by demonstrating business skills. Most fail because they are not employee champions or respected advisors and, therefore, not very effective business partners.

The outstanding HR executives see the people implications in business strategies and impact on the income statement, balance sheet, and cash flow statement.

BUSINESS PARTNER

Being a successful business partner as an HR executive requires assisting management in the optimal organization of work that provides the greatest value added, namely, output minus costs. To date, most HR functions

126

are better at identifying costs than defining output. To be an effective business partner, the HR executive has to do a better job in quantifying output. It is difficult to justify additional expenses without showing increased output. This means HR executives have to be able to determine the financial impact of proposed actions of the three levers of change (described next) on the income statement, balance sheet, and cash flow statement. The successful HR business partner is one who knows not only the cost of action but also the value added, for if there is no value added, why should there be a cost?

The challenge in workforce structuring is putting the right person in the right place at the right time. This challenge can be better described in terms of the three powerful management levers of organizational change: (1) recruit/select, (2) train/develop, and (3) reward/penalize. Each has a required HR skill base enabling HR to become an effective business partner. It will be virtually impossible to stay at the management table without doing these three very well.

Recruit/Select

The recruit/select lever begins with the HR executive assisting in identifying those positions that support the core competencies. For these positions, the desired skills (and values) needed to do the work (and fit within the company culture) are identified. The HR executive must then help identify the best sources for such candidates and (if necessary) the best outside experts who can help in this identification and in reaching desired individuals. This step is critical to ensuring a cost-effective approach to obtaining a pool of desirable talent.

From the recruited pool of candidates, selection of those to be hired is made by a multirater assessment against described standards or screens based on a historical assessment of successes and failures by management and HR. The screens address both values and job skills recognizing that it is easier to train individuals to acquire needed skills than to get them to alter their values. Because these screens are intended to predict success in core competency work, they should be subjected to strenuous tests of validity and reliability.

Furthermore, these screens should be carefully guarded because they are the basis for a competitive advantage. From these very specific screens, it will be necessary to develop more general, nonconfidential screens that can be used in the recruiting effort if it is outsourced.

Outstanding HR executives ensure that the company is always able to hire outstanding talent. The best time to capitalize on adding outstanding talent is when other companies are laying off because of economic downturns. This may mean having some work done by outside contractors in the interim.

Train/Develop

The senior HR executive should take the initiative to ensure that internal training programs are developed for key positions identified as internal searches to maximize their potential. These programs for core competencies should be treated as intellectual property and protected. They provide the company a competitive advantage. Conversely, those positions externally searched are candidates for external training programs run by associations, educational institutions, and other companies. Such programs need to be supplemented to some extent by internal programs to conform to company policies and procedures. Focus training on what individuals do well (not poorly), making them even better, and redesign the work, removing those responsibilities they don't do very well. The HR executive can make a valuable contribution to the company by appropriately blending these opportunities.

Training covers both work and culture. Culture training requires an ongoing series of programs that describe and reinforce how work is done and people are treated. Work training is focused on how to get work done, including what is done, when it is done, and by whom is it done. Culture training is *all the time;* work training is *just in time.*

While training is focused on the current assignment, development focuses on future opportunities, both in the current assignment and for greater responsibilities. HR must reinforce the idea that employees are responsible for their career planning; employers are responsible for indicating the best method of being prepared and offering those courses and assignments.

Reward/Penalize

The reward/penalize lever addresses the reinforcement of desired outcomes by rewarding positive results and penalizing negative ones. Positive reinforcements (or rewards) come in the form of increased responsibilities and/or pay. Penalization takes the form of withheld or reduced bonuses, no job advancements, and possibly even termination.

While the intellectual property for recruit/select and train/develop can and should be carefully protected, it will be more difficult to do so for reward/penalize. From CEO down through the organization, the pay plans fall into the public domain. At the CEO level, the Securities and Exchange Commission (SEC) requires disclosure. And in other parts of the organization, individuals leaving the company will be able to describe the reward system. The same applies to the penalize portion, which ranges from withholding a salary increase or bonus to termination. But because pay delivery systems should be specific to the needs of the company, they are of little value to other organizations unless they have identical needs. This basic point is missed by HR executives who seek to copycat other company programs.

Because the design of pay delivery systems requires a significant knowledge base, those responsible internally for these systems should engage outstanding pay designers to help create the optimum plan for each segment of the workforce rather than attempt it themselves unless they are uniquely qualified. Be careful to keep a firewall between the designer and proprietary company information. It is critical that top HR people have a sound understanding of pay programs and how they can improve organizational effectiveness. Otherwise, how can the HR professional add value to the process in defining and assessing the validity of deliverables? The most effective senior HR executives have a strong base in pay systems, especially executive pay.

It is critical that an ongoing performance management process be in place to identify shortfalls as well as successes. Shortfalls initially result in withholding pay increases and ultimately in termination if not adjusted. Between these two extremes, HR should be trying to help the individual succeed. Is training the answer? Should the person work for a different supervisor (most leave because they do not like their manager)? Should the person be in a different job? Only after exploring these alternatives (and doing so quickly) should the person be terminated if still not meeting standards. And then it should be done generously and with dignity. Others will be watching.

EMPLOYEE CHAMPION

Many companies proudly profess, "Employees are our most valued assets." But, companies do not own employees. Employees rent their skills to employers in exchange for acceptable conditions of employment. Thus the HR executive should ensure that the company not only promises but also delivers the following:

- Everyone has the opportunity to be the best he or she can be.
- The work environment is one in which everyone is treated with dignity and respect, including the speedy resolution of problems and complaints.
- Reasonable accommodation is made for individual needs.
- The workforce is informed in a timely manner of all things that may affect their work within a culture that promotes two-way communication.
- Protecting employee health and safety is ensured.
- Reward and recognition are based on performance.
- Opportunity is provided to balance work and personal life.
- Training and development opportunities are provided on company time and at company expense.
- Continued employment is a reasonable expectation for those who excel.
- Lawful and ethical behavior overrides all workforce actions.

Living up to these objectives is not easy, especially when one or more conflict with expedient business action. But if it were easy, the company would not need an HR function. HR cannot simply side with business in all situations. It must speak up for the individual. While the "workforce" is a faceless, aggregate descriptor, we must remember it consists of individuals. Doing so makes it easier to reinforce the principles identified earlier.

Being an employee champion does not mean being "soft." In exchange for treating employees fairly and with respect, all individuals must understand that in exchange the company expects them to be the best they can be. The company will provide the support and tools to facilitate this result, but the onus is on the person. Continuous improvement, helping others do their best, and doing the right things the right way—these must be ingrained in the company culture. These are the screens for recruiting, selecting, training, and development. And this is the culture that will be rewarded. Failures will be penalized financially and ultimately with loss of employment.

The importance of being an employee champion is answered by this question: How important are employees (or whatever they are called)? Name an organization that is successful without employees or with unhappy ones. Management gurus (e.g., Ed Lawler) and business studies (e.g., by Sears) have demonstrated that employees transfer how they are treated to how they treat the customer. This may be radical thinking to those industrial relations professionals who seem to believe employees, like auto parts, are interchangeable. But without hard-working employees, the company will fail.

Therefore, it is critical that the HR executive ensure that not only does the company have a code of conduct that includes treating employees with dignity and respect, but also the code permeates conduct within the organization. Positive actions are to be rewarded, and inappropriate actions are to be penalized. HR should be the paragon of virtue, setting the example for both honesty and integrity. Some may not want to be the "conduct cop," but if HR does not accept the role it may not be done. If employees believe they can trust representatives of the company to treat them properly, the company and its shareholders will profit.

RESPECTED ADVISOR

HR leaders who have achieved the top rung in the organization are viewed as having made it, but they have a tremendous responsibility: to tell it like it is. Unfortunately, it seems that some are more concerned about job security than job responsibility. Those who do not give honest opinions should be removed from office because they not only are not creating value but also may be destroying it by serving as "yes-sirs."

Additionally, it is critical that HR executives respect confidences, which means not sharing information received from the CEO as well as not breaking confidences of those on the same organizational level or lower. This gets a little trickier when it is something the CEO should know. If it is something that can truly be anonymous, fine; if not, then the source has to be encouraged to either pass it on directly or permit the HR executive to do so.

The HR executive can be especially helpful in getting a new CEO up to speed. It is also critical for the HR executive because the new CEO is also determining whether the person will be on the team. The first 30 days are important; the first week is crucial. The outstanding HR executive will have the schedule prepared and the action scripted before the CEO takes the job. The old clique, "You never get a second chance to make a first impression," is critical for both the CEO and the HR executive.

Much has been written about greedy, arrogant CEOs who believe they are not accountable to anyone—not the board, not the shareholders, and not the law. A HR person stepping into this situation has an almost impossible transformational change challenge. But does that mean blind obedience and even support for unethical, if not illegal, activities? Obviously not! And if the HR executive cannot change the CEO's view, it would be appropriate to seek career alternatives elsewhere. Unfortunately, a few HR executives seem more swayed by hefty bonuses and stock options than by doing the right thing.

If cost reduction is required, start at the top. It's difficult to get much support from the workforce losing jobs when the top executives not only keep theirs but also get a bonus for cutting costs. The workforce is more than "human resources." They are individuals. Remember that when reducing "headcount."

Fortunately, most CEOs do look for and value the advice of someone they can trust—a person with good judgment and an ability to keep confidences. The really smart ones look for those who believe honesty is more important than silent compliance. The senior HR executive is the logical choice to be this advisor. He or she is similar to the consigliore to the mafia don. The nature of the function is that its constituency is the workforce, the prime factor in determining company success. How business decisions are going to affect them will affect the success of the company. The HR executive must remember that to be truly outstanding in the job, the individual must be respected and trusted throughout the organization, not simply at the top. And without integrity, how can there be trust? At all times, executives must be open, honest, and deliver on promises. It is absurd to believe workers will give their best if they do not feel appreciated. Treat employees right, and they will treat the company right. It may be tempting to agree with the CEO rather than stand up for the workforce. But an HR executive who sells out the workforce should be removed from the position because the workforce will know they lack a champion, and their underperformance will significantly affect the success of the business.

CONCLUSION

For decades the cry was heard from HR people that they deserved a seat at the management table as a business partner. And, surprise: Many companies concluded this was appropriate. But few have been prepared to take on this responsibility. They are still focused on transactions, not transitions. Rather than eliminating non-value-added work, they attend conferences and programs to be more proficient in doing non-value-added work.

Unless these individuals take on development opportunities to understand what is required to be a successful business partner and employee champion, they will forever be in the category of a "never-will-wannabe." Service providers have to ask themselves whether they are providing the right programs for those interested in taking on learning responsibilities to prepare themselves to be an outstanding HR professional, rather than simply focusing on non-value-added transactional work.

Was it not Lord Tennyson who wrote, "to strive, to seek, to find, and not to yield"? Being an outstanding HR executive is not easy, but it is very important to the workforce and, therefore, to the company. And doing it well is both professionally and personally rewarding.

CHAPTER 16

EVOLUTION AND REVOLUTION IN THE TWENTY-FIRST CENTURY: REVOLUTIONARY NEW RULES FOR ORGANIZATIONS AND MANAGING HUMAN RESOURCES

RUSS ROBERTS AND PAUL HIRSCH

In this chapter, we consider how new rules for organizational success in a radically different world necessitate a fundamental rethinking of the expectations for the HR function and HR professionals. We identify changing organizational critical success factors, new expectations for HR, and the changing roles and capabilities of HR professionals.

A growing swell of "sea changes" has played havoc with our rules for generating strong organizational performance. In this environment, new organizational needs arise that don't readily fit into any of today's traditional functional areas but imply a broader mandate for HR. The need for a reconceived, higher value-added HR capability has emerged.

This need, combined with recent insights into practices that unleash superior "people" performance, gives HR both the mandate and many of the tools for a profound role reinvention. We propose the revolutionary new role of the *chief organization effectiveness officer* (COEO), which encompasses, but goes well beyond, today's top HR job to include:

- Enabling capable and courageous leadership
- Building a very strong and adaptive organizational culture
- Strengthening organizational productivity and performance

- Fostering creative innovations, products, and solutions
- Building exceptionally high customer loyalty

THE HEIGHTENED NEED FOR LEADERSHIP

Throughout the business cycle, different growth stages demand a different mix of individual capabilities. Success in the embryonic, launch, and early rapid-growth stages demands strong entrepreneurial thinking and behavior. The power and inspiration of visionary leadership with the ability to discover and apply the rules for success are critical. As businesses mature, leadership skill requirements change. Management that can stay the course, work the plan, refine processes, sweat the details, and carefully monitor progress is critical. When the business cycle is moving toward decline, organizations again benefit from visionary leaders with the awareness and courage to say, "We're on a burning platform. We either put out the fire right away, or we find a new strategic direction that can win market acceptance. I don't know the right way to go, but I'm going to lead us in discovering it together."

Figure 16.1 illustrates how the required leadership and management skills vary with the stage of development. With new strategic eras developing faster and business cycles ending sooner, organizations spend increasing time in development stages that cry out for strong leadership. Few organizations understand or are prepared for this challenge.

Organizations are run by managers. People can be taught management skills. Leadership, however, is more elusive. As Warren Bennis (1994) says in *On Becoming a Leader:*

> More leaders have been made by accident, circumstance, sheer grit, or will, than have been made by all the leadership courses put together. Leadership courses can only teach skills. They can't teach character or vision, and indeed they don't even try. Developing character and vision is the way leaders invent themselves. (p. 42)

While skilled, experienced managers are in more ample supply, organizations desperately need more visionary, passionate, courageous, and enabling leaders. As Jim Collins (2001) explained in *Good to Great,* leadership is the most important element in moving organizations from average to excellent performance.

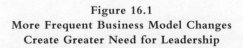

Figure 16.1
More Frequent Business Model Changes
Create Greater Need for Leadership

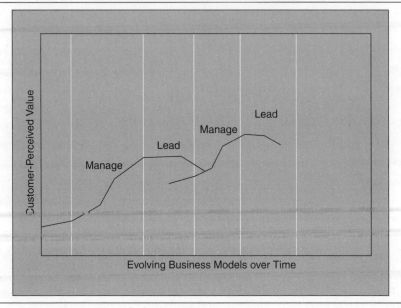

Unfortunately, the ability to create great leaders has been weakened by the evolution to leaner, flatter organizations, which provide less opportunity for development and mentoring. Further, a rebalancing toward family-friendly lifestyles has caused high-potential future leaders to decline taking developmental assignments that uproot and relocate their families. These trends, coupled with organizations seeking every possible place to cut costs, have resulted in work environments less conducive to building great leaders.

THE NEW FRONTIER: BUILDING MORE CAPABLE AND EFFECTIVE ORGANIZATIONS

Recent studies have measured the economic benefit of various organizational and HR best practices. There is now substantial data linking such practices to improved bottom line performance. Some findings are surprisingly powerful, yet most haven't attained broad awareness at the CEO and chief HR levels. Therefore, there remains potential for organizations to achieve substantial performance gains by implementing these practices. As these findings become widespread, the revolutionary thinking about the future of HR will grow.

BUILDING POWERFUL ORGANIZATIONS: FIVE WAYS TO STRENGTHEN PERFORMANCE AND A NEW POSITION TO HEAD IT

Five areas are ripe for generating improved organizational performance. Most organizations could reap significant strategic and financial returns by:

1. Enabling capable and courageous leadership
2. Building a very strong and adaptive organizational culture
3. Strengthening organizational productivity and performance
4. Fostering creative innovations, products, and solutions
5. Building exceptionally high customer loyalty

Other than customer loyalty, none of these areas enjoys a champion in most organizations. Who should own these? We believe here is a profound need for a COEO. This role would encompass and expand on the top HR job. The knowledge and proven approaches for mining the five areas already exist. We next lay out the issues that this new position should address and the results to be achieved in each area.

ENABLING CAPABLE AND COURAGEOUS LEADERSHIP

Effective leaders determine organizational success. They make or prevent things from happening. They stand up to critical issues or not, and encourage important communication or impede it. We tend to assume that chosen leaders will "have what it takes" to succeed. Yet, most senior leaders have not received a performance appraisal or coaching in the past five years. Most lack any means to improve their leadership effectiveness.

Highly successful leaders possess five key attributes:

1. They are driven by a strong, personal vision of effective leadership.
2. They lay out a vision of success and engage others in the process of how to achieve it.
3. They are firmly rooted in the values and behaviors required of them.
4. They muster the courage to do what's right and necessary.
5. They are modest, servant leaders dedicated to enabling their people to succeed.

No leader is perfect, nor is perfection required. Still, when leaders possess all of these attributes, it is a stroke of good fortune. Good people are routinely thrown into key leadership roles absent some of these attributes, unaware of their importance. Leaders often feel alone, without a dialogue partner or mentor. They are expected to demonstrate strength, skill, optimism, and bravado. They are nonetheless human and struggle with their role on the inside. Leaders are expected to nurture and coach, but where do they go for help?

Evolving from the chief HR job to the COEO encompasses strengthening leadership capabilities and performance. Leaders depend on their heads of marketing, finance, and legal for counsel. We believe the COEO must provide meaningful assistance on leadership. Once leadership becomes an explicit COEO accountability, the CEO is free to ask, "How are you helping people to strengthen their leadership abilities? Is there anything I could learn or do differently?" The door is now open for a genuinely welcomed dialogue.

COEOs can assist leaders without being inappropriate. One form of assistance is to tell rich stories about well-known leaders, the struggles they faced, and how they approached them successfully. As a situation arises, a COEO can slip readily into an appropriate story; for example, "Darwin Smith had a similar problem at Kimberly-Clark and what he did . . ."

BUILDING A VERY STRONG AND ADAPTIVE ORGANIZATIONAL CULTURE

Companies with strong and adaptive cultures earn a significant premium over their cohorts, making the cultivation of such cultures extremely desirable. Collins and Porras's (1994) "visionary" companies outperformed the S&P by a wide margin in total return to shareholders. A separate study of 207 companies in 22 countries found that adaptive companies grew revenue four times greater than nonadaptive companies and achieved 12 times the stock price performance (Kotter and Heskett, 1992). *Built to Last* (Collins and Porras, 1994) characterizes companies with strong cultures as having:

- A deep-seated, powerful ideology or set of core beliefs in which employees are thoroughly indoctrinated, with an insistence on "walking the talk"
- A special bond or "organizational glue" that holds people together
- Leaders who were recruited young, carefully developed, and promoted from within (going to extremes to develop people thoughtfully)

Adaptive cultures can be characterized as having:

- Challenging, stretch performance goals
- The ability to embrace change—through gradual evolution or placing big strategic bets
- Encouraging trial and error, opportunism, or "purposeful accidents"
- A penchant for self-improvement even if they are already best in class

Strengthening Organizational Productivity and Performance

Top-performing companies place special emphasis on direction and alignment, emphasizing four areas: (1) core beliefs, (2) strategic management and performance improvement, (3) culture, and (4) organizational development and change mastery. Expanding the chief HR officer to COEO is in keeping with what is important to sustained excellence companies. HR consultants and academics have recently sought to calibrate the economic benefit of identified best practices that fit into the four areas in Figure 16.2. Their findings validate the potential for gain in creating a top organization effectiveness officer.

Figure 16.2
The Highest Performing Companies
Place Unusual Emphasis on Four Areas

Areas of Focus	Alignment	
	Systems and Structures	Style and Shared Values
Who We Are (Direction)	I Core Beliefs	III Culture
How We Will Succeed	II Strategic Management and Performance Improvement	IV Organizational Development and Change Mastery

Source: Based on work from Collins and Porras. (1994). *Built to Last.*

FOSTERING CREATIVE INNOVATIONS, PRODUCTS, AND SOLUTIONS

The best way to encourage creative new ideas is to articulate the need, encourage people to cut loose, provide some upside opportunity for a big success, and get out of the way. Most organizations are reluctant to provide such freedom. They fear people will lose track of the goal, veer off course, make bad decisions, waste time, and accomplish little or nothing. This is what kills empowerment in organizations today. What to do?

Organizations most effective at fostering creativity and innovation know that what their company stands for, where it is going, and how it does business have been deeply implanted in the hearts and minds of their employees. These are organizations with remarkably strong cultures and belief systems that keep people from going too far astray. As Jim Collins (2001) notes:

All companies have a culture, some companies have discipline, but few companies have a culture of discipline. When you have disciplined people, you don't need hierarchy. When you have disciplined thought, you don't need bureaucracy. When you have disciplined action, you don't need excessive controls. When you combine a culture of discipline with an ethic of entrepreneurship, you get the magical alchemy of great performance. (p. 13)

In *Thriving on Chaos,* Tom Peters (1991) said that surviving and thriving amidst chaos would become a defining characteristic of successful companies. Indeed, McKinsey & Company, where Peters got his start, is comfortable in the belief that a certain degree of controlled chaos within their organization can have a beneficial effect. McKinsey avoids overly managing its business and its consultants. It sets a direction, guides behaviors, and trusts in the individual judgment of its people. The culture of discipline McKinsey creates, similar to GE's, empowers its people, without worrying that they will go too far astray. This is the model for future success.

BUILDING EXCEPTIONALLY HIGH CUSTOMER LOYALTY

A successful COEO can drive higher customer loyalty. In his groundbreaking book, *The Loyalty Effect,* Frederick Reichheld (1996) found that customers, unless they are true apostles for your company, are ripe for being wooed away—even if surveys say they are very satisfied with your organization. Reichheld also found that very strong customer loyalty is directly correlated with very high employee tenure. As HR professionals know, employee loyalty is strengthened by challenging and satisfying work; opportunity for growth and advancement; recognition for achievements; a stimulating, enjoyable work environment; and fair and competitive compensation. These loyalty motivators are the business of HR. Reichheld's work is mandatory reading for future COEOs.

SUGGESTED ACCOUNTABILITIES

If these changes are accomplished under the leadership of the proposed COEO, we expect strong results, which should be measurable through the following set of accountabilities. We expect the COEO to have:

- Enhanced levels of human performance and organizational effectiveness to achieve exceptional health and earnings
- Enabled leaders to maximize their effectiveness so that all can achieve to the best of their ability
- Built an exceptionally strong, supportive, and adaptive culture that embraces and thrives on change and adapts readily to the demands of the changing environment
- Achieved a very high employee loyalty and fulfillment, leading to very high customer loyalty and maximizing customer lifetime value
- Stimulated creative, innovative ideas and breakthrough solutions that enrich the organization and win favor in the marketplace
- Ensured that strategic choices are achievable given organizational and individual capabilities to execute strategy successfully
- Provided the people and development programs that make the preceding results possible

ON PREPARING FOR THE NEW TOP JOB

How do you prepare for the top job that doesn't exist today? As Wayne Gretzky says, "Go to where the puck is going to be." Learn how organizations work. Get some broad experience spent in several functions providing insights across the organization. Learn the more consultative and change-oriented aspects of human resources. Read about culture, leadership, organization effectiveness, performance improvement, and best practices. Experience as a management consultant can be extremely valuable. A graduate management education will clarify how everything fits together and provide important knowledge, skills, and abilities.

REFERENCES

Bennis, Warren. (1994, paperback ed.). *On Becoming a Leader*. Reading, MA: Addison Wesley.

Collins, James C., and Jerry I. Porras. (1994) *Built to Last*. New York: HarperCollins Publishers.

Collins, Jim. (2001). *Good to Great*. New York: HarperCollins Publishers.

Kotter, John P., and James L. Heskitt. (1992). *Corporate Culture and Performance*. New York: Free Press, a Division of Simon & Schuster.

Peters, Tom. (1991). *Thriving on Chaos*. New York: HarperCollins Publishers, Harper Perennial Edition.

Reichheld, Frederick F. (1996). *The Loyalty Effect: The Hidden Force Behind Growth Profits and Lasting Value*. Cambridge, MA: Harvard Business School Press.

CHAPTER 17

FROM HUMAN RESOURCES MANAGEMENT TO ORGANIZATIONAL EFFECTIVENESS

EDWARD E. LAWLER III

For at least the past decade, virtually every book, article, and speech on the future of the HR function in corporations has emphasized the need for change. There is nearly a unanimous view that HR can and should add more value to corporations and that the best way to do this is by being a business partner. In other words, it needs to move beyond performing the many administrative and legally mandated tasks that traditional personnel functions have performed to adding value through directly improving the performance of the business. There also is agreement that HR can add more value by effective talent management, helping with change management, influencing business strategy, and a host of other high-value-added activities that impact organizational effectiveness.

A number of strong arguments suggest that now is a particularly favorable time for HR to become more of a business partner in large organizations. Many are highly dependent on their human capital for their competitive advantage. Their market value increasingly depends on their intangible assets, such as their knowledge, core competencies, and organizational capabilities (Ulrich and Smallwood, 2003). In addition, change seems to be almost a constant today, so that organizations have an increased need for expertise in change management and the implementation of new business policies, practices, and strategies. Thus, there is a clear need for the kind of business partner services HR could deliver.

The problem is that HR does not seem to be able to position itself as a business partner. Even the most recent studies of its position in major corporations suggest that it is struggling to be more than an administrative function that is viewed as a cost center, rather than as a value-added, strategic function (Lawler and Mohrman, 2003). This view is in contrast to some of the other staff functions of large corporations, most notably finance and marketing, which play key strategic roles.

A useful way to analyze the problem HR has in transitioning to a new role is to think of it as a business. The HR function in most large corporations has many of the characteristics of a business. It has competitors, both internal and external; products; and costs. It also has customers who need a variety of services and who have feelings of satisfaction and dissatisfaction with the services offered. In some cases, they are able to decline to use the services that HR offers.

Thinking of HR as a business leads immediately to the critical question: What products should it offer? Potentially, it can offer three product lines (Table 17.1). The first product line is the traditional one that it has offered for decades—the reason the function was created in the first place. The other two, business partner and strategic partner, are newer and the ones that HR seems to have the most trouble delivering. In some corporations, it clearly does deliver on the business partner role, but rarely does it deliver on the strategic partner role.

Table 17.1
HR as a Business with Three Product Lines

1. Basic Administrative Services and Transactions involved with compensating, hiring, training and staffing

   —*Emphasis on resource efficiency and service quality.*

2. Business Partner Services involved with developing effective HR systems and helping implement business plans, talent management

   —*Emphasis on knowing the business and exercising influence—solving problems, designing effective systems to ensure needed competencies.*

3. Strategic Partner Role contributing to business strategy based on considerations of human capital, organizational capabilities, readiness, developing HR practices as strategic differentiators

   —*Emphasis on deep and broad knowledge of HR and of the business, competition, market, and business strategies.*

Figure 17.1
Business Partner

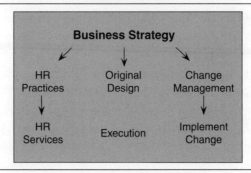

Figures 17.1 and 17.2 amplify the distinction between the business and strategic partner roles. Although they have some of the same deliverables, the strategic partner role does more. It provides strong input and direction to the formation of business strategy, something that does not happen with the business partner role. To be able to deliver on this part of the product line, HR needs to have good metrics and analytic data about human capital, organizational capabilities, and core competencies. These metrics and data are also useful in delivering on the business partner role but are less important for the strategic role.

Figure 17.2
Strategic Partner

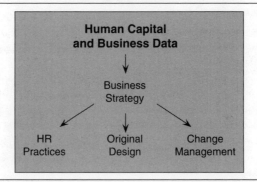

ORGANIZATION DESIGN

If HR is to deliver the three product lines that have been identified, it needs to be structured to do so. Most HR functions are designed to deliver a single product line, HR administrative services. Research on organization design suggests that to deliver three related, but different, product lines, an organization needs to be structured differently than if it is delivering a single product line. Relatively independent units need to be established to deliver multiple product lines because the skills, competencies, capabilities, and relationships that are required to deliver the product lines are different. However, they cannot be entirely independent when they go to the same customer and influence each other, as with the HR function. Admittedly, the customer for administrative services is the entire organization, while customers for the strategic partner services are likely to be only the very senior people in the organization. Nevertheless, each product line needs to interface comfortably with and support the others.

Most HR organizations have struggled with the issue of how to organize to deliver three product lines. Indeed, it is likely that their failure to organize properly is one of the reasons they have had trouble developing a strategic role. Let's examine how HR can best deliver each of its three product lines.

ADMINISTRATIVE SERVICES

Historically, the administrative services that are delivered by HR organizations have been paper and labor intensive. In many cases, the work has been repetitive and high touch. The HR staff members who do this work usually are located close to the customers, that is, employees. Over the past few decades, more and more elements of HR administration have been done by outsourcers on a process-by-process basis. The internal HR function still manages the HR outsourcers. Favored candidates for outsourcing have been benefits administration, payroll, and recruiting.

There are two increasingly popular alternatives to outsourcing HR administration to multiple vendors. Both of these are possible because of the growing capability of e-HR systems. Organizations can increasingly create electronically enabled HR systems that are largely self-service when it comes to basic HR administration. There is little doubt that a strong Web capability is the cheapest and fastest way to provide HR administrative services.

The key question is not whether e-enabling HR administration is the best solution; it is whether it should be outsourced to an HR business process outsourcer (BPO) or performed internally by corporate centers of excellence and service centers. In either case, economies of scale can be captured by having common administrative processes across an entire corporation. An organizationwide HR information system also has the advantage of potentially providing useful human capital data to the HR organization that can be used in its other product lines. It is beyond the scope of this chapter to compare the advantages of an HR BPO approach with an internally managed e-HR system with centers of excellence (for this analysis, see Lawler, Ulrich, Fitz-enz, and Madden, 2004). Both are viable approaches to delivering administrative services. A good guess is that HR BPO will grow rapidly and ultimately provide lower cost services and, potentially, higher quality services.

Even if an HR BPO model is chosen, an organization needs to maintain expertise in the processes that are outsourced, as well as have the internal capability to evaluate the outsourcer's performance, both financially and administratively. In short, although HR BPO should lead to a much smaller HR administrative staff, HR still needs to have a substantial level of expertise in processes such as employee development, benefits administration, compensation, and recruitment. It also needs the ability to analyze the effectiveness of its programs, transfer processes from one outsourcer to another, and be able to negotiate service level contracts with outsourcers.

BUSINESS PARTNER

The skills that are needed for HR to provide services concerning business support and execution are significantly different from those needed for personnel services and HR administration. For this reason, different people need to be involved, and the organization's structure needs to be designed to provide these services. The structural feature that most organizations have used to make HR a business partner involves establishing senior HR managers, often referred to as *generalists,* in most of the key business units of the organization. The HR generalist is the major interface between the HR organization and the business unit. The generalist is available to help with picking the right HR practices, developing change management strategies, advising on talent development and deployment, and the other HR issues and organizational effectiveness issues that come up as line managers try to implement strategy and effectively manage their business units. Typically, the generalists who are in this role report jointly to the business unit manager, as well as to the HR VP. They, in effect, are the part of the HR function that is responsible for the second HR product line.

To execute this role effectively, HR generalists need considerable support. First and foremost, they need to be able to draw on depth expertise. This expertise can come from corporate centers of expertise in areas such as change management, leadership development, staffing and metrics, and analytics, or it can come from external consultants.

In many cases where the generalist role has been established, the generalists have not been able to act as business partners, often because of their lack of a depth of knowledge of the business. In some cases, it has to do with the resources that are available to them. They simply do not have the ability to access either the internal resources or the external resources they need in order to deliver on some of the complex issues that they face. They also often find it difficult to report to both the HR VP and a business unit head.

Finally, although much of what they need to deliver cannot be delivered by an e-HR system, increasingly, some of it can. Some of the new products that are available can help coach line managers on how to handle change, how to do performance management, and, generally, how to implement their business plans. Thus, establishing e-HR-based systems can help the HR function deliver its business support product line.

STRATEGIC PARTNER

The strategic partner product line is the one that is least well developed in most corporations and the newest. It also is the one that has the potential to add the most value. It is rapidly increasing in importance because of the growing importance of intangibles and human capital. Because business strategy is typically developed at the corporate level in most organizations and the strategy implementation process begins there, this product line needs to be delivered to the senior executives of the corporation. Basically, this product line needs to include input to business strategy, analysis of the organization's strategic readiness, and its strategy implementation. In order to deliver the strategic partner product line, HR needs individuals who can interact with senior executives as well as HR generalists who can help with the development and implementation of the strategy. Thus, staff is needed at the corporate level that is focused on strategy analysis and strategy development—in effect, an organizational effectiveness unit that has a small, full-time staff. This unit also needs to be chartered to draw on HR resources (e.g., generalists) from elsewhere in the organization to help with strategy development and strategy implementation.

What should an organizational effectiveness unit look like? It needs to be a multidiscipline center of excellence that focuses on business strategy, organization design, and human capital development. It should be staffed by individuals who have expertise in business strategy, organization design, organization capability development, knowledge management, HR analytics and metrics, financial modeling, and utility analysis. In short, it should have a broad range of analytic skills so that it can evaluate different strategic options and alternatives for the business, assess how effectively the current strategy is being implemented, and develop recommendations about how to improve the strategic position of the organization and the implementation of its current strategy.

ORGANIZATIONAL EFFECTIVENESS

Now that we have identified the organizational units that are responsible for delivering the product lines that should be in the HR function, we can address the issue of how the three product lines can be integrated and managed. One alternative, and probably the one that most organizations will choose, is to have all of them report to an HR VP and have the HR generalists report to the head of their business unit. This approach keeps in place the traditional position of HR VP as a senior individual who reports to the CEO or COO.

An interesting question is whether the head of the three product lines should be called the *HR VP* or the *chief organizational effectiveness officer* (COEO) or perhaps *Organizational Effectiveness Vice President* (OE VP). The latter options are more descriptive of what the role involves given the fact that it would have all three product lines, not just traditional HR administration reporting to it. It seems like a much superior alternative to having a position called the *chief administrative officer* to which HR and "other" administrative functions report.

An alternative to having a single head of the three product lines who reports to the CEO or COO is to have a separate head of the organizational effectiveness unit who reports directly to the CEO while having an HR VP who is responsible for the business partner relationships and HR administration. Depending on the situation, the HR VP might report to the CEO or to the VP for OE. One precedent for the latter approach is the case of marketing and finance. Marketing and finance have separated themselves from sales and accounting by their reporting relationships. They are typically separate strategic units that play a major role in strategy formulation and development. The transactional work in their areas is done by the accounting function and the sales function. Following that pattern with respect to HR would suggest that the HR administration activities would report in at a lower level than the organizational effectiveness activities. This would create a world in which HR is to organizational effectiveness as accounting is to finance and as sales is to marketing. Once and for all, it would recognize the critical role that decisions concerning the acquisition, development, and organization of human capital play in determining the effectiveness of organizations.

By itself, changing the structure of the HR function is not enough to make it a strategic partner. It is a necessary, but not sufficient, step. New skills and competencies need to be developed. The metrics and analytics that are used by HR need to be expanded and improved on, and, perhaps most important, executives need to see HR as having the capability to be a strategic partner.

REFERENCES

Lawler, E. E., III, and S. A. Mohrman. (2003). *Creating a Strategic Human Resources Organization: An Assessment of Trends and New Directions.* Palo Alto: Stanford University Press.

Lawler, E. E., III, D. Ulrich, J. Fitz-enz, and J. C. Madden. (2004). *Human Resources Business Process Outsourcing: Transforming How HR Gets Its Work Done.* San Francisco: Jossey-Bass.

Ulrich, D., and N. Smallwood. (2003). *Why the Bottom Line Isn't! How to Build Value Through People and Organization.* Hoboken, NJ: John Wiley & Sons.

SECTION IV

DISCERN, CREATE, AND ADAPT CULTURE TO BUSINESS CONDITIONS

Imagine being a fly on the wall at corporate headquarters of JetBlue or the Ritz-Carlton, watching the day-to-day operations unfold. Now imagine being a fly on the wall at the headquarters of almost any other airline or hotel chain. What's one of the first things you'll notice? Probably the difference in the culture—the personality of the organization.

An organization's culture shapes who wants to come to work at the company, and it shapes how they act and react once they get there. The right culture can be the oil that makes the organization's internal mechanisms work more smoothly and seamlessly. The wrong culture can act like sand in the oil, causing disruption and uneven or failing performance.

Culture can be nurtured and created. It drives behaviors and unites employees. HR professionals help create and deliver it. When done well, the culture that's created can become a positive firm brand, or the identity, of an organization. This firm brand affects employees inside and customers and investors outside the organization.

In this section, the authors examine what HR can do to help create or at times transform a culture of success.

Fairbairn in Chapter 18 describes how, through appreciative inquiry, HR was able to lead a cultural transformation effort at American Express. With HR leadership, American Express began a search for what was best about the company, envisioned what might be, discussed what should be, and began moving the company in that direction.

Pfeffer in Chapter 19 points to how HR can help change mental models or mind-sets within organizations, thereby changing cultures. Pfeffer outlines a process for HR to help diagnose and change the mental models that individuals often bring with them to the workplace.

Rao and Dewar in Chapter 20 focus on six levers to create a market-focused culture, exploring how Washington Mutual created a market-focused culture when the customer became the responsibility of the entire organization. The authors highlight the importance of creating an employment brand that's consistent with the customer brand.

Sartain explains in Chapter 21 how an HR professional can leverage and link the company's brand to the employment brand. She shares how an HR professional can develop an initiative across the organization, looking at the brand promise, engaging the employees, and using powerful key words, all to help create a culture.

Soupata in Chapter 22 recounts the UPS experience and UPS's efforts to create a "winning team" culture that is based on core values of integrity, employee ownership, performance, respect, innovation, personal growth, and service excellence.

Collectively, these chapters, by both practitioners and academics, highlight an emerging and critical role for HR professionals. Culture should not "just happen" within organizations. HR can and must play a key role in developing and nurturing an organization's culture and must be willing to lead change in a culture when change is needed

CHAPTER 18

HR as a Strategic Partner: Culture Change as a Case Study

URSULA F. FAIRBAIRN

Culture does not change because we desire to change it. Culture changes when the organization is transformed; the culture reflects the realities of people working together every day.

—*Frances Hesselbein*

As a strategic business partner, HR can have a powerful impact on a company's operational and financial outcomes by leading a cultural transformation. This role, which has been well documented (Beatty and Schneier, 1997; Beer, 1997), will be even more critical for HR in the future.

In this chapter, I discuss our experience as a strategic partner in a recent effort to strengthen American Express' culture and renew its corporate values. I focus on why this initiative was important, how we reviewed company culture and implemented culture change strategy, and what early results showed.

The Importance of Corporate Culture

A *corporate culture* is the combination of the values and characteristics that define an organization. It influences the way employees relate to one

The effort to strengthen American Express' culture and renew its corporate values was made possible thanks to the work of dozens of employees around the world. In particular, I would like to acknowledge the leadership and dedication of the following individuals: Gabriella Giglio, Tom Leitko, Gordon Smith, Lori Sundberg, and Christopher Yates. I would also like to thank Fran Goldstein for her assistance in writing this chapter.

another, to customers, to shareholders, and to business partners. It drives behaviors and unites employees around a shared set of values. It can lift our performance and improve our work environment.

Companies with strong, formally articulated values that are focused on the needs of their constituencies have an important advantage over those without such values. For example, over its 155-year history, American Express has developed a strong sense of itself and what it stands for. Time and again, our people have demonstrated their deep commitment to a consistent set of core values that has become an invaluable asset. Our values have helped to keep the company on course, regardless of challenges, and have helped American Express stand out in the marketplace.

OUR CALL TO ACTION

Past achievements don't guarantee future success. Companies must regularly take the pulse of their organizations to make sure they have a clear sense of who they are, what they stand for, and what behaviors their people must exhibit for the enterprise to be successful.

American Express put its values in writing in 1990, explicitly stating its commitment to customers, quality, people, integrity, teamwork, and good citizenship.

During the decade that followed, the company underwent substantial changes to strengthen its organization and improve its performance—including divesting of businesses that were not core to its brand, reengineering to reduce costs and gain greater flexibility, globalizing lines of business, launching hundreds of new products, and expanding business through partnerships. By the end of the decade, the company also had a relatively new and larger workforce—75 percent of the company's 78,000 employees were not with American Express when the values were first codified.

In 2002—given the dramatic changes in the competitive landscape, customers' expectations, and the economic and geopolitical environment— American Express had to take even more bold moves to fuel growth over the long term. By improving the underlying economics of our business, lowering our risk profile, and increasing investments in business-building activities, we created a more flexible and adaptable business that was less reliant on robust market conditions to deliver strong results.

In light of these changes and the competitive landscape ahead, the time was right to take stock of our culture. The idea was not that we had to fix something that was broken. Rather, we wanted to ensure that our culture reflected and supported the behaviors needed to win in the marketplace and to accelerate growth. In addition, our CEO, Ken Chenault, wanted to inspire employees to stretch themselves and perform at the peak of their abilities.

Our Approach: Appreciative Inquiry

> *Appreciative Inquiry (AI) is, in my view, an exciting*
> *breakthrough, one that signals a change in the way we think*
> *about change. . . . We are looking at something important. AI*
> *will be of enduring consequence, an energizing innovation for the*
> *field. That's my prediction.*
> —*Richard Beckhard, Academy of Management Meeting, 1999*

By the time these words were uttered by Richard Beckhard, a founder of the field of organizational development and a pioneering consultant on issues of managing change, appreciative inquiry had already emerged as a revolutionary approach to organizational change.

The original theory and vision for AI was articulated in 1987 by two professors at the Weatherhead School of Management at Case Western Reserve University. In their landmark article, "Appreciative Inquiry in Organizational Life," David Cooperrider and Suresh Srivastva called for a shift in the way people approach change. Rather than focus on problems to be solved and gaps to be closed, they hypothesized that whatever you want more of already exists in an organization (Hall and Hammond, 1998). Thus, they encouraged the search for the best in people, their organizations, and the relevant world around them. The key is to discover your strengths by asking people "unconditionally positive questions" about the organization (Cooperrider and Whitney, 2001).

This method is in contrast to traditional methods for gathering information from employees, which tend to focus on problem solving and lead to an expectation that management would solve the problems (Table 18.1).

AI's positive approach to organizational change appealed to us on many levels. First, Ken believed that any change must reflect the realities and

Table 18.1
Traditional Problem Solving versus Appreciative Inquiry

Problem Solving	Appreciative Inquiry
"Felt Need" Identification of Problem	Appreciating and Valuing the Best of "What Is"
↓	↓
Analysis of Causes	Envisioning "What Might Be"
↓	↓
Action Planning (Treatment)	Dialoguing "What Should Be"
↓	↓
Basic Assumption: An organization is a problem to be solved.	Basic Assumption: An organization is a mystery to be embraced.

expectations of stakeholder groups, including employees, customers, and shareholders. Moreover, we wanted our approach to be forward looking and aspirational.

Therefore, in reexamining American Express' values and organizational behaviors, we decided to loosely follow the four stages of AI:

I. *Discovery:* In the discovery, or inquiry, phase, you discover and appreciate the best of what already exists in an organization.

We spent nine months conducting more than 30 focus groups with hundreds of employees representing all levels and businesses around the world. Our goal was to answer fundamental questions, such as:

- What are the best attributes of the company's culture today?
- What behaviors are most important to achieving business goals and to bringing the core values to life?
- What attributes should be emphasized more to help reach the next level as a high-growth company?
- What management processes can more effectively foster those desired behaviors and attributes?
- What can be done better to attract and retain highly talented employees?

The culture review revealed several clear trends. Chief among them was that American Express had strong core values that contributed greatly to the company's historical success and that remain relevant today. Employees were resoundingly proud of the company's outstanding brand and reputation and of how the company conducts business. They also cited a number of reasons they like working at American Express, especially the spirit of teamwork and mutual respect, the work environment, and opportunities for growth and advancement.

II. *Dream:* During the dream phase, the interview stories and insights are analyzed, and you begin to envision and articulate what the future might look like either through a vision or a compelling strategy statement.

Asked to envision what American Express should look like in five years, employees said they would like to see a company that:

- Outperforms the global market and has a significantly larger customer base,
- Is faster, nimbler, and more proactive, and
- Is in a position to attract and retain the most talented people through superior advancement opportunities and more pay-for-performance incentives.

To achieve this vision, employees felt American Express needed a greater focus on two characteristics deemed critical to helping us grow the company:

1. *A will to win:* Increase the focus on delivering products of superior value, understanding our competitors and capitalizing on their weaknesses, and knowing and serving our customers better than anyone else.
2. *Being personally accountable for the company's success:* Deliver on commitments but also challenge others—including your superiors—if you believe something is not right.

III. *Design:* In the design phase, images of the future emerge based on concrete positive examples from the organization's past.

Design/Part 1: *Reinvention*

Our HR team conducted *culture forums* with employees across the company to analyze the results of the focus groups and determine how to create a culture that brings the two new attributes to life. It was clear that we had to better articulate the values and principles that guide business decisions, while emphasizing that our updated values represented an evolution, not a fundamental revision of the company's traditional values.

We decided to restate our existing values in ways that made them more concrete, actionable, and measurable than in the past. For example, "Treat employees with respect and dignity" became, "We value our people, encourage their development, and reward their performance." In addition, we introduced two new values (having a strong will to win in everything we do and taking personal accountability for delivering on our commitments).

Design/Part 2: *Implementation*

With the new values codified, we developed an implementation plan that included a change management strategy focused initially on shifting the mind-sets of leaders, many of whom, given the company's success, did not see a need for change. Because our employee satisfaction (as measured by an annual survey) was already on a continued upward trajectory, we were often asked, "Why fix it if it isn't broken?"

After announcing the changes in May 2003 at our annual senior leadership conference, we provided leaders with talking points and training materials to enable them to discuss the changes. This was particularly important because we didn't want people to misconstrue what the new values meant. For example, having a strong will to win does not mean winning at all costs. It means winning the right way, with absolute integrity in all that we do.

This was followed by an employee communications plan that included an announcement from Ken to all employees around the world and a broad effort to stimulate dialogue among employees about what the values meant to them and how the culture efforts related to their work. We also produced publications, an internal web site, and even the obligatory banners and flyers, all of which highlighted and reinforced the culture work and the new values.

Most importantly, we had to translate the words into actions so employees did not perceive the reintroduction of our values as merely an exercise in semantics.

HR cannot lead a cultural transformation on its own. Strong partnerships with business leaders are critical for success. We worked very closely with individuals and teams in the businesses to assess how to best implement cultural change in their respective areas and reviewed management processes to ensure that they were aligned with and helped support the behaviors we were trying to drive throughout the organization.

Over the following year, we established HR processes and tools to reinforce and maintain the behavior changes. We revised our leadership competencies (which spell out desired behaviors at various levels of performance) to reflect both the restated traditional values and the new ones. We also revamped the entire performance management process to make sure people are being evaluated, and ultimately compensated, according to these new competencies. For example, excellence in personal accountability would mean that a leader "makes timely decisions on critical implementation issues" and "speaks up and shares views." A high performer in the will-to-win category "anticipates changing customer needs and seeks to create value for the customer" and "knows the business models and key levers that drive performance and profitability."

To ensure that our annual employee survey continues to accurately measure employees' perception of how well we are living the renewed values, we added new questions and recategorized others.

We also increased our focus on retention by establishing quantifiable accountability at the senior levels of the organization for retaining high-performing vice presidents and customer service representatives.

On the recruitment side, we launched a new campaign that reinforces American Express' strong will to win in the marketplace through our brand and commitment to premium products and customer service excellence.

IV. *Destiny:* The last stage of AI focuses on identifying ways to sustain an organization's strengths and, in a sense, create its destiny.

In many ways, we're still in this stage and will be for several years. One measure of success is imitation. For example, when our colleagues in the finance organization identified the need to transform their planning process, they understood that process changes must be supported by mind-set and behavior changes. They are now turning an unwieldy financial planning process into one that is more timely, flexible, responsive to external conditions, and focused on shared goals.

We also saw indications of early success in the results of our 2003 employee survey, which measured for the first time the company's two new values as distinct dimensions. Personal accountability scored 83 percent favorable, and will to win scored 66 percent favorable. In general, there is greater recognition that we must increase our focus on performance and execution. At the same time, employees continue to feel valued, motivated, and proud to be with the company.

The linkages between the cultural transformation and actual business performance improvements are difficult to quantify. But 2003 and 2004 were outstanding years for American Express. There is no doubt that the right culture can make a great difference in a company's ability to compete, succeed, and grow.

The steps that we took at American Express to renew our corporate values and strengthen our culture will undoubtedly help the company continue to earn the loyalty of our customers, attract and retain satisfied employees, and ultimately drive business growth in the future. And, I'm proud to say, HR was at the strategy-planning table every step of the way.

REFERENCES

Beatty, R. W., and C. E. Schneier. (1997). New Human Resources Roles to Impact Organizational Performance: From "Partners" to "Players." In D. Ulrich, M. Losey, and G. Lake (Eds.), *Tomorrow's (HR) Management: 48 Thought Leaders Call for Change* (pp. 69–83). New York: John Wiley & Sons.

Beer, M. (1997). The Transformation of the Human Resources Function: Resolving the Tension Between a Traditional Administrative and a New Strategic Role. In D. Ulrich, M. Losey, and G. Lake (Eds.), *Tomorrow's (HR) Management: 48 Thought Leaders Call for Change* (pp. 84–95). New York: John Wiley & Sons.

Cooperrider, D. L., and D. Whitney. (2001). A Positive Revolution in Change: Appreciative Inquiry. In D. L. Cooperrider, P. F. Sorensen, D. Whitney, and T. Yaeger (Eds.), *Appreciative Inquiry: An Emerging Direction for Organizational Development.* Champaign, IL: Stipes Publishing LLC.

Hall, J., and S. Hammond. (1998). What is Appreciative Inquiry? Retrieved June 10, 2004, from www.thinbook.com.

Hesselbein, Frances. "The Key to Cultural Transformation" *Leader to Leader,* No. 12 (Spring 1999), pp. 6–7.

CHAPTER 19

CHANGING MENTAL MODELS: HR'S MOST IMPORTANT TASK

JEFFREY PFEFFER

Here is a paradox. In the financial markets, investment information is rapidly and efficiently diffused. New product and service innovations, be they junk bonds, new forms of options, or debt securities that allocate and price risk in an innovative fashion, get rapidly copied by competitors. But in the "managerial knowledge" marketplace, there is little evidence of much diffusion of ideas, innovative business models, and management practices. How can I say this in a world in which there are entire industries—for example, publishing and management consulting—that are devoted to spreading concepts and best practices and where management is occasionally accused of being too fad driven? Although there is certainly rapid diffusion of language—the language of quality or six-sigma, the language of empowerment and putting people first, the language of employee and customer loyalty, and so forth—in many cases, not much changes in terms of what occurs on a day-to-day basis and in fundamental organizational business models.

A few examples illustrate the point about how long it takes to successfully imitate effective management models. Southwest Airlines was the most successful, productive, and profitable U.S. airline, and its success was widely described in books, cases, and articles literally decades before JetBlue, ATA, and a few others both in the United States and in Europe and Asia finally began to successfully imitate its approach. Or, as described in an article in *Fortune,* Toyota has been world class and ahead of its competitors in automobile quality and productivity for many years, and this competitive advantage persists even though the company gives plant tours to its competitors and its approach has been extensively described and analyzed in books and research articles.[1] Nevertheless, its rivals seem to have trouble learning from and about Toyota and catching up.

In the gambling business, Harrah's Entertainment has used evidence, gathered from its customer database and from running numerous small experiments, to turn conventional wisdom about how to make money in the casino business upside down.[2] Although Harrah's has outperformed its rivals and its approach has been widely documented and praised, once again there is little evidence of successful imitation of its management techniques by others in the industry.

Another example is Whole Foods, the natural foods grocery store chain whose stock sells (as of summer 2004) at a price-earnings ratio of about 40—for a grocery store, no less—and has a five-year return to shareholders of over 330 percent. Whole Foods's big insight that somehow others can't quite copy is that people will pay more for food that is of high quality and that they want to eat. This strategic insight entails customizing both prepared food and even packaged goods selections for the local market in recognition that tastes in food vary, in the process giving up on the idea of driving product costs down as much as possible but enhancing margins in the process.

In considering these and many other, similar cases of organizations confronting either *knowing-doing* problems—not implementing what they know they should be doing based on experience and insight—or *doing-knowing* problems—companies not acting on the basis of the best available evidence—one factor looms large as an explanation for the difficulties: the mental models or mind-sets of senior leaders. As a colleague, Mary Kathryn Clubb, formerly a senior partner at Accenture, puts it: "To get different results, you need to do different things." Most readers are familiar with the definition of insanity: doing the same thing over and over again but expecting different results. Clubb's insight was that to do different things, at least on a consistent, systematic basis over a sustained time period, companies and their people must begin to think differently. That's why mental models affect organizational performance and why they are a high leverage place for HR to focus its organizational interventions.

Thus, Toyota's success has much less to do with the specific techniques of its quality process—cords to stop the production lines if there are defects, just-in-time inventory systems, and particular statistical techniques—and much more to do with a philosophy that supports quality (and productivity and innovative product design). The techniques and specific practices can be, and are, copied. The philosophy is much more difficult to inculcate. Southwest Airlines' success is not simply a result of putting its flight attendants in shorts, not serving meals, or flying only 737s on short hauls, something many other airlines have imitated. Instead, the key to Southwest's performance is great service and outstanding productivity produced by a strong culture built on a value system that puts employees first, customers second, and shareholders third, along with a way of thinking about and treating employees that has built loyalty and commitment even with a heavily unionized workforce.

Whole Foods has a different conception of its business, captured in part in its "Declaration of Interdependence," that permits it to operate differently and innovate to maintain its position as the leading natural foods grocery store chain. And Harrah's success is premised on a different way of *thinking* about the gambling business and what its strategy is. While other companies in the gaming industry build "attractions" and are increasingly hotel, convention, and show businesses with some gambling thrown in, Harrah's remains focused on gambling and on systematically understanding how to make money in that industry, in part by offering a higher level of customer service. Also, Harrah's focuses less on high rollers or families with small children (who have neither lots of free time nor a lot of discretionary money) and does not try to get people to come by "comping" rooms. Instead, it has identified and focused on its best customers, older players who live nearby, see gambling as entertainment, and are much more interested in free chips than free rooms.

An emphasis on the importance of mind-set and mental models as a way of understanding the foundation of organizational success makes intuitive sense. Every organizational intervention or management practice—be it some form of incentive compensation, performance management system, or set of measurement practices—necessarily relies on some implicit or explicit model of human behavior and beliefs about the determinants of individual and organizational performance. It is, therefore, just logical that (1) success or failure is determined, in part, by these mental models or ways of viewing people and organizations; and (2) to change practices and interventions, mind-sets or mental models must inevitably be an important focus of attention.

Where do these mental models or mind-sets come from? First, most of our models of business and behavior are unconscious and implicit. This fact suggests that the first practical step is to get people thinking about the implicit models of human behavior, organizational performance, and strategy that are implied by their organization's ongoing practices. Second, a lot of what we do is based on simply repeating what we have done before, carrying the past into the future. Companies also copy what others do—called *benchmarking*—sometimes without carefully considering whether their circumstances are different and whether the experience of others, therefore, will generalize to them. And belief and ideology play a large role in management decisions. Incentive pay ought to work, people need to take more responsibility for their benefits decisions, and the grocery business is a low-margin business, so we have to drive down product and people costs—and we all too infrequently examine the evidence for and the assumptions underlying these beliefs.

There are some straightforward implications of these ideas for the HR function and for HR professionals. One implication is that the HR function needs to intervene somewhat less using programs and particular techniques and practices and instead focus much more on helping both itself and senior organizational leaders both see and, when necessary, change their mental models. An implication for HR professionals and their skills and professional development is that the ability to identify and help others discover their mind-sets and mental models and the capability to change those mind-sets when necessary are possibly among the most critical capabilities an HR professional can have or acquire.

Many people apparently believe that mental models or mind-sets are not a very useful focus for organizational intervention because this sort of approach is seldom employed. There are some reasons for this belief. First, changing how people think is going to be more difficult than just changing what they do because assumptions and mind-sets are often deeply embedded and below the surface of conscious thought. Second, to some people this type of intervention seems "softer" than the more typical HR interventions such as redesigning incentive plans, implementing new performance management programs, and introducing HR information systems such as automated applicant tracking and computerized hiring systems. But in spite of the apparent difficulty and its less tangible nature, changing the way people think about situations is, in fact, the most powerful and useful way to ultimately change behavior and thereby affect organizational results.

AN EXAMPLE: THE "RESPONSIBILITY" MIND-SET

It is, in fact, possible to uncover and change mind-sets and mental models and to do so reasonably efficiently, reliably, and predictably. To make the earlier discussion somewhat more concrete, let me provide one specific example of how to diagnose and intervene to change one particular mind-set. The general framework and process can be applied to other mind-sets and mental models.

Some colleagues at a small boutique strategy implementation consulting company, The Trium Group, headquartered in San Francisco, have been reasonably successful at helping companies make mind-set transitions and, in the process, enhancing the companies' effectiveness and helping in their strategy implementation,[3] Although their work focuses on a number of mental models, one important focus is on what they call the "responsibility" mind-set, which they contrast with the "victim" perspective.

Responsibility is *not* the same as accountability. Responsibility is probably a good thing for companies and their cultures, but accountability is somewhat more problematic. Accountability is an idea very much in vogue these days—people in companies and even children in schools are supposed to be held accountable for their decisions and actions—what they do has consequences and they need to feel those consequences, be they positive or negative. There is a lot of evidence, however, that the growing emphasis on individual accountability—something, by the way, that is completely inconsistent with the lessons of the quality movement—hinders learning and even discovering mistakes.

The downside of the emphasis on *individual* accountability is nicely illustrated by Jody Hoffer Gittell's research on Southwest and American Airlines during the mid-1990s.[4] American Airlines' then-CEO, Robert Crandall, insisted that delays come to his attention and that the delays get assigned to individuals and departments, so they would be accountable for their results and, moreover, would compete with one another to avoid creating problems. One field manager told Gittell that when a plane making a connection was late, "Crandall wants to see the corpse." The result of this approach was to create a culture of fear and infighting as people and units tried to pin the blame for problems on others. Little learning occurred and on-time performance continued to lag. At Southwest Airlines, the view was that delays were everyone's problem and when they occurred, people needed to work together to learn as much as possible so that, to the extent possible, delays and other operational problems could be prevented in the future. Gittell's research showed that the Southwest system produced more learning and more teamwork, resulting in better system performance, than the American Airlines' approach with its emphasis on assigning individual or departmental accountability and blame.

Responsibility implies something different. Responsibility entails feeling efficacious and believing that you have some obligation to make the world, including the organizational world, in which you live a better place. Building a responsibility mind-set, or for that matter, changing mind-sets in general, is a process that requires two things: (1) getting people to acknowledge and accept that how they think about situations is under their volitional control—choice is possible—and (2) having them both emotionally experience and think about the pros and cons of alternative ways of thinking about situations.

Trium has people pair up with someone attending the same workshop or meeting. One person in the pair is then told to tell the other a story that has the following characteristics: (1) The incident is real, (2) it is work related, and (3) the person telling the story felt like a victim—not in control, that things were happening to the person, there was little or nothing he or she could do about what was occurring, and the person was unhappy with what occurred. Participants are told to tell the story in as convincing a way as possible, so that their partner believes the story and feels their emotions. Then the roles are reversed, and the partner tells his or her "victim" story to the other person.

The questions posed are: What does it feel like to be a victim, and what are the advantages and disadvantages of the victim role? One advantage of being in a victim role is that the person gets sympathy, and, in fact, we often see people in subunits who bemoan their shared and unfortunate fate with one another, thereby building social solidarity. Certainly this feeling must be familiar to HR professionals, who often tell stories to one another about how their chief financial officer or other senior executive refused to let them do the right thing or prevented them from implementing some culture-building program or practice that might have enhanced the organization's performance.

The next step in the mind-set change process is to have the partners tell the same stories they just told each other, but in this instance, trying to imagine what it would be like to be more in control or more responsible for what transpired. Being in control does not mean that things would have necessarily turned out perfectly—organizations are interdependent systems and almost no one gets to have his or her way all the time. But the responsibility mind-set is simply seeing yourself as an actor affecting, or trying to affect, what goes on rather than being in a more passive role of having things happen to you.

The debrief then continues by having people think about the emotions they experienced with this responsibility mind-set and again discussing the advantages and disadvantages of adopting a responsibility mental model. Not everything is great about being responsible—it is, for instance, hard work and can feel burdensome. Feeling responsible also has many positive emotions and advantages associated with it, including feeling more powerful and more connected.

The point of the exercise is not to have people necessarily come to believe that one way of thinking is better than another. The objective is to have people recognize that each of us has a choice—actually a series of choices—that we make each day about how we approach the world and the problems and opportunities it presents to us. We can be victims or responsible. In a similar fashion, we can choose how we view opponents and rivals, and we can choose what assumptions we make and hold about people and organizations and their capabilities and potential. We can choose to see the grocery industry as a low margin business where minimizing costs is the only way to compete or consider a different approach. We can see casinos as hotels with gambling or, as Harrah's does, see hotel rooms as places for gamblers to sleep, restaurants as places for gamblers to eat, parking lots as places for gamblers to park their vehicles, and so forth. Each of these choices has consequences—for how we feel and, more importantly, for what we do, the decisions we make, and how we act in the situations we confront in seeking to make our organizations more effective and successful.

HOW HR MIGHT INTERVENE IN ORGANIZATIONS

For many good and understandable reasons—for instance, that the urgent pressures of day-to-day operations drive out the long-term planning and strategic thinking and the important but more fundamental changes that get pushed into the future—HR in many organizations is mostly involved in systems, operations, and the pressing issues of setting pay, recruiting, and developing people. Even when HR adopts a more strategic role, that role is mostly focused on designing specific systems to produce higher levels of performance in the immediate future.

There is certainly nothing wrong with these activities or focusing on critical processes that are key to organizational success and, by the way, dimensions that are used to evaluate the performance of the HR function. All of these things have to get done and, moreover, when they are done well, can contribute to the organization's performance and success. Hiring, retaining, and developing people are critical activities in a world in which intellectual capital and organizational capabilities are the key source of competitive advantage, so working on incentive pay plans and improving recruiting and hiring systems are important activities.

But, there may be a potentially even more important activity for HR—the diagnosing and changing of mind-sets and mental models as described in this chapter. Because, as my colleague Karl Weick once noted, "Believing is seeing," intervening to affect mental models may be one of the more efficient ways of making the changes that HR so often advocates to build a high-performing culture. In an environment in which there are many tasks, this task—of helping to uncover and change mental models—may be the most high leverage and, therefore, the most important.

Moreover, it is possible to measure and monitor the results of this process. Surveys and interviews can reveal whether there is consensus in how people understand the causes of organizational performance and the company's strategy. And, surveys and interviews can also reveal the mental models people use in thinking about their role and work as well as other dimensions of their work environment and the company's business model. Assessed over time, it is possible to chart the results of various interventions on the mental models people use and, for that matter, the actions and decisions they take.

HR has, at times, been described as one of the important keepers and analysts of an organization's culture. Culture is a crucial determinant of many dimensions of organizational performance, and HR's cultural role is significant. What I have argued here is that there is another, possibly even more crucial role for HR: In addition to being concerned with the company culture, HR needs to be concerned with the mental models and mind-sets of the people in the company and particularly its leaders. Because what we do comes from what and how we think, intervening to uncover and affect mental models may be the most important and high-leverage activity that HR can perform.

NOTES

1. Alex Taylor III, "How Toyota Defies Gravity," *Fortune* (December 1997), 100–108.
2. Gary Loveman, "Diamonds in the Data Mine," *Harvard Business Review, 81* (May 2003).
3. I have recommended Trium over the past few years and meet with them occasionally to discuss ideas. They were the ones who came up with this particular intervention and who first introduced me to their views on the importance of mental models and mind-sets and how to think about changing them.
4. Jody Hoffer Gittell, *The Southwest Airlines Way* (New York: McGraw-Hill, 2003).

CHAPTER 20

BUILDING A
MARKET-FOCUSED CULTURE

HAYAGREEVA RAO AND ROBERT D. DEWAR

Market-focused organizations carefully segment and then select specific target markets. They then create an *experience* of value for these target customers. This experience in turn builds and supports their brand. However, truly market-focused organizations must also pursue more than a sound market strategy. They must align all aspects of their business, especially their culture, with the target customer value experience. *The result is that the employee experience is deeply intertwined with the target customer value experience.* In these organizations, everyone, regardless of position or function, knows what the market strategy means for his or her job and makes decisions consistent with this strategy. A recent study showed that market-focused organizations outperformed their competitors by 33 percent in customer retention, 51 percent in sales growth, and 38 percent in profitability (Day, 2002).

Most organizations typically think about the four Ps of marketing—Product, Price, Promotion, and Place. Market-focused organizations think of the fifth P—People—and in such organizations, the HR function partners actively with the marketing function in creating an employment brand that is consistent with and reinforces the customer brand.

Indeed, market-focused organizations excel in customer attraction and retention because they develop capabilities to sense customer needs, they

172

have a configuration to serve the customer, and, above all, they nurture a culture that emphasizes building the value experience for the target customer. Indeed, the key norm in the market-focused company is one that says the customer is the responsibility of the entire organization, not just a problem for marketing and sales. Without a customer-centric mind-set in the company's DNA, capabilities languish from disuse and systems become ceremonial edifices, so much so that Lou Gerstner (2002) said, "Until I came to IBM, I probably would have told you that culture was just one among several important elements in any organization's makeup and success—along with vision, strategy, marketing, financials, and the like. I came to see, in my time at IBM, that culture isn't just one aspect of the game; it is the game."

In this chapter, we draw on a program of inductive, case-based research that we have begun at the Kellogg School (Dewar and Rao, 2003) to argue that the heart of building a market-focused culture is to create an employment brand that is consistent with the customer brand. A corollary is that the HR function in any organization should do more than see other functions within the firm as customers—instead, they ought to play a leading role in infusing a customer-centric mind-set. The creation of an employment brand that is consistent with the customer brand starts with translating the target value proposition into desired employee behaviors and then aligning six levers to ensure consistency: *recruitment and retention, talent development, job design, top manager modeling, information sharing and empowerment, and measurement and reward systems.* Figure 20.1 depicts the levers for building a market-focused culture and sustaining an employment brand.

We provide an example drawn from our program of case-based research—the Occasio project initiated at Washington Mutual (WaMu)—the Seattle-based bank with $275 billion in assets and 60,000 employees—to jumpstart its transformation from traditional bank branches into retail financial stores. The Occasio project is a long-term effort to transform the retail banking arm of WaMu, and we, therefore, do not discuss its commercial lending side or the mortgage banking side. The Occasio project is a work in progress, rather, and we hope its lessons can diffuse to the commercial and mortgage banking sides of WaMu.

Figure 20.1
Levers for Building a Market-Focused Culture

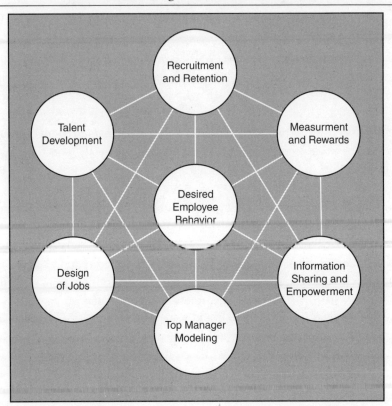

THE OCCASIO PROJECT AT WAMU: DEFINING THE BRAND

WaMu's customer brand is built on the premise, "Great value with friendly service for everyone." Its retail banking business focuses squarely on middle and lower income customers. WaMu likes to think of itself as a "Wal-Mart with a heart." After a retreat in 2000, WaMu executives decided that the WaMu experience for employees and customers could be distilled into several adjectives that could be easily concretized for customers and employees:

1. *Fair:* For customers, WaMu dropped ATM fees before being ordered to do so by courts in California and found that it was a good way to recruit customers.

2. *Caring:* WaMu seeks to build communities in which it does business. Employees are given four hours of paid time a month, not overtime, to volunteer for local charities, fund drives, and K through 12 educational programs.

3. *Human:* Even ATMs display messages that look like what a person, not a machine, would say. Kerry Killinger, CEO, says, "We're just real people talking to real people." So in every store, that is, a branch, concierges greet customers.

4. *Dynamic and driven:* WaMu seeks to innovate (e.g., changing branches into retail stores) and is driven in the sense that it seeks to accomplish changes quickly.

OCCASIO: MAKING BRANCHES INTO RETAIL STORES

How does WaMu translate these brand values into a culture? For example, if you want your bank branches to really be seen as retail stores and you want employees to see and feel this so that customers think they are visiting a "store," not a branch, how does an organization do this? Killinger and other senior executives noticed how Starbucks had transformed drinking a cup of coffee into an "experience." Nordstrom had achieved similar results with its stellar customer service. Killinger thought the customers' experience with their bank could be similarly transformed. WaMu executives started with researching the customer's perception of a typical bank—"cold, stone, vaults, cages." Their objective was then to transform branches into stores that offered fair, caring, human service, but were driven and dynamic. WaMu calls branches *stores* to emphasize they are really retailers. Tellers are called *personal financial representatives,* and branch managers are referred to as *store managers.* Our intensive study of WaMu revealed that the success of the branch transformation project was the result of focusing attention on six HR levers and creating extraordinary consistency among them.

Recruitment and Retention

WaMu, borrowing from Nordstrom, began to hire for the brand, not for banking skills. Killinger said, "If we can hire the right personality, we can teach them banking, but we can't teach someone to have a friendly, sales driven personality" (Dewar and Rao, 2003, p. 7). For example, when faced with the challenge of opening 70 branches in the Chicago region, the regional manager visited a number of retailers and observed their salespeople. When he noticed salespeople "running," he targeted these retailers for his hiring efforts. He also ensured that their employee base mirrored the demographic makeup of WaMu's targeted customers. Store managers conduct the interviews, asking the interviewee to sell something, for example, a pencil lying on the desk. WaMu also grows through acquisitions. Officers and managers of acquired firms are taken to a WaMu store first rather than the corporate office. Acquired employees are paired up with buddies, WaMu personnel at their level who coach them on the job how to use the WaMu systems. Employees and managers alike are allowed to remain on their old compensation scheme for one year, but they also receive a report detailing what they would have made under the WaMu plan. WaMu's incentive compensation is highly performance based. Those not wishing to put a large percentage of their salary at risk self-select out after seeing these reports. The "right kind" of people, from WaMu's perspective, stay.

Talent Development

New recruits are trained in banking and service skills. Introductory training is as intense as you would expect, and it never ends. One store manager conducts a weekly training lunch after the busy lunch hour. The focus is on sharing service ideas (e.g., how to explain a denial and coach the customer what to do to prevent it from happening again), sales techniques, and new regulations and requirements. Employees also undergo training in multiple areas because they are measured on cross-selling a variety of products. Training is an integral part of talent development, and WaMu treats talent development plans as an integral part of business planning, and the whole process goes until the top management level—even Killinger, the CEO—is accountable to the board for a talent development plan.

Job Design

A striking feature of the WaMu approach to building a market-focused organizational culture is that jobs are designed from the perspective of the customer. A position of concierge was established to meet and direct people entering the store because research indicated that customers intending to make a complex transaction (e.g., wiring money) expected to wait longer in line than those with simple tasks—80 percent of transactions are simple cash deposits or withdrawals. As a consequence, the concierge routed customers to different lines depending on the length of transaction. This arrangement was found to dramatically increase customer satisfaction because people with complex transactions expect to wait longer while those with simple transactions hate to wait. Retail sales associates do not count cash—instead, ATM technology is harnessed for them to deliver cash to customers with a few keystrokes. The result is that they save 40 seconds per transaction and can talk to customers to find out what else they need and whether they should be sent to the store manager if they need additional products. Similarly, retail sales associates don't spend time balancing the books—the back office does that, saving 40 minutes of time at the end of the day and freeing up even more time for store personnel to interact with customers.

Information Sharing and Empowerment

A key element of information sharing is the brand rally. Here employees meet, learn about upcoming advertising campaigns, and even view customer complaint videos. Brand rallies are also used to enable employees from an acquired firm to mingle with WaMu personnel at their same level to learn about how the incentive program really works, what they think of WaMu's benefits, how they like the WaMu performance-driven culture—in short, how the reality of WaMu measures up against the official presentation made at the brand rally. WaMu has nothing to hide. Brand rallies involve people from all areas of the bank, front line and back office. Employees from the call centers interact with store employees and realize how they are all part of WaMu. Brand rallies are also used as great celebration occasions that highlight brand values and motivate the troops just before opening stores in new markets.

Store managers feel a sense of empowerment because they decide the number of employees needed for the store to accomplish their performance goals; they hire and train their own employees. This tradition of "empowering" the store manager goes back to 1987. During a senior management meeting, the executives were engaged in their annual approval process for branch-specific, requested variances to the standard staffing model. One manager stopped the process, asking why people at the top level should be wasting their time doing this. Why not let the branch managers decide how many staff they need? They were on the scene; they knew their market's revenue potential; and given proper performance goals and incentives to reach them, they could be trusted to staff appropriately to achieve these goals. The standard staffing model was eliminated, and senior management then devoted its time to setting the goals and to developing WaMu's highly leveraged pay system. Two months after the elimination of the model and the introduction of the new incentives, sales dramatically increased and headcount of tellers dropped by 300.

Measurement and Rewards

One store manager commented, "The great thing about managing a 'store' (or even older branches not yet converted) is that you know exactly what's expected of you. You have plenty of support and autonomy to accomplish it and can make a significant amount of money if you accomplish your goals." WaMu pays on the average close to market rates, but the big difference is the variance around this mean. The variance comes from the large percentage of uncapped incentive compensation. Less than half of a manager's pay is guaranteed. The rest depends on performance. Store managers' base pay has six levels. These levels are determined by three key performance indicators: cross-selling, customer service (measured by surveys and mystery shoppers), and revenue per employee. Incentive pay is based on profit per full-time equivalent employee in the branch. The store manager is free to hire any number of employees, train them in as many banking skills as they are willing to learn (especially cross-selling), hire for attributes he or she thinks will sell best in that particular store, and outplace those who do not contribute sufficiently to store profit. Corporate and regional HR is there to help detect good applicants and to supply training, but never to dictate to the store manager. All store managers receive a daily printout showing where their store ranks with all other WaMu stores on the three key performance indicators. At the end of the year, the top 1 percent of managers attend an incentive trip to Hawaii with their spouses. The cross-selling initiative began when it was found that only a small number of mortgage customers had checking accounts and that 70 percent of the mortgages came from mortgage brokers, not WaMu employees. Today the cross-sell goal is set at 5.4 products per customer, and this goal is closely linked with incentive compensation. WaMu has a panel of top performers that act as an internal focus group to vet proposals for modifications of performance goals and changes in incentives. The idea is to find out if the proposed change will allow them to do even better.

Top Manager Modeling

The top managers at WaMu model the behaviors. If store managers have incentives contingent on store performance, the CEO and direct reports also have a small base and large percentage of incentive compensation, which is based 100 percent on the total performance of the company. Killinger noted this goes a long way to driving team behavior. Killinger and his senior managers lead brand rallies, visit stores, and are always listening to the customer and exhorting the rest of the organization. When a new call center opened to support retail banking in New Jersey, Killinger flew there to lead the brand rally.

An important learning from WaMu is the importance of deliberate alignment among the six levers because each lever multiplies the effect of the others. The result is one consistent message rather than a barrage of contradictory signals that impede execution. The emphasis on customer focus even extends to call centers (each call center is led by someone with store experience, employees are trained to never say no) and to the finance department (they did an analysis to justify dropping ATM charges for nonbank customers and approved it because they found it was an excellent method of attracting new customers).

THE ROLE OF HR IN BUILDING A MARKET-FOCUSED CULTURE

One implication of the Occasio project at WaMu is that the HR department is far from a support function but is, instead, a central player in institutionalizing the market-focused culture. The mission of the HR department ought to be to synchronize the employment brand with the customers' brand. A starting point for HR professionals is to understand the customer brand and then make a strong effort to bring the voice of the customer inside the HR department through customer visits and the observation and understanding of customer experiences. Once the voice of the customer is brought inside the organization, it can serve as a basis to articulate what kind of employee experience and behaviors are required to support the customer experience and what employee value proposition best fits the customer value proposition. Thereafter, the HR department's senior managers should model the desired behaviors, rethink recruitment and retention criteria from the vantage point of the customer, reorganize training and talent development with a view toward enhancing skills demanded by the customer, redesign jobs from the customer's point of view, provide information about the customer and empower employees, and construct metrics and rewards that reinforce customer-relevant behaviors. In short, the whole HR architecture should be configured from a customer's point of view so that the organization becomes customer-centric. This requires HR to forge a close partnership with the marketing function if organizations are to become market focused and outperform their peers.

REFERENCES

Day, G. S. (2002). "Winning the Competition for Customer Relationships." Wharton School.

Dewar, R., and Hayagreeva Rao. (2003). "The Washington Mutual Case: A Very Old Bank Can Grow—A Lot." Kellogg School of Management.

Gerstner, Louis. (2002). "Who Says Elephants Can't Dance: Inside IBM's Historic Turnaround." New York: HarperBusiness, 181.

CHAPTER 21

BRANDING FROM THE INSIDE OUT: HR'S ROLE AS BRAND BUILDER

LIBBY SARTAIN

Every day, thousands of companies spend millions of dollars to build external brand identity and customer loyalty. Branding implies more than just selling a product or service; the best companies sell a promise that goes with the product. If we believe what we watch on television, certain pills will give us not only relaxing moments in beautiful settings but also happy relationships and more meaningful lives. There is a strong emotional connection between the message and the product. The brand attaches meaning, the lifestyle, the transformation, the potential, the joy, and the fulfillment to the product. The message engages, enchants, and compels the customer to give the product a chance.

But branding efforts fail or, at best, achieve only minimal success unless the company invests just as carefully in nurturing its internal brand. Employees make or break the company's brand and, ultimately, the company's results. In fact, the company that overlooks its internal brand significantly reduces the potential impact of its external brand. Just one negative customer experience can undermine the investment in marketing to promote an external brand promise. And, customers not only expect but also demand the promised experience while price competitiveness and commoditization erode traditional concepts of brand loyalty, placing more pressure on organizations to deliver easy-to-differentiate products or services. Internally, increasing pressure to deliver that promise erodes employee belief in the fundamentals for which an organization stands, which can severely impact effort to recruit and retain internal staff. Today, the stakes are too high for any organization to leave brand delivery to chance.

181

Adding to this pressure is the impending war for talent among companies. The jobless recovery is over, talent will become scarce, and retention will become as important as recruiting. According to recent research by HotJobs, a division of Yahoo!, nearly one-half of U.S. employees surveyed will search for new employment in the next 12 months. And, unlike the last war for talent in the 1990s, this one is likely to be fought on less tangible issues than financial rewards—including employee perceptions of security, organizational pride and individual recognition, and other dimensions of an internal brand.

For this and many other reasons, people issues occupy the top of the business agenda, and this provides us as HR leaders with a high-profile mandate: to deliver value. Today, competing for employees is as difficult as competing for customers, building employee loyalty is as important as building customer loyalty, and treating employees right is the key to treating shareholders right.

HR can borrow the lessons and principles from product branding to extend their branding efforts internally or, better yet, start internally first when developing an external brand. Marketers have research tools to determine what customers will value and then craft a value proposition that serves as a basis for brand promotion and advertising messages. The same premise can be used as a springboard for an internal branding strategy and a springboard for change inside an organization (Tosti and Stotz, 2000). By branding the meaning, promise, and overall employee experience, organizations can engage and enchant employees and give deeper meaning to the promise that lies behind their daily efforts that give their jobs a deeper resonance and results in an emotional connection that compels commitment.

In a study of 20 HR practices that increase shareholder value (and one that didn't; Pfau and Kay, 2001), the authors related that the best organizations use employee branding to pinpoint, distinguish, and tout the unique values, systems, policies, and behaviors that are manifested in a culture and to communicate that differentiated culture and envisioned future to employees and prospects. In a 2001 study, The Conference Board (Report Number 1288) noted that employer branding is being used more widely to attract, retain, and align talent around the promises made to the customer.

Branding internally is not just a way to attract and retain employees. It is a way to bring employees together under a shared sense of mission and values; the brand promise constantly broadcasts the external brand promise, and that message continues to attract other like-minded candidates who identify with the values that the organization stands for and offers. Branding inside the organization is a way to constantly rerecruit an existing workforce in a way that doesn't feel like hollow propaganda.

The communication of an employer brand using consistent voice, look, feel, and tone—throughout the entire employment relationship—is the most powerful tool I have discovered for HR. Branding can be the "secret sauce" for HR. It helps keep all the many parts moving smoothly, but it also gives HR a way to tie our programming directly to the business, speaking the language of business versus HR jargon, and it can be a very tangible way to add value. Instead of selling your latest "HR program," internal branders are selling brand building inside the organization and the entire employee experience and value proposition to the people.

Southwest Airlines determined that the strongest differentiator between Southwest and its competitors was the spirit of its people. So the company decided to use that differentiator externally as its competitive advantage. Finding and keeping the best talent in the airline industry became the secret weapon from the earliest days.

Over the years the marketing strategy proved so effective that Southwest became a major national airline. At that point, Southwest needed a more powerful brand. Its marketers chose, *Symbol of Freedom*. Southwest's mission to deliver low-cost air travel had given Americans the freedom to fly. We in management knew we needed our employees to catch the passion and power behind this vision of opening up travel to everyday Americans. We embarked on an internal branding campaign designed to make the freedom message come to life for employees first so they could deliver on this promise. We wanted to send the message that working for Southwest was unique. But the challenge was to figure out a way of making this message real, not just another one-dimensional piece of propaganda.

Working with a cross-functional team from advertising, public relations, marketing, operations, and HR, we went to work cataloging the products, services, and experiences offered by the company that employees wouldn't get if they worked somewhere else. These items were categorized and shared with focus groups of employees for their reactions. When we finished, we had defined the entire employee experience and could now brand it under eight basic freedoms with corresponding brand icons: Freedom to pursue good health, to create financial security, to learn and grow, to make a positive difference, to travel, to work hard and have fun, to create and innovate, and to stay connected. Our internal brand message was, "At Southwest, Freedom begins with me."

Like those emotionally engaging advertisements, we then translated our freedoms into outcomes, always linking those outcomes back to the freedoms in all our messages. Working in partnership with our ad agencies, benefits consultants, employment partners, and so on, we created great employee-related products and services and tied them together under the Freedom theme with creative, on-brand packaging (Sartain and Finney, 2003).

At Yahoo!, internal branding was part of an entire rebranding initiative designed to position the company for a bigger future. In preparation, we defined our mission and values. This process began with an employee survey, a series of meetings with founders, employees, and executives. We wanted to answer for employees the question, "What does Yahoo! want to be when we grow up?" Corporate values seemed too traditional for such an irreverent young company. One of our founders asked us, "Why do we have to have a list of values; why can't we just have a list of 'what sucks'?" And, that is exactly how we marketed the values, paired with a "what sucks and aren't you glad you won't find these at Yahoo!?" list.

The values became the foundation for our new brand. As we launched our rebranding, our marketers conducted an inside-out and outside-in review of the company with HR as part of the internal review team. Internal workshops were held to explore brand characteristics, competencies, values, and territories. A brand audit was conducted with internal stakeholders through one-on-one interviews. Extensive marketing research tools were used to learn what our customers thought about the company and our brand. This led to the identification of our core competencies and core experiences for customers. We defined our target customer as an intensive Internet user (we say they have a special Y! gene) seeking efficiency, engagement, and expansion—and Yahoo! as the *Life Engine* with everything a customer needs or wants to do.

To introduce our new brand internally, we gave every employee a chance to advertise what makes Yahoo! his or her life engine by giving out license plate frames that are customized: "My _____ fill in the blank _____ Engine." We also held an essay contest for employees and customers to describe how Yahoo! is their life engine with a Harley-Davidson as the prize.

The Life Engine brand worked as well internally, so we began our efforts to make it come to life for Yahoos (our employees). This effort would involve finding the unique attributes that attract the right people, creating the right experience for Yahoos, so that we bring out the best in our people and they can bring their best to their work. We began with an online survey to determine which Yahoo! benefits, amenities, affinities, and experiences our employees valued most.

As I write this, we are working on our internal brand positioning and applying it to every dimension of the employee experience. We want to find and keep Yahoos with the "Y! gene," and we want the employee experience to fuel their life engines and their careers. We can do this by making it easy for Yahoos to get things done and engage by offering tools for life, guides to make it easier to navigate through the company, and special amenities that create the "Wow" experience for Yahoos. A newly branded product will be a repackaging of our benefits under the label *My Life: My Benefits.* This program will describe our offerings by life stages to make them real. Our efforts have just begun. We anticipate adding other My Life: My _____ products, including my career, my rewards, my perks, and so on.

Internal branding will change the way you design, deliver, and communicate HR products and services. Aligning the employee experience with the customer experience and the brand promise is a powerful way to establish a new relationship with employees. Various moments of truth provide the opportunity to connect with employees in a branded experience from the moment a candidate begins to think of an organization as a potential employer to the time an employee exits the organization as an alumni. HR can create and enhance the internal brand through these interactions with employees by providing branded HR products and services (compensation, benefits, career opportunities, learning experiences, internal communications), branded processes (hiring, on-boarding, promotion, exiting), and branded infrastructure (self-service, HRIS) to support the experience.

Steps for Internal Branding in Your Company

1. *Don't work in silos.* Successful internal branding must involve all constituencies. Involve marketing, public relations, advertising, corporate communications, talent acquisition, learning and development, compensation and benefits, facilities, and any other group that delivers products, experiences, or amenities to employees. Internal branding fails if it is one dimensional, for example, just an employment brand or a benefits brand. The entire employee experience is the value proposition.

2. *Start with your brand promise.* Be sure you understand what your external brand promise is to your customers. If this is a brand that your marketing, advertising, and public relations departments intend to continue using for the future, you can build your internal message on a foundation that has already been built to reach out to the public. If your brand is due for an overhaul, use this opportunity to create a brand message that can be translated into meaningful ways both externally and internally. You can begin to brand internally without a clearly defined external brand by focusing on your corporate mission, vision, and existing products and services. For example, at Yahoo! we created a series of guides to working at the company with the look and feel of our Yahoo! Maps products. Be careful not to tread too far away from the branding your organization is already using.

3. *Think like a marketer.* Use the expertise and the techniques of your marketing, communications, advertising, and public relations people to comprehend how employees currently perceive the company, what they want, and how you can help them experience the company in a more positive way. Focus groups are one example of classic marketing tools that will give you extraordinary insight.

4. *Engage your employees.* To make sure your messages sustain their meaning and credibility, keep your employees involved. Answer these three questions for employees: What does the company stand for? How will the company deliver on its stand consistently? How can the employee help the company deliver what we promise?

5. *Use powerful key words.* Link all your messages to powerful one- or two-word messages. Southwest used *Freedom*. Yahoo! chose *Life Engine*.

6. *Be authentic.* Develop a narrative proclamation of how your organization will carry out the promise and uphold the values in the employment relationship. Don't overpromise and underdeliver. Your brand promise should be powerful and emotionally evocative. But it must be tightly connected (and connectable) to your employees' daily experience with the company.

7. *Update your packaging.* The promise statement can be used day to day to inform and guide decisions that impact the employment relationship. All communication materials—from recruiting advertisement, to compensation and benefits, to retirement—should be expressed following brand communication guidelines.

8. *Market the internal brand externally.* Use your internal brand to let the community, customers, and potential candidates know what it's like to work at your company.

9. *Create internal brand standards.* For every touch point of the employee experience, there should be corresponding metrics to track performance against standards. For example, measure whether you deliver the right candidate experience by surveying candidates, including those you didn't hire. Ask departing employees whether their exit experience left them feeling good about the organization.

10. *Build and enhance the brand.* Every brand evolves over time. Keep your messaging fresh and new. Each year, HR should plan and carry out repackaging and messaging to keep the message exciting and fun.

REFERENCES

Employer Branding: It's Not Just for Good Times. *JWT Specialized Communications,* February 2003.

Engaging Your Employees Through Your Brand. *The Conference Board Report,* Number 1288, 2001.

Pfau, Bruce N., and Ira T. Kay (Eds.), The Human Capital Edge: 21 People Management Practices Your Company Must Implement (or Avoid) to Maximize Shareholder Value, *McGraw-Hill Professional,* December 2001.

Rogers, Fiona. Engaging Employees to Live the Brand, Towers Perrin, *Strategic HR Review,* Volume 2, Issue 6, September/October 2003.

Sartain, Libby, and Martha I. Finney. *HR from the Heart: Inspiring Stories and Strategies for Building the People Side of Great Business.* New York: AMA-COM, March 2003.

Tosti, Donald T., and Rodger Stotz. Internal Branding: Using Performance Technology to Create an Organization Focused on Customer Value, *Performance Improvement,* Volume 39, Number 9, October 2000.

CHAPTER 22

THE WINNING TEAM: A STRATEGIC IMPERATIVE

LEA SOUPATA

> *Good management is not just organization. It is an attitude inspired by the will to do right. Good management is taking a sincere interest in the welfare of the people you work with. It is the ability to make people feel that you and they are the company—not merely employees of it. Good management is your worthiness to have and hold the confidence of others.*
>
> —*J. E. Casey, 1949*[1]

A century of experience confirms that any large organizational strategy must be grounded in the company's culture and aligned with its business goals. At UPS, the companywide vision is based on its founder, Jim Casey, his philosophy of good management, and on UPS principles and priorities. This chapter focuses on a specific strategic imperative (critical organizational outcome) that aligns with overall corporate goals. The *Winning Team* strategic imperative is an HR effort to attract, develop, and retain a skilled, motivated, and diverse global workforce. The Winning Team strives to develop not only an effective workforce but also one whose interests and values align with UPS, which consequently results in engaged employees. It also is intended to preserve and build on UPS's culture and legacy of integrity, ownership, performance, respect, innovation, personal growth, and service excellence.

UPS was founded in 1907 in Seattle, Washington, as a messenger company and has now grown into the world's largest package delivery company and a leading global provider of specialized transportation and logistics services with over $33 billion in revenue. UPS enables global commerce in

189

more than 200 countries and territories worldwide. The company continues to develop the leading edge of logistics, supply chain management, and e-commerce by integrating the three flows of goods, information, and funds and by maintaining a positive global reputation through its sustainability effort. UPS emphasizes the importance of environmental and social health. Through the UPS Foundation, the philanthropic arm of the company, UPS champions innovative solutions to social problems by focusing on literacy, hunger, and effective volunteerism. UPS is a model for global community involvement and corporate citizenship.

Currently, there are over 370,000 UPS employees throughout the United States, Canada, Asia, Europe, Africa, and Latin America. Although UPS is constantly expanding, its strength exists in the commitment and dedication employees have to the company's success. Today, UPS is publicly traded, but it is still predominantly an employee-owned company. One of the company's missions is to be financially sound *with broad employee ownership,* offering a long-term, competitive return to shareowners. This ownership culture is very strong at UPS. It is demonstrated through ownership guidelines for managers and supervisors and employee stock programs, which include the Discounted Employee Stock Purchase Plan (DESPP), Managers Incentive Program (MIP), and the Long-Term Incentive Program. This ownership culture is vigorously communicated throughout UPS through a variety of communication channels. Employee ownership is core to UPS culture, and it translates into a strong work ethic with employees engaged in growing the business and committed to the company's success.

The Winning Team works in combination with other strategic imperatives, which rely on a strong Winning Team effort, including *Value-Added Solutions, Customer Focus,* and *Enterprise Excellence.* These imperatives are supported by a number of initiatives, each monitored through standard measures.

UPS uses metrics that are based on industry standards, UPS historical trends, and challenging stretch goals to measure success of the Winning Team effort. For example, turnover is a retention metric. Because retention is a workforce planning initiative, other groups have measures tailored to their own areas of responsibilities. The resulting key initiatives, based on measures and goals, consist of programs, projects, and functional initiatives.

A Winning Team critical initiative example is, "Establish a workplace environment based on a supportive relationship with our employees." To tackle this goal, the company developed many functional initiatives such as dynamic communications with employees through an employee web portal project. The Winning Team metrics coincide with key metrics used to keep track of progress in reaching business goals. These success indicators include: revenue growth, operating income growth, net income growth, operating economic value added (EVA) growth, customer satisfaction index (CSI) improvement, employer of choice index (ECI) improvement, and service quality index (SQI) improvement.

The Winning Team strategic imperative, in alignment with other imperatives, comprises UPS's strategy as it enables global commerce. To enable global commerce, all functional processes, business unit programs, projects, and initiatives align. Any new programs, projects, and initiatives are developed with the intent of contributing significantly, in a measurable way. Departments within HR have unique responsibilities in successfully meeting the Winning Team imperative. Areas within HR that contribute to this strategic imperative include health and safety, employee communications, employee relations, and learning and development. The following paragraphs discuss each area's contributions to the outcome in more detail.

The significance of UPS's success in meeting the business goals of the strategic imperative requires a broad communicative effort. Employees must know what UPS is doing, why, and what their role is in making the business successful. They also need to understand the principles that are guiding the imperatives. These are found in the UPS Charter. The Charter, which includes the company's strategy, mission, purpose, and values, sets forth the principles that guide decisions and solutions developed every day at UPS. The strategic imperatives grew from the vision of the Charter.

In creating a thorough understanding of the Winning Team initiative and developing supporting relationships throughout UPS, a number of media and deliverables are used. There are frequent communication meetings throughout the operating districts among staff, operations, managers, and first-line employees. In addition, UPSers.com, the employee portal, provides the most up-to-date information about UPS, technology, industry news, employee services, and business initiatives. This communication channel, which employees can access from work or home, is needed because with over 70,000 drivers, UPS is truly a mobile workforce. UPSers.com includes links to the medical, dental, vision, and prescription carriers, as well as other benefit providers for U.S. employees. It also includes links to the administrator for the UPS Savings Advantage (401k plan) and the DESPP. There is also a site where employees can view executive speech summaries and bios to better understand who the UPS leaders are and what they are saying to the public about the business.

UPS views the relationship with its more than 230,000 union employees as an opportunity to protect and grow its business. There are numerous activities that accomplish this goal; however, three are mentioned here: *One vision, Project LEAD,* and *Comprehensive Health and Safety Process (CHSP).* One vision is an hour-long, one-to-one conversation between the supervisors and first-line union employees that focuses on topics such as UPS's competition, technology, health and safety, opinion survey feedback, UPS supply chain solutions, stock purchasing, and recognition. An important part of the One vision discussion focuses on how the managers, supervisors, and first-line union employees can work together in maintaining an environment of openness and trust. Company success depends on a commitment to building trust and improving employee relations by relying on integrity, ability, and character. During discussions, the supervisor explains the UPS open-door policy, which means all management people are available at any time for workplace issues, questions, or concerns. The supervisor also engages the union employee in a discussion about building and improving trust.

In short, this conversation states what UPS has done, where UPS is presently, and the future of UPS. It is seen as a forum for the supervisor and first-line union employee to communicate openly with each other, talk about the challenges the company faces, business initiatives, and how all can work together for success.

Project LEAD also is a critical part of building a Winning Team with employees. Project LEAD seeks to motivate all UPS employees to take an initiative in seeking new business by discussing service offerings with current and potential customers. Project LEAD gives financial rewards to employees, including union employees, who obtain quality sales leads for the company. Frequent meetings also take place between the sales force and delivery drivers to discuss pending sales leads and prospects for future leads.

Through Project LEAD, the workforce is engaged in protecting and growing UPS's business.

The CHSP is an all-encompassing system to prevent occupational injuries and auto accidents through the development of workplace health and safety programs. The core function of CHSP is to find and fix hazards that could potentially cause injuries or auto accidents and implement systems that eliminate or control the hazards from recurring. What make the CHSP so effective are the Cochaired Employee Health and Safety Committees. These committees are cochaired by a management employee and a union employee who work side by side to create a safer working environment at UPS. As a testament to their effectiveness, in 2003, over 3,500 UPS drivers had at least 25 years of service without a traffic accident.

Along with a more supportive and safer workplace, the Winning Team attempts to build on an integrated talent management program, because employees are a competitive advantage to any organization. Succession planning, career development planning discussions, management performance improvements, and retaining talent are essential. UPS encourages promotion from within the organization and believes in cultivating talent. Succession planning is a long-range process that is important for UPS leadership continuity in critical positions and for fostering individual employee development. Succession planning is aligned with the Winning Team because merely making financial goals does not ensure an individual's promotion to greater responsibility. Rather, the individual's ability to manage people effectively (using the historic Employee Relations Index scores as a measure) plays a key role in UPS's promotion decisions. Career development planning discussions are critical to ensure that employees set appropriate goals and develop plans to help them attain necessary skills and experiences that are in line with the organization's needs and that will eventually fill essential competency gaps. Performance improvement plans also are used to guide and assist managers and supervisors in creating a strategy to improve employee performance that is consistent, specific, clear, and documented.

It is necessary for UPS to identify, align, and retain diverse talent to grow and exceed the competitors. UPS believes diverse people, ideas, and points of view are critical to the success and growth of the company. However, just having a diverse workforce is not enough; people must be able to effectively manage that diversity. Diversity training that emphasizes terms such as *trust, respect, relationships, acceptance, inclusion, working together,* and *team* supports the Winning Team imperative. Employment and retention processes, practices, and criteria accommodate workforce stability and development to retain the diverse talent. Training and development processes help UPS to continuously develop this talent.

The Winning Team strategic imperative is grounded in UPS ideals. It provides initiatives for HR practices that preserve the culture and legacy of UPS and engage employees in the success of UPS. UPS continues to align HR activities with critical organizational outcomes, such as Winning Team. To do so, first-line managers and supervisors must be able to respond to constant change and innovation.

Metrics that measure the improvement of initiatives associated with the Winning Team assist the company in determining success by comparing its progress to the planned results. These indicators ensure that the HR practices advance UPS while supporting the vision found in the UPS Charter. This vision guides UPS and has helped it to grow into one of the most admired companies in the world.

NOTE

1. This quote from Jim Casey can be found in "Our Partnership Legacy: Jim Casey," copyright United Parcel Service of America, Inc., 1985.

SECTION V

RETHINK ORGANIZATIONS AS CAPABILITIES, NOT STRUCTURES

If we were to ask 10 people to "draw" an organization, they would likely all depict some form of an organization chart, with boxes to represent the hierarchy and structure. But, when we ask people to name organizations they admire, they often pick firms based on the reputation of the firm, not the structure of the firm. A firm's reputation is not embedded in its structure, but its capabilities. GE has the ability to develop leaders, 3M innovates, Southwest Airlines operates efficiently, and Disney gives guests an escape experience. These organizations are known more for what they are able to do than how they are structured.

The distinction between structure and capabilities is important for HR professionals. It is easy to seek structural solutions to business problems and reorganize by removing layers, downsizing, changing reporting relationships, or changing processes. Focusing on capabilities starts by figuring out the desired identity for the organization in the mind of its key stakeholders such as customers, investors, and employees. Once the desired identity is defined, HR professionals may design HR practices to build those desired capabilities.

The chapters in this section point out some of the possible capabilities that organizations might possess and the HR role in their application.

Beatty and Schneier in Chapter 23 focus on an organization's ability to build a workforce strategy to connect business strategy to HR strategy. Workforce strategy includes differentiating employees, creating a workplace philosophy, and decisions made by line managers. HR professionals have primary responsibility to draft a workforce strategy to link business and HR practices.

Hewitt proposes strategic clarity as a capability in Chapter 24. *Strategic clarity* means that leaders have the ability to redefine the nature of competition, demonstrate clear analytical frameworks for strategic positioning, and encourage cross-unit collaboration and disciplined entrepreneurship. HR professionals may help advocate for strategic clarity rather than link their HR plans to flawed strategic assumptions.

Joyce, Nohria, and Roberson review their research that leads to 4+2 capabilities in Chapter 25. Their work finds that successful organizations must have four foundation capabilities: to focus strategy, execute flawlessly, maintain a performance-oriented culture, and build a flexible organization. In addition, successful firms either manage talent, engage leaders, innovate, or manage partnerships. HR professionals help implement these winning practices.

Ulrich and Smallwood show in Chapter 26 that the desired capabilities may also be seen as intangibles that investors value. These intangibles become the new "return" for HR work. A return on intangibles index helps HR professionals track measures that matter most to line managers.

Chapters 27, 28, and 29 raise a new reality about organizations: duality or paradox. Rather than have a defined and single capability, complex realities require complex and paradoxical capabilities.

Dyer and Ericksen in Chapter 27 suggest that in rapidly changing marketplaces, the ability to get the right number of the right types of people in the right place at the right time (HR scalability) is increasingly difficult. To manage internal fluidity, HR professionals should build both (1) freedom and flexibility and (2) discipline and order. HR professionals may establish principles to help make these paradoxical capabilities happen.

Miles, Miles, and Snow in Chapter 28 introduce a new organizational form, the collaborative multifirm network. This organization archetype innovates continually by flowing information and resources to key projects. HR professionals may help create protocols to simultaneously share information across units and focus accountability within units.

In Chapter 29, Wright and Snell propose that organizations must simultaneously create value as defined by stakeholders, deliver value by aligning with and driving issues critical to the business, and live values by being the guardians of the morés within the company. HR professionals play a central role in each of these value-contributing activities.

HR professionals who focus on capability more than structure work to figure out the desired identity of the firm in the mind of the investor and customer. They then create HR practices that create and sustain these capabilities throughout the organization. This section suggests possible capabilities of the future organization and how HR might play in their creation and maintenance. "Human" resources is not just about people, but about the organizations in which people operate. And, increasingly, organizations may be characterized more by their capabilities than their structures.

CHAPTER 23

WORKFORCE STRATEGY: A MISSING LINK IN HR'S FUTURE SUCCESS

RICHARD W. BEATTY AND CRAIG ERIC SCHNEIER

There has been growing acceptance of the importance of the HR function's role as a strategic partner within firms, but only occasional recognition of HR as a strategic player. If HR is to be invited to participate in top-level strategic decision making, it needs to become a strategic player (Ulrich and Beatty, 2001), which requires the ability to "score"-that is, impact the business scorecard. Figure 23.1 modifies the traditional business scorecard by adding workforce success to demonstrate where and how HR can score and suggesting metrics indicative of HR's success. HR can become a player by focusing on three strategies: the business strategy, the workforce strategy, and the HR strategy. By mastering these three strategies, HR can contribute significantly to successful execution of the business strategy. To begin with, HR must understand the firm's business strategy to be able to align HR strategy to it. Common sense dictates that HR's time, effort, and resources be devoted to successfully attaining the business priorities. Unfortunately, such alignment is rare, for two reasons: First, much of HR's efforts are still focused on transaction processing and advocating for employees who may not be strategic contributors. Second, there is an analytical "missing link" between business strategy and HR strategy: workforce strategy.

199

Figure 23.1
The Business Scorecard

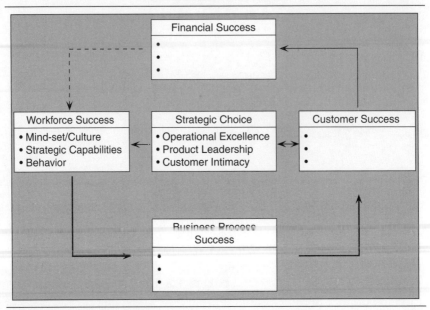

WORKFORCE STRATEGY AS DIFFERENTIATING INTERNALLY AND OPERATIONALLY

A workforce strategy exists conceptually between an HR strategy and a business strategy. The concept is simple: If a firm's competitive advantage consists of differentiating itself from other firms externally (i.e., in the marketplace), a firm must similarly differentiate internally with respect to the focus and allocation of resources. The firm's workforce is not only one of its costly resources but also often *the* most expensive resource. Thus, a strategy for addressing this critical resource is essential. Only when a workforce strategy is known and understood can the HR strategy be effectively articulated. HR strategy (e.g., the design and operation of practices such as compensation or appraisal) in the absence of workforce strategy (e.g., how to move the best people to the key positions) and business strategy is meaningless. Figure 23.2 illustrates the relationship of the three strategies. Business strategy focuses on how the firm creates its competitive advantage—how it differentiates itself in its

Figure 23.2
The Prerequisites for Effective Strategy Execution

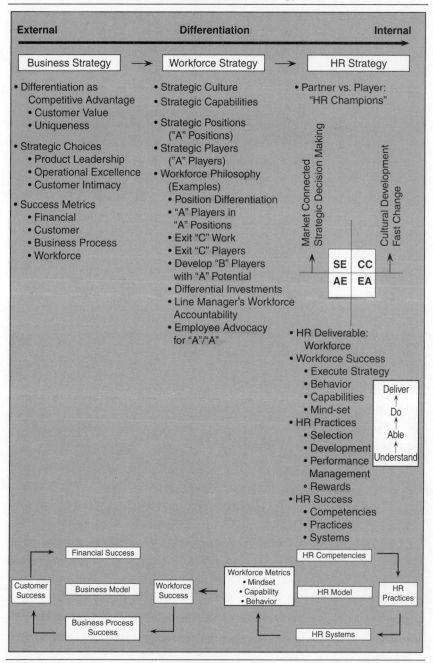

marketplace. For discussion purposes, we find the approach of Treacy and Wiersema (1995) to nondiversified firms a useful starting point. They posit three basic strategic choices firms make: operational excellence, product leadership, or customer intimacy. These three distinct choices are designed to differentiate the firm in its marketplace, although successful firms generally have a second, supporting strategy. For simplicity, we focus on nondiversified firms because diversified firms present many additional complicated issues, implying additional complexity for the HR role. In any case, both types of firms require a workforce strategy.

WORKFORCE STRATEGY COMPONENTS

A workforce strategy is developed by identifying the strategy of the business and the firm culture necessary to effectively execute that strategy. Workforce strategy also includes an organization's philosophy regarding strategic capabilities, the strategic positions, and strategic players (see Figure 23.2). Consideration of the interaction of these components is also required. Once this analysis is carried out, the firm is ready to develop a workforce philosophy, the firm's rules of governance with respect to creating and delivering a workforce that maximizes the realization of the firm's business strategy. At this point, a strategy for the HR function can be articulated.

The most important "deliverable" of the HR function is the workforce, but not just any workforce. It must be an internally differentiated workforce, one that can successfully deliver the business strategy *externally*. This notion of differentiation is inherent in the HR function. If a company's workforce is an undifferentiated collection of individuals, why would it need the HR function? But HR professionals, and the systems and processes they design with and for managers and employees, do indeed differentiate. They differentiate, for example, in selection, development, performance management, and rewards. HR's job is also to take the lead in the design of systems that enable firms to optimally differentiate their workforces in delivering the strategy of the firm. HR cannot differentiate effectively without understanding this role and the link between business strategy and HR strategy.

In his cogent analysis of the HR function, *Human Resource Champions,* Dave Ulrich (1999) speaks of four primary roles for HR: administrative efficiency, employee advocacy, strategy execution, and culture change. Because strategy execution (via HR strategy) and culture change (a component of workforce strategy) are critical to delivering strategy in the future, we advocate that most of HR's time, effort, and professional development be devoted to these areas. This is where HR can truly differentiate itself and become a player (see also Beatty and Schneier, 1995).

Firms don't change; people do, and it is people who change organizations. HR, therefore, has a major responsibility to facilitate the change process. Nearly 70 percent of many firms' expenditures relate to their workforce. The major challenge for HR in the future is not reducing its cost or increasing administrative efficiency. Why? The HR function typically accounts for less than 1 percent of a firm's total expenditures; HR cannot help the firm save its way to prosperity. HR cannot save enough to make a real difference in the firm's economics. But HR can make a significant difference in the firm's economics if it facilitates the development of a workforce that delivers–executes–the firm's business strategy.

DEVELOPING A WORKFORCE PHILOSOPHY TO GOVERN WORKFORCE DECISIONS

Another important aspect of workforce strategy is developing a workforce philosophy. Such a philosophy serves as a system of governance for decision making with respect to the workforce by both line managers and HR. By implication, line management and HR must be held jointly accountable for managing the workforce.

Figure 23.3 illustrates some of the types of choices firms make in developing a workforce philosophy. The HR function can help by constructing a similar set of choices tailored to a firm's specific needs. Some choices may reflect past practices or decisions; others will be more forward looking. By surfacing such issues, HR can compel the firm's leaders to consider whether they will conduct "business as usual" or whether it is necessary to move in a new direction. Some choices may be easy (e.g.,

Figure 23.3

Workforce Strategy: Developing a Strategically Successful Workforce

What Is Your Workforce Philosophy?

Workforce Strategy: Developing a Strategically Successful Workforce
Which choices must your firm make to deliver its competitive advantage?

Listed below are examples of principles that could be the basis of a workforce strategy. They are intended to stimulate your thinking as you consider how to design and build the best workforce to deliver your firm's strategy. Please check (P) those that represent our firm now and those you believe are necessary to deliver our firm's strategy and to build the *most* successful workforce in our industry.

NOW FUTURE

1. All employees deserve "lifetime job security."
2. All employees are entitled to an annual increase.
3. Equality is more important than equity.
4. Replacement planning for all top positions is critical.
5. Employee advocacy is critical.
6. Staffing strategic capabilities is an imperative.
7. Successful staffing of "A" positions is critical.
8. Leadership competencies for top positions should be based on our leaders today.
9. Corporate "owns" and manages the careers of most "A" positions.
10. Developmental investment should be made in "A" players in "A" positions.
11. Developmental investments in "B" players with "A" potential are critical.
12. Performance management is a tool to execute our strategy.
13. "C" players must be developed or exited.
14. All employees must contribute to customer/consumer success.
15. No employee "owns" a position.
16. Line managers have workforce responsibilities: mindset, competency growth, and employee behavior.
17. Line management is to execute workforce strategy.
18. We must topgrade in all "A" positions.
19. "A" players must be in "A" positions.
20. Competency growth is required in all positions.
21. All employees either are strategic resources, operational resources or surplus.

NOW FUTURE

22. Generating ideas and high levels of performance are the criteria for advancement.
23. Annual improvement of each employee's performance is critical.
24. Having effective leaders at all levels is critical to strategic success.
25. Every employee must contribute more value to the firm than they receive from it.
26. Differential investment in employees is necessary.
27. "B" players are expected in "B" positions.
28. "C" positions must be eliminated.
29. Managers must be accountable for their workforces.
30. Knowledge sharing is indispensable to strategic success.
31. Retention of "A" players in "A" positions is vital.
32. Our workforce is HR's major deliverable.
33. Management of the workforce should represent at least 25% of line manager or executive's performance evaluation.
34. Active learners in all "A" positions are needed.
35. "A" positions are not hierarchical, but based on strategy value to the firm.
36. All employees must be given timely, candid feedback on their performance.
37. Managers should be the advocate of their employees based on their performance.
38. Employees should be their own advocates.
39. Replacement planning for all strategic positions is critical.
40. Building a deep, broad succession pool is critical.
41. "A" positions should have a midpoint at the 75th percentile, "B" positions at the 50th, and "C" positions (if we must have a few) no higher than the 25th percentile.

204

committing to a diverse workforce); others may be extremely difficult or controversial (e.g., moving solid performers with no potential out of the firm). Decisions antithetical to the status quo bring the most resistance. It is important to stay focused on the question of whether the firm has the right workforce allocation (e.g., headcount at various levels and functions), alignment (e.g., objectives and priorities, as well as interactions), and cost structure (e.g., compensation) to win its future. When action becomes necessary, we must have in place guidelines for strategic decision making with respect to the workforce and ensure that the guidelines are followed consistently by all line managers and by HR.

THE ROLE OF METRICS

Ensuring accountability for strategic decision making requires a system of metrics to hold line managers accountable for implementing that specific workforce philosophy determined to leverage competitive advantage. For example, accountability calls for making decisions that are often ignored or delayed-for example, what to do about long-term "C" (nonstrategic) people or "C" (nonstrategic) work.

At a more fundamental level, a firm may need different strategic capabilities to win in the future. Here we follow Ulrich and Smallwood (2004) and use the term *strategic capabilities* to refer to those bundles of information, technology, *and* people that create a firm's competitive advantage, not the capability of individuals (or "competencies" in common HR usage). The leadership should identify those strategic capabilities required to execute strategy, level of performance on each-objectively-to determine what competitive advantages it has (see Figure 23.2). Today's strengths may not be tomorrow's. Thus, the firm needs to consider which strategic positions (or "A" work) should be significantly increased, as well as the implications for selection, development, performance management, and rewards. HR must work to ensure their attention is devoted to the firm's "A" positions and obtaining "A"-level performance. If we fully understand the business strategy, have in place appropriate metrics, and have built-in consequences for both HR and line managers for performance against those metrics, workforce success can best be realized.

Integrated Business and HR Scorecards

Workforce success must be determined via the scorecard of the business, just as financial success, customer success, and operational success are determined. Workforce success is influenced not only by HR but also by line managers. Therefore, as noted earlier, line managers and HR must share common metrics and targets, for which both are held accountable. For example, such metrics might include workforce "mind-set" (see Figure 23.1). That is, does the workforce know and understand the firm's strategic position, where it is going, and what must be done to ensure that the strategy is executed? Other metrics refer to usage of our best talent. Do we have individuals in "A" positions who deliver "A" work? Another potential metric relates to workforce behavior-whether it's leader behavior or customer service behavior-and ensuring that the workforce is behaving in ways that deliver the firm's competitive advantage.

We have argued here that the HR of the future will look to mastering business strategy, workforce strategy, and HR strategy. However, the emphasis should be on workforce strategy, a missing link. Workforce strategy focuses on the deliverable of HR: the workforce. A workforce strategy encompasses the culture of the workforce, its strategic capabilities, strategic positions, strategic players, and a philosophy to serve as guidelines for strategic decision making. The components of the workforce philosophy should be driven by the firm's strategy in both the short and long term. For example, if the firm is facing adverse circumstances in the short term, it may elect highly differentiating (i.e., new) workforce practices related to its culture, capabilities, positions, and employees. A firm whose competitive advantage is threatened, a circumstance that all maturing firms eventually face, will anticipate the threat and seek to differentiate its workforce in new ways that better fit its emergent strategy.

REFERENCES

Beatty, R. W., and C. E. Schneier. (1995). Making Culture Change Happen and Making It Last: Using Structure, Systems and Skills as Change Levers. In L. A. Berger (Ed.), *Handbook of Culture Change*. Business One/Irwin.

Treacy, M., and F. Wiersema. (1995). *The Discipline of Market Leaders*. Reading, MA: Addison-Wesley.

Ulrich, D. (1999). *Human Resource Champions: The Next Agenda for Adding Value and Delivering Results*. Cambridge, MA: Harvard Business Press.

Ulrich, D., and R. W. Beatty. (2001). From Partners to Players: Extending the HR Playing Field. *Human Resource Management Journal*. Vol. 40 (4), 2001, pp. 293–307.

Ulrich, D., and N. Smallwood. (2004). Capitalizing on Capabilities. *Harvard Business Review,* June 2004.

CHAPTER 24

CONNECTING STRATEGY AND HR: ESTABLISHING A NEW LOGIC OF PARTNERSHIP

GORDON HEWITT

How do we find a compelling connection between the changing worlds of business strategy and HR? How can HR professionals add distinctive value to the competitive agenda and capabilities of the organizations they support? In what ways can they enable businesses to compete and create value at a higher level or in new forms? What is required for HR to become a genuine and meaningful *strategic partner*?

At any gathering of HR professionals, these questions increasingly dominate the agenda and reflect both a sense of aspiration and apprehension. The questions are clear and challenging. The answers, however, are more elusive and varied. They illustrate a dilemma in clarifying both what being *strategic* is all about in today's competitive landscape and the logic and basis of a *partnership*.

This dilemma may lie partly in the way the HR function has traditionally defined its role and value added. If HR starts with the question, "Given the strategy of the business, how can we develop a set of supporting processes and capabilities?" two doubts immediately arise. First is the assumption that a robust strategy (as distinct from a set of operational targets) is genuinely in place. Second, the proposition puts HR in reactive mode, delivering value as part of the executional arm of strategy rather than cocreating it and enabling the business to *resolve strategic dilemmas*.

In many ways, HR executives deserve much sympathy. At the very time they are trying to find an agenda that connects more closely with strategy, the logic and legacy of the strategy process are under significant pressure to adapt to more dynamic and complex forces of competition in the global business system. So often, the reality of strategy in practice has constrained the HR contribution for three reasons:

1. What many businesses eloquently describe as their "strategy" may, on deeper investigation, turn out to be little more than a medium-term operating plan.
2. The statement of "strategic vision" hanging proudly on the office walls rarely goes beyond a generic list of obligations to stakeholders and in today's competitive environment fails to provide sufficient *direction and traction*.
3. Typically, the language of strategy fails to inspire confidence and credibility and may even encourage cynicism. Describing a proposal as strategic often sends a coded message that returns are unlikely in our lifetime and that risk is not for the fainthearted.

HR should also be wary of aligning itself uncritically with the in vogue sentiment, "It's all about execution." Great ideas that lack an implementation capability remain simply great ideas. In today's competitive landscape, however, the nature of the execution challenge goes well beyond establishing disciplines for consistently meeting performance targets.

For example, corporations such as GE and Rolls-Royce are competing to create unique solutions for airlines that integrate aircraft engines, service and logistics systems, finance, and informatics. Sony is attempting to morph the evolving worlds of consumer electronics and digital entertainment. Drug companies are trying to harness the growth of genomic sciences and targeted therapeutic diagnostics to their traditional blockbuster drug business models. Intel and Microsoft are seeking to create new engines of profitable growth beyond their homeland of the personal computer.

Such strategic journeys are becoming more typical of the challenge facing corporations worldwide. They should cause us to rethink the simplistic dichotomy between *formulation* and *execution* of strategy. Additionally, so much of the strategic debate in corporations has focused on the question of how we play. The emerging dynamics of global competition should also encourage us to think deeply about the nature of the game and the rules.

Enabling a business, however well intentioned, to develop a capability to play the wrong game better is an outcome HR should seek to avoid. In that sense, speed of execution is today's double-edge sword of competitive capability. If a corporation is on the highway to hell, it needs to take its foot off the accelerator and acquire a dependable compass.

What are the issues that should form the basis of dialog between strategy and HR and a new logic of partnership? To address this question, we need to start with some competitive pathology and understand what is driving a period of unprecedented volatility in business performance, corporate reputation, and CEO credibility. The widely fluctuating recent track record of firms such as Sony, Ford, Nokia, and Time Warner testify to that volatility.

While the experience of Enron, WorldCom, Tyco, and others raised new concerns about the ethical credibility of top executives, today's competitive system is posing more widespread and enduring questions about *strategic credibility*—the capacity to lead an enterprise often in a new and uncharted direction supported by new organizational competencies. The challenge that connects strategy and HR is much more about developing new mind-sets for new games, rather than more efficient processes for existing games.

THE EMERGING CHALLENGES

The components of the challenge, as summarized in Figure 24.1, are:

Issue 1: Radical changes in the competitive landscape are challenging conventional views about the nature of competition and the relevance of "experience."

Managers today are confronted with a new and uncomfortable reality. Their competitive landscape is altering not only at a rapid pace but also in unfamiliar patterns. Many "industries" now lack clear boundaries and even definition and are becoming highly fluid spaces whose features are constantly morphing. Telecommunications, energy, health care, financial services, information, and entertainment are examples of arenas whose boundaries and structure are no longer established and agreed to by existing, known competitors.

Figure 24.1
Components of the Challenge

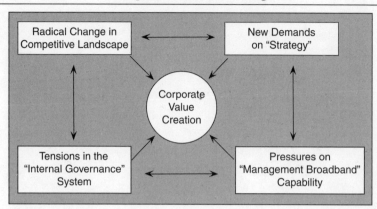

Additionally, many industries are evolving like "complex adaptive systems" in which the pattern of interaction between different competitive variables can move the whole system in a direction that is difficult to predict (see Figure 24.2).

This interaction can cause noise inside the executive brain for several reasons. First, value chains are being replaced by value networks in which customers, competitors, suppliers, and collaborators perform multiple, overlapping roles. Second, it implies that today's events can significantly affect the way the whole industry game will look in the future. Therefore, having a top management point of view about how to shape the evolution of an industry may be as important as the accuracy of their forecasts. Third, it suggests that strategy has intensely short-term features in terms of making moves and placing bets, rather than being an exercise in long-term visioning.

In the mid-1970s, James March (March, 1999; March and Olsen, 1976), one of the pioneers of complexity analysis, observed that aspects of the world in which we have to make decisions are simply beyond our understanding. Therefore, some strategic decisions will be based on "knowable impact"—our experience of similar actions in known circumstances—and partly a "journey of discovery."

Figure 24.2
The Emerging Competitive Landscape

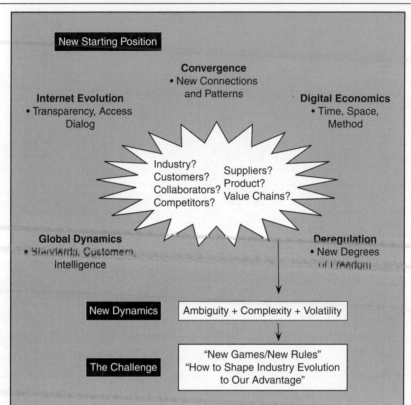

If today's competitive landscape is being driven more by the combined forces of *ambiguity, complexity, and volatility* than conventional explanations of structural and cyclical change, then maybe the balance is shifting toward discovery. This shift has powerful implications for the nature of strategy, risk, execution, and the whole basis of executive development. It also highlights the limits of top management experience. As one CEO confided to me recently, "Life can be really unkind. . . . You can arrive at the top of a corporation just when everything you know is irrelevant to the future."

Issue 2: New demands are being placed on strategy, both as a set of analytical frameworks and organizational processes.

Why is it that despite possessing more comprehensive data about industry trends than ever before, more accurate forecasting systems and scenario plans, plus world-class executive development programs, so many corporations are deeply disturbed by *inflection points* (changes that fundamentally alter the basis of competition and traditional sources of advantage)? The current troubles facing the world's recorded music industry provide a sobering example.

From the 1970s to the 1990s, major players such as EMI, Warner, and Bertelsmann successfully adapted to significant technology shifts in the format of recorded music—from gramophone records to audiotapes to compact discs. Changes that are disruptive physically, however, may not be disruptive intellectually. During the music industry's voyage of technology discovery, they did not embark on an equivalent challenge to rethink the validity of business and industry models. The assumption structure about how music was recorded, stored, accessed, distributed, bought, and owned remained firmly rooted in "old game" competitive logic.

The disruption that was ignited in the late 1990s by the Fraunhofer Institute's dissemination of a compression standard for digital sound that led to MP3, Napster, and a host of followers challenged every one of the music industry's assumptions. For years, the traditional players seemed unable to mount a "new game" strategic response, especially because they diagnosed the key issue as "piracy." Eventually, the breakthrough (as so often happens) came from outside the industry via the I-Pod technology developed by the Apple Corporation. This technology resolved so many of the dilemmas with a new micropayments pricing model—99 cents per song downloaded.

The implication of this example for HR is clear. If HR practices are themselves rooted in old game logic, they may unintentionally reinforce old game assumptions. Every organization needs an internal, healthy, ongoing process to challenge and revalidate its value-creation assumptions and orthodoxies. This is a key role for HR in a genuine strategic partnership.

Issue 3: There are pressures and tensions in the *internal governance* systems of organizations to create value in new ways.

Many corporations have organized themselves as a portfolio of relatively autonomous business units. In many ways, HR has followed this trend by having a corporate concept of HR based at headquarters but with significant decentralization of HR activity in separate businesses.

Often, however, powerful opportunities to discover new game logic span multiple businesses or lie at the connection points between them. Consider Sony's approach to the digital entertainment revolution. Should Sony allow its TV, PC, and PlayStation groups to develop separate views about the home entertainment platform for the future or encourage one cross-divisional, corporate perspective? The dilemma is illustrated in Figure 24.3.

The challenge is how to resolve the internal governance tension between achieving strong business unit performance and at the same time creating horizontal linkages that go beyond old-fashioned synergy to access new opportunities. The traditional measurement and resource allocation system, however, is firmly based on the vertical pillars of the enterprise.

Figure 24.3
Value Creation and Organizational Productivity

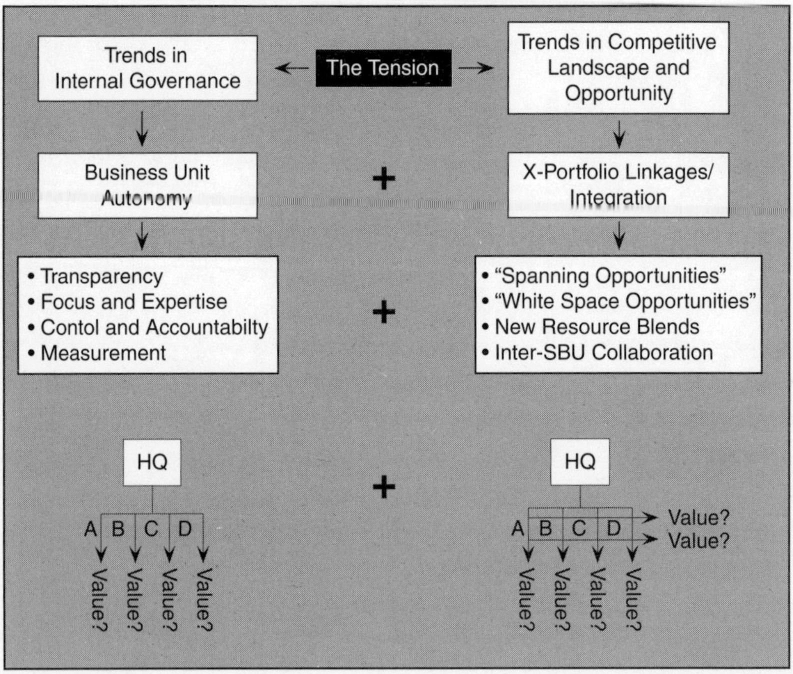

Trends in Internal Governance	← The Tension →	Trends in Competitive Landscape and Opportunity
Business Unit Autonomy	+	X-Portfolio Linkages/ Integration
• Transparency • Focus and Expertise • Contol and Accountabilty • Measurement	+	• "Spanning Opportunities" • "White Space Opportunities" • New Resource Blends • Inter-SBU Collaboration

HQ

A B C D

Value? Value? Value? Value?

+

HQ

A B C D → Value?
→ Value?

Value? Value? Value? Value?

The challenge for HR is whether it can build layers of horizontal capabilities and metrics that encourage intense interbusiness collaboration and the sharing of risk, opportunity, and reward. HR may have to take the lead in symbolically demonstrating that it can resolve its own internal governance tensions to allow this to happen. Organizations need to develop corporate disciplines to leverage resources, not just to allocate them.

Issue 4: Building both vertical and horizontal streams of value creates new pressures on "leadership broadband."

Executives of the future need to be developed with a deep understanding of, and comfort with, Issue 3. This implies showing deep respect for organizational boundaries and yet behaving as if none existed. There seem to be four preconditions, all of which can be impacted by HR practices, called the *Four Shareds:*

1. *Shared mind-set:* Deeply held views by executives across businesses about the ambition and direction of the enterprise as a whole
2. *Shared logic:* Widely agreed assumptions about the nature of cross-divisional opportunity, the emergence of new business models, the need to create new advantages rather than simply defending existing ones
3. *Shared disciplines:* How to collaborate without losing business unit focus, how to challenge orthodoxies, how to create new knowledge across the enterprise, not just transfer existing knowledge
4. *Shared language:* Agreed frameworks and terminology for implanting new capabilities such as relationship management, solutions, becoming global, customer centric, and so on

Further, executives have traditionally been developed in a world in which strategy formulation and execution were two very different activities. Formulation was the preserve of top management; execution was the responsibility of lower levels. Moreover, strategy was seen as moving a business from point A to point B. In an era in which strategy has often been an exercise in operational improvement, such as achieving six-sigma standards, the A to B analogy works.

The competitive challenge facing today's executives, however, looks radically different. Point B is more likely to be a moving target and may not be completely understood when the journey begins. Nor is the path to the future likely to be linear and sequential. As my colleague C. K. Prahalad and I have argued for some time, strategy becomes a *process of discovery*.

CONCLUSION

For HR to become a strategic partner, the challenge begins by addressing the new reality that strategy is as much about discovery as positioning and that partnerships imply mutual agenda building—not just translating targets into processes. This challenge potentially impacts everything the HR function does to develop individuals and organizations, appraise and evaluate behavior, and reward performance. HR professionals themselves may have to begin by developing new mind-sets for new games.

REFERENCES

March, James G. (1999). *The Pursuit of Organizational Intelligence*. Cambridge, MA: Blackwell.

March, James G., and J. P. Olsen. (1976). *Ambiguity and Choice in Organizations*. Bergen: Universitetsforlaget.

CHAPTER 25

What Really Works?
HR's Role in Building
the 4+2 Organization

WILLIAM JOYCE, NITIN NOHRIA, AND BRUCE ROBERSON

What really works? For firms that are doing well, ensuring continued success is on everyone's mind. For a company in trouble, the challenges are even more critical. Many of the critical issues facing organizations today are human issues. HR must lead in addressing these issues. Leading means building organizations that consistently and predictably outperform their competitors. But what are these organizations like, and how can HR professionals contribute?

Literally thousands of books and papers have been published attempting to answer these questions. And most have failed. We learn, too late, that many of the "excellent" companies are no longer excellent, "best" practices are "worst" practices when used in different contexts, and today's fad may be tomorrow's ticket to oblivion. What really works, consistently and predictably in different situations and industries, remained a mystery—until now.

In 1997, we began a study to determine what would really work to obtain and ensure continued high levels of economic performance. There was some degree of hubris in our search for the answer to the question that has eluded management consultants, researchers, and authors for decades. But there was also the reassurance that we were going to approach the problem differently and in a manner that would be likely to really produce an answer to the critical question, "What *really* works?"

How could we hope to succeed where so many talented researchers and managers had failed? We believed that most of these failures could be attributed to four causes: (1) limited resources, (2) separating theory from

217

practice, (3) relying on preconceived "truth" about success, and (4) under-estimating the difficulty of the problem.

The research that we conducted (summarized in our book *What Really Works: The 4+2 Formula for Sustained Business Success*) was designed to avoid these problems. It is the largest study of its kind ever undertaken. We analyzed over 60,000 pages of information from 200 firms in multiple industries. In all, 10 years of data were collected. The firms that were stud-ied varied in size, and we complemented these broad, extensive analyses with focused, in-depth exploration of issues of special interest. Both re-searchers and practitioners were involved. Fourteen prominent academics from Dartmouth, Harvard, Wharton, and other leading business schools were involved. Twenty-one practitioners implemented the study in coor-dination with the academic researchers. We interviewed journalists, exec-utives, and Wall Street analysts. We let the answers come from the data and then tested specific hypotheses to explore promising possibilities. And fi-nally, we invented new statistical methodology that is appropriate to this level of complexity. It worked. This almost superhuman effort has resulted in the first true answer to the question, "What *really* works?"

WHAT REALLY WORKS?

Each company in our study was assigned to an industry subgroup such as retailing, consumer electronics, or energy (40 in all) and then given a spe-cific performance designation in that subgroup based on its performance relative to peers. These performance differences identified each firm as a winner, climber, tumbler, or loser over the 10-year time frame of the study. Winners started out strong and got even better. Tumblers started strong and then faltered. Climbers and losers both began with weak performance. However, climbers were able to overcome their problems and rise to a high level of performance by the end of the 10-year period. Losers muddled along, never rising above mediocre performance.

What distinguished winners from losers and climbers from tumblers? Surprisingly, the answer could be summarized in a relatively simple formula for success. Only four foundation practices (focused strategy, execution, performance culture, and fast and flat organization) and four secondary practices (securing talent, committed leadership, industry-transforming in-novation, and growth through mergers and partnerships) were found to be necessary to produce extraordinary returns to shareholders. Specifically, success required performing well in all four foundation areas plus at least two of the secondary areas—we called this the *4+2 formula for sustained business success*. Firms that were unable to meet the requirements of the 4+2 formula dramatically increased their chances of failure. In fact, failing to achieve just one of the foundation practices increased the probability of failure by 90 percent.

The differences in performance among these firms were remarkable. Winners produced total returns to shareholders (TRS) of 945 percent over the 10-year period of the study, whereas losers were able to grow TRS only 62 percent. Sales rose 415 percent for winners, but only 83 percent for losers. Similar results held for operating income and asset growth.

HR's Role in Building the 4+2 Organization

Our research indicates that organizations flourish and performance abounds in organizations that embody the winning practices that we identified. These 4+2 organizations do not simply happen, however; they must be built and sustained, and there are many challenges along the way. Many of these practices are fundamentally human in nature, and HR must play a critical role in implementing them. Let's look at each practice and what HR can do:

1. *Strategy: Devise and maintain an engaging, focused strategy.* Winners had strategies that focused the organization on a clear, engaging set of shared goals. Even though they might operate extensively, there was a focus on a clear business model. And perhaps even more importantly, this strategy was shared and meaningful to those within the company. Many companies manage their strategic planning activities so that the "strategic" goals are only the goals of management and not the organization. HR can lead the process of building a shared strategy throughout the organization. Without this, our research indicates that performance will falter.

2. *Execution: Develop and maintain flawless operations and customer focus.* Winners and climbers paid attention to their customers and constantly sought reductions in cost and improvements in productivity.

For climbers, this was often the early focus on regaining a high-performance position in their industry. Execution is at the core of business success and forms a foundation for applying the firm's competence. HR can lead the execution process through initiatives such as Work-Out! (at General Electric) and GoFast! (at General Motors). In these processes, workers at all levels are engaged in a participative process of identifying performance opportunities and taking initiative for solving them.

3. *Culture: Develop and maintain a performance-oriented culture.* Essentially, this means building a culture that is meaningful to all of the employees of the firm. Allowing them to grow and to be part of something bigger than their own contributions, treating them fairly, and rewarding their contributions are essential. When the whole organization is engaged, performance follows. HR has already taken on this critical function, and my colleagues Dave Ulrich and Wayne Brockbank are pioneering HR practices to achieve this result.

4. *Structure: Build and maintain a fast, flexible, flat organization.* Organizations must choose structures that facilitate execution and serve their strategies. The structures that were adopted by winners and climbers radically simplify the way that work is done and reduce bureaucracy. In contrast, losers and tumblers seem to almost consciously erect barriers to success. Excessive rules and procedures, old and outdated processes, and unnecessary organizational units slow us down and frustrate those who are really trying to get things done. Unfortunately, HR has lagged in this area. Organization design still remains almost the exclusive domain of line managers. Yet, how can this be done effectively without the knowledge of the human organization that HR possesses? HR must work proactively to introduce this perspective into all decisions about organization design.

Successful firms had all of the four foundation practices. Winners and climbers also used at least two of the remaining four complementary practices. There was more latitude with respect to the complementary practices. Two practices were necessary for success, but firms were free to choose which two made the most sense for their firms and industry. HR must promote:

1. *Talent: Hold on to talented employees and find more.* Winners grew their own talent. Climbers had to find it, sometimes outside their organizations. Once they had it, they worked hard to keep it. Tumblers and losers lost it or were never able to obtain it from any source. As climbers pulled out of their low performance position, they developed HR systems that helped them to continue to develop and retain talent. HR has already taken up this challenge and innovations are being made every day. This effort must continue.

2. *Leadership: Keep leaders and directors committed.* Our study showed that CEOs, on average, influence 15 percent of the variance in corporate performance. The board chooses CEOs, so it is important to have directors that make good selections. When these directors have a significant financial stake in the company and are committed to its success, they seem to make better choices of CEOs. HR can help by being involved in executive compensation decisions and by being sure that the decisions that are being made support the strategy of the firm. Once again, HR must be involved in strategy at the highest levels of the firm.

3. *Innovation: Make industry-transforming innovations.* Winners tend to anticipate, and even cause, major industry disruptions, whereas losers tend to be much more reactive. As a consequence, they are able to exploit the opportunities that occur in these disruptions. They are able to lead and not follow. These first-mover advantages give them an early head start in relation to competitors, one that is often difficult to catch up with. Being good at innovation means creating the conditions in which innovation is likely to flourish. For HR, this means ensuring a "fit" among strategy, flat organizations, and talent that encourages, rather than discourages, innovation.

4. *Mergers and partnerships: Make growth happen.* Companies that can master mergers and acquisitions are more likely to be winners, as long as these deals are compatible with the focus mandate of the strategy foundation practice. Doing smaller, more frequent deals seems to allow this strategy. Losers, like winners, also engaged in many acquisitions, as if they could buy their way out of trouble. Many of the failed acquisitions and mergers failed because of problems with post-merger acquisition. HR professionals can contribute to success by

ensuring that a broad view of integration is taken. It is not just a matter of the right person in the right job. Success requires integrated strategy, flat organizations, and a new culture—and HR can provide the critical expertise to achieve this success.

FOCUS ON THE FUTURE

The 4+2 formula is essentially a human formula—it makes abundantly clear the relationship between winning in the marketplace and the human side of the enterprise. Over the past few years, HR has become more and more strategic in its orientation. Culture change has become a central aspect of enlightened HR practice. Yet, we have still not come far enough. The 4+2 formula shows that merely being more strategic or adept at cultural change is not enough. Winning means achieving all of the four foundation practices *simultaneously*, and this can be a difficult balancing act.

Thus, just as there is evidence of progress, there is also evidence of more to be done. In particular, we notice a peculiar absence of HR initiatives in organizational design, relative to the other three foundation practices. This seems to be an area of great opportunity for HR professionals because senior line managers need and want help with these problems, and HR, with its understanding of organization, is uniquely positioned to provide it. Organizational design is precisely where strategy and the human side of the enterprise meet. It is a logical place for HR professionals to contribute as they move from traditional roles to that of a true strategic partner.

Beyond this clear need, HR professionals also need to become more adept at managing large, complex transformations, as opposed to transitions. Being good at one or two things such as cultural change or strategy is not enough. The 4+2 formula makes it clear that simultaneously bringing together *all four* of the winning foundation practices at one time is essential. The days of managing separate transitions are over. We must now be good at managing a total, integrated *set* of transitions that culminates in a total transformation embodying the 4+2 mandates.

HR executives are faced with a bewildering array of choices for achieving success, along with the reality of limited resources. The question is how best to apply our resources to achieve our strategic aims. *What Really Works: The 4+2 Formula for Sustained Business Success* answers this critical question. The challenge for HR professionals is how to implement these winning practices—to build the 4+2 organization. Most of the work in this area falls squarely in the domain of HR. We must take up these challenges and lead in building the 4+2 organization.

REFERENCE

Joyce, William, Nitin Nohria, and Bruce Roberson. (2003, May). *What Really Works: The 4+2 Formula for Sustained Business Success*. New York: HarperBusiness.

CHAPTER 26

HUMAN RESOURCES' NEW ROI: RETURN ON INTANGIBLES

DAVE ULRICH AND NORM SMALLWOOD

The search for the Holy Grail of HR continues. We want the indisputable proof that HR departments, practices, and professionals matter. Just as with the Holy Grail, evidence is all around us that we can "see" only if we know how to look. There is evidence of the value of HR all around us. We know that investments in HR practices will increase employee commitment, and increased employee commitment is a lead indicator of customer commitment, which is a lead indicator of profitability (Ricci, Kern, and Quinn, 1998). We know that firms that invest in some HR practices are more likely to have financial returns than firms that do not invest in these HR practices (Pfau and Kay, 2001; Wyatt, 2001). We know that HR practices shape an organization's culture, identity, reputation, and brand (Kotter and Heskett, 1992; Sartain and Finney, 2003). We also know that investments in HR deliver more than they cost through break-even analyses (Fitz-enz and Davison, 2001).

Each of these paths to HR's Grail offers insights. We do not disagree with any of them, but we want to suggest another. A new human resource ROI can be identified, HR's *return on intangibles*. Intangibles represent the hidden value of a firm—shareholder value not determined by financial results. Intangibles are not new to a firm's overall market value, but they are becoming an increasingly important portion of a firm's total market capitalization (Lev, 2001). Intangibles affect firms as diverse as Wal-Mart and Microsoft, each having captured intangible value in their industry. Intangibles can be positive or negative, and without being grounded, they can disappear as easily as hot air in a balloon. Intangibles also affect government and not-for-profit agencies in the form of goodwill and contributions to these agencies' success. Measures of intabgibles for not-for-profits might include alumni donation, contributions, retention of association, and political capital. In this chapter, we suggest six actions HR professionals can take to create sustainable intangible value (Ulrich and Brockbank, 2005).

Become Investor Literate

For HR professionals to deliver intangible value, they must first learn who the investors are and why they are investing in the organization. We suggest an investor literacy test:

- Who are your five major shareholders? How much of you do they each own?
- Why do they own you? What are their investing criteria (e.g., dividend stock, growth stock)?
- What is your price to earnings (P/E) ratio for the past decade, and how does it compare to your industry average and to the firm with the highest P/E ratio in your industry?
- Who are the top analysts who follow your industry? How do they view your company versus your competitor(s)?
- How are you including key investors and analysts in the design and delivery of your HR practices (e.g., succession planning, leadership development, reward and recognition)?
- How well does your board govern itself, not just on the institutional shareholder service criteria but also on the process for good board governance?

We have found few senior HR executives who can answer all of these questions. Yet, these questions form the basis of knowledge that enables HR professionals to link their work to investors.

Understand the Importance of Intangibles

Recent research by accounting professors Baruch Lev and Paul Zarowin at Stern School of Business, New York University, shows that the regression between earnings and shareholder value has traditionally (1960 through 1990) been between 75 percent and 90 percent (Lev, 2001). Therefore, 75 percent to 90 percent of the market value of a firm (stock price × shares outstanding) could be predicted by the financial performance of the firm. However, since 1990, this percentage has dropped to about 50 percent in both up and down markets. Thus, an increasingly large portion of the market value of a firm is not directly tied to present earnings; it is tied to what the financial community calls *intangibles*. Intangibles represent the value of an organization not directly derived from physical assets.

Many leadership actions lead to intangible value. Often, leaders focus on what is easy to measure such as investments in R&D, technology, or brand more than on investments in organization and people. Leadership can also erode intangible value when investors lose confidence in leaders. Ethical violations are among the most visible and immediate ways to destroy value. Organization and people become intangible assets when they give investors confidence in future earnings and when they can be made tangible.

CREATE A FRAMEWORK FOR ORGANIZATION AND PEOPLE PRACTICES THAT INCREASE INTANGIBLE VALUE

We propose a pattern in the techniques that leaders use to increase their organizations' intangibles, beginning with the basic essentials at Level 1 and proceeding upward to more complex concepts. We call this the *architecture for intangibles* (Table 26.1; Ulrich and Smallwood, 2003).

This architecture is progressive. Keeping promises is what builds trust and delivers credibility, so it has to come first. With credibility, trusted leaders can envision a future state that captures imagination and generates enthusiasm, which means they can hope to bring it into existence.

A compelling strategy builds confidence in the future. This vision of the future must turn into today's action, or the hope will prove false. Leaders must invest in aligning core competencies to fold their future into their present. Yet, core competencies are not enough, either. Ultimately, an or-

Table 26.1
Architecture for Intangibles

Level	Area of Focus	Action Potential
1	Keep your promises	Build and defend a reputation among external and internal stakeholders for doing what you say you will do.
2	Compelling strategy	Define growth strategy and manage trade-offs in customer intimacy, product innovation, and geographic expansion to achieve growth.
3	Aligned technical competencies	Provide concrete support for intangibles by building core competencies in R&D, technology, sales and marketing, logistics, manufacturing, and the like.
4	Build value through organization and people	Develop capabilities of shared mindset, talent, collaboration, speed, accountability, learning, leadership, and the like throughout the organization.

ganization must be sustained by enduring capabilities embedded in its people and organization.

This process is sequential. Without trust, visions lack authority; without core competencies, visions will be unrealized; and without capabilities, core competencies and visions lie dormant. In contrast, kept promises allow credible visions to be crafted, credible visions lead to informed investments that ensure core competencies, and core competencies enable capabilities to be realized.

An organization's capabilities are the deliverables from HR work. These capabilities give investors confidence (or lack therefore) in future earnings and increase (or decrease) market capitalization. HR professionals who link their work to capabilities and who then find ways to communicate those capabilities to investors deliver shareholder value. A typical list of capabilities includes: talent, speed of change, shared mind-set, accountability, collaboration, learning, and leadership.

Clearly, these are not the only capabilities that may be required of an organization, they are indicative of the types of capabilities that make intangible tangible. They delight customers, engage employees, establish reputations among investors, and provide long-term, sustainable value. HR professionals should be architects and thought leaders in defining and creating capabilities.

HIGHLIGHT THE IMPORTANCE OF INTANGIBLE VALUE TO TOTAL SHAREHOLDER RETURN

At times, HR professionals have trouble talking about HR issues in financial terms that directly connect to the thinking patterns of business leaders. With a spotlight on shareholder value and intangibles, HR professionals may create charts that highlight the importance of intangibles.

Earnings and Shareholder Value

Go through the past 10 or 15 years of your firm, and plot earnings and stock price (or total market capitalization) by quarter. This chart will show whether market value is above or below the earnings line—whether the firm has a net positive or negative intangible reputation.

Price/Earnings Ratio of Your Firm versus Largest Competitor

Plot for 10 or 15 years your firm's P/E ratio with that of your most successful competitor. This trend line offers an overall report card on how investors perceive your firm's leadership versus its leading competitor. We did this in one firm and found that the firm had a P/E ratio consistently 20 percent below the largest competitor. Investors were less confident in the firm's management team than the competitors, and the gap existed over time. This firm's market value was about $20 billion at the time, and we made the bold argument that the top management team's reputation cost the firm about $4 billion. While the management team did not like the data, they could not run away from it.

CONDUCT AN INTANGIBLES AUDIT THAT ASSESSES WHERE LEADERS SHOULD FOCUS VALUE CREATION

HR professionals can be the architects of intangible audits that define, assess, invest, and improve on each of the four levels of intangibles (Table

26.1). These intangibles give investors confidence in future earnings and increase the market value of similar earnings. Just as financial audits allow leaders to monitor cash flow and leadership 360s assess leadership behaviors, intangible audits allow leaders to turn intangibles into tangibles. In the June 2004 *Harvard Business Review* "Capitalize Your Capabilities," we describe how an intangibles audit assesses what leaders must do to deliver investor value given the organization's history and strategy, measures how well each level of intangibles is being delivered, and leads to an action plan for improving intangibles. An intangibles audit serves leaders at all levels of the organization: It helps the board of directors assess overall firm intangibles, senior leadership define strategy, mid-level managers execute strategy, and front-line leaders make things happen.

ALIGN HR PRACTICES AND INVESTORS

Traditionally, HR practices focus on what is done inside the organization. However, by focusing on the investors, these traditional practices take on a different focus. When investors are included in HR, a new set of questions and actions follows.

Investors and Staffing

What if investors could vote on individuals hired and/or promoted in the firm? In some limited cases, investors do so through the surrogate voice of the board. But what if some of the large institutional investors participated in the interviews for senior officers? What questions would they ask? What leadership and management qualities would they look for? What types of individuals would give them confidence that the management team possessed the capacity to make correct decisions? Alternatively, what if institutional investors reviewed competence models used as candidate screens in the hiring process? Would the institutional investors focus on the same attributes as the traditional hiring manager? Would their interview questions be different?

These questions suggest that HR professionals find ways to engage targeted investors for hiring and promotion decisions. Using investor criteria and participation in the staffing process brings a rigor and discipline often overlooked. In addition, if investors participate in the selection of the management team, they may be more committed to this team's decisions and choices. At first, involving investors in management practices may seem awkward, but over time investor insights may become an increasing part of HR decision-making processes.

Investors and Training and Development

In a seminar for chief learning officers, we posed the following scenario: Assume a representative of the largest single investor in your firm sat through the past five-day leadership program you offered. What would be his or her investment response (buy, hold, sell) at the end of the week? This question forces a new filter on what is taught, how it is taught, and what participants in training leave with at the end of the week. We predict that most investors would be more positive if participants invested their training time focusing on real business issues within their firm rather than case studies of other firms, facing their competitive realities in candid conversation with thoughtful responses laid out, and leaving with clear and specific actions that would be taken as a result of the training experience. The ultimate impact of such training is to show investors that the leadership team knows what needs to be done, understands strategic choices, and is willing to make and implement bold decisions.

Investors and Appraisal and Rewards

Many firms already tie management behaviors to investor-focused rewards. Putting a larger percentage of total compensation into stock-based incentives (grants, options, etc.) links management actions to investors. Many claim that CEO pay relative to average employee pay is excessive. Such arguments are less tenable when the CEO pay is linked to stock. The boundary between managers and investors is removed when managers become investors. In addition, the wider and deeper the investment mind-set is throughout a firm, the more managers act and think like investors.

Investors and Governance and Communication

Investors of publicly traded firms have traditionally been hands-off. They do not participate in teams, help develop processes, or work to set and accomplish strategy. However, when investors realize that the intangibles predict shareholder value as much as the financial performance, they will begin to explore these intangibles. Thus, investors may help diagnose how well the organization makes decisions, allocates responsibilities, and meets commitments. Peter Lynch has suggested that smart investors recognize firms that provide customers what they want (e.g., Toys "R" Us).

As these and other HR practices are applied through an investor filter, investors gain confidence in the organization's ability to deliver future earnings.

SUMMARY

HR professionals have a new ROI—return on intangibles. It is not the Holy Grail, but it offers a different path and approach. Too often, HR professionals are not sure how to make this connection, and their fear of financials keeps them from being fully engaged. It is time to put away these fears and connect HR work to investor value. The emerging focus on intangibles opens the way for HR professionals to more readily link their work to shareholder value.

REFERENCES

Fitz-enz, Jac and Barbara Davison. (2001). *How to Measure Human Resource Management*. New York: McGraw Hill.

Kotter, J., and J. Heskett. (1992). *Corporate Culture and Performance*. New York: Free Press.

Lev, Baruch. (2001). *Intangibles: Management, Measuring, and Reporting*. Washington, DC: Brookings Institute.

Pfau, Bruce, and Ira Kay. (2001). *Human Capital Edge: 21 Practices Your Company Must Implement (or Avoid) to Maximize Shareholder Value*. New York: McGraw Hill.

Rucci, Anthony, Steven Kirn, and Richard Quinn. (1998). "The Employee-Customer-Profit Chain at Sears," *Harvard Business Review,* January/February: 82–99.

Sartain, Libby, and Martha Finney. (2003). *HR From the Heart: Inspiring Stories and Strategies for Building the People Side of Great Business*. New York: AMACOM.

Ulrich, Dave, and Wayne Brockbank. (2005). *The HR Value Proposition*. Boston: Harvard Publishing Company.

Ulrich, Dave, and Norm Smallwood. (2003). *Why The Bottom Line Isn't*. Hoboken, NJ: John Wiley & Sons.

Wyatt, Watson. (2001). "Human Capital Index: Human Capital as a Lead Indicator of Shareholder Value," www.watsonwyatt.com/research/resrender .asp?id=W-488&page=1.

CHAPTER 27

IN PURSUIT OF MARKETPLACE AGILITY: APPLYING PRECEPTS OF SELF-ORGANIZING SYSTEMS TO OPTIMIZE HUMAN RESOURCE SCALABILITY

LEE DYER AND JEFF ERICKSEN

Increasingly, firms find themselves, either by choice or circumstances, operating in turbulent and highly unpredictable environments. For them, competitiveness is a constantly moving target, and many stumble or fall because they lack the organizational capacity to keep pace. In response, some are exploring and even experimenting with new, more agile organizational forms that are, in turn, replete with a host of exciting HR challenges (Dyer and Shafer, 1999, 2003). Here we explore just one of these, the issue of HR scalability—an organization's capacity to get the right numbers of the right types of people to the right places at the right times.

For firms operating in relatively stable and predictable environments with sustained business ventures, HR scalability is a "hygiene" factor. It is a problem if done poorly but usually not a source of competitive advantage because it is relatively easy to do and, thus, for competitors to match. For agile enterprises, however, the situation is quite different. Strategically, they strive to leapfrog and outmaneuver current and potential competitors by generating ever-changing portfolios of products, service offerings, or

Funding for the research underlying this chapter was provided by the Center for Advanced Human Resource Studies, ILR School, Cornell University, Ithaca, New York.

even business models hoping to attain a series of temporary competitive advantages that add up to success over time. The constant pursuit of marketplace agility requires (among many other things) an ability to make rapid and seamless transitions from one configuration of HR to another, and then another and another, ad infinitum. This is HR scalability on steroids. It is, to be sure, a major challenge, and we know of no organization that has it nailed, which means that it has the potential to be a source of competitive advantage for those that figure it out first.

But this agility will take verve and nerve because huge leaps in HR scalability are unlikely to result from tweaking conventional processes. What is needed instead is a totally new way of approaching the problem. One promising possibility lies in the precepts of complexity science and, in particular, the notion of self-organizing systems. We explore this possibility, beginning with a brief description of the emerging paradigm and then offering some preliminary thoughts on how it might be used to significantly enhance both dimensions of HR scalability: internal fluidity and numerical flexibility.

THE ESSENCE OF SELF-ORGANIZING SYSTEMS

Organizations are typically, even instinctively, premised on mechanistic, or linear, assumptions descending from Newtonian physics and what has been learned from over two millennia of futzing with various bureaucratic forms. Self-organizing systems, in contrast, are organic manifestations of causally intricate, or nonlinear, dynamics uncovered by students of chaos and complexity science by observing and modeling the emergence of order in natural settings such as ant hills, termite colonies, and, more recently, social settings such as business organizations (for an elegant and illuminating review of this literature, see Holbrook, 2003). Basically, the latter view characterizes firms as complex adaptive, or living, systems populated not by automatons to be manipulated, but by autonomous free agents who can and will, under the right conditions, purposefully improvise to do whatever it takes to promote system survival. Further, this perspective postulates that in turbulent and unpredictable environments, self-organizing systems are superior to top-down organizations when it comes to allocating resources to their most productive uses. They are more widely attuned to the outside world and, as a consequence, better at uncovering and exploring potential opportunities and threats. And, like open markets, they are relatively unemotional and apolitical about what goes where when and, especially, about abandoning legacy commitments that no longer make sense (Foster and Kaplan, 2001; Surowiecki, 2004).

Emergence is often observed at work in environments characterized by crisis: in hospital emergency rooms overrun with accident victims, among teams from various electric utilities following major ice storms or hurricanes, and in the military when units in the field become cut off from their chains of command (and more recently in the U.S. Army as a routine way of operating in certain combat conditions; see Pascale, Millemann, and Goija, 2000, pp. 135–147). In these instances, the people involved are expected to, and do, take personal responsibility for determining what has to be done, spontaneously collaborating, attaining the information and other resources they need, improvising to deal with unanticipated obstacles, focusing furiously on the task at hand, and disengaging when their contributions are no longer required—precisely what needs to happen in agile enterprises.

What, then, would it take to make these things happen on an ongoing basis?

OPTIMIZING INTERNAL FLUIDITY

Internal fluidity refers to the ease and speed with which the continuous self-allocation of existing talent and effort occurs. In this context, complexity science favors minimalism over specification; self-organizing systems cannot be managed or directed, only nudged and disturbed. Further, the science suggests that this type of emergence happens best when a system is operating "at the edge of chaos." This is perceived as a state, not a point, which is attained when forces favoring initiative, spontaneity, and improvisation are delicately balanced, or paradoxically paired, with forces favoring focus and direction. Accordingly, the task of system designers, and ultimately all system participants, is to devise and revise a bare minimum of guiding principles that on the one hand promote freedom and flexibility and on the other provide enough discipline and order to keep the system from spinning aimlessly out of control (see Figure 27.1).

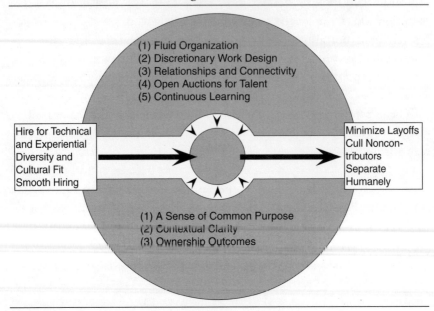

Figure 27.1
Context for Fostering Human Resource Scalability

Guiding Principles to Promote
Freedom and Flexibility

The goal of these principles is to create virtually limitless options for employee initiative:

Principle 1: Fluid organization: Define *organization design* as an action verb, not a noun—as what everyone in the organization does, not a place where they all do it. Minimize hierarchy; create a huge hierarchical vacuum to force leadership to emerge when and where it is needed. Instill a mental model of emergence, of employees constantly creating, pursuing, and abandoning ventures (products, services, business models) by organizing and reorganizing teams and temporary alliances (in evolving networks of firms). Resist all temptations to draw static organization charts.

Principle 2: Discretionary-based work design: Eradicate jobs and, with it, TIMJ ("That isn't my job," Bridges, 1994). Frame work in terms of voluntarily assumed temporary assignments rather than hierarchically defined and protected fiefdoms. Envision ever-expanding zones of discretion where employees are expected not only to determine what needs to be done but also to make sure it gets done. Favor soft- over hard-wired business processes and templates over standard operating procedures. Pare the number of assigned tasks to a bare minimum. (Do not confuse discretionary-based work design with traditional notions of job enrichment or empowerment in which managers expand subordinates' jobs by assigning them a handful of previously forbidden activities or responsibilities.)

Principle 3: Relationships and connectivity: Encourage the formation and reformation of in-groups and fringe groups. Jumble physical and conceptual proximity to ward off coagulation. Design workplaces to be adaptable and expansive (tensile and modular or mobile buildings, movable panels instead of walls, open offices, nomadic workstations, plug-and-play technologies), with a variety of spaces for informal social interactions. Enhance electronic linkages through distributive information systems. Remove barriers to free and open 360-degree communication.

Principle 4: Open auctions for talent: Post *all* needs for talent as ventures and teams emerge, evolve, and die, emphasizing requisite competencies. Minimize barriers to self-nominations (e.g., restrictions on who can apply for what when) and to mobility (e.g., limitations on buyers and bidders regarding the negotiation of terms and conditions). Encourage open discussions of career opportunities and aspirations. Kill clustering (i.e., the tendency for the same people to want to work together time after time).

Principle 5: Serial incompetence: Foster a relentless drive for development (in dynamic environments, standing pat is tantamount to falling behind). Celebrate serial incompetence (i.e., frequent, temporary bouts of less than full proficiency as people explore new horizons; Godin, 2000). Treat errors as learning opportunities (no recriminations). Shuffle team memberships on long-standing ventures. Establish communities of practice (i.e., where those with common interests and competencies can easily congregate, physically or virtually, to help one another get or stay up to speed). (Note that with open auctions for talent, paradoxically, both perennial and serial incompetents find themselves on the outside looking in. In the former case, this situation is fine because it encourages continuous learning. But in the latter, active intervention is required to ensure ample opportunities for on-the-job development.)

Guiding Principles to Promote Discipline and Order

The goal of these principles is to direct and restrain the pandemonium that can result from the unfettered pursuit of boundless opportunity:

Principle 1: A sense of common purpose: Have a vision. Embed it deeply in the organization. Have core values. Embed them deeply, too. Have a small set of common performance metrics. Base rewards, in part, on goals around these metrics. Change the vision, values, and common performance metrics only very reluctantly and thus rarely.

Principle 2: Contextual clarity: Clarify competitive realities. Open the books. Help people understand how and why optimal HR scalability matters. Encourage the systematic use of performance feedback (i.e., examples of when and how HR scalability helped or hindered organizational performance). Celebrate improvements.

Principle 3: Ownership of outcomes: Facilitate coordination through personal accountability. Consummate every major change of assignment with an authentically negotiated commitment among the parties involved as to the expected outcomes (i.e., who will deliver what to whom by when; for a protocol, see Haeckel, 1999, pp. 148–154). Ensure that commitments are kept.

A sense of common purpose creates a common identity among employees, a feeling that each embodies the whole, and a strong natural pull to act in the best interests of the entire enterprise (in contrast, e.g., to the system at Enron where employees were encouraged to follow their personal interests rather than pursue the organization's overall goals). Contextual clarity makes it possible for employees, thus motivated, to make wise choices when deciding where to put their attentions and efforts. And ownership of outcomes avoids situations where everybody is responsible for everything and no one is responsible for anything. It puts accountability the only place it can be in self-organizing systems—squarely on each individual. When commitments are made and kept, trust results. And in social systems, trust is the essential bond that makes self-organizing possible.

Inducing Numerical Flexibility

Over time, agile enterprises must add and release (and will involuntarily lose) people, making numerical flexibility an integral component of HR scalability. Thus, agile enterprises require guiding principles that encourage the inflow and outflow of talent in ways that preferably facilitate, but otherwise only minimally disrupt, internal fluidity. The search is for a middle ground. On the one hand, there is a need for new blood to avoid the groupthink and habituation that tend to imbue inbred social systems. Too much churn, on the other hand, undermines the mutual understanding and trust that grease the skids of internal fluidity. Again, finding and attaining this middle ground is no easy matter. Following is a brief (given space lmitations) rundown of a set of potentially useful guiding principles (refer again to Figure 27.1).

On the intake side, hire for technical and experiential diversity but also for cultural fit (in the sense of accepting only applicants who are comfortable with ambiguity and change) and, wherever possible, smooth hiring (to avoid an influx of nescient members who overwhelm the system). With respect to losses, minimize layoffs (to avoid tearing the social fabric and inducing mistrust), systematically cull noncontributors (to keep the damage done by the inevitable misfits to a minimum and to induce some churn in nongrowth situations), and conduct all involuntary separations with over-the-top fairness and humanity (to avoid traumatizing and evoking risk aversion among those who remain).

Conclusion

Firms whose survival depends on marketplace agility face a Hobson's choice: to prod the extant system for a few additional fragments of flexibility or take a bold step into the abyss of self-organization. While the new way offers considerable promise, there are risks. One, perhaps more illusory than real, is the dreaded fear of losing managerial control. Another, indisputably real, is born of ignorance. While the literature offers glowing accounts of tentative and small-scale experiments along the lines explored here (see, e.g., Lewin and Regine, 2001 and Pedzinger, 1999) and a few intriguing success stories (e.g., Oticon, W. L. Gore, and Capital One), the specter of failure lurks (Enron comes immediately to mind) because of the incredible complexities involved. Our modest efforts to unravel these complexities are tentative and, we assume, ephemeral. We hope, however, that the putative promise of this approach spurs additional experimentation with, and concomitant research into, the essentials of self-organizing systems and, in particular, the lessons they hold for generating quantum leaps in HR scalability.

REFERENCES

Bridges, W. (1994). *Job Shift*. Reading, MA: Addison-Wesley.

Dyer, L., and R. Shafer. (2003). "Dynamic Organizations: Achieving Marketplace and Organizational Agility with People." In R. S. Peterson and E. A. Mannix (Eds.), *Leading and Managing People in the Dynamic Organization*. Mahwah, NJ: Lawrence Erlbaum Associates: 7–40.

Dyer, L., and R. Shafer. (1999). "From Human Resource Strategy to Organizational Effectiveness: Lessons from Research on Agile Organizations." In P. Wright, L. Dyer, J. Boudreau, and G. Milkovich (Eds.), *Research in Personnel and Human Resource Management* (Supplement 4. Strategic Human Resource Management in the 21st Century). Stamford, CT: JAI Press: 145–174.

Foster, R., and S. Kaplan. (2001). *Creative Destruction: Why Companies That Are Built to Last Underperform the Market and How to Successfully Transform Them*. New York: Currency.

Godin, S. (2000). "In the Face of Change the Competent Are Helpless." *Fast Company* January/February: 230–234.

Haeckel, S. H. (1999). *Adaptive Enterprise: Creating and Leading the Sense and Respond Organization*. Boston: Harvard Business School Press.

Holbrook, M. B. (2003). "Adventures in Complexity: An Essay on Dynamic Open Complex Adaptive Systems, Butterfly Effects, Self-Organizing Order, Coevolution, the Ecological Perspective, Fitness Landscapes, Market Spaces, Emergent Beauty at the Edge of Chaos, and All That Jazz." *Academy of Marketing Science Review*, 6 (online version): 181 pages.

Lewin, R., and B. Regine. (2001). *Weaving Complexity and Business: Engaging the Soul at Work*. New York: Texere.

Pascale, R., M. Millemann, and L. Goija. (2000). *Surfing on the Edge of Chaos*. New York: Crown Business.

Pedzinger, T. Jr. (1999). *The New Pioneers*. New York: Simon & Schuster.

Surowiecki, J. (2004). *The Wisdom of Crowds*. New York: Doubleday.

CHAPTER 28

CREATING THE CAPABILITY FOR COLLABORATIVE ENTREPRENEURSHIP: HR'S ROLE IN THE DEVELOPMENT OF A NEW ORGANIZATIONAL FORM

RAYMOND E. MILES, GRANT MILES, AND CHARLES C. SNOW

The United States and other advanced economies, virtually all observers agree, will compete in the twenty-first century increasingly at the downstream end of the value chain. That is, many firms will succeed to the extent that they can use their superior know-how and capabilities to generate a continuous stream of innovative products and services. However, most business organizations in advanced economies today are able to tap into only a small fraction of their knowledge-driven innovation potential (Kaser and Miles, 2002).

The growing recognition of this anomaly is leading perceptive managers to search for a means of unlocking their firms' innovative potential. Those managers realize that the knowledge needed to continuously create new products and services, and to move into new markets, is as likely to be located outside their firms as inside (Chesbrough, 2003). Therefore, the challenge managers face is to create an approach that permits a firm to extend its organizational reach—to develop a community of like-minded firms that can share their knowledge for the purpose of creating economic wealth. We call this emergent organizational form the *collaborative multifirm network* (Miles, Miles, and Snow, 2005), and it will take shape as forward-thinking managers, with the support of HR professionals, forge the unique capabilities required to operate it.

THE ROLE OF HR IN THE DEVELOPMENT OF NEW ORGANIZATIONAL FORMS

Historically, successful new organizational forms have helped turn under-utilized resources into economic wealth. At the same time, each new form has generated its own HR requirements that HR professionals must antic-ipate and help to meet. For example, Andrew Carnegie, Henry Ford, and other management pioneers created a new organizational form at the turn of the twentieth century that brought new power sources, abundant raw materials, and an army of underskilled workers into alignment with a growing market for efficiently produced, standardized products. They de-signed the functional organization that assigned workers to carefully coor-dinated, specialized, repetitive tasks that could be quickly mastered. This new structure not only demanded large investments in special-purpose equipment but also created the need for personnel systems that could attract, train, and maintain a stable workforce. It became the task of a new group of personnel specialists to design approaches to recruiting, training, and su-pervision that would provide this stability, which in turn created the po-tential for scale economies that allow a firm's products to be priced to stimulate consumer demand.

Similarly, toward the middle of the twentieth century, some managers began looking for new arenas in which they could apply their firms' accu-mulated design, production, and marketing know-how. Firms such as General Motors, Sears, Johnson & Johnson, General Electric, and Hewlett-Packard created and honed the new multidivisional form of organization that could focus resources and know-how on not one but a series of related markets. New managerial skills in delegation and participative decision making were essential to the operation of this new organizational form, and HR specialists created new approaches to management training and development, along with information and reward systems, that could sus-tain decentralized operations.

During the past two decades, managers across many industries have learned how to rapidly assemble and efficiently link specialized firms along a value chain. Called a multifirm network (Miles and Snow, 1986), this or-ganizational form can be both efficient and responsive. As before, the ef-fective management of network organizations demanded new skills, in this case, team building and interfirm project management. Again, HR played a crucial role in encouraging and designing new ways to create self-managing coordination systems within and across firms.

A NEW ORGANIZATIONAL FORM TO SUPPORT A STRATEGY OF CONTINUOUS INNOVATION

To meet today's increasing expectation of continuous innovation, a new type of network organization will emerge around groups of independent firms, operating in diverse but complementary markets, and collaboratively sharing a common, ever-expanding knowledge base. The opportunity for ideas to flow across firms and markets will generate a continuous flow of innovative products and services, many if not most of which would never have found life within existing business models. Indeed, most would have failed to reach the surface in the traditional hierarchically managed firm. Moreover, even in those firms that did encourage innovation, many ideas would have perished because they had no clear relevance to the firms' existing markets.

The new multifirm collaborative network form that we envision will be assembled over time with a core group of organizations adding new firms based on common values and on complementary technologies and market reach. Within the network, know-how and ongoing research will be electronically assembled and accessible only to network member firms. It will be exchanged and developed through self-managed projects among two or more network firms. These voluntary interfirm innovation efforts will differ from current "strategic alliances" in two important ways. First, they will be based on collaborative capabilities rather than negotiated cooperative agreements such as a joint venture. Second, they will be initiated, managed, and completed using broad protocols specifically developed to build trust and facilitate self-governance among member firms. Such protocols will be used in place of the policies and rules normally created to integrate different hierarchically organized firms.

As opposed to cooperative agreements, which try to spell out in advance the contributions and returns of the parties involved, collaborative approaches are based on trust supported by a common commitment to the equitable sharing of returns. This is a crucial distinction because much of the sharing that drives innovation deals with knowledge that is tacit and fragmented rather than explicit and integrated. A process whose effectiveness hinges on the full sharing of knowledge, and in which one thought often triggers another, cannot be hierarchically guided by traditional types of reward systems.

Today, true collaborative sharing tends to occur primarily in nonbusiness settings and within knowledge-based communities. For example, knowledge is freely shared in scientific and academic communities because it is supported by the commonly held value of scholarly recognition—the recipient of knowledge is obligated to recognize all of the contributions to that knowledge. A similar commitment is a crucial ingredient in "open innovation" communities such as that supporting the Linux operating system. Within firms, members with common interests and problems often voluntarily share their know-how outside formal communications channels.

In a business setting, knowledge sharing demands trust that the fruits of innovation will be equitably shared among the collaborating firms. We are just beginning to find examples of interfirm collaboration, including "industrial symbiosis" in Kalundborg, Denmark; partnering in the U.S. civil construction industry; and the worldwide "business federation" model used by Acer, a large Taiwan-based information technology firm (Miles, Miles, and Snow, 2005). With shared knowledge driving unforeseen product innovations toward unanticipated markets, returns can seldom be calculated in advance. Thus, the creation of mechanisms that build and maintain trust, along with the development of collaborative skills and abilities both within and across member firms, is a key HR requirement of the new network form. An even more demanding HR challenge is that of designing reward systems that encourage and sustain collaboration rather than thwart its development, as with most current reward practices.

Sophisticated HR departments are already skilled at developing team self-management capability. Those skills can be expanded to include approaches to trust-building and trust-signaling across interfirm teams. Our research shows that groups can develop and apply protocols that promote trustworthiness and guide the establishment of knowledge-sharing relationships (Miles, Snow, and Miles, 2000). However, to sustain trust, teams and firms must demonstrate their full commitment to the equitable sharing of returns, a commitment that appears to be at odds with the internal reward systems found in most firms.

Knowledge sharing within self-directed and innovation-focused work teams is exciting and intrinsically satisfying. However, most reward system designs focus attention not on the creation of useful new products and services but rather on capturing and allocating the returns from those innovations. Reward systems that promote the precalculation of returns direct people's attention toward mechanisms that protect against opportunistic behavior rather than encourage trust-building relationships. Interfirm alliances traditionally have had a high failure rate largely because of efforts, real or expected, by one firm or the other to capture a disproportionate share of the returns.

Indeed, it seems likely that the key features of reward systems that encourage trust and knowledge sharing will turn out to be almost exactly the opposite of those that have become popular in recent decades. That is, knowledge sharing occurs most readily when participants enjoy superior, ensured salaries and benefits and when their innovation activities are not tied directly and immediately to monetary incentives. Reward systems that provide for current well-being and security and ensure the search for equitable returns are well within our design capability. Such reward systems minimize the need for precalculation, encourage collaborative sharing, and focus attention on innovation-driven wealth creation.

CONCLUSION

A new organizational form is beginning to emerge—one that will allow a growing network of firms to share knowledge in collaborative efforts that generate a steady stream of both planned and unanticipated products and create wealth across myriad complementary markets. HR professionals, as in previous eras, will help design this new multifirm network structure and its supporting management system.

Within individual firms, HR's task will focus on reward system design and team building to create and enhance collaborative skills. Across the network as a whole, managers and HR professionals will have a unique role in recruiting and orienting new firms—assisting them in mastering the values and protocols that guide interfirm collaborative efforts. And, as has been true of previous organizational forms, HR professionals will help make the investment decisions that create the human competencies, such as trust-building and collaborative attitudes and skills, which the new form will require.

REFERENCES

Chesbrough, Henry. (2003). *Open Innovation: The New Imperative for Creating and Profiting from Technology* (Boston, MA: Harvard Business School Press).

Kaser, Philipp A. W., and Raymond E. Miles. (2002). "Understanding Knowledge Activists' Successes and Failures." *Long-Range Planning,* 35: 9–28.

Miles, Raymond E., Grant Miles, and Charles C. Snow. (2005). *Collaborative Entrepreneurship: How Groups of Networked Firms Use Continuous Innovation to Create Economic Wealth* (Stanford, CA: Stanford University Press).

Miles, Raymond E., Charles C. Snow, and Grant Miles. (2000). TheFuture.org. *Long-Range Planning,* 33: 300–321.

Miles, Raymond E., and Charles C. Snow. (1986). "Network Organizations: New Concepts for New Forms." *California Management Review,* 28: 62–73.

CHAPTER 29

PARTNER OR GUARDIAN? HR'S CHALLENGE IN BALANCING VALUE AND VALUES

PATRICK M. WRIGHT AND SCOTT A. SNELL

Two roads diverged in a wood, and I—I took the one less traveled by. And that has made all the difference.
—Robert Frost

Is HR at a crossroad? A number of signs seem to be pointing that way. Increasingly, HR executives are faced with a critical decision: Will they continue on their journey to be business leaders, with full sway and equal influence in organizational decision making, or will they take the shortcut by sacrificing professional ethics and values for a "seat at the table"? This challenge is exemplified by the story of Delta Air Lines.

Since its founding, Delta Air Lines has been distinct in its ability to deliver outstanding service to its customers and in its family atmosphere, which attracted and retained the most talented people in the industry. However, in the early 1980s, deregulation enabled low-cost entrants to establish a foothold in Delta's major markets. In the early 1990s, the globalization of the industry prodded Delta to expand by purchasing Pan Am's European routes. Finally, the changing information technologies were resulting in price competition within the industry. Faced with these challenges, Delta embarked on a strategic change called *Leadership 7.5* (Brannigan and Lisser, 1996).

Leadership 7.5 was a massive effort to reduce Delta's costs from 10 cents per available seat mile to match Southwest's 7.5 cents. It entailed massive workforce transformation, with highly skilled, committed, and experienced workers being shed and replaced by a lower paid contingent workforce lacking in skills, commitment, and experience. The effort resulted in Delta's return to profitability, however, with an organization that was only a shadow of its former self (Brannigan and White, 1997).

Where has this transformation led? Today Delta's revenue growth lags that of the rest of the industry. Their core business customer fled for Continental years ago. The unions have been knocking on Delta's doors, and employees have been ready to answer it. And, as of April 2004, talent is fleeing, with three of five top executives and at least six vice-presidents having left Delta or announced departure plans in the previous six months (Grantham, 2003).

What happened at Delta? Most of us would recognize—perhaps in retrospect—the detrimental effects of these HR decisions at Delta. But would we have a deep understanding of the firm's economic model to articulate the negative outcomes in a way that is compelling to the executive leadership? Perhaps more importantly, would we have the courage to be the voice of dissent that has sway in the strategic decision? In many ways, this story serves as a real-life allegory that illustrates the past mistakes of one organization while also laying out the three future challenges faced by the field of HR.

The first challenge refers to *value creation* and describes the almost "perfect storm" of influences that have called into question the viability of every firm's preexisting business model. Creating value in a global economy requires that HR executives clearly understand the confluence of economic, social, and technological forces that drives industry competition. Do we? The second challenge, *value delivery,* deals with the pressing need for HR functions to demonstrate its tangible impact by aligning with and driving the issues critical to the business. Finally, *living values* recalls us as a profession to rediscover that we are not just order takers or implementers, but the guardians of our organizations. We guard and preserve its strategic capability, we guard its people, and we guard its values. When we fail to guard these things, our firms fail—financially, strategically, legally, and morally.

In this chapter, we examine these challenges and provide a model for understanding how the competing demands placed on HR create both organizational and professional conflict. To do so, we first address the current trends in firms' competitive environments and how these trends are revolutionizing the demands placed on HR professionals and organizations. We then discuss the need for HR functions to balance their needs to execute for the business while investing in their own functional capability. We propose the *SELF* (strategic, ethical, legal, and financial) model as a framework for identifying some of the main demands placed on HR as well as how these demands often conflict with one another, resulting in tremendous challenges for HR professionals. Finally, we discuss the implications of these competing demands for the future of the profession.

THE VALUE CREATION CHALLENGE

Over the past decade, numerous researchers have attempted to reveal the future trends impacting organizations. In 1995, Ulrich and Eichinger identified globalization and technological change as two of the major environmental developments that would influence organizations during the late 1990s. Caimano, Canavan, and Hill (1998) identified the same basic issues in their canvassing of the trends that would impact organizations and HR. Based on interviews and surveys of over 150 HR thought leaders worldwide, Wright, Dyer, and Takla (1998) identified globalization, increased competition, and technological change as the three major trends that would impact organizations.

It is interesting that, regardless of methodology, researchers, or scope, certain trends stand out. First, globalization seems to top the list of concerns for just about every organization today. In some cases, the concern arises as firms increasingly seek to maximize their global presence. The increase in global presence stems in part from the desire to better distribute and sell their products, but increasingly also derives from aspiring to capitalize on labor cost advantages. In other cases, firms in domestic markets increasingly face competition from global competitors.

Second, no one argues with the fact that technological change has driven, and continues to drive, competition. Again, in some cases, firms such as Intel or Microsoft seek to drive the changing technologies, forcing others to play catch up. In other cases, firms such as Amazon or Wal-Mart seek to leverage the new technologies being developed in order to change the nature of the competitive environment.

While other trends may be unique to particular industries or product markets, these trends universally influence the competitive landscape: globalization, increased competition, and technological change. The synergistic result of these forces is to commoditize the marketplace for products and services. Consider that Toys "R" Us faces Wal-Mart; IBM faces Dell; and Delta Air Lines faces Southwest, JetBlue, and ATA. Over the past few years, the low-price competitors have tended to dominate every industry, making price an important, if not the most significant, criterion in the buying choice. How can firms create value for customers, shareholders, and employees in a world of commoditization?

The commoditization process drives firms to reduce their cost base, having a number of implications for HR. First, because labor costs usually comprise a firm's largest single controllable cost, this area becomes the focus of a number of strategies and tactics. Firms seek to limit the increase in hourly wages through small wage increases and by requiring employees to increase their contributions to health care premiums. Firms also seek to move more and more work offshore to capitalize on the lower labor costs. Finally, the labor cost pressure leads firms to increasingly manage costs by more quickly downsizing in response to decreased product demands. Second, this has heightened the role and accountability of the HR function for actually delivering value.

Here's the challenge: Without a real understanding of the firm's business drivers, HR executives can become complicit in the cost-cutting game. This game has three detrimental effects of the sustainability of a firm's business model. First, it cuts the core talent that leads to value creation. Second, it trades short-term costs for long-term (total) costs. Third, it diminishes the potential for real innovation. While forces toward commoditization are driving the economics of business, the requirements for innovation and product development are changing the pace and structure of industries.

Delta Air Lines exemplifies the risk in this cost reduction emphasis. While cost pressures require cost control, cutting too deeply in costs at some point cuts too deeply into a firm's strategic capability. Such decision making simultaneously increases a firm's short-term survival while decreasing its long-term viability.

THE VALUE DELIVERY CHALLENGE

With a heightened sensitivity to the very real tangible costs of supporting an HR function compared to the less tangible benefits accrued, HR organizations will continue to face the challenge of delivering value.

This value must be demonstrated both quantitatively and qualitatively. The recent focus on developing a set of comprehensive HR metrics exemplifies the importance that HR functions place on providing quantitative data to demonstrate the value of HR. However, regardless of how extensive these metrics become and how useful they are for internal HR assessment and decision making, they still seem to fall short of fully convincing those outside HR of its value. Rather, as firms seek to attract, motivate, and retain talent and to build organizational capability for leadership, the qualitative value that HR delivers seems to become more readily apparent.

In addition, the perceived value emanating from HR clearly increases with HR's improvement in the execution of HR activities. Such execution currently focuses on two aspects: doing the right things and doing things right. Doing the right things requires focusing time and energy on the most important value-creating or value-impacting dimensions of HR. Doing things right entails providing near-perfect execution in all those activities.

Finally, meeting the value delivery challenge requires managing the HR function as a business, with as much attention paid to building the core competence of the function as to the actual delivery of products and services to customers. But firms have to be careful not to outsource the competence to cut costs. Particularly over the past few years, as the economy has suffered, HR functions have obsessed about doing whatever is asked by the line, whenever it is asked, while virtually ignoring the activities that build HR capability. We often hear about HR being so focused on fighting fires that they cannot engage in strategizing, but this obsession is worse. In essence, our functions have become like marathon runners that keep running and running but never stop to eat. It can last for only so long, and sooner or later, the runner, or the function, collapses.

The story of Delta Air Lines again demonstrates the value delivery challenge. Delivering value must focus on the long-term, as opposed to short-term, value. The HR function certainly delivered short-term value through replacing their *capability* workforce with a *commodity* workforce.

However, this action failed to deliver long-term value as can be seen by their situation today.

THE LIVING VALUES CHALLENGE

The final and most pressing challenge is for HR to rise up to truly live, model, and promote the values that have historically characterized our profession but that are also necessary for long-term organizational success. To do so will continue to increase in difficulty as organizations become more and more cost focused and demand more and more accountability from HR.

The problem is described by what we heard at a meeting of some senior VPs of HR. Before the session began, these executives, who all knew one another, began what we might describe as a therapy session or, better yet, a catharsis. We heard one executive bemoaning his organization's downsizing effort because, in spite of all the data they had showing that the best predictor of same store sales was the average tenure of the sales associates, those were the people being targeted by top managers' layoffs. We heard an executive complaining about how top managers were requiring an extra $500 contribution for hourly employee health care coverage, while they weren't even willing to entertain the notion that they should pay anything for their top-hat coverage. We heard an executive, whose company met none of its goals and whose average bonus payout was 10 percent of target, complain of the compensation committee's obstinate insistence that the CEO receive 100 percent of his target bonus because, "It's a retention issue." In each case, what did the executive do? What would you do?

As we have listened to these and a number of other stories, we have found that they often describe the conflict that occurs when competing values conflict with one another. What are these values? We suggest that, while not exhaustive, the most predominant are strategic, ethical, legal, and financial.

Strategic value is concerned with building an organization that is capable of delivering customer outcomes. The priorities of this value system consist of processes, technologies, culture, and the skills and commitment of the workforce. Ethical values relate to doing what is morally right. Such values place priority on social responsibility, organizational values, and individual integrity. Legal values focus on not violating the law. Priority is given to compliance with existing legal and regulatory systems and the avoidance of lawsuits and legal proceedings. Finally, financial values aim at increasing shareholder wealth. Such values give priority to cost control, margin management, and return on investment.

All of these values share legitimacy, but problems often arise because they really or seemingly become mutually exclusive with regard to particular decisions. For instance, consider the recent travails of Boeing. According to recent *BusinessWeek* articles (Holmes, 2004; Holmes and France, 2004), years ago internal HR professionals at Boeing discovered some pay disparities between the male and female engineers. Now, consider what your options might be as an HR executive. First, you could come forward and admit the disparities and consequently raise the female pay to achieve equity. However, to do so would come at considerable *financial* cost and would open the firm up to *legal* liability for past inequities (with additional financial costs). Second, you could try to keep it secret while you attempted to raise the pay to equitable levels over time. This might reduce the *financial* cost but leave you open to *legal* liability (if discovered), and it would raise *ethical* questions (Is it right to knowingly let female workers be underpaid for the time frame during which you will work to achieve equity?). The point is not to single out Boeing (indeed, many companies face similar challenges) or to suggest any wrongdoing on Boeing's part, but rather to illustrate how the competing values create tensions and challenges for HR professionals. As we manage these tensions, we must make choices, and each choice becomes the first step down a path. Do we know where that path leads organizationally, professionally, or personally?

In contrast, consider Eaton Corporation, a highly values-driven company. A former student related a story of how when selling a plant, Eaton used part of the sale price to fully fund the pensions of the employees of the plant, even though it was at financial cost to the company and there was no legal obligation to do so. When we questioned Eaton's senior VP of HR, Sue Cook, about it, she looked somewhat confused—not because she didn't remember it, but because she didn't know to which of the many instances we referred. "We do that quite frequently. We do it because it's the right thing to do," she said. When asked what their shareholders thought of it, the answer was, "That's why they buy Eaton stock. They know the way we run the company will pay off in the long term."

CONCLUSION

The HR profession has reached a critical juncture in its history. We are being asked to be business partners and business driven, yet we frequently face situations where our historic values conflict with short-term decisions made in the business. Bill George, retired CEO of Medtronic, argues that deviating from values can be costly. To illustrate, he relates this story:

> Recently I used the Enron-Arthur Andersen debacle to make this point with a class of MBA students. I described Arthur Andersen as a tragedy, saying, "You can spend fifty years in establishing your reputation, and lose it in a day." A Dutch student challenged my characterization: "No, Bill, Andersen didn't lose it all in a day. They sold their soul to their clients over the last five to ten years by compromising their values more and more, just to make money. What looks to you like a giant step in destroying documents was to them just another step in sacrificing values for greed." He was right. What appears to be a compromise of values in a single instance is usually the final act in a series of compromises. (George, 2003, p. 75)

This story, as well as the stories of Delta and Boeing, challenges the HR profession. We seek to be business partners, but if we take the shortcut by sacrificing our values and integrity for a seat "at the table," we may end up playing a significant role in the demise of our organizations. Instead, HR leaders require the vision and courage to integrate the different value systems in an organization for its long-term viability.

This is not blue-sky idealism. Although competitive realities require that HR organizations be business oriented, HR leaders need to distinguish between decisions that are driven *by the business* and decisions driven *for the business*. A focus on short-term financial returns for fickle investors may be made at the long-term cost of organizational viability. As the Delta story shows, HR leaders need to be the guardians of our firms' strategic capability. As the Boeing story shows, HR leaders need to be the guardians of our firms' ethical and moral integrity. As we increasingly are asked to play a significant role in these types of decisions, let us hope that no one ever need ask, *"Quis custodiet ipsos custodies?"* ("Who must guard the guardians?" from *Satires of Juvenal*).

REFERENCES

Brannigan, M., and E. Lisser. (1996). "Ground Control: Cost Cutting at Delta Raises Stock Price but Lowers the Service." *Wall Street Journal,* June 20, 1996.

Brannigan, M., and J. White. (1997). "'So Be It:' Why Delta Airlines Decided It Was Time for CEO to Take Off." *Wall Street Journal,* May 30, 1997, A1.

Caimano, V., P. Canavan, and L. Hill. (1998). *1988 State-of-the-Art & Practice (SOTA/P) Report.* New York: HRPS.

George, B. (2003). *Authentic Leadership: Rediscovering the Secrets to Creating Lasting Value.* San Francisco, CA: Jossey Bass.

Grantham, R. (2003, April 16). "Delta's Bonuses Fail to Stop Execs' Flight." *Atlanta Journal-Constitution,* p. 1A.

Holmes, S. (2004). "A New Black Eye for Boeing? Internal Documents Suggest Years of Serious Compensation Gaps for Women." *BusinessWeek,* April 26, 2004, p. 90.

Holmes, S, and M. France. (2004). "Coverup at Boeing?" *BusinessWeek,* June 28, 2004, 84–90.

Ulrich, D., and R. Eichinger. (1995). *1995 State-of-the-Art & Practice (SOTA/P) Report.* New York: HRPS.

Wright, P., L. Dyer, and M. Takla. (1998). *1998 State-of-the-Art & Practice (SOTA/P) Report.* New York: HRPS.

SECTION VI

SEE HR AS A DECISION SCIENCE AND BRING DISCIPLINE TO IT

We have all recognized the snickers when we present our HR recommendations and our beneficiaries think, "HR is just common sense." Nonsense. As the theory and research on HR escalates, common sense answers are no longer acceptable. Platitudes and maxims such as, "We pay for performance," "When people participate they feel ownership," or "We hire only the best," can and should be replaced by rigorous theory and research. Criteria for specifying performance can be defined in explicit ways and rewards, measured by both behaviors and outcomes, and configured in a range of options from compensation to nonfinancial remuneration. Participation can occur through teams, technology, and management style, and the results of participation may be satisfaction, loyalty, or commitment. Hiring the best requires a clear definition of *best,* and that definition may vary by strategy, organization capability, and existing talent. Hiring may now include an array of options from full-time employment to employment contracts. The HR world has become more complex.

In this complexity, the authors in this section each propose that HR should develop an analytical rigor and become a decision science. These authors are well suited to defining the science of HR and to suggesting what this science would entail. Each of these authors has written numerous books and articles showing the empirical precision of HR and its impact on business results. They now turn their attention to how HR can use measurement analytics to define, make, and accomplish decisions with exactness and confidence.

Fitz-enz in Chapter 30 suggests a science of HR in retailing. He shows that scientific analysis in retailing can improve selection decisions and ensure that firms have front-line sales personnel who deliver higher sales per hour. Experience, preferences, and potential can be specified and tested to ensure a science in HR.

Flamholtz has defined the field of human resource accounting (HRA). He shows in Chapter 31 how the rigor of HRA is the backbone for human capital management. With HRA, the value of an individual can be ascertained and improved. He also shows future areas for applying HRA to performance management and corporate culture.

Huselid and Becker in Chapter 32 draw on the creative work going on in baseball where the book *Moneyball* captured how the Oakland A's manager Billy Bean changed the nature of baseball by bringing science to the game. They suggest a similar analytic literacy in HR. They suggest that this rigor will require understanding of business logic, causal relationships, intermediate outcomes, and new modes of analysis.

Lewin has written for decades about the impact of HR. In Chapter 33, he presents a dual theory of HR where core employees are treated differently from periphery employees. Core employees should be addressed with high-involvement HR practices that are tailored to employees and engage their attitudes and shape their behaviors. Peripheral employees may be better dealt with through low-involvement HR practices that are more standardized, routine, and delivered more efficiently. His data show that alignment of the HR practice with employee group leads to business results.

John Boudreau and Peter Ramstad in Chapter 34 advance the concept of *sustainability*. Rather than organizational orientation to short-term interests, sustainability is defined as promoting development of the enterprise to meet the needs of the present without compromising the ability of future generations to meet their own needs. What is needed, they suggest, is a well-developed decision science for human capital talent or "talentship," again, given the need for sustainability.

Collectively, these chapters suggest a new discipline for the HR profession. Common sense can be supplemented with rigorous analysis. The science of HR should never replace the art of HR, and professional instinct will always have a significant place in the profession; but without the scientific grounding, HR will not reach its full potential. The impact of HR as a decision science is huge. It will affect those coming into the profession. Certification is not just a title on a business card, but an assurance that the new HR practitioner has mastered the decision rules. It will affect those recommending HR practices. Rather than making recommendations based on personal preference, recommendations can be made with data and evidence of the proven impact. The impact of HR as a decision science will also change what HR professionals take to the strategy table, and it will change expectations of senior HR leaders on presentations made by staff specialists. With the decision science, variance and risk in HR investments should be reduced.

CHAPTER 30

SCIENCE EXPLODES HUMAN CAPITAL MYTHOLOGY

JAC FITZ-ENZ

Every industry has its folklore—its set of legends, myths, and experiences that shapes enduring beliefs, values, and attitudes—for better or worse. These belief systems cover all aspects of an enterprise but none more so than the management of its human capital. From time to time, someone with great imagination, ceaseless curiosity, undaunted courage, and a profound desire to push the system forward points out a fallacy within the belief system. Often, he or she is confronted with resistance from CEO to first-line supervisor. Apathy, skepticism, and even derision can be the rewards of venturing into this arena. Nevertheless, eventually new ideas prove out, the word circulates, and slowly a myth disappears. The bad news is that systems and processes change, but many of the conscious and subconscious human biases don't.

HOME FIELD OF HUMAN CAPITAL MYTHOLOGY

Service businesses are profoundly dependent on the behavior of employees. Yet, nowhere is there a more obsolescent belief system than in the retailing segment of the service industry. *Retailing* covers any business wherein a high percentage of total personnel are interfacing directly with customers and prospects, including department, grocery, drug, convenience, and specialty stores such as home improvement or office products as well as restaurants, banks, hotels, and car rental agencies.

In these businesses, it is accepted theory that turnover runs from, for example, 40 percent for bank tellers to 1,000 percent for convenience store help. Turnover in many department and specialty stores runs over 70 percent with some suffering triple digit annual losses of personnel.

Mythology in Action

Most retailers view people as an expense and see advertising and merchandising as the twin drivers of sales. To an extent, this view can be true. Yet, consider retail stores today. What two things do they all have in common?

1. The word *Sale!* Everyday is sale day. Customers now act like vultures. They have learned to circle above the stores waiting for ads on the major items they want and then descend to shop for those items only on sales days.
2. High turnover of front-line personnel—lowly paid, untrained, marginally motivated sales associates. When you can find a sales clerk, often he or she has very limited knowledge of the store or the relative quality of the stock. In the end, a significant portion of advertising cost is wasted at the point of sale.

Most clerks, or sales associates as they are often titled, would like to be helpful. Helping someone does fulfill basic human ego and social needs. The problem resides in the management practice of selling the staff by cheerleading rather than through better selection, training, and pay for performance systems. A recent example from a major department store confirms management's disregard for people. One of the sections of this store had reached or exceeded its sales target for seven straight months and was earning a quarterly bonus. In fact, it outsold the same section in every other store in the chain. As a reward, the bonus was cut in half.

Belief behind the Practice

Despite what managers and supervisors say, their actions confirm their belief that front-line people are interchangeable. If they lose one today, they know they can find what they perceive to be another equally unmotivated one tomorrow. This has become a self-perpetuating practice.

Forty years ago, Douglas McGregor at MIT published what he called *Theories X and Y*. Theory X claimed that people are lazy, don't really want to contribute, and are motivated only by a paycheck. Theory Y was the opposite view: People wanted to add value, and money was only part of the attraction.

One of our favorite true Theory X stories comes from a retail executive who gave his managerial staff a "practical" lesson in employee relations, paraphrased here:

> When it comes to a decision about employees, there are two alternatives. One is to claim that people are our greatest asset and are dedicated to personal service. The other is to make them informed and motivated associates. The first is easy. It requires only a little advertising. The second is quite expensive, demanding an investment in better methods of selecting, supporting, and training employees. Are there any questions?

Although few will admit it, their practices confirm that they believe in path number one.

HR's Concern

This endemic staffing problem is of particular interest to HR professionals on two levels. Tactically, it is HR that designs staffing processes. Matters of sourcing and selection are largely the province of HR. Obviously, hiring the best starts with selecting the best candidates from the applicant pool. HR is also concerned with talent retention. Research shows that people chosen using decision science methods perform better and stay much longer than traditional process hires.

The strategic issue is culture management. HR is the corporate culture manager. A substantial part of culture management is hiring people who "fit." Again, decision science is helping to pick out not only talent but also candidates who have a high probability of long-term success within the culture.

Signs of Progress

Consistently, research has shown by case examples that people are intrinsically motivated to make a positive contribution at work. Achievement is a fundamental human desire. Deming proved that management practices and flawed processes inhibit human effort. Although executives and managers at all levels clearly want to create competitive advantage, their subconscious Theory X beliefs sometimes contaminate their efforts. Enter science.

Decision science tools have advanced to the point that retailers now have an opportunity to select and retain a higher percentage of top talent. Most managers are well-educated people who tend to believe in scientific methods. The stumbling block is cost. Good science costs money. Good science applied to a high-volume situation such as selection can be a significant investment. Executives often balk at human capital investments that cost a fraction of what they spend on information technology.

The reason behind this reluctance seems to be visibility. Executives can see computers, reports, evidence of databases, and other physical paraphernalia indigenous to information technology. What they can't see and touch is the intelligence, attitudes, and motivation of their people—those factors that make the difference in performance. Linking that myopia to a negative mythology kills many a human capital project. Fortunately, that is changing.

RECENT APPLICATIONS

There are now long-running cases of companies that have applied scientific analysis to HR programs. The more impressive examples are found in hiring, specifically, within the selection process. The latest methods go well beyond a set of questions designed to tease out suitable candidates from a mass of applications. In most cases, they can foretell the likelihood of success in different roles. Additionally, there is substantial evidence of their ability to predict incremental gains in time to standard performance as well as differentials in performance.

A typical example is that an assessment-based hire reaches standard sales per hour 60 percent faster and sells at least 20 percent more than a hire coming through traditional methods. Considering that at least 75 percent of the sales positions turn over annually, within one year the former traditionally hired employees could be replaced by scientifically hired sales associates. If $120 per hour is the standard sales associates target and if you employed 100 sales associates, you would replace at least 75 per year, about one-third for substandard performance. It takes 180 days for the average associate to reach the target level. Some never do and are replaced. Depending on certain assumptions, if you used scientific selection methods, your sales would increase by more than 100 percent in the first 180 days and continue to run about 50 more the rest of the year.

Mediocre performance and high turnover have always plagued retail sales positions. In recent years, a number of *Fortune* 500 retailers such as Nordstrom, Neiman Marcus, Radio Shack, LensCrafters, Target, CVS Pharmacies, Best Buy, Circuit City, Border Books, Lowe's, and Blockbuster have applied assessment tools to selection of front-line sales personnel. They consistently report significant savings in interview time, increases in sales per hour, and reductions in shrinkage, accidents, and turnover.

The executives in these pace-setting firms now recognize that the person at the point of sale is more important than the advertisement that attracted the shopper. The ad might bring in a lady who has been waiting for a shoe sale. The average salesperson probably will sell the shoes and let it go at that. The scientifically selected salesperson more likely will also sell a second pair of shoes in a different color, a matching purse, or maybe two, and possibly complementary hosiery or other accessories such as a scarf. The salesperson might even mention a sale on dresses in another department that would go well with the style of shoes the shopper has chosen. Recently, a friend went to buy a suit on sale at one of the stores mentioned earlier. Through the skill of the salesperson, my friend walked out with three suits, a sport coat, three shirts and ties, slacks, and two pairs of shoes totaling over $3,000.

The success rate with front-line sales personnel has been so consistent and the benefits so visible that now the methodology is advancing into the managerial ranks. This is a much more complex assessment exercise. Nevertheless, the lessons learned are accelerating the development of an assessment science for management.

ABOUT THE SCIENCE

Assessment tools systematically measure candidate variables that are critical to job performance. They test for experience, preferences, and potential. The combination of these variables drives performance on the job and predicts performance, assuming the company does its part. Ultimately, it is the responsibility of management to establish a culture and train supervisors to support the potential identified through assessment. The variables work together as discussed in the following sections.

Experience

Background information unlocks the applicant's past to evaluate qualifications and achievements along with evidence of behavior patterns. A combination of instruments and behaviorally based interviews indicates whether the person has the knowledge and skills needed to quickly become proficient in a given job. But these instruments and interviews do not tell the employer much about the candidate's ability to perform different roles in the future.

Preferences

This data deal with interests, motives, and values. They tell what a person wants to do and the kinds of situations in which they are most comfortable. This brings into play motivation and organizational culture and implies degrees of fit. Preference data are very effective for predicting job satisfaction, commitment, and retention. However, preference and performance do not always correlate in that wanting to do and being able to do sometimes do not coincide. Still, preference data are useful in identifying possible career paths.

Potential

Here we delve into fundamental characteristics such as personality and ability. They tell an employer what a person can do under normal conditions. In addition, because the future is the focus of potential data, it can provide insights into work areas previously not experienced. Potential is also useful in employee development programs that seek to build on inherent strengths.

CAUTION

Look before leaping. Some search and software firms are hiring a psychologist or two to build selection instruments. There is no telling if the work is of a high order or simply a rehashing of old preference tests. Simply applying personality tests can be misleading and even dangerous. The effectiveness of the tools depends on how they are designed. Their construct and empirical validity should be thoroughly tested prior to application. Failure to address validity and reliability can lead to misuse and, in severe cases, lawsuits over alleged discrimination.

THE FUTURE FOR HR

Despite the threat of me-too, trailing-edge vendors, it is clear that scientific methods are proving their value in human capital management. They are generating both indirect and direct returns on investment. Indirectly, hiring the right person cuts down on the drag created by unsuccessful people. Coworkers and supervisors can focus on value-adding work rather than having to support a substandard individual. Moreover, the cost of turnover and retraining are avoided with effective hiring. On the direct side, productivity, quality, and customer service all improve at a financially measurable rate.

New industries outside retailing are now being targeted. Health care and financial services are the next most likely users of this advanced decision science. Any business that depends on a large number of front-line staff to serve customers is a likely candidate for proven objective approaches. We are witnessing the scientific method slowly erode a 50-year-old mythology about human capital value.

HR professionals must become conversant with assessment tools just as they had to learn to apply computer automation to administrative tasks. Automation freed them to spend more time on higher level work. Assessment offers a quantum leap from dealing with past data to beginning to predict returns on investment in the future.

More importantly, it has become clear that culture is the most important driver of organizational performance. As the corporation's culture managers, HR professionals are finding themselves at the culture epicenter. We can take people out for all types of training, but when we toss them back into the culture, it must reinforce the new knowledge and skills. HR leaders are becoming more culture managers than anything else. If HR truly wants to be a strategic business partner that impacts organizational performance, there is no better place to start than with the organization's culture.

CHAPTER 31

HUMAN RESOURCE ACCOUNTING, HUMAN CAPITAL MANAGEMENT, AND THE BOTTOM LINE

ERIC G. FLAMHOLTZ

The purpose of this chapter is to provide a brief overview of the role that a technology known as *Human Resource Accounting* can play in the management of people in organizations. It addresses the question: What does the forward-thinking senior HR professional need to know about this technology and its potential usefulness and impact on human resource management?

TOWARD HUMAN CAPITAL MANAGEMENT

The field of HR management is in transition, and the sophisticated HR professional will want to understand and take advantage of this. It is well recognized that the human resource management function (HRM) has been changing (Albers-Mohrman and Lawler, 1997; Ulrich, 1997). It has been evolving from an administrative function to a strategic partner whose value proposition is the contribution to an organization's financial performance or bottom line (Becker, Huselid, Pickus, and Spratt, 1997). What is less recognized is that a critical dimension of this transition is the need to change the perspective of HRM from a behavioral field anchored in social and organizational psychology to a field rooted in measurement and analytical tools. This change requires a paradigm shift from the traditional perspective to a *human capital management* perspective (Becker et al., 1997).

The historical shift from a personnel approach to a human resource management approach for managing people was profoundly important. It implied that people, though not owned by organizations, represent an important resource.

The next stage of the evolution of the HRM function is to make the transition to human capital management. Although related to the notion of HRM, there is a subtle and significant difference in the perspectives. The notion of human capital emphasizes the essential idea that people are an asset of an organization rather than an expense. Although in principle this could be the connotation of the concept of human resources, it has been lost or at least attenuated by conventional practice.

A human capital perspective implies a different view of the nature and therefore the management of people in organizations. It implies that they are assets to be employed or used in an optimum manner instead of expenses to be minimized. This is a wonderful concept, but it is of limited value unless it can be operationalized. Without measurement, the human capital notion is just a concept and difficult to apply in the real world.

The key to making this concept operational and practical is the measurement of the costs, replacement cost, and economic value of human resources or human capital. This is the focus of Human Resource Accounting and has been in development since the early 1960s (Flamholtz, 1999).

DEFINITIONS

Human Resource Accounting can be defined as "accounting for people as organizational resources." Operationally defined, this means measuring the cost, replacement cost, and economic value of people as organizational resources for facilitating human resource management, decision making, and control as well as the reporting of human capital in financial statements.

There is a dual aspect to Human Resource Accounting (HRA) measurement: (1) the actual measurements (numbers derived) of the historical cost, replacement cost, and economic value of people per se, and (2) the use of the HRA measurement framework as a lens for HRM planning and decisions.

HISTORICAL CONTEXT AND RATIONALE OF HUMAN RESOURCE ACCOUNTING

The development of Human Resource Accounting began in the mid-1960s. The impetus came from several areas simultaneously. Rensis Likert, the noted organizational psychologist, argued that it was necessary to develop measures for valuing human resources to demonstrate that participative leadership was more cost-effective than an autocratic style. Likert (1967) submitted that without measurements of the changes in the value of human resources of a firm, managers would be motivated to put undue pressure on people for short-term gains in productivity while liquidating invisible human assets. Personnel theorists such as George Odiorne (1963) began to argue for an economic approach to personnel administration with a calculation of costs and values. The same omission was noticed by economists such as Nobel Prize winner Theodore Schultz (1961), who argued for the development of an economic theory of human capital. Similarly, the accounting field began to recognize that financial statements were incomplete and misleading without an explicit recognition of human assets (Hermanson, 1964).

Since the 1970s this, in turn, has led to a flurry of research to develop methods of measuring human resource cost and value that would account for human resources (Flamholtz, 1999). Some of the key concepts and ideas are summarized here for HR professionals.

THE ROLE AND IMPACT OF HRA MEASUREMENTS

Without data, all you have is opinions, and without measurement you cannot really have significant data. The primary role of HRA measurement is to provide data or information for human resource management. There has been much research to develop methods of measuring human resources as well as to assess their impact on management and investor decisions (Flamholtz, 1999; Hansson, 1997).

Although the development of these measurement methods is a work in progress, it can still affect the management of people. A recent unpublished MBA field study (required for completion of a degree at the Anderson School, University of California–Los Angeles) on the cost, financial impact, and cause of turnover indicated that turnover was costing an organization more than $7.6 million per year. This was based on a very conservative estimate of the cost of turnover per employee ($1,330). The study also indicated that by reducing turnover to the industry average turnover would generate a net after-tax savings of $1.4 million or 1.4 percent of net income. Since this was a retail organization that operates with very low margins, even this seemingly small amount of cost savings was sufficient to get management to consider changes in human resource management practices.

From this example, the HR professional can see how the measurement of information about human resource costs resulting from turnover can have much more of an impact on management than merely the reporting of turnover rates.

THE HUMAN RESOURCE ACCOUNTING PERSPECTIVE OR LENS FOR HRM

Another use of HRA is as a strategic lens to help HR professionals think differently about the management of people as human capital. This kind of lens is found in economic theory but not in the HR world.

Economic theory is built on certain concepts such as opportunity cost, elasticity of demand, and utility. In the real world, these constructs are difficult to measure, but they are useful as an analytical perspective to think about economic problems.

Like economic theory, human resources accounting also provides a set of constructs for thinking about the management of human capital in a firm. The measurement of the cost and value of people as organizational resources requires the development of valuation formulas. These formulas can be used for human resource management planning, decision making, and control (Flamholtz, 1999). This function of HRA exists independently of the actual numbers generated by HRA measurement systems per se.

As shown in Figure 31.1, three constructs of an individual's value to organization (taken together) provide an analytical framework for HRM planning and decision making that is analogous to microeconomic theory.

Under human resource value theory (Flamholtz, 1999), the value of an individual to a firm depends on (1) the value of the economic services the person can potentially provide, and (2) the likelihood that those services will be realized by the enterprise. The potential value of an individual to a firm is termed *expected conditional value*. This construct ignores the possibility of turnover and therefore represents the maximum potential (theoretical) value of an individual to an enterprise. Since turnover is always

Figure 31.1
Determinants of Individual Value

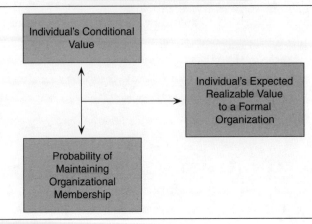

possible, we also use the construct of *expected realizable value* to represent the value that an organization expects to derive, given the possibility of turnover. If the possibility of turnover is greater than zero, then the expected conditional value must be greater than the expected realizable value. The probability of a person remaining in a firm is represented as 1 − the probability of turnover.

The mathematical statement of the preceding concepts, in algebraic terms, is as follows:

$$ERV = ECV \times P®$$
$$P® = 1 - P \times T$$

where   ERV = Expected realizable value
        ECV = Expected conditional value
         P® = Probability of maintaining organizational membership
    P × T = Probability of turnover

This then means that there is a potential opportunity cost of turnover, which is represented as OCT = ECV − ERV, where OCT = Opportunity cost of turnover.

This small set of equations provides the foundation for viewing the management of human resources in analytical terms and, in turn, provides the basis for the theory of human capital management. These constructs might be used as criteria for selection decisions. They raise the issue of whether it is preferable to base selection decisions on a criterion of expected conditional or expected realizable value to an organization. Stated differently, should an organization select a job candidate: (1) with the greatest expected potential value to the firm if we ignore the person's chances of leaving (greatest expected conditional value) or (2) should it select the person who has less potential value but is less likely to leave the firm (the greatest expected realizable value)? This is a key decision, and it is possible to think about it analytically if we quantify the variables involved.

Similarly, these criteria can be used in making personnel investment decisions, such as investments in training and development. These constructs can be used to quantify the expected return on investment from management development programs, as I have demonstrated elsewhere (Flamholtz et al., 2003).

THE BOTTOM LINE

The basic implication is that there is a clear and present need to change the perspective of HRM to one that is more closely aligned with a human capital management perspective. This, in turn, will require the further development and application of the measurement tools and lens of HRA.

Future Directions of Human Resource Accounting and Human Resource Management

The development of what might be termed *human capital management theory* and its companion tool—human resource accounting—is a work in progress. There are several future directions for HRA and HRM in their continuing development.

Further Development of Human Resource Value Theory

An avenue of future research and development is fleshing out a more definitive theory of human resource value. This would conceptualize the value of people in organizational resources and capital. The human capital of a firm comprises three components: (1) the value of the knowledge and skill of its workforce as individuals, (2) the differential performance value of people working as a true team or traditional group instead of as a set of individuals, and (3) the differential economic value of a strong corporate culture. At present, most human resource management and even human resource accounting is based on the general notion that people are a valuable resource, without a definitive look at what constitutes the components of human resource value. The preliminary work to develop a theory of human resource value (Flamholtz, 1999), is not definitive.

Use in Measuring Return on Investments in Human Resource Management

Most HRM decisions are made without the calculation of the related costs and benefits. For example, investments in training are understood to be investments in building human capital but they are not made in the way of other capital investment decisions. HRA provides a potential tool to make investments in human capital on the basis of expected returns on investment (see Flamholtz, Bullen, and Hua, 2003).

Use in Performance Management Systems

Human resource accounting has a potential future application as a component of a corporate or strategic business unit's control system (Flamholtz, 1996). A *control system* can be viewed as a *performance management* system for an organization or component, such as a division or department or even an individual. The basic notion of a control system is that there must be goals, measurements, evaluations, and related rewards for all critical aspects of performance.

These critical aspects of performance are known as *Key Result Areas*. Most control systems either do not include measurements of human resources or only include measurement of employee attitude surveys.

HRA can potentially provide measurements of the financial aspects of human capital management, including turnover cost and changes in the economic value of people. This, in turn, might improve the validity and utility of such concepts as the *Balanced Scorecard* (Flamholtz, 2003).

The concept of the Balanced Scorecard (BSC) proposed by Kaplan and Norton (1992, 1993, 1996a, 1996b) was a significant step in the right direction of moving performance management away from the tyranny of a single-minded focus on the bottom line of net income. Instead of a single perspective of financial performance, Kaplan and Norton proposed three additional perspectives: "customer satisfaction," "internal business processes," and "learning and growth." This fourth perspective is the closest to a focus on human resources. However, Kaplan and Norton (1996) do not really deal with human resources, except perhaps as buried in internal business processes. Perhaps this omission is due to the difficulties of measuring human resources. Whatever the reason, the omission of human resources as a critical component of performance management is a major problem and limitation of the BSC (Turner, 2000).

Measurement of the Economic Value of Corporate Culture

Another potential future direction for HRA and Human Resource Capital Management Theory is to measure the economic value of corporate culture and to conceptualize corporate culture as a component of human capital. Recent evidence has indicated that corporate culture can have an impact on financial performance (Flamholtz, 2001; Kotter and Heskit, 1992).

What has not yet been done is to make the case that corporate culture is actually a component of the value of human capital. What creates the difference in value in firms that sell the same products (e.g., Wal-Mart and Kmart), if not the differences in intangible assets such as corporate culture?

Some preliminary research has been conducted to measure the economic value of corporate culture (Flamholtz, 2001). This research involves the following four steps:

1. Management must develop an explicit statement of an organization's values. This can range from statements such as "people are our most important asset" to the way customers ought to be treated.
2. These statements are then measured using a Likert Scale to determine the extent to which there is agreement with the stated or desired culture throughout the organization.
3. Another measurement is also made of the extent to which actual behavior is consistent with the proposed or desired culture.

4. The differences between (2) and (3), provide a culture gap score that is then used in a regression against a measure of company profitability by organizational units.

In the research study conducted by Flamholtz (2001), a statistically significant relationship was observed between divisional agreement with the desired corporate culture and the financial performance of the business units. The R-square was 45.5 percent, suggesting that about 46 percent of financial performance is attributable to corporate culture and that this methodology might be used to value corporate culture and changes over time.

Conclusion

As we begin the new millennium, it is increasingly clear that the core strategic asset of enterprises as well as the new foundation of the wealth of nations is human capital. Without the ability to measure these assets, their management is unlikely to be either rational or optimal. Although the development of human resource accounting is not complete, some progress has been made.

Given the importance of the underlying issues, we can expect continuing progress in the future. We look forward to the day when human capital receives the same recognition as other assets in accounting practice as well as in the overall management paradigm.

At this point in the development of HRA, saying that the human resource accounting lens is a paradigm, or shared model, is too strong a statement. It has the potential, however, to provide the analytical basis for a new paradigm of human capital management.

References

Albers-Mohrman, S., and E. Lawler. (1997). Transforming the Human Resources Function. In D. Ulrich, M. Losey, and G. Lake (Eds.), *Tomorrow's HR Management*. New York: John Wiley & Sons.

Becker, B. E., M. A. Hueselid, P. S. Pickus, and M. F. Spratt. (1997). Human Resources as a Source of Shareholder Value: Research and Recommendations. In D. Ulrich, M. Losey, and G. Lake (Eds.), *Tomorrow's HR Management*. New York: John Wiley & Sons.

Flamholtz, E. G. (1996). *Effective Management Control: Theory and Practice.* Boston: Kluwer Academic Publishers.

Flamholtz, E. G. (1999). *Human Resource Accounting: Advances in Concepts, Methods, and Applications,* 3rd ed. Boston: Kluwer Academic Publishers.

Flamholtz, E. G. (2001). Corporate Culture and the Bottom Line. *European Management Journal,* June, pp. 268–275.

Flamholtz, E. G. (2003, Autumn). Putting Balance and Validity into the Balanced Scorecard. *Journal of Human Resource Costing & Accounting,* pp. 15–26.

Flamholtz, E. G., M. L. Bullen, and W. Hua. (2003, Spring). Measuring the ROI of Management Development: An Application of the Stochastic Rewards Valuation Model. *Journal of Human Resource Costing & Accounting,* pp. 21–40.

Hansson, B. (1997). Personnel Investments and Abnormal Return: Knowledge-Based Firms and Human Resource Accounting. *Journal of Human Resource Costing and Accounting,* Vol. 2, No. 2, pp. 9–29.

Hermanson, R. H. (1964). Accounting for Human Assets. Michigan State University.

Kaplan, R. S., and D. P. Norton. (1992). The Balanced Scorecard: Measures That Drive Performance. *Harvard Business Review,* January/February, pp. 71–79.

Kaplan, R. S., and D. P. Norton. (1993, September/October). Putting the Balanced Scorecard to Work. *Harvard Business Review,* pp. 134–147.

Kaplan, R. S., and D. P. Norton. (1996a). *The Balanced Scorecard.* Boston, MA: Harvard Business School Press.

Kaplan, R. S., and D. P. Norton. (1996b, January/February). Using the Balanced Scorecard as a Strategic Management System. *Harvard Business Review,* pp. 75–85.

Kotter, J. P., and J. L. Heskett. (1992). *Corporate Culture and Performance.* New York: The Free Press.

Likert, R. (1967). *The Human Organization: Its Management and Value.* New York: McGraw-Hill.

Odiorne, G. S. (1963). *Personnel Policy: Issues and Practices.* Columbus, Ohio: Merrill.

Schultz, T. (1961, March). Investment in Human Capital, *American Economic Review,* pp. 1–17.

Turner, G. (2000). Using Human Resource Accounting to Bring Balance to the Balanced Scorecard. *Journal of Human Resource Costing and Accounting,* Vol. 5, No. 2, pp. 31–34.

Ulrich, D. (1997). Human Resources of the Future: Conclusions and Observations. In D. Ulrich, M. Losey, and G. Lake (Eds.), *Tomorrow's HR Management.* New York: John Wiley & Sons.

CHAPTER 32

IMPROVING HUMAN RESOURCES' ANALYTICAL LITERACY: LESSONS FROM *MONEYBALL*

MARK A. HUSELID AND BRIAN E. BECKER

Moneyball, the bestseller by Michael Lewis (2003), recounts how one organization achieved a sustained performance advantage over its competitors. The Oakland Athletics were able to become one of the most successful franchises in major league baseball, despite having one of the smallest payrolls in the league. What is surprising about the Oakland As, however, is not *what* they did, but *how* they did it. In a break with baseball tradition, senior executives brought a new analytical literacy to their strategic decision making and redefined *what matters and how to measure* it. It is a lesson that has direct application to other organizations and in particular to senior executives (both HR professionals and line managers) attempting to build the workforce and the HR function into a strategic asset.

HR professionals are in the midst of revolutionary change with the increasing importance of intangibles as drivers of firm performance. Our research over the past decade, involving nearly 3,000 firms, has consistently shown that a *high performance* HR system can increase shareholder value. Taking advantage of these strategic opportunities in their own firms presents an important challenge for HR professionals. In *The HR Scorecard* and in our forthcoming book *The Workforce Scorecard,* we argue that HR professionals require a much different perspective on their strategic role (Becker, Huselid, and Ulrich, 2001; Huselid, Becker, and Beatty, 2005). A firm's capability to execute its strategy is perhaps its foremost source

278

of competitive advantage. In this world, it is not enough for HR professionals to be good HR managers—they need to be good strategy managers. Like the Oakland As, they need to redefine *what matters.*

Once HR professionals have redefined what matters and are focused on how HR drives successful strategy execution, there are direct implications for *what to measure* and *how to measure* it. HR's strategic goals should map directly onto the imperatives of successful strategy execution. There should be a clear line of sight between achieving HR's strategic goals and successful execution of the organization's strategy, and this line of sight should be reflected in HR's measures of strategic performance. This means new measures and new ways to measure. New measures mean that conventional metrics such as cost per hire, recruiting cycle time, cost per trainee, or overall levels of turnover rarely qualify. New ways to measure mean that benchmarking is not the answer. The human capital demands of an organization are as unique as the system of strategy drivers underlying successful strategy execution. Measures that capture the strategic value and contribution of either the workforce or HR will be as unique as the system of strategy drivers in the organization. As a result, those measures will not be found by comparing efficiency and activity measures with a benchmarking survey.

DEVELOPING ANALYTICAL LITERACY

The development of HR's strategic role has been an evolution. The first stage required a better understanding of business problems, as opposed to HR problems. This required new competencies on the part of HR professionals, and HR professionals are much more business savvy than they were a decade ago. The next step in that evolution is for HR professionals, and particularly senior HR professionals, to develop what we call *analytical literacy*. The need for greater analytical literacy reflects several trends. First, because technology allows organizations to more easily and cheaply collect data, key organizational decisions are much more data driven than in the past. Second, intangible assets and in particular human capital influence firm performance through a complex system of relationships. Quarterly employee surveys, activity reports, and turnover data rarely measure the strategic relationships that must be managed. Finally, other functional areas (finance, marketing, etc.) increasingly rely on more sophisticated analyses, and line managers expect HR professionals to be comfortable with these terms.

Does analytical literacy mean you have to have a graduate degree in statistics? No. Being a strategy manager means HR professionals should be asking a whole new set of questions about HR and human capital. Measures and their analysis provide answers to questions, and analytical literacy gives HR professionals the competency to recognize the appropriate measures, and the appropriate analyses, for the strategic questions confronting them. *Moneyball* is not about senior executives personally conducting sophisticated data analysis. But it is about senior executives understanding the analytics "well enough to use their conclusions" (Lewis, 2003, p. 57).

Moneyball offers three important lessons about analytical literacy that are applicable to HR professionals in their role as strategy manager.

Business logic drives measurement. Moneyball is not about new measures that just appeared by luck. They are in large part the result of a new perspective on what constitutes success in baseball and what is important about player (workforce) performance. *Moneyball* describes a new theory of the business, of how value is created; and the measures that are used to manage that business follow directly from the new business logic. While the strategic goals may include scoring runs and winning games, the strategic focus in an individual game that will most likely lead to strategic success over a season is minimizing the chances of making an out in each inning. Therefore, "on base percentage" (the probability of not making an out) is a more important measure of player performance than batting average.

The lesson for HR professionals is that an analysis of what is important and what should be measured is a top-down process, not a bottom-up process. The Oakland As figured out what it took for the team to be successful and then defined player performance, and the measures of that performance, in terms of their logical contribution to that success. HR professionals often do just the opposite in their efforts to demonstrate their strategic contribution. They start with the measure, often focusing on operational and administrative efficiency, and attempt to make a bottom-up argument. The business logic is superficial and neither the execution of the firm's strategy nor the credibility of the HR function is well served.

HR professionals, however, face a more difficult challenge than major league baseball executives. In baseball, the game had not changed—the challenge was to find a more successful strategy for the same game. For most HR professionals, the increasing importance of intangibles as sources of competitive advantage, and in particular the role of human capital, is an entirely new game!

Thinking in terms of causal relationships. Human capital rarely has a direct effect on firm performance. This is particularly true when the business logic of HR's effect requires that human capital drive firm performance through its contribution to effective strategy execution. Instead of looking for the strategic holy grail of HR's impact on shareholder value, HR professionals (and line managers) need to recognize that effective strategy execution is the basis of shareholder value and that effective strategy execution is a system of *intermediate* outcomes. Thinking like a strategy manager means recognizing the importance of the causal relationships between HR decisions and these intermediate outcomes that ultimately drive strategic success in your organization.

This causal thinking about relationships is illustrated in *Moneyball* with the following simple example. Starting pitchers are generally more effective than relief pitchers, so a team will be more successful if it can get the opposing team to remove its starting pitcher and bring in a relief pitcher. The chances of a starting pitcher being removed increase with the number of pitches he has to throw. So batters contribute to team success, not only when they get on base, but also when they make the opposing pitcher throw a lot of pitches before they eventually get on base. There is a business logic that describes success and a system of relationships linking individual performance to team success.

The notion of the intermediate outcome, the strategic performance driver that is the precursor of successful financial performance, is HR's neglected strategic "return." *Moneyball* is described as a story about efficiency, of achieving more success from a limited budget. Efficiency measures, however, are typically a measure of gain divided by cost. HR professionals too often focus only on the cost dimension of efficiency—the denominator. The story of *Moneyball* is not about how an organization achieved success by driving down costs; it is about how it dramatically increased gains with a relatively modest and stable cost base. The executives in *Moneyball* excelled at numerator management more than at denominator management. HR professionals need to radically redefine their concept of the numerator when they think of the return on HR or human capital. The impact of human capital and HR decisions on your organization's system of strategy drivers should be your numerator focus.

We like to use a simple example from the retail industry to illustrate this focus on numerator management. Assume that a retail firm's strategy to increase revenue growth depends on expanding market share, which in turn requires increased customer satisfaction. A marketing study concludes that customer satisfaction is largely driven by the customer buying experience, which is a function of front line staff who are knowledgeable, courteous, and timely. Developing those performance behaviors is a strategic responsibility for HR, but the return to those HR initiatives should be measured in terms of improved customer buying experience and customer satisfaction. Moreover, the analysis that is the basis for those HR initiatives requires HR professionals to think in terms of causal relationships from revenue growth back down through intermediate outcomes to the necessary strategic performance behaviors.

New modes of analysis are required. Finally, analytical literacy includes an appreciation and understanding of the notion that many of the HR solutions that might be proposed to drive a firm's strategy are merely hypotheses. They are the best estimate of what will work at the time, but they are not guaranteed to work. As hypotheses, however, the results of these decisions need to be examined in light of the results. Again from *Moneyball,* the general manager of the Oakland Athletics "concluded that everything from on-field strategies to player evaluation was better conducted by scientific investigation—hypotheses tested by analysis of historical statistical baseball data—than by reference to the collective wisdom of old baseball men" (Lewis, 2003, pp. 56–57).

The results of interest should be the *relationship* between human capital or HR decisions and key business outcomes. For example, a leading insurance company has implemented a leadership competency model. Does it make a difference? The measure of success is not how cheaply it was implemented, or how quickly or even how widely it was rolled out. The measure of success is whether managers with more of these leadership competencies had more business success than those managers with less of these competencies. The evidence showed a strong positive relationship between leadership competencies and key intermediate strategic outcomes: client satisfaction and policy renewals.

Just as the Oakland As had to move away from modes of analysis emphasizing "gut feelings," HR professionals need to develop more sophisticated modes of analysis. According to Sandy Alderson, former general manager of the Oakland As, "I couldn't do a regression analysis, but I knew what one was. And the results of them made sense to me" (Lewis, 2003, p. 57). Developing this capability may mean bringing it in-house, as at Allstate or with the Sun HR Labs. Or, like Cardinal Health, the organization may rely largely on outside expertise for more sophisticated analysis. But in each case, as with the Oakland As, the senior executives were literate with this kind of analysis and knew how to take advantage of the results.

We need to emphasize that these more sophisticated methods of analysis follow directly from the first two dimensions of analytical literacy, using business logic as the foundation of measurement and thinking in terms of causal relations. Strategic performance measurement is based on the relationship between human capital and the unique strategic performance drivers in your organization. Therefore, benchmarking HR performance using traditional efficiency measures such as cost per hire or recruiting cycle time, is not the solution (Becker and Huselid, 2003). Neither is constructing measures like "human capital value added" that are nothing more than combinations of old measures with new names. HR and human capital strategic performance require new numerators and they will largely be unique to the system of strategy drivers required to execute your firm's strategy.

AN IMPORTANT CAVEAT

There is good news and bad news in drawing lessons from *Moneyball*. The bad news is that the strategic implications of analytical literacy in major league baseball are very different from those in most industries. In baseball, every team is playing the same game. *Moneyball* is largely a story of market inefficiency. One team discovers a better strategy and achieves a competitive advantage. But since all the teams are playing the same game, another team can simply copy what the Oakland team has done and expect to improve their performance. As more teams adopt this new strategy, and several have already begun to do so, they will erode Oakland's competitive advantage.

Most HR professionals do not work in this type of industry setting. The system of strategy drivers, the employee mind-set, culture, and workforce performance required to execute one firm's strategy is often quite different from that of other firms in your industry. That the games you are playing differ from those of your competitors is a mixed blessing. On the one hand, it is bad news because HR professionals need to develop a differentiated workforce strategy that is unique to their own organization. Despite the allure of benchmarking, they cannot simply copy the same performance measures and initiatives used in an industry success story and hope for the same results. The good news is that this differentiation means that if they are successful in their own organization, it should provide a relatively sustainable source of competitive advantage. The foundation of this approach will be a new emphasis on analytical literacy.

REFERENCES

Becker, Brian E., and Mark A. Huselid. (2003, December). "Measuring HR? Benchmarking Is NOT the Answer." *HR Magazine,* pp. 56–61.

Becker, Brian E., Mark A. Huselid, and Dave Ulrich. (2001). *The HR Scorecard: Linking People, Strategy and Performance.* Cambridge, MA: Harvard Business School Press.

Huselid, Mark A., Brian E. Becker, and Richard W. Beatty. (2005, March). *The Workforce Scorecard.* Cambridge, MA: Harvard Business School Press.

Lewis, Michael. (2003). *Moneyball.* New York: Norton.

CHAPTER 33

THE DUAL THEORY OF HUMAN RESOURCE MANAGEMENT AND BUSINESS PERFORMANCE: LESSONS FOR HR EXECUTIVES

DAVID LEWIN

Contemporary human resource management (HRM) research, including studies based on North American, European, and Asian data, finds that certain *high involvement* HRM (HIHRM) practices have significant positive effects on such business performance measures as market value, rate of return on capital employed, revenue growth, revenue per employee, productivity, product/service quality, and even organizational survival (Lewin, 2004). That HIHRM practices leverage business performance appears to be well known to human resource (HR) executives.

HIHRM practices, however, constitute only one way of managing human resources to leverage business performance. Another way to achieve enhanced business performance is by managing human resources for expense control. Consequently, certain *low involvement* HRM (LIHRM) practices may best fit some organizations and employees. Taken together, HIHRM and LIHRM practices form the building blocks for a *dual theory of HRM and business performance,* with consequent lessons for HR executives.

THE DUAL THEORY ELABORATED

Consider that a business's workforce comprises two distinct segments: a *core* and a *periphery* (Lewin and Mitchell, 1995). Members of the core workforce typically are employed full time; paid a regular salary or wage; covered by fringe benefits; have training, development, and promotion opportunities along well-defined career paths; and participate in decision making through work teams and a decentralized organization structure. The core workforce is also carefully selected, has employment security and some performance-based pay, and regularly receives information about the business. Unlike the core workforce, the peripheral workforce consists of part-time, temporary, contract, vendored, and outsourced employees who are generally paid a fixed wage, salary, or lump sum, are partially or not at all covered by fringe benefits, and have little or no training, development, or promotion opportunities. The peripheral workforce also typically does not participate in decision making through work teams or organizational decentralization, has little performance-based pay or employment security, and receives little business-specific information.

This core-peripheral workforce distinction provides the conceptual foundation for the dual theory of HRM and business performance. Expenditures on the core workforce should (present accounting conventions aside) be treated as an investment intended to increase the value added to the business by employees in this segment. Expenditures on the peripheral workforce should (following present accounting conventions) be treated as an expense that the business seeks to contain or reduce and, in this way, also add value to the business. In both cases, the key task facing the business is to maximize return, or value, over cost. Ideally, applying HIHRM to core employees and LIHRM to peripheral employees should result in larger profit margins than would result from following conventional HRM practices in which few or no distinctions are made between core and peripheral employees. There is evidence to support this dual theory of HRM and business performance, as briefly summarized in the following section.

HIHRM/LIHRM EMPLOYEE COVERAGE AND BUSINESS PERFORMANCE

A recent study that sampled 289 (U.S.) companies, 313 company business units, 457 manufacturing plants, and 249 sales and service field offices of a national insurance company found that HIHRM practices were applied significantly more to core employees than to peripheral employees (Lewin, 2004, 2001b).[1] Among eight specific HIHRM practices—employment continuity, selective hiring, training/development, teams/participation, variable pay, performance management, promotion opportunity, and business information sharing—that provided the basis for this comparison, each was significantly more widely used for core than for peripheral employees. Collectively, these HIHRM practices were two and one-half times more likely to be used for core than for peripheral employees (with means of 4.1 and 1.5, respectively, for "all practices" on a 1 = low, 5 = high rating scale). Therefore, and despite variation among the sampled businesses in their uses of HIHRM practices, it appears that peripheral employment is low involvement employment and that core employment is high involvement employment.

This same study also analyzed LIHRM practices for their effects on business performance. In doing so, an index of LIHRM practices was constructed that measured the proportion of an organization's workforce consisting of part-time, temporary, and contract employees as well as employees who were placed with vendors and employees leased from outsourcing firms.[2] The data for determining the LIHRM index score at a point in time (1998) and changes over time (1995 to 1998) came from surveys administered to each company, business unit, manufacturing plant, and sales and service field office. Business performance data were obtained from secondary sources in the cases of the company and business unit samples, and from the surveys in the cases of the manufacturing plant and insurance company field office samples. The variation in performance among each of the four sets of business entities was then subjected to multivariate analysis that included the LIHRM index as the main independent variable and several control variables (e.g., organizational size, capital-labor ratio, and unionization). The following paragraphs describe the main findings from this quantitative analysis.

For the company sample, the LIHRM index was *positively* associated with return on capital employed, market value, and revenue per employee in the single-year analysis, and with changes in each of these business performance measures in the multiyear analysis. These findings imply that a one standard deviation increase in LIHRM was associated with a significant 1.5 percent increase in return on capital employed, a 2.7 percent increase in market value, and a 3.2 percent increase in revenue per employee. For the business unit sample, the LIHRM index was *positively* associated with return on capital employed and revenue per employee, both at a point in time and over time. These findings imply that a one standard deviation increase in LIHRM was associated with a significant 2.2 percent increase in return on capital employed and a 4.1 percent increase in revenue per employee in these business units.

For the manufacturing plant sample, the LIHRM index was *negatively* associated with total labor cost as a proportion of total operating cost at a point in time and with the change in this operating performance measure over time. These findings imply that a one standard deviation increase in LIHRM was associated with a significant 5.8 percent reduction in manufacturing plant labor cost as a proportion of total operating cost. Notably, the LIHRM index was *not* associated with productivity or product quality at a point in time or over time. Contrary to expectations, these manufacturing plants apparently did *not* experience lower productivity or product quality as a result of employing peripheral workers and managing them with LIHRM practices.

For the insurance company field office sample, the LIHRM index was *negatively* associated with the ratio of payroll cost to sales revenue, both at a point in time and over time. These findings imply that a one standard deviation increase in LIHRM was associated with a significant 4.8 percent decrease in the ratio of payroll cost to sales revenue in these field offices. By contrast, the LIHRM index was not associated with revenue growth, quality of service, or customer satisfaction. Consequently, and again contrary to expectations, these insurance sales and service field offices apparently did not experience lower revenue growth, service quality, or customer satisfaction as a result of employing peripheral workers and managing them in a low involvement fashion.

These four analyses were then extended to include an eight-item HIHRM index, which was found to be positively associated with long run (that is, changes in) company financial performance, short- and long-run business unit financial performance, and short- and long-run manufacturing plant operating performance. Most important, and in each case, the LIHRM index remained positively associated with business performance measures when these businesses' HIHRM practices were taken into account. Therefore, it appears that LIHRM practices also leverage business performance.

LESSONS FOR HR EXECUTIVES

These empirical findings support the dual theory of HRM and business performance, especially because businesses typically use HIHRM *and* LIHRM practices simultaneously. To illustrate, among all the business entities included in the aforementioned study ($n = 1,308$), more than 95 percent reported having some peripheral employment (in 1998), and their average score on the HIHRM index, which ranged from 8 to 40, was 25.5. Therefore, most businesses make use of core employees to whom HIHRM practices are applied and peripheral employees to whom LIHRM practices are applied. Since both HRM practices have positive effects on business performance, an important lesson for HR executives is that a business can manage one segment of its workforce by investing in HIHRM practices and obtaining net value added, and also manage another segment of its workforce through LIHRM practices that add value through labor expense control.

Given this conclusion, one can ask, "Is there an optimal balance of core and peripheral workforce segments for a business?" To answer this question, additional quantitative analysis was undertaken in which the ratio of peripheral employment to total employment for each business entity in each of the four samples served as the dependent variable, and the various business performance measures served as independent variables—in effect, reverse regression analyses. The findings showed that the better performing companies, business units, manufacturing plants, and insurance company sales and services field offices made greater use of peripheral employment than the poorer performing companies, and also increased their use of peripheral employment significantly more than poorer performing companies.

These findings do not, however, mean that business entities should simply or linearly increase their ratios of peripheral employment to total employment. When the company, business unit, manufacturing plant, and sales and service field office samples were separated into quartiles based on changes (during 1995 to 1998) in their financial performance, the top-performing quartile in each sample had an average ratio of peripheral employment to total employment of .34 compared with ratios of .17 for the worst-performing quartile, .26 for the second-worst performing quartile, and .40 for the second-best performing quartile. In other words, the gain in business performance from increased use of peripheral employment was greatest when the ratio of peripheral employment to total employment rose from about one-quarter to one-third; increases in the ratio beyond this point were associated with declining business performance. The lesson for HR executives, therefore, is that a balance of one-third peripheral employment and two-thirds core employment appears optimal.[3]

The findings from LIHRM-business performance research also provide lessons for HR executives about globalization, organizational change, and the HR function. There are many countries in which certain HIHRM practices apparently do not fit because they run afoul of cultural values, custom, history, and legal constraints. Variable pay, business information sharing with employees, and decentralized, team-based work are among such practices. Similarly, certain LIHRM practices, such as part-time, fixed contract, and outsourced employment, do not appear to fit well with many nations. Yet it was only recently that these HIHRM and LIHRM practices were virtually unknown in the United States, where individually designed work for a fixed rate of pay in a high-control organization predominated. The lesson here for HR executives is that these historical U.S. HRM practices were substantially altered by market globalization and that further globalization will likely result in businesses outside the United States making greater use of LIHRM practices.

Regarding organizational change, researcher and practitioner attention has focused predominantly on such global environmental factors as technology, deregulation, customers, and competitors as key drivers of change. But from time to time, new ideas and new evidence about human behavior at work can drive organizational change. Historical examples include the emergence and expansion of free labor markets in the nineteenth century, the scientific management and Hawthorne-inspired human relations movements of the early twentieth century, and the total quality and work process reengineering innovations of the late twentieth century (Lewin, 2001a). Each of these developments brought about major changes in the design of work and the management of people at work (i.e., major organizational change) both in the United States and abroad. Hence, the dual theory of HRM and business performance offers to HR executives worldwide the lesson that, when it comes to managing people, one size or set of best practices does not fit all.

Finally, the dominant role of the HR function in the business enterprise has frequently changed to emphasize social welfare services, union avoidance, organizational rule enforcement, compliance with regulation, and record keeping (Lewin, Mitchell, and Zaidi, 1997). Only relatively recently has the HR function's principal role been characterized as that of a business partner or change agent. The capability of the HR function—of HR executives and professionals—to fulfill either or both of these newer roles, however, is called into question by the creation of organizational learning functions and executive positions in several prominent businesses. In these businesses, and perhaps many others, the HR function continues to be viewed not as a key business partner or change agent but, instead, as largely fulfilling one or more of its older, traditional roles. Thus, *the key lesson here is that to lead HR functions that occupy the role of key business partner and/or change agent, HR executives must grasp and especially apply the knowledge of LIHRM and HIHRM practices derived from the dual theory of HRM and business performance.*

NOTES

1. Additional detail about the study design, surveys, and sampling frames is provided in Lewin (2004, 2001b).
2. For the four samples as a whole, peripheral employment accounted for just under 32 percent of total full-time equivalent employment in 1998, closely approximating the extent of peripheral employment at that time in the broad U.S. economy. Between 1995 and 1998, peripheral employment increased by about 14 percent in the company sample, 15 percent in the business unit sample, 16 percent in the manufacturing plant sample, and 15 percent in the insurance sales and service field office sample. For further details, including changes in specific categories of peripheral employment in these four samples of business entities, see Lewin (2004).
3. Not included in this calculation, however, is the potential or hidden cost to a business if its (relatively low cost) peripheral workforce becomes so large that it seeks to become part of its (higher cost) core workforce.

REFERENCES

Lewin, D. (2001a). IR and HR Perspectives on Workplace Conflict: What Can Each Learn from the Other? *Human Resource Management Review,* 11, 453–485.

Lewin, D. (2001b). Low Involvement Work Practices and Business Performance. *Proceedings of the 53rd Annual Meeting,* Industrial Relations Research Association. Champaign, IL: IRRA, pp. 275–292.

Lewin, D. (2004). HRM and Business Performance Research: Empiricism in Search of Theory. *Paper presented to the 62nd Annual Meeting of the Academy of Management,* Denver, CO, 2002, revised.

Lewin, D., and D. J. B. Mitchell. (1995). *Human Resource Management: An Economic Approach,* 2nd ed. Cincinnati, OH: South-Western.

Lewin, D., D. J. B. Mitchell, and M. A. Zaidi. (1997). Separating Ideas and Bubbles in Human Resource Management. In D. Lewin, D. J. B. Mitchell, and M. A. Zaidi (Eds.), *The Human Resource Management Handbook, Part I.* Greenwich, CT: JAI Press, pp. 1–31.

CHAPTER 34

TALENTSHIP, TALENT SEGMENTATION, AND SUSTAINABILITY: A NEW HR DECISION SCIENCE PARADIGM FOR A NEW STRATEGY DEFINITION

JOHN W. BOUDREAU AND PETER M. RAMSTAD

What are the talent pools (e.g., jobs, roles, or competencies) in your organization, where a 20 percent improvement in quality or availability would make the biggest difference to organizational success? The answer reveals the "pivotal talent pools," which are the vital targets for HR investments and leader attention. Yet, today most organizations have many opinions and little logic or data to answer this fundamental question. In addition, the task is about to become much more difficult because the very definition of organization success changes from strictly financial to *sustainability*.

This chapter describes two paradigm shifts and how to address them. The first paradigm shift is *Talentship:* HR and business leaders must broaden their traditional focus beyond just HR services, toward a "decision science" that enhances decisions about human capital, wherever they are made (Boudreau and Ramstad, in press-b). Talentship has many implications for HR strategy, organizational design, service delivery, and competencies. One implication is that "talent segmentation" is as vital as "customer segmentation" (Boudreau and Ramstad, in press-a). Part of talent segmentation is identifying "pivotal talent pools"—where human capital makes the biggest

Thanks to John Hofmeister for helpful comments.

difference to strategic success. The second paradigm shift is that HR and business leaders increasingly define organizational effectiveness beyond traditional financial and shareholder outcomes to encompass *sustainability*—achieving success today without compromising the needs of the future.

Fortunately, a common strategic human capital logic can reveal pivotal talent under both definitions and thus uncover important insights about the talent implications of the shifting definition of strategic success.

THE TRADITIONAL "PRIZE" OF FINANCIAL RETURNS IS SHIFTING TOWARD SUSTAINABILITY: IS HR READY?

The traditional business paradigm strives to achieve financial returns—or maximize shareholder value—through competition. Human resource management (HRM) responds with "strategic" logic showing HR's contribution, also defined in financial terms. Yet, even as the HRM profession works diligently to understand the business in traditional financial terms, the very definition of organization success is changing. The shareholder value paradigm is challenged by the argument that organizations should strive for an expanded prize—sustainability. The World Commission on Environment and Development defines sustainability as "development that meets the needs of the present without compromising the ability of future generations to meet their own needs" (World Commission on Environment and Development, 1987).

Sustainability is just emerging, but it includes values, governance, transparency, and ethics, as well as goals such as diversity, social responsibility, supporting human and employee rights, protecting the environment, and contributing to the community. Sustainability includes the bottom line, because financial viability is necessary for organizational survival, but it defines success beyond financial results. For example, the working conditions of employers and their suppliers have become a de facto standard for many firms because sweatshop scandals have hurt a number of famous brands.

Sustainability is not a fringe issue. Corporate heavyweights like Shell, BP, and DuPont, as well as the United Nations (UN) and International Labor Organization (ILO), are all embracing sustainability. It is particularly relevant to mission-driven organizations such as governments, charities, and universities. Sustainability rarely appears in strategic HR plans, and its implications for strategic HRM have received less attention. Yet, as organizations increasingly embrace sustainability, so must HR.

THE TRADITIONAL HR PARADIGM APPLIED TO FINANCIAL VERSUS SUSTAINABILITY GOALS

The traditional HR paradigm defines HR contribution as supporting organization goals through aligned HR policies, practices, and programs. Combined with traditional financial goals, this HR paradigm emphasizes *compliance* with legal regulations (e.g., reducing risks of costly legal actions), *efficiency* in HR processes (e.g., minimizing cost per hire, HR staff per employee, and the time to train), *client satisfaction* with HR practices, and (more rarely) *effectiveness* of HR programs in enhancing employee characteristics (capabilities, culture, attitudes, or motivation). Perhaps the best example is measuring return on investment (ROI) in HR programs, such as showing that training costs are offset by improved sales knowledge related to increased sales.

The traditional HR paradigm of service delivery is also the typical way HR connects to sustainability. The ILO Declaration urges the elimination of child labor, forced or compulsory labor, employment discrimination, and the promotion of free association and collective bargaining.[1] The UN Global Compact adds that companies should protect internationally proclaimed human rights and ensure they are not complicit in human rights abuses.[2] HR programs such as performance management, selection, and training can reflect fair treatment, respect for collective association rights, work-family balance, and reward not only economic performance but also community involvement or reduced environmental emissions. HR can measure sustainability-related knowledge, behaviors, attitudes, and motivation, as well as collective activity, community involvement, and employee health and safety. Such measures often appear in corporate sustainability or social responsibility reports to investors.

These actions are important, but the HR paradigm is still traditional—applying sustainability to the policies, practices, and activities *within the HR function*. Other important connections go beyond HR practices and can be understood only with a more strategic HR paradigm that connects human capital to sustainable strategic success.

A New Paradigm for Strategic HR: The Talentship Decision Science

HR has struggled to define what it means to be *strategic*. The answer lies not just in benchmarking HR organizations, but in the evolution of more strategic functions such as finance and marketing (Boudreau and Ramstad, 1997, 2003). The marketing decision science enhances decisions about customers, and the finance decision science enhances decisions about money, so a talent decision science should enhance decisions about talent, both within and outside the HR function.

The finance decision science provides well-articulated logic, models, and methods that use accounting data to improve decisions about deploying financial assets. The finance department doesn't make most of these decisions—they are made by managers across the organization. The finance decision science is different from accounting, but accounting remains a critical professional practice.

Today's HR is similar to accounting. It is and will remain a critical and important professional practice. Yet, we still lack a well-developed decision science for human capital or "talent." This is not surprising. Modern accounting is 400 years old, but finance evolved around 1900 (Johnson and Kaplan, 1991). The professional practice of sales goes back to ancient times, but the decision science of marketing emerged only in the twentieth century (Howard, 1957). Yet, a talent decision science is vitally needed today for all the well-known reasons that it is increasingly important to enhance talent decisions, including structures, behaviors, capability, learning, collaboration, shared culture, and so on. In several companies, we have labeled it *Talentship* because it focuses on decisions that improve the stewardship of the hidden and apparent talents of employees. This chapter illustrates one Talentship, showing the human capital implications of defining organization as purely financial versus as sustainability.

One element of any decision science is the logic that connects decisions about the resource to organization success. In finance, the formula for ROI produces a number, but its more important purpose is to articulate what factors are relevant to financial investment decisions and how they combine. In this case, it is economic inflows and outflows, matched over time, and appropriately discounted to reflect future risk and inflation. Similarly, a talent decision science requires frameworks that show what factors are relevant to decisions about talent and how they combine. HR investments affect "pivotal talent segments" that enhance the processes and resources that most affect sustainable strategic success. Research in areas as diverse as industrial psychology, sociology, and operations management increasingly focuses on these connections (Boudreau, 2004). The HC BRidge framework, discussed next, is a model that articulates those connections.

THE HC BRIDGE FRAMEWORK

Boudreau and Ramstad created a model, the HC BRidge Decision Framework,[3] that outlines the logical connections supporting talentship. The HC BRidge framework is based on three anchor points: impact, effectiveness, and efficiency that are common to all business decision sciences (Figure 34.1).

Efficiency asks, "What resources are used to produce our HR policies and practices?" Typical indicators of efficiency are cost-per-hire and time-to-fill vacancies. As noted earlier, when applied to sustainability, efficiency would focus on the resources used to bring HR practices into compliance or to provide incentives that reflect community, environmental, or social goals.

Effectiveness asks, "How do our HR policies and practices affect the talent pools and organization structures to which they are directed?" Effectiveness refers to the effects of HR policies and practices on human capacity (a combination of capability, opportunity, and motivation) and the resulting aligned actions of the target talent pools. In the traditional HR paradigm, effectiveness would include trainees' increased knowledge or performance ratings of those receiving incentives. Effectiveness applied to sustainability draws attention to human capacity and aligned actions that go beyond traditional job and performance requirements. Capability might include knowledge about the organization's social responsibility and ethics codes, opportunity might include time off from work to do volunteer tasks in the local community, and motivation might include employee perceptions that activities related to sustainability are noticed and rewarded.

Figure 34.1
HC Bridge® Decision Framework

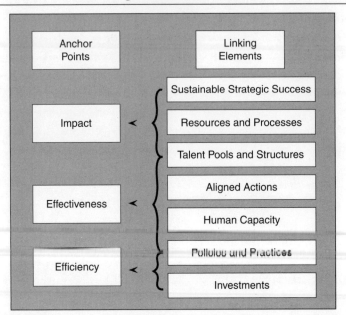

Impact reflects the hardest question of the three and most vividly illustrates the fundamental differences revealed by a focus on talent decisions, beyond simply HR service delivery. Impact asks, "How do differences in the quality or availability of different talent pools affect strategic success?" This question is a component of talent segmentation, just as in marketing a component of market segmentation asks, "How do differences in the buying behavior of different customer groups affect strategic success?"

Even using the traditional financial definition of success, impact can reveal surprising results. One organization initially believed the most important talent pool was sales representatives because revenue was important. Working through the impact elements of HC BRidge revealed that there was relatively little to be gained in improving the quality of sales reps. This talent pool had received much attention already. They were high performing, making further improvements difficult. HR investments *would* make a bigger difference in the talent pools affecting product development, which had been relatively ignored, and thus offered ample improvement opportunity. Applying the impact question to sustainability can reveal similar unseen talent contributions and new directions for HR.

There are some key lessons here about Talentship and talent segmentation. First, they are not about dropping HR's focus on efficiency and effectiveness but rather about adding impact. Second, they suggest that HR programs applied across the board may be more focused, making HR investments in the talent pools that produce the best return. Third, Talentship breaks the traditional HR silos by clearly showing that it takes a mix of interventions to improve the performance of the pivotal talent (e.g., the sales support staff). Now, let's apply HC BRidge to the role of HR in sustainability, achieving today's goals without compromising the needs of the future.

COMBINING THE NEW PARADIGMS: TALENTSHIP PLUS SUSTAINABILITY

We can summarize our discussion about HR and sustainability along two dimensions: first, whether the "prize" is primarily profits or sustainability and, second, whether the HR paradigm reflects the traditional one of service delivery or the new paradigm of a decision science (Figure 34.2).

Each quadrant provides opportunities for HR contribution as we have seen, but the most untapped area is the top right, where Talentship is applied to sustainability. Organizations can use the same HC BRidge framework that connects talent to financial goals to understand where talent connects to sustainability goals.

In the upper-right quadrant, the impact question now becomes, "In which talent pools will HR interventions have the most impact on sustainability?" The pivotal talent pools for traditional financial goals vary with organizations' strategies and competitive challenges, and it's the same with sustainability. Each organization must work through the impact elements to find the pivotal talent for sustainability. An example from DuPont will show how Talentship and HC BRidge reveal strategic talent differences between exclusively financial and sustainability goals.

In 2000, DuPont and three other large agricultural companies agreed to share technology, free of charge, with African scientists to increase food

Figure 34.2
How the Talent Paradigm and the Organizational Prize
Define the Strategic Talent Questions

		Organizational Prize	
		Traditional: Financial	Emerging: Sustainability
Talent Paradigm	**Emerging: Talent Decisions –Talentship**	Do we make excellent decisions about the talent resources that are pivotal to our financial results?	Do we make excellent decisions about the talent resources that are pivotal to sustainable strategic success?
	Traditional: HR Service Excellence	Are our HR policies and practices efficient, and do they produce acceptable returns on investment?	Are our HR policies and practices consistent and compliant with sustainable employment relationships?

production in areas where mass starvation is a recurring threat. They would donate patent rights, seed varieties, laboratory know-how, and other aid to African agricultural scientists working with small farmers to battle plant disease, insects, and drought (Holliday, 2003).

A traditional strategic analysis reflecting only financial outcomes and competition would identify patent rights, seed varieties, and laboratory know-how as strategic resources. It would identify processes such as commercialization (transforming discoveries into product/service features that customers will pay for and applying them to high-profit and/or high-volume products) and protection (creating legal or physical barriers around intellectual property to keep competition at a disadvantage). In the impact analysis of the traditional financially driven strategy, pivotal talent would include research scientists and intellectual property lawyers. The key aligned actions for scientists would be to direct their research toward discoveries that yield highly profitable product features. For lawyers, aligned actions would be to create patent or other legal protections against competitive espionage and copying.

Applying Talentship and HC BRidge to the sustainability objective of alleviating hunger in Africa uncovers different talent implications. The resources of laboratory know-how and seed varieties are still important, but now it is for their effectiveness in hunger reduction, not just profits. Patent rights may actually be detrimental because starvation reduction requires knowledge that is *unprotected*, so that collaborating companies and African communities can easily copy and disseminate it. Commercialization is less critical than transforming discoveries into product/service features that provide the greatest nutrition and applying them to low-cost and easily used products. Protection is less critical than dissemination (making knowledge easily copied, transmitted, and applied to maximize collaboration). The aligned actions for DuPont's scientists would now be to discover what starvation-preventing product features can be cheaply and easily deployed. DuPont's laboratory talent must not only develop seed varieties that can be profitably cultivated in Africa but also find seed varieties that thrive in starvation-prone areas and that produce food products that efficiently alleviate starvation. A pivotal talent pool will be translators and trainers, whose aligned actions would be to transfer knowledge quickly and widely, not only to the communities that must apply it but even to *competitors*.

WHERE NEXT FOR HR AND SUSTAINABILITY?

The movement to seek sustainability, not just financial returns, is embryonic in the United States, but has significant momentum globally. Decision makers, opinion leaders, voters, and employees care about sustainability. They want corporations to reduce the externalities that burden future generations. Sustainability is not just good ethics; it's potentially good long-term economics, as executives in major global multinational organizations have stated. HR has an important role to play in sustainability.

Compliance and social accountability for HR programs are an important beginning. However, organizations will achieve sustainability more effectively if they adopt a decision science that helps them better understand and articulate the connections between talent and sustainability. The deep line of sight created by a decision science provides the alignment necessary to drive execution through effective decisions about human capital, within and beyond the HR function.

Leading organizations are using frameworks such as Talentship, HC BRidge, and talent segmentation to enhance execution of traditional financial goals. A talent decision science, built on these ideas, applies equally well to sustainability goals. Using a common, logical, decision-based framework for both financial and sustainability goals makes the implications for talent decisions vividly apparent. This takes the debate about HR's role in strategy and sustainability beyond rhetoric and toward logical analysis and consistent execution.

NOTES

1. http://www.ilo.org/dyn/declaris/DECLARATIONWEB.INDEXPAGE.
2. http://www.unglobalcompact.org/Portal/?NavigationTarget=/roles /portal_user/aboutTheGC/nf/nf/theNinePrinciples.
3. HC BRidge is a trademark of the Boudreau-Ramstad Partnership, http://www.hcbridge.com.

REFERENCES

J. W. Boudreau. (2004). "Organizational Behavior, Strategy, Performance and Design in Management Science," *Management Science*.

J. W. Boudreau and P. M. Ramstad. (1997). "Measuring Intellectual Capital: Learning from Financial History," *Human Resource Management, 36*, 3, pp. 343–356.

J. W. Boudreau and P. M. Ramstad. (2003). "Strategic HRM Measurement in the 21st Century: From Justifying HR to Strategic Talent Leadership." In *HRM in the 21st Century,* Marshall Goldsmith, Robert P. Gandossy, and Marc S. Efron (Eds.), 79–90. Hoboken, NJ: John Wiley & Sons.

J. W. Boudreau and P. M. Ramstad. (in press-a). "Talent Segmentation: The Logic and Power of Differentiating Human Capital," working paper, Center for Effective Organizations. University of Southern California, Los Angeles, CA.

J. W. Boudreau and P. M. Ramstad. (in press-b). "Talentship and the Evolution of Human Resource Management: From 'Professional Practices' to 'Strategic Talent Decision Science,'" working paper, Center for Effective Organizations, University of Southern California, Los Angeles, CA.

C. Holliday. (2003, March 29). "Corporate Social Responsibility, Sustainability, and Markets." Speech delivered to the Wharton China Business Forum. Available from the World Business Council for Sustainable Development, www.wbcsd.ch.

J. A. Howard. (1957), *Marketing Management; Analysis and Decision.* Homewood, IL: R. D. Irwin.

H. T. Johnson and R. S. Kaplan. (1991). *Relevance Lost: The Rise and Fall of Management Accounting.* Boston: Harvard Business School Press.

World Commission on Environment and Development. (1987). *Our Common Future.* Oxford, UK: Oxford University Press.

SECTION VII

CREATE MUTUALLY
COLLABORATIVE VENTURES

When we ask employees in large U.S. corporations, "What do you do for work?" the responses are often finance, marketing, manufacturing, sales, or human resources. Each answer defines work as the functional silo where the employee works. In contrast, Japanese employees who are asked the same question often respond, "Toyota, Nissan, NEC," or the name of the company. The Japanese mind-set is to work across silos in a company; the U.S. mind-set is often to develop functional expertise and work within a silo. Silos divide and separate. They often make for good parts that do not work well together. Collaboration comes through unity and sharing.

Collaboration makes the whole more than the sum of the individual parts in two ways. First, combining resources increases efficiency. Efficient use of resources includes purchasing, technology, and organization. HR professionals in shared services find ways to streamline and more efficiently accomplish work. Second, by leveraging ideas and information, the whole becomes stronger. HR helps share knowledge through facilitating movement of people, shaping and sharing processes, and creating communities of practices and learning experiences.

Indeed, collaboration is the work of HR. Collaboration and cooperation are among the hallmarks of successful organizations, and HR must help the whole be greater than the parts. HR practices and professionals may help different units work together, help employees understand how it all comes together, and help employees view themselves as part of the larger organization, not a single unit or division.

In this section, the authors propose some models to enhance collaboration and cooperation. Culbert and Coget propose that true teamwork

305

within an organization requires two-sided accountability, with vertical collaboration between managers and employees. They explain that creating truly effective teamwork involves not only managers telling subordinates how they are doing, but subordinates providing input on how they see a situation and what they need to get their jobs done.

Gratton describes how cooperative ventures come from creating ties across units and establishing tools within units. Using Nokia as an example, Gratton highlights the crucial role HR plays in designing the practices, processes, and structures that create levers for working horizontally.

Seemann delves into the issue of power within organizations, and stresses that power should not be viewed as a nasty word. Power ensures cooperation and collaboration. A cross-departmental team, without clarity regarding its power, will not be productive. HR has a role in creating the conditions, structure, and processes to ensure that power can be delegated, assumed, and shared appropriately and effectively.

These chapters all highlight that collaboration and cooperation across organizations should not be left to chance or allowed to stagnate. Organizations are in many ways organic—constantly changing, sometimes growing, sometimes shrinking, with new people and departing people. HR must play a leadership role in ensuring that an organization is structured and operates with systems, processes, and conditions designed to maximize the free flow of information and ideas within it.

CHAPTER 35

TEAMWORK: THE NEW EMPHASIS ON TWO-SIDED ACCOUNTABILITY

SAMUEL A. CULBERT AND JEAN-FRANÇOIS COGET

Accountability! Stop and think about it. How often do you worry about holding someone accountable when you see the person performing sensibly, appearing on course to deliver the results you expect? Probably never. The construct *accountability* usually gets used only when we see people not giving us what we want or when we have evidence that they are letting us and the organization down. Then accountability becomes a finger-pointing construct for placing blame on others and meting out penalties that we think will deter repeat performances. No matter how high-minded and organizationally essential our cause, however, in almost every instance distrust becomes the predictable second-order outcome. Thus, the connection to HR is apparent. Inside the corporation, HR should be in the fair-play, trust building, and team-building business, all elements of performance assurance and accountability.

Until recently, holding someone accountable was a privilege reserved for hierarchical superiors wanting to take the moral high ground to claim that an errant subordinate, who knew better, had not performed as there was good reason to expect. But why did the subordinate fail to produce the wanted results? Did that person think he or she had the resources, perspectives, opportunities, and jurisdictions to do so? Probably not. Thus, in corporate settings, the intellectually well-intentioned mechanism of accountability deteriorates to people lower down in the hierarchy being blamed for not producing what a higher-up wants. Meanwhile, the alleged nonperformer futilely blames those whose actions or inaction made it impossible to produce what was wanted, with the buck passing around and down the hierarchical chain. But how does this glitch get resolved? Certainly it is a situation that begs for HR leadership and intervention.

Traditionally HR has acted as the "enforcer," siding with the finger-pointer who has the most hierarchical power. By invoking procedures, methods, and review processes to justify penalties proposed and meted out, HR implicitly endorsed an outmoded hierarchical model. It allowed bosses to unilaterally hold accountable the very people they hired and whose success they were supposed to ensure. But isn't the standard charge for bosses to guide, coach, support, and provide oversight and critique to the people to whom they assign work and who report to them? Thus, shouldn't any performance failure also be considered a failure in staging, guidance, and oversight caused by insufficient teamwork from the top?

Approaching this issue another way, you can say whatever you want about intraorganizational cooperation and teamwork, but the one team that has to work well is the boss teaming up with his or her direct reports. However, the conventional use of accountability belies this taking place; too many bosses find a way to succeed while the people they recruited, whose success they were supposed to ensure, falter and fail. Hence the opportunity for human resource professionals. They need to change the emphasis of company-wide evaluation procedures that attempt to exact accountability after an errant performance has been made, to focus on progressive teamwork thinking and the implementation of two-sided accountable boss-subordinate relationships that weld the boss to his or her role in assuring that organizationally appropriate and competent performances are being made.

We have found getting the organization chart straight to be the starting point for implementing effective, teamwork-oriented systems of accountability. The guidelines and logic for getting the chart straight are matter of fact and grounded in positive answers to a few simple questions. First, are core functions clearly stipulated and nonredundantly described so that chart viewers can readily determine which person has responsibility for what function? Core functions sometimes are split up—marketing into advertising and sales, or advertising into business and creative, or engineering into engineering, international engineering, and manufacturing engineering, without functions converging on a single individual. Attempts at getting people to stand accountable for negative results may then quickly deteriorate into jurisdictional disputes as people point fingers to avoid accepting responsibility for what fell through the cracks because jurisdictions never came together on the chart.[1]

Second, do people portrayed on the chart as responsible for a function actually have the authority to make decisions bearing on that responsibility? If they do not, you can never be confident that they will stand accountable. Worse than that, you can expect systemic close-mindedness and defensiveness as operatives who lack decision-making authority excessively defend the courses they would like to take in order to purchase authorization and buy-in from above. If they knew in advance that the decision was theirs to make, they would be less quick to counterargue alternative suggestions even before they heard them out. They would be more likely to open-mindedly seek out the reasoning behind the ideas of others realizing that before-the-fact rejection of good ideas would be held against them if end results proved insufficient.

Third, are the superiors' actions when providing oversight and direction sufficiently documented to allow failures of guidance, lack of support, or reversals of subordinate-made decisions to be traced back to them? For the hierarchical chain of command to operate effectively, no boss should have the ability to separate him- or herself from the efforts, results, and commitments of direct reports. Accountability needs to be thought of as a reciprocal, two-sided relationship activity. Now we are at the crux of our prescription. How do you get two-sided accountability? How does such a relationship work?

Whereas a clear and clean hierarchical chart is the basic tool for enforcing accountability, the commonplace practice of importing hierarchy into managerial relationships is the deal-breaker. Hierarchical relationships, not hierarchical structure, make subordinates bend the truth to tell superiors what they want to hear. Such relationships also allow superiors to believe they heard information straight while bending the truth themselves for consumption to their own superiors. When it comes to accountability, a well-done hierarchical chart may be essential, but hierarchical relationships corrupt the process.

The defining characteristic of hierarchical relationships is one-sided accountability—bosses with the motives and means to hold subordinates accountable without subordinates having the reciprocal.[2] HR professionals have been honing in on this issue for years and coming up with a succession of evaluation plans aimed at getting accountability from bosses, such as 360-degree reviews and team effectiveness surveys. In practice, however, most of the formats used amount to no more than sophisticated spy systems, providing power to HR professionals who reserve the right to interpret "confidential" comments and to score them. Two-sided accountability requires direct face-to-face, boss-subordinate relationships, not power-taking intermediaries.

When restructuring relationships for two-sided accountability, it is important to remember that two-sided means reciprocal, not mirrored. Accountability is different for operatives and overseers. On the one hand, operatives should be accountable for making the right inputs correctly, for achieving results even when they require inputs that were not previously specified, and for commitments to the organizational objectives underlying the operation at hand while observing socially prescribed rules for fair play and human conduct. On the other hand, overseers should be accountable for focusing goals and framing objectives, for creating and fixing the systems, establishing the conditions and circumstances for people to operate without distraction, and for providing operatives the resources to advance on organizational objectives effectively. Adding upward accountability to downward accountability produces organizational accountability and system connectedness while staging people for teamwork and personal effectiveness. This is why we say teamwork at the top is essential. Without it, evaluation and performance do not connect.

To get this connection, the conventional boss-subordinate relationship needs revising. Structures that support self-honest consciousness, candid give-and-take, and truthful statements of what participants think and believe, need to be in place prior to the person with decision-making authority deciding on a course of action. What we are aiming for is a boss-subordinate two-sided communication that embodies teamwork at the top.

Conventional practice has bosses attempting to establish accountability by asking operatives, before the fact, "Are you clear about what we expect in the way of results?" Two-sided accountability adds a teamwork-producing question, "What do you need *from me,* for you to do what you believe you need to do, to produce the results you are after?" And, we might add that the boss should further request, "Could you be more precise about what you are after and specifically how you plan to get it?" The key issue in connecting evaluation and performance to create teamwork at the top, is finding out how the person on whom you and the organization are depending for positive results sees the situation and, importantly, what supports that person will need. Using this logic, you quickly see that the optimal time to think about organizational accountability is before an activity takes place, not after. When there are disappointments, the accountability questions should, two-sidedly, include inquiry to determine whether, where, and how the boss let the errant performer down.

Finally, and we cannot emphasize this strongly enough, accountability is an empty concept without consequences. Most often consequences mean penalties, but they can and should include a recitation of lessons learned and personal resolve to operate differently with visible evidence to demonstrate implementation is actually doable. The latter can be substituted for penalties. When lessons learned are put to use, in contrast to lip-service acknowledgment, the organization benefits from having enlightened resources that supplant a previous liability. For that to take place, however, lessons learned need to go up the hierarchical chain, not just down. The tide of actions that produce disappointing results and accountability glitches are stemmed only after each level of the hierarchy performs its own reconnaissance of self- and domain-lessons learned.

Because these thinking patterns and format are not standard operating practices today, there is a role for HR as system enhancers to vet organization charts. They need to see that organizations conform to the previously mentioned list of accountability stipulations. Human resource consultants can help managers and operatives to extricate themselves from years of practiced incompetence in stepping up to two-sided relationships that provide accountable teamwork from the top.

NOTES

1. A vivid example of this is seen in the Abu Ghraib prison outrage where the guards, MPs, and civilian interrogators (aka CIA) each reported to different commands. These functions did not come together on a single chart so that after-the-fact attempts to place accountability became an exercise in scapegoat futility.
2. For a more thoroughgoing analysis of this phenomenon and exemplar remedies proposed, see S. A. Culbert and J. B. Ullmen, *Don't Kill the Bosses!* San Francisco: Berrett-Koehler, 2001.

CHAPTER 36

MANAGING COOPERATIVELY WITHIN ORGANIZATIONS

LYNDA GRATTON

One of the most challenging issues an executive team will face over the next decade is how to encourage cooperative working within teams, and across the internal and external boundaries of the company. The reason is simple. Much of the value creation opportunities within an organization occur when people work cooperatively across boundaries. This became clear to us as my colleagues and I researched a group of high-performing companies. Here I consider four of these high performers: the mobile phone company Nokia, the oil company BP, the advertising company OgilvyOne, and Royal Bank of Scotland (RBS), the retail bank. Our research into these companies shows that in each one, the executive team believed the capacity to work cooperatively across borders was a key to the company's success.

At Nokia, we heard CEO Jorma Ollila describe how the innovative capacity of the company increasingly springs from multifunctional teams working together to bring new insights into products and services. At BP, CEO John Browne described the peer group process, which he believes to be key to the company's performance. He is certain that the real knowledge sharing from "best in class" across BP requires the business unit managers from all the 120 companies of BP to actively share their knowledge, insights, and wisdom with each other. At OgilvyOne, CEO Reimer Theddens described how their global clients, such as American Express, increasingly judge their suppliers and partners on their capacity to stitch together the parts of the company to create a seamless global service. CEO

Fred Goodwin, at RBS, explained that the full extent of the best-in-world cost base enjoyed by RBS has only been realized because the various businesses and functions of RBS are all committed and able to operate from common shared platforms. Managing these horizontal boundaries, between functions, between businesses, and between geographies is a key feature in the topography of companies, and their management is a key source of competitive advantage.[1]

In managing across these horizontal boundaries, what role, if any, can the HR function play? In each of these four companies, the HR function played a crucial role in designing the practices, processes, and structures that create the levers for horizontal working. But to do so, these HR professionals had to learn a whole new vocabulary and a new lens by which they viewed their company.

To understand this lens, we need to look at research in organizational effectiveness. For some years now, academic researchers have been fascinated in understanding cooperative working within and across teams. We have used the term *social capital* to describe the extent of these positive cooperative relationships. Through the lens of social capital, we are describing the company as a complex network of acquaintances and friendships, some of which bridge across groups.

THE VOCABULARY OF SOCIAL CAPITAL

To understand cooperative, cross-boundary working, let us take a closer look at the theory of social capital.[2] Cross-boundary working is essentially about the quality and extent of the relationship between people. The building blocks are the relationship ties that develop initially between two people. These begin as *weak ties* when people are merely acquaintances. Over time, some of these ties will remain weak or decay; others will strengthen and become *strong ties* if people have an opportunity to spend time with each other as they are engaged in a shared task, and if they begin to like and trust each other. The network ties within groups are called *bonding ties;* those between groups are called *bridging ties*. Tie strength and tie formations are described in more detail in Table 36.1. We have discovered that the extent and the combination of strong and weak bridging ties are what is essential to the cooperative, cross-boundary working.

Table 36.1
The Elements of Social Capital

	Tie Strength
Strong ties	Created when two people know each other well. There is trust between them, and they have some affection for each other. Occurs when people have an opportunity to spend time with each other on a shared task.
Weak ties	Formed when people are acquainted with each other but have spent little time with each other. These relationships are positive but not as affectionate as strong ties. Some weak ties will be the result of historical strong ties that have now decayed. Others will remain weak ties over time, while a proportion will form into strong ties as people spend more time with each other.
	Tie Formation
Bridging ties	Relationship ties between two people who are in different groups. Within the company, they could be from different functions, different businesses, or live in different countries. They could also be with people from outside the company.
Bonding ties	Relationship ties between people in the same group. These are ties within rather than across boundaries.

We have also discovered that there is no one optimal structure of net-work ties for all companies. The optimal structure depends on the specific tasks of the group and the pace of change. However, the savvy HR professional should consider several design parameters:

- Strong, bonding ties are appropriate in groups where the task is to share and develop complex, tacit knowledge. The depth and strength of these relationships between people within teams enable them to share and discuss knowledge at a deep level. At OgilvyOne, strong bonding ties were maintained within the design teams whose members had worked together for many years on a client account.
- Strong, bridging ties are essential where there is a need to share complex information across groups. The twelve business unit managers in each peer group at BP meet frequently to exchange ideas and insights.
- Weak bridging ties enable what has been termed an *adaptive field* to emerge when there are many bridging ties across the boundaries of

the company. We found this adaptive field at Nokia. Here the network of ties both within and outside the company to partners and research establishments across the world, enabled the company to adapt quickly to the fast-changing environment in which Nokia operates.

The Levers and Tools That Can Affect the Creation of Network Ties

I am interested in the role, if any, that the HR teams in these companies played in the creating network ties. These ties cannot be forced. The HR teams were clear that bringing people together in task forces, for example, may not necessarily result in members of the task force actually liking one another and being prepared to cooperate with each other in the future. They had learned that serendipity played an important role. So the role of the HR professional is to create the space and circumstances for serendipity to occur. Four levers are available for them to do this:

1. Through the active management of *proximity* (who meets whom)
2. Through the provision of *time* (how much time do people spend together)
3. By crafting a *motivation* for people to work together through shared tasks (what is it the people are working on)
4. With a *culture* of trust and respect (how at ease are people with each other, and what is their propensity to trust each other)

How then do the executive team and the HR group actually work these four levers? We found that two sets of tools appeared to be crucially important. The first was the *organizational architecture* of the company. This structural architecture—who reports to whom—establishes the power and decision-making structure of the company, and therefore impacts the lever of motivation. The structural architecture also influences the formation of teams and task forces (hence influencing the lever of proximity); consider here the peer group structure at BP. Finally, the frequency of changes in the organizational architecture determines the speed with which the teams and boundaries are reconfigured (and therefore the lever of time).

Figure 36.1
A Model for Considering Ties

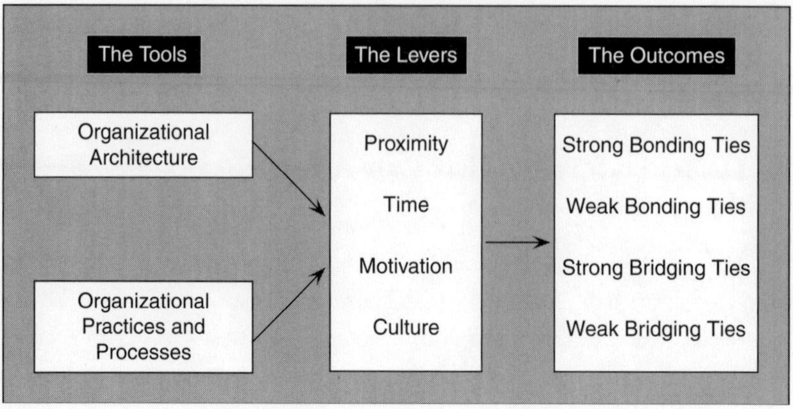

The second set of tools in the kit bag of the HR team are the *practices and processes* of the company that establish the day-to-day routines. These practices and processes can create the task forces and project teams that establish proximity and build motivation through an exciting, shared goal. We saw this at RBS where the HR team is adept at building task forces around managing change. Practices and processes can also build the motivation to collaborate. The remuneration system at BP encourages and rewards business unit managers to work cooperatively in bridging roles (see Figure 36.1).

BUILDING NETWORK TIES AT NOKIA

We found that Nokia had five key tools that seemed to be crucial in supporting the serendipitous creation of strong and weak bonding and bridging ties. One was an aspect of the organizational architecture of Nokia (the modular structure). Two were organizational practices (the practice of creating business strategy through the strategy road map practice, and the practice of linking into universities). Three were HR processes (job rotation and induction). We considered the extent to which each of these five tools affected tie strength, and the extent to which they affected tie formation. Each was then placed on the tie strength/tie formation matrix shown in Figure 36.2. The shape of each circular form approximates the impact it has

Figure 36.2
The Formation of Network Ties at Nokia

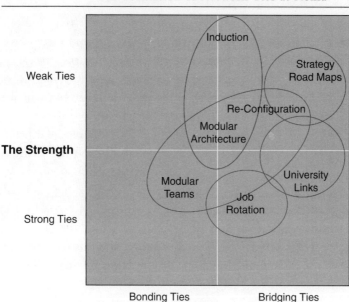

on network formation. In the case of the modular structure, the two elements (within modular team and reconfiguration) are shown separately.

The modular architecture, the structural architecture of Nokia, makes a significant contribution to the creation of what we earlier called an adaptive field. This is a mix of both strong and weak bonding and bridging ties. To achieve this mix, the structural architecture of Nokia is essentially modular in its form. As Mikko Kosonen, senior vice president (SVP) of Strategy and Business Information, describes it:

> One of the distinctive characteristics of Nokia is the organizational architecture. It is avant garde. It fits with the turbulence and an opportunity rich environment. Reconfigurable, modularity, re-usable capabilities.[3]

Beneath this modularity lies a common global platform that delivers a single system for logistics, human resources, finances, and other transactions.

Sitting on this common platform are the modules that combine business groups and core horizontal processes. Following the 2004 reorganization of Nokia, the company had four customer-orientated business areas (mobile phones, multimedia, networks, and enterprise solutions) and three horizontal entities (customer and operations; technology platforms; research, venturing, and business infrastructure). This structure was made up of many modular teams of people who remain within their teams but who are reconfigured with other teams.

So, despite the rapid reorganizations of Nokia, the basic modular teams working on an aspect of the business remain the same. Even in the midst of reorganization, the strong bonding ties within the modular teams remain intact (see Figure 36.2). These modular teams, which can be as small as 20 people for some subprocesses, typically have worked together for as little as 6 months, and as long as 12 years. During this time they have developed a high degree of expertise and shared tacit knowledge. In a sense, these modular teams with strong bonding ties are the guardians of the key process knowledge at Nokia.

Yet, while the intact modular teams remain together for an extended period, the boundaries between the teams change as they are relocated. These relocations involve the modular teams working with people from other modular teams on a common process or task. So with each successive reorganization, the members of the team trail behind them some of the old bridging ties they established in the previous structure. Those relationships that are sufficiently strong may well remain as strong bridging ties. Others will decay over time as lack of proximity and a joint project erodes the basis of the relationship.

The strategic road mappings, by which the people across Nokia create the maps for the future, serve to build an environment for forming weak bridging ties. This practice creates an opportunity for people from all parts of the company to work with each other intensely on a common topic over a relatively short period. As a consequence, strategy creation makes use of the levers of proximity, time, and the motivation of a shared topic. The strategic road mapping begins every six months with the executive team identifying the five to fifteen issues they believe will be crucial to Nokia's success going forward. Around each issue, the sponsoring senior executive handpicks a multifunctional team of 10 to 20 people to work intensely with each other for a four-month period. These teams then have conversations with each other and with people within Nokia, with Nokia's partners, and with external individuals. So, during the course of a year, about 400 people across Nokia have the opportunity to create weak bridging ties with many other people. Some of these ties will become strong as team members meet people whom they like and want to continue being associated with after the completion of the project.

The practice of linking to universities, of building links to universities, ensures that there are strong bridging ties between members of the firm and the faculties of up to twenty prime universities around the world. These relationships are deepened by faculty members of these prime universities and members of Nokia meeting frequently to exchange ideas. Weaker bridging ties are formed between members of Nokia and faculty from a further one hundred universities. Students from all these universities are invited to participate in summer internships and to work with the Nokia teams.

The induction process, for every new member of Nokia and an employee new to a team, has the potential to create weak ties between those new to a job and those around them. Managers are obliged to formally introduce all new joiners of their team to at least 15 people from within and outside the team. Those ties with people outside the team will begin as weak bridging ties, but over time, some will strengthen into strong bridging ties as the joiners build stronger relationships with people outside the group whom they trust and respect.

The job rotation process, the way in which people are inducted into their roles, creates the context for creating bridging ties. The same is true of the practice of job rotation. A hallmark of the internal labor market at Nokia is the preference, in the words of one senior executive, to "put people into coats that are much too large for them." The company abounds with stories of relatively young people assuming positions in which they have very limited experience. The philosophy is clear: After three to five years, most people are operating in their comfort zones and it is time for them to do something completely different. These job leaps typically take place across countries, across functions, or across the processes of the company. Occasionally, they involve jumping all three boundaries at one time. As these jumps across boundaries occur, people trail with them some of the old bonding ties they had established within their previous team. In their move, these old bonding ties will become bridging ties. At the same time, the job movers may well introduce colleagues from their previous team to members of their current team. This begins to build weak bridging ties.

THE HR ROLE IN BUILDING NETWORK TIES

In attempting to build network ties, the HR professional is faced with two challenges. First, there is no ideal network structure that can be the template for their interventions. Like much in HR, the key is to think contextually; what matters is whether the networks are in sync with the company tasks and goals. However, we do know that for companies operating in dynamic environments, the combination of strong and weak bridging ties (the adaptive field) may be crucial to their success. The second challenge is the nature of social capital, and the network ties that create it. Social capital is essentially a by-product of other processes. It arises through serendipity, not as a result of mechanistic interventions.

So given these two challenges, what opportunities are open to managers and HR professionals to make a difference in this area of organizational competence? Most crucially, they need to begin to understand what social capital is, and become familiar with the models that frame its creation. Taking a look at the model presented earlier, there are three sets of issues and questions the HR professional should discuss and reflect on:

1. Taking the goals of the company as a starting point, they can begin to map what sort of configuration of network ties would be most useful to meet these goals. There will be tasks of the company in which long-term bonding ties are critical; there will be others where bridging ties would make a real difference. The question here is, "To meet the goals of the company, who needs to know whom (bonding and bridging ties) and how well do they need to know and respect each other (weak and strong ties)."

2. Next, they need to consider the four points of leverage available to them. With regard to proximity, the question would be, "Are the people who need to get to know each other physically located

together (bonding ties), or alternatively, do they have an opportunity to frequently meet (bridging ties)?" With regard to time, the question will be, "Are people who need to get to know each other well (create strong ties) given the time and space to do so?" For motivation, the question will be, "Are the tasks in which people are engaged sufficiently exciting and the goals sufficiently clear and aspiring for people to really want to collaborate with each other?" In terms of culture, the question is, "Is the culture sufficiently respectful and trusting for people to naturally cooperate with each other?"

3. Finally, they can take a look at the practices and processes of the company in the light of their understanding of the outcomes and the levers. The questions for reflection are, "Are there current practices and processes that are destroying social capital?" (e.g., combative succession processes and individual remuneration schemes that pit people against each other will destroy goodwill and a collaborative mind-set). Next, "What are we currently doing that enhances network ties and that we could strengthen over time?" (e.g., the peer groups at BP are the product of years of enhancing and strengthening a rather simple process of group sharing that John Browne and his team developed over a decade ago). Finally, "What new practices and processes can we develop that will really make a difference?"

In considering how the HR function can make a difference to this crucial area of organizational performance, I have followed my own biases on the role of the function. My first bias is that HR members should and must become initially familiar with, and later sophisticated in, leading-edge thinking. The field of social capital and network configuration represents such an opportunity. Next, my bias is to move from the goals of the company and take these as a starting point. In that sense I am essentially contextual in my view instead of "one size fits all." Finally, the focus should be primarily on building and enhancing what the organization is currently capable of, not on importing vast swathes of "best practice" from other companies that may or may not be appropriate.

NOTES

1. The importance of the forces of integration has been described in S. Ghoshal and L. Gratton, 2002, Integrating the Enterprise, *Sloan Management Review,* 44: 31–38.
2. There is a growing body of academic research on social capital. A recent review of the literature is provided in P. Adler and S. W. Kwon, 2002, Social Capital: Prospects for a New Concept, *Academy of Management Review,* 27: 17–40. The idea of task directed and serendipitous development has been explored by M. Kilduff and W. Tsai, 2003, *Social Networks in Organizations.* London: Sage.
3. Kosonen, Mikko. (2004). Nokia: The Challenge of Continuous Renewal, London Business Case.

CHAPTER 37

POWER, THE LAST
CORPORATE TABOO

PATRICIA SEEMANN

Leadership is a great thing. We all want some, lots of it, so any company worth its salt has some kind of leadership program going. Some are better than others, but they all stop short at tackling a key issue: power. Yet, well-exercised power is fundamental to the performance of the firm because it provides predictability and reliability.

The most important signs of well-exercised power are: (1) There is a clear sense of direction throughout the firm, (2) promises are kept, and (3) accountability and responsibility are clear and unequivocal.

Leadership programs have the vital purpose of embedding a common understanding of the company's norms and values, a description of the attributes of what the firm defines as good leadership, and how that will contribute to its business performance.

To achieve full impact, leadership programs should be complemented with a clear view of power, how it is achieved, acceptable ways of exerting it, the responsibilities that go with it, what to do when it is abused, and what we do when some fail to take the responsibility to exercise power commensurate with their position and role.

There are different kinds of power in an organization. For instance, some are institutional ("I am the boss; you are not"), some are inherent to the person ("He's the kind of guy I'd like to work for"), and some are often both. In this chapter, we focus on the institutionalized power of the CEO because how he or she deals with it models many behaviors in the firm and, therefore, has critical and lasting consequences. We discuss the issues the CEO must tackle and how HR executives can support that process.

WHY IS POWER SO DIFFICULT TO DEAL WITH?

Power is an uncomfortable topic. Power is emotional—there is no indifference in the presence of power. Those who don't have it often fear its presence or grow intensely jealous of the ones who do. Those who have it are sometimes frightened by the responsibility it brings. Many enjoy having it, some are obsessed by it, and some just get plain drunk on it. Some amass as much as possible and ferociously defend it. Others try to keep as little as possible, limiting themselves to what is absolutely necessary to get the job done.

The other issue is that power is usually associated in people's minds mainly (sometimes only) with its abuse. In the political and corporate realm, power raises suspicion. Perhaps only religious leaders have a chance to avoid the accusation of seeking and using power to further their own agendas.

Yet, we confer power on people every day—in the public realm by electing them and in the corporate realm by appointing them to an office. A CEO, for instance, has a huge amount of power in the organization. CEOs are given that power with a purpose and as a responsibility, not as a perk. They are vested with power so that they can get things done—to achieve purpose so they can lead. Thus, a CEO's effectiveness in using power is pivotal to the firm's (and his or her) success.

WHY SHOULD HR EXECUTIVES CARE?

HR professionals play an important role in ensuring that power is exercised well and in the best interest of the firm. They often are confidants of the CEO, especially if they are competent. HR executives tend to have a very good sense of the state of mind of the firm. Also, they are "safe" to confide in because they are rarely contestants for the CEO's job.

But it is not only the CEO who is more likely to seek the advice of HR leaders. HR touches all functions, which gives HR leaders a unique perspective on the firm, one that bridges functions and departments.

Finally, HR executives themselves hold a considerable amount of power. For instance, they have significant influence on so many issues people at work care about: compensation and benefits, employment and promotions, training and career development, supervision and employee relations, diversity, culture, ethics, and so on.

POWER MATTERS FOR PERFORMANCE

It is puzzling that power is hardly ever addressed explicitly. Certainly, it usually grabs the headlines in daily corridor gossip about corporate politics (Who is really in charge here? Who has the boss's ear? Who is trying to trip up whom? Who is getting ahead, why, and how?).

E. Rosabeth Moss Kanter, the Ernest L. Arbuckle Professor of Business Administration at Harvard Business School, once said that power is America's last four-letter word—that we can use any four-letter word today, in pretty much any setting, but power is only whispered, alluded to, and vaguely hinted at, as if it were an indecent or, at the very least, unsavory topic.

It is important to make power an explicit object of debate and attention. Do not leave it as a dark force veiled behind politically correct statements by, for example, exhorting the "team" when really one person is in charge—and that person has no intention of working through others. This is as good a breeding ground for nefarious politics as standing water is for the mosquitoes in Maine.

Well-defined, exercised, and controlled power is fundamental to the smooth and effective workings in an organization. For instance, hesitation or reluctance in addressing and using power can be just as problematic as its abuse (which is what we usually worry about). When a CEO does not exercise power even though he or she should, others will—leading to confusion and eroding confidence among employees because the way in which the firm works becomes unpredictable and unreliable. And predictability and reliability are the key foundations of trust in an organization.

What power is used for, how it is applied and projected into the firm, how its abuse is hedged against and sanctioned, and so on hugely influence the culture of a firm. Whether people sense that the leaders in the organization use power for their personal aggrandizement or for the betterment of the firm defines in great measure how work gets done, how decisions are made, and what kind of loyalty and commitment people will develop.

In more formal terms, the underlying purpose of corporate hierarchies (VP, supervisor, etc.) is to articulate who has the power to issue what kind of orders, make decisions, assume responsibility (that, too, is a form of power), and who has to be subservient to them.

HOW DO YOU WRAP YOUR HEAD AROUND THE ISSUE OF POWER?

Let's start with the power that American CEOs are given (it can be different in other countries, according to local jurisdiction) and what they can do with it. They have three types of power: the power to set expectations, the power to delegate decision making, and the power to control and demand accountability.

To project power into the organization, they do essentially three things: set the direction of the firm, select its leadership team and determine its culture, and manage and guard the reputation (as in brand, communications, etc.) of the organization.

To be helpful to the CEO, HR executives must have the right to inform, warn, and encourage. This may sound obvious, but it isn't. Often, we see CEOs who don't think that it is HR's "place" to address these issues proactively, and, in other instances, we see HR executives who hesitate because they don't think it is their role. But we think it most definitely is. Even if the CEO chooses to hire an external coach, the coaching process will be so much more effective if collaboration with HR works well.

There are three key roles for HR in helping CEOs think through and decide on issues surrounding their power.

First is making sure that CEOs have all the information and knowledge they need to think this power issue through and to the greatest extent possible can understand and anticipate the consequences of the way they exercise power. HR executives need to have a sound understanding of the goals and aspirations of the CEOs and the empathy and ability (as well as the courage) to push back productively to warn, encourage, and support their CEO.

Second, once CEOs make up their minds about power, either on their own (preferably not) or through intense debate with their team and the people in the firm (better), HR needs to help translate this decision throughout the firm and understand and stay current with how the exercise of power influences the subtle and yet strong cultural dynamics.

The third role is to help the CEO create structures, systems, and processes that ensure that power can be delegated, assumed, and shared appropriately and effectively.

Power, Responsibility, and Corporate Impotence

One of the key things to consider is that power and responsibility go together. Power is not only a right; it is also a responsibility. When you separate the two, anger, frustration, and confusion result.

If someone is responsible for a decision, activity, or process, you must allow the necessary power to go along with that responsibility. Often, people are asked to make decisions but have no power to enforce them, or they find themselves endlessly second-guessed by someone else in the chain of command.

Consider the role of the project manager of large, complex projects such as developing drugs. A frequent source of frustration is being responsible for time lines to be met but having no power over the project team members. This situation is one of the great dilemmas of matrix organizations, and it is what has given the concept such a bad name.

Checks, Balances, and Corporate Swamps

Often, responsibility and power are segregated in the interest of so-called checks and balances. Checks and balances are supposed to ensure control and guard against abuse or malfeasance. However, often they proliferate. No one is in charge, no one takes charge, no one is responsible, and everybody who wishes to do so can hide behind the vague mass of people and debates in an organization.

If the concern driving the construction of organizational systems is corporate malfeasance, we should remind ourselves that nothing is more discouraging of improper behavior than the knowledge that responsibility and accountability can always be tracked to an individual.

Power, Experts, and 800-Pound Gorillas

If the concern is the quality of decision, then we need to be careful that only people who are respected by their peers and valued for their contributions, expertise, and leadership are involved in decision making. Often, though, we see that people can involve themselves in (or interfere with) decision-making processes mainly because they want to demonstrate their impor-tance and status. This situation is highly frustrating and at times insulting to those who really add value.

Consider again the situation of experts in drug development. In a reengi-neering project at a major pharmaceutical firm, it became apparent that 52 people had to sign off on reports of clinical studies. Only about 5 were in a position to judge the content. Yet, 47 others had the "chance" (and some-times took it just for the sake of drawing attention to themselves) to delay the projects, either, for example, by just not getting around to signing or by giving uninformed opinions that would throw the entire project into an-other round of discussions and arguments. The latter scenario was the more prevalent the more senior the signing executives were.

HELPING THE CEO, A WORK
LIST OF SORTS

As stated, HR executives need to have the right to inform, warn, and en-courage their CEOs in the use of power. HR should work with the CEO and, in an adapted form, anyone with power in an organization to answer the following questions as a first phase:

- What values and responsibility do I attach to power? For instance, do I see it as a right, a responsibility, or a burden?

    —People around a person with power will sense this power, no matter what is said. Authenticity is a critical component of the re-spect a person with power commands.
- What is the purpose of my power? Value creation for shareholders? A work life of dignity and meaning for the employees?

    —The use to which power is applied hugely influences the culture of a firm. Value creation for shareholders is likely to generate a very tough, short-term, pragmatic culture; a dignified, meaningful work life is likely to generate a softer, empowering, and longer term working environment.
- What kind of power do I need? What can I delegate?

    —Power generates resistance. Thus, delegate as much as possible. After all, any exercise of power in some way limits what others can do because a decision in which a particular course of action is chosen eliminates the others. Some may not agree and try to get into a position where they can challenge power.

- Given the culture of the firm, how is power best exercised? What do people expect?

    —What may be seen as assertive, for example, in the military, may be considered coercive in a different setting. Understanding the culture is important. The way in which power is exercised can nurture, change, disrupt, and destroy a culture. Depending on the culture, the company needs to develop to successfully pursue its strategic intent. The way in which power is exercised is an important tool in bringing about change, even if you didn't intend to.

- Where do I hesitate to exercise my power? Why?

    —Is it in firing people who are obstructing the strategy, in speaking my mind, or in reaching out to support? Understanding where those hesitations are and knowing how to deal with them are critical for the effective exercise of power.

- How do I make sure that I stay real—that I don't lose touch with the reality of those who are subjected to or rely on my power?

    —The boss who has lost reality is a caricature. But we all know it happens—and never believe it can happen to us. Yet, leaders need to make sure that they have personal power hygiene processes. For example, make sure that they expose themselves at times to social settings where the fact that they are a CEO is irrelevant.

- How will I deal with disloyalty and betrayal?

    —Often, people in power do not even entertain the possibility of disloyalty or betrayal, either because they are naïve (people around me are too decent to do that) or arrogant (they couldn't get it together even if they wanted to) or inexperienced. Power is a highly desired commodity; therefore, betrayal is an inherent risk to anyone in power, so think this possibility through like any other risk and be clear how you would deal with it if it occurs.

    —One thing is for sure: Tolerating disloyalty or even betrayal severely weakens the person in charge. Those who are loyal (often at a cost to themselves) feel betrayed because toleration suggests that disloyalty is fine and invites imitators to break promises, to mislead, and to be less than truthful—which is toxic to any organization.

SUMMARY

The effective and appropriate use of power is a critical element in ensuring a firm's reliability and predictability. HR executives are best positioned to:

- Help a CEO think through and decide how he or she intends to use and project the power. HR executives are the ones who can provide the context that CEOs need to make the right decision. They have the right to inform, warn, and encourage the CEO.
- Support the design and implementation of effective and appropriate organizational structures, which ensure that power is delegated in such a way that it supports high-quality decision making throughout the firm.
- Be the whistleblowers on inappropriate use (or lack of effective use) in the organization.

HR has been quite successful in recent years in bringing the topic of leadership to the fore and in improving standards and norms. Now could be the time to go a step further and to take a hard look at power to ensure that it is exercised to the benefit of the firm and its stakeholders.

SECTION VIII

RESPONDING TO SOCIAL EXPECTATIONS AND PUBLIC POLICY AND THE RENEWED IMPORTANCE OF ETHICS

In our prior book, *Tomorrow's HR Management: 48 Thought Leaders Call for Change* (New York: John Wiley & Sons, 1997), we stressed that advocacy and ethics were critical HR requirements. Since then, management ethical lapses and corporate fraud have shown just how much damage can be done when such standards are compromised and violated.

Many HR professionals have been tested through these difficult times. Some have found it necessary to put themselves at risk to maintain their ethical standards. Unfortunately, others have compromised the profession's ethical standards. A perverse benefit to some HR professionals was being spared simply because they were not considered important enough to be part of the senior management team who acted unethically.

We have sadly learned that ethics is not merely morality but also impacts credibility and eventually firm success. This happens when the lack of ethical conduct leads to an erosion of trust by those who depend on or contribute to organizational achievement. Employees leave or lose motivation. Customers chose to go elsewhere. Those who invest money based on intangibles such as trust as much as financial returns are quick to depart as well. Clear, viable, and practical ethical conduct can increase employee commitment, customer share, and investor confidence.

331

HR must play an important and fundamental role in organizational ethics and public policy. For instance, HR must play a role in:

- Helping determine an organization's ethics and other public policies.
- Developing supportive procedures, training, and communications.
- Creating a culture where ethics and related, proactive conduct are valued.
- Fostering an environment where violations will be reported.
- Conducting investigations and applying discipline, when needed.

Also, HR must be sufficiently involved in organizational operations to be able to recognize and act on ethical violations and other important public policy issues. Only then will HR be viewed as a responsible management group to whom, for instance, violations can be reported.

In this section, Richard Beaumont draws on his many years of experience to suggest that HR leaders are the most appropriate management representatives to help develop a more systematic approach to social and public policy issues. In Chapter 38, Dick reviews an approach to how to identify those issues that have little visibility today but could become significant public and/or government concerns in the future.

Frances Hasselbein in Chapter 39 sees HR moving across the whole organization with total involvement. Dynamic changes, she advances, will cause HR to help develop and protect employees who are, after all, any organization's greatest asset.

Patricia Harned suggests in Chapter 40 that ethics is part and parcel of HR. But she also highlights the contradiction of many HR professionals' feeling that although they are not "part of the ethics infrastructure," they are tasked with "cleaning up the ethical messes." Her chapter lays out a plan for HR to take a leading role.

Ethics has always been an integral part of defining a legitimate profession. Current events and anticipated challenges will make ethics and public policy issue even more important.

In addition to discussing the educational, skill, and managerial requirements of the profession, the chapters in this section highlight how HR can frame its contribution to organizational ethics and public policy success.

CHAPTER 38

A CHALLENGE TO HR: BUILDING THE COMPANY'S EXTERNAL DIMENSION

RICHARD A. BEAUMONT

Over some 45 years of experience, working with and in companies and the federal government, I have learned that, for all the folklore about the power of management and all the talent and might of large companies, they are less effective than they should be in dealing with public and social policy developments at both the national and international levels. It is not that companies lack an interest in many of these issues; typical corporate organization does not allow for a clear focus on many issues, especially when they develop over long periods of time.

In this chapter, I argue that HR leaders are the most appropriate ones to help develop a more systematic approach to social and public policy issues. And the matter is urgent to deal with—illustrated by the growing public attention currently being given to the behavior of a few companies that clearly violated both written and unwritten ethical standards of business conduct in the United States and abroad.

Increasing global and national competition puts many demands on an organization. And it is generally agreed that HR will play an increasingly important role contributing to the achievement of business objectives. Unfortunately, operating results have sometimes been trumped by the lack of foresight and action on public policy and social issues.

The recent business ethics scandals are but a current example—causing many organizations catastrophic, permanent damage. The toll on individuals, employees, shareholders, and communities for this lack of management foresight is an even greater cost.

333

These experiences fortify my conclusion that social and public policy issues are not remote "soft" issues. They are "hard" issues requiring management attention, focus, and skill. This conclusion has encouraged me to
suggest that the HR function is the place in the corporation where the initiative for social and public policy issues must rest.

CHALLENGES—FROM THE COALMINES TO THE GLOBAL WORLD

At the dawn of the corporate era, the biggest businesses were managed by
their owners. And the most farsighted of these hands-on owners recognized
the societal responsibilities of their organizations. The most prominent of
these "welfare capitalism" advocates was John D. Rockefeller Jr., after he
learned firsthand about the importance of social policy from his own company's experience in the coalmines of Colorado and the ugly and unfortunate Ludlow Massacre. One challenge is whether now, with corporate
ownership and management split, corporate leaders can have the perspective and freedom to deal with social and public policy issues in a way that
can give business a meaningful and effective human face. I believe they can.

Another challenge is the human ability to foresee major, especially long-
term, societal developments. Also, two cents off the consensus view of a
quarter's results is a disaster. Thus, most organizations are highly focused
on the near term. Results dominate management attention. Even in HR,
the experience of the past blurs the capability to consider and predict the
future. Many of us did not see the extent and depth of globalization and its
unparalleled impact on management and its employee relations needs and
requirements. It has underscored the essential importance for business to
attend to its external relationships, and in large measure this has meant
growing responsibilities for the HR function.

In 1975, a distinguished group of managers in the HR field were nom-
inated to participate in a year-long study group to project what issues would
dominate the field 10 years in the future.[1] Eighteen of these individuals
were selected from leading large, prominent, American companies in all
major industries. Many of the companies were gleaning more than half their
revenue from offshore markets. But significantly, they did not think of
themselves as "global" companies.

The group spent a year interviewing academics and practitioners, labor union officials, government officials, and "futurologist" consultants. They debated their learnings and developed a report to be presented to their functional seniors. With hindsight, the resulting report missed many of the salient issues that began to dominate the field just a few years later. Among the key new developments *not* projected in the study were:

- The growth of competitiveness from foreign companies in what had been "protected" domestic markets.
- A new and intense focus on costs and productivity at all organizational levels, which gave rise to the new field of organizational development.
- The growth of new industries based on electronics and other new technologies that required new organizational and motivational strategies.
- The beginnings of a drop in the ability of unions to organize in the private sector, which began the evolution of personnel organizations to HR.
- The need for economies of scale when competing in world markets, which demanded new insights into a multicultural workforce.
- The depth of the social and cultural issues in specific countries calling for new attention to diversity, continued emphasis on civil rights in the United States, dealing with South Africa's apartheid requirements, and so on.

These executives did not fail because they lacked intelligence. They failed because they lacked a management system to develop a knowledge base and agenda to anticipate and react effectively. The personnel leaders in this group had arrived at their positions from a labor relations background. But, in the early to mid-1980s and beyond, the world required a new and different emphasis to deal with the issues of growth, productivity, internationalization, and the introduction of new marketing principles as well as new technologies in a new, competitive environment.

It was in response to these changes that the concept of *human resources* began to come into existence. And in the changing environment, professionals in the field set as their mantra the need to serve their company's business interests and started to demand and get a seat at the top management table.

THE SCOPE OF HUMAN RESOURCES— SO FAR

More sophistication was required in dealing with the new issues of managing increasingly global companies, addressing new levels of competitiveness, and helping management integrate new technology in all aspects of the business as it operated in different cultures. But there was also the need for more willingness to take risk. HR people began to seek new roles or to enable/require new skills to be brought to bear on the function in support of management objectives.

These developments in support of the requirements of management called for newly developed HR competencies. Moreover, because less energy was directed toward labor relations, the HR function tended to become more inwardly focused. At about the same time in Europe, starting in the 1980s, the European Community (EC) was debating various proposals regarding worker participation in the management process. Employers in general opposed many of these proposals, but the HR function was largely absent from the table.

While each company had its own structure of organization and responsibility for responses to these matters, this external role was often allocated to public affairs or legal departments. And in many debates it was the perspective of the finance function that prevailed because of its key concern with tax policy and cross-border trade.

There were even observable incidents of internal disarray. I had the unusual experience of being called to the office of a CEO of a prominent U.S.-based global company to help moderate a discussion at which the European American profit center manager supported his European HR head's plan to agree voluntarily to a European Directorate proposal on dealing with unions that was in direct opposition to company policy. He was able to take such a position because his sector was producing excellent business results at the time. Other U.S. company representatives in Europe, as members of an American Chamber of Commerce, also represented viewpoints that were not always consistent with corporate positions.

What was going on? Often, companies had not decided on a company position in the rapidly evolving arena of social policy in Europe, so corporate positions were not developed strategically but on an ad hoc basis. In other cases, internal politics were subverting a company's effectiveness in the external arena, and it was only when a crisis developed that issues were brought to headquarters for resolution. The business of running a truly global company was a challenge for which most companies were not fully prepared—or structured.

Globalization, however, is just one of the larger societal issues challenging large corporations. Today, HR generally does not play a central, unifying role in responding to (let alone, leading) corporate social policy concerns. Many large companies use ad hoc committees or task forces to bring together the skills needed to manage and monitor major developing issues such as health care costs, pension costs, funding issues, pending legislation, and, most recently, organizing and managing corporate response to terrorism and working with the new Department of Homeland Security. Too often, however, politics, fuzzy delegations, or the absence of pinpointed responsibility means that there is too little clarity to manage issues effectively, even when all in management are well intentioned.

ORGANIZING HR FOR CORPORATE SOCIAL POLICY RESPONSES

In general, companies have managed, but not always early or well enough, to take leadership positions of enlightened self-interest on a variety of current issues. In the broad area of corporate social responsibility, nongovernmental organizations (NGOs) took the lead on issues related to the environment and various social causes. Regarding the current issues of compensation and governance, companies clearly failed to anticipate the societal and governmental reaction, not only to corporate misbehavior but also to what had been standard, competitive, comparative practices (especially concerning executive pay).

But the story is not complete. The nature of the world is that many issues that have little visibility today can become significant public and/or governmental concerns in the future. How should a company best be organized to be alert to new trends, to effectively read the tealeaves, and, therefore, marshal its resources to meet new external challenges that will make an operating difference? How can a company do a better job of overcoming parochialism, improving the level of understanding of what is important, and cohering management attitudes?

In some companies, there may be a "philosopher king" who plays this role, or members of the board may do so. But philosopher kings and board members that have an interest, while helpful, cannot substitute for an ongoing management system. Perhaps some functional head can step into the role, but it is a role of peril for it is a difficult and contentious one.

Do we need a new function? And if we do, how will it gain the level of organizational acceptance and credibility to do the job? Years ago, John Dunlop, noted Harvard professor and former U.S. Secretary of Labor, advanced the thesis that industrial relations (HR) is an integrative function in that it seeks to blend law, organizational objectives, and human reactions and aspirations to advance the goals of institutions and people. So should this role rest with HR today? Yes! By building further around the concept of HR as an integrator, the functions role can be broadened. The ultimate questions are whether HR leaders are ready to take on such a role and whether their organizations are ready for such a role to be played.

On many issues, HR has been generally effective in getting a seat at the table. It has demonstrated that it can cope with knotty workplace issues, succession planning processes, management and talent acquisition, and development strategies. Could it also take the lead in identifying and managing public and social policy issues that are on the table or on the horizon today?

First, there are caveats. To play the role envisioned here, HR leadership needs to be able to manage the process of the evaluation of evolving issues and to be bold enough to try to convince management of the need to change a policy, views, or corporate behavior in the best, longer term interests of the corporation. How many were willing to tackle this job in the early civil rights days or regarding plant shutdown notification or in bloated executive reward programs? But if HR is to be a true business partner, its contribution must be based not only on competency. It must be willing to take risks for the longer term health of the business.

This is not a simple sell, but it is possible that a structured approach would be easier to sell, especially because most organizations rely on structures to help management identify and solve problems. Budgeting, long-term business planning, and succession planning all are systematic processes that take known current data and assumptions about the future along with best estimates and hunches and run them through a structured system to help management focus, increase communications, and minimize uncertainty in planning to deal with the future.

Given this background, consider HR leadership in a process (borrowing from the environmental scanning process prevalent in some companies in the past) that falls into eight steps and might be called the *business environmental planning process (BEPP):*

1. Gain management understanding and agreement that:
   - Public and social policy issues can have a cost, especially if management does not engage in the debate and resolution of such issues.
   - It is a management responsibility to systematically organize and identify the important issues and be prepared to take proactive approaches and speak out on issues of significance to the company and its related stakeholders.
2. Based on management agreement, charge HR with developing a structured program to identify and organize such issues recognizing that accountability for this effort must rest at the highest level.
3. Draw up an annual list of issues that qualify for consideration in the BEPP and circulate them to appropriate managers and functional areas for their information, review, and suggestions.
4. Structure the BEPP to precede but parallel the structure of the annual budgeting and planning process and provide for the involvement of top management in selecting from the list those issues to be candidates for company attention and action.
5. Ensure that the BEPP involves management by assigning issues to high potentials as "issue managers," and appropriately reward such managers for the results achieved.
6. Report on the priority issues at subsequent management meetings, recognizing the need to limit the focus to a manageable number of issues.
7. Take responsibility, at the end of each planning/budgeting cycle, for HR to summarize where the issue is and what the company has done to have an impact. Also determine whether the issue will remain in the BEPP for the next year.

8. Ensure that individuals who have contributed to company business objectives through this process are identified in succession planning reviews with senior management and the board.

This outlined approach needs tailoring to a specific company's circumstances, but many elements of the proposed approach exist in companies possibly not as integrated as proposed here. Experience has revealed that issues left to flourish and develop without proactive involvement can become costly and disruptive to companies and to a democratic, free market society. Rather than playing catch up, what is proposed here is good business practice. It is proactive management planning.

Based on all the experience with public policy that has often caused problems for management, including the growth in extragovernmental organization attempts (Organization for Economic Cooperation and Development, International Labor Organization, European Commission, United Nations) to constrain management rights and behavior, it is time to get organized. It is time for HR leadership to step up and give attention to the external world and help management manage this increasingly complex and contentious area.

HR as an increasingly important function in the management process is the only function that can play the role of coordinator and stimulator in helping the organization. Public and social policy issues have become too important to take a secondary role, especially as they now reach into every nook and cranny of our economic, business, and social structure. Can there be any more important area in which HR could step forward and take on a new, broadened responsibility for the benefit of all?

NOTE

1. *People, Progress, and Employee Relations: Proceedings of the Fiftieth Anniversary Conference of Industrial Relations Counselors, Inc., University of Virginia, June 9, 10, and 11, 1976,* University of Virginia Press, 1976.

CHAPTER 39

LEADING CHANGE: AN IMPERATIVE OF LEADERSHIP

FRANCES HESSELBEIN

Discerning the future of HR brings us more challenges than opportunities, more questions than answers. Long ago Peter Drucker (1997) was asked how he could have predicted the reunification of Germany when no one else did so. He replied, "I never predict. I just look out the window and see what is visible but not yet seen." In today's world, with the HR landscape changing faster than most of its architects can anticipate, it throws all of us back to Peter's "I just look out the window and see what is visible but not yet seen."

So, we look out the window with new eyes, straining to see the promises and challenges of HR of the future.

I remember talking with Max DePree when he was just leaving Herman Miller as its chairman. I told him how inspiring it was to know he had a vice-president for people—not vice-president for HR. His reply was, "If I had stayed longer, it would have been vice-president for people and families."

Later, as we were developing our Drucker Foundation book, *The Organization of the Future* (1997), I invited Lewis Platt, then chairman of Hewlett-Packard, to write a chapter for the new book. Instead of writing on the wonders of the new technology or cyberspace, he said, "I would like to write on employee work-life balance, one of the greatest challenges to corporations today. And if we ever get it right, it will be win-win for everyone." It was a great chapter that readers in all three sectors—corporate, government, and social—found inspiring and motivating (pp. 314–323).

341

And Peter Drucker most recently shocked some when the title of one of his many *Harvard Business Review* articles flat-footedly stated, "They're Not Employees, They're People." (2002).

Now we are deep in HR 2005–2010, trying to peer into a murky future. The old questions do not generate the new answers required, and I look forward to all the great HR thought leaders writing for this book to provide the questions we should be asking if our organizations in all three sectors are to be viable, relevant, or even present in 2010.

As we scan that environment for those straws in the wind that may portend major shifts or change, in the backdrop for our introspection are some messages from our HR past with powerful implications for the HR of the future. Max DePree, Lewis Platt, and Peter Drucker all remind us to be people focused—to keep a human face on human resources.

A DEVIL'S BARGAIN?

Who knows what we will be writing about HR in 2010? How will the landscape have changed in the world outside? What will be the state of the HR leaders within? What of the morale, spirit, motivation, and productivity of the people of the enterprise? No one can predict, but the HR leaders who respond to "They're Not Employees, They're People," and help the total organization—governance and management included—to appreciate the people and function of HR may be leading all three sectors.

The Conference Board's Summer 2004 newsletter front-page article, "HR Outsourcing Here to Stay," states:

Some 76% of the surveyed firms currently outsource one or more major HR functions. Nearly ¾ (71%) of the companies that currently outsource HR say they will extend or renegotiate contracts with their current outsourcing providers, and 29% say they will put their existing outsourced services out for a new bid—but none will be taking these services back in-house.

More than ¾ of executives at large North American and European companies that currently outsource one or more major human resources functions say they would do so again, according to a Conference Board survey sponsored by Accenture.

If "we look out the window and see what is visible but not yet seen," what is our response? I do not pretend to know what lies beyond the horizon or is visible but not yet seen, but the outsourcing of North American major HR functions now and in the future raises new challenges to a function that can well determine the success or failure of the enterprise.

As Drucker wrote in his *Harvard Business Review* article, "Developing talent is business's most important task—the sine qua non of competition in a knowledge economy. If by off-loading employee relations, organizations also lose their capacity to develop people, they will have made a devil's bargain indeed" (p. 71).

What are the other special challenges to the leaders of an enterprise that outsources some of its HR functions? If indeed the people of the organization are its greatest asset, how do we plan for the day when they are leaving their positions within the organization? How are they notified? What are the plans for outplacement support?

The answers to these and other questions will help measure the quality of HR and the leadership of the organization. When and where the jobs are outsourced is not the primary question. The governance and management of the organization have the primary responsibility for their people whose jobs will leave the organization and perhaps the country.

Governance must ask of management:

- How are they informed?
- When are they informed?
- What outplacement services are provided? What are the benefits provided?
- What support does HR provide to its people as it moves them and the organization forward in an uncertain economic climate?

At a time such as this, many of us are moving out some of the people whose work-life balance used to be our concern and retaining those people who may now see their workplace in a different way. I do not attempt to describe their reaction because they differ just as organizations' plans, procedures, and communications differ. Simply, the future will be different for the people and their workplace.

THE CALL OF GREAT LEADERS

This is the time for HR teams to take the lead, look out the window, and see what is visible but not yet seen.

In the past, we've had Peter, Max, and Lewis reminding us that people come first. Can we say that today? One vision of HR in 2005 to 2010 will reflect that the people are first, families are first, heeding the call of great leaders. This call was based not on theory, but success—measurable, tested—not just in the workplace, but back home where families who know they are people flourish. And workplace morale and productivity soar as the people of the enterprise make its mission, values, and goals their own.

Perhaps as you read this, you sense a cultural disconnect. What kind of workplace am I describing? Surely not the workplace of some downsized, outsourced organization where the notice of positions eliminated comes by the ubiquitous e-mail. (Unfortunately, this is a real example.)

Perhaps at a time such as this, some HR directors, vice-presidents, authorities, experts, and observers find themselves in an exhilarating position of swimming against the tide, demonstrating that indeed it is the people of the organization who will determine the future of the enterprise. By their powerful example, leaders at every level of the organization dispersed leadership at work right across the company, unleashing the energy, the innovation, and the powerful spirit that move the enterprise beyond the old walls into a future built on the successes of the past, the strengths of the past, but not repeating the past. This is what the people of the organization can accomplish where the leaders of the organization and the HR team indeed see the organization as its people—not numbers or faceless, nameless "employees."

CHALLENGE THE GOSPEL

Outsourcing is being addressed in many ways by its proponents and its critics. It is just one of the challenges HR leaders are struggling with today. A far greater challenge is finding the courage to question the gospel of the status quo within the organization—and this requires HR leaders to examine every policy, practice, procedure, and assumption affecting our people.

We throw out the practices that were appropriate in the past, perhaps adequate today, but which we know will have little relevance in the future. We examine the policies affecting the organization's people and challenge governance and management to replace those that are no longer viable, relevant, or part of a new and tenuous future. Until we get our house in order and until we have only those policies, practices, procedures, and assumptions exactly right for the organization, its people, and the future, it will be difficult to chart our journey.

My picture of the organization of the future shows HR as moving across the total organization with total involvement. HR takes the lead in describing the who and why of the big picture before we determine the whats and hows. Overarching redefining the future of the organization is a powerful revisiting of the mission by governance and management. A redefined mission, solely why we do what we do, or a positive endorsement of the present mission, with a few powerful goals to further the mission helps redefine the future of the organization. Then our HR team translates this clear and inspiring direction into a clear and powerful response—how to mobilize the people of the enterprise around the mission, why they do what they do, their reason for being. Nothing releases the energy, the human spirit, or the sense of ownership better than inclusion that is circular and total.

If this description does not sound much like the old hierarchy, it isn't. New demands, new threats and opportunities, and new ambiguities call for a renewal of leadership, perhaps even a redefining of leadership congruent with a society changing so rapidly that, as Warren Bennis (1994) wrote, "Change is now our weather."

The organization that remembers, "Tis the set of the sails and not the gales that determine the way we go," will do far more than weather the change upon us. This organization will not just lead in redefining the organization and its future but also help lead as the society is redefining the future.

THE INDISPENSABLE ASSET

All the physical assets—the things owned, the structures, and systems—pale beside the newly energized, motivated, determined workforce of the future, the men and women, the people of the organization.

Of all groups and teams within the enterprise, the most critical, most challenged, and most indispensable group is HR, the people part of the organization. For, in the end, success or failure will be measured by the people, that is, the human resources, of the enterprise.

When we reach checkpoint 2010, then 2020, there will be new voices, new stirring examples of the organizations of the future and the leaders of the future leading into a new era, a new age of communication, opportunity, diversity, inclusion, and success when the people led the way.

HR, in addition to all the usual long list of accountabilities, carries a unique accountability: communication—translating all the messages from management into human terms—and connecting the communication of the moment to the message of the moment, communication that is heard.

Nuts and bolts, the how-tos, fail to inspire. The why of the hardware in human terms connects, includes, and builds cohesion and community within the walls where the people are.

And, today, who can forget Jim Collins's (2001) *Good to Great* and his big yellow bus, destination "Success," and his unforgettable "Do practice the discipline of 'first who': first get the right people on the bus, the wrong people off the bus, and the right people in the right seats, then you figure out where to drive the bus."

Here we have a great thought leader, the author of *Good to Great* describing a concept common to great thought leaders who have gone before him. It is the people on the bus, the people within the organization, and those we bring in who indeed are the indispensable asset, who "figure out the best path to greatness."

Thus, HR of the future, the how to, whats, and whens must change, but why we do what we do never changes. The people of the enterprise, the people on the bus, indeed will determine where our bus is headed into the future—"destination Success." This is part of the big picture of HR in the future.

Today, I can offer no easy answers, only the belief that indeed our people are our greatest asset. And when our organizational culture, "the beliefs and values practiced by an organization," is palpable with how we value our people, the results will be high morale, high productivity, and high sense of appreciation, and it will be circular.

We face tough times today, yes, but in times such as these, great HR leaders will take the lead in redefining HR of the future even as they take the lead in redefining the organization of the future and beyond the walls, the society of the future. The society of the future is not faceless, nameless numbers; it is people.

Ten years from now, we will be looking back at a period that tested our organization with new and powerful challenges. I hope we will find that our response defined HR of the future in human and powerful terms that strengthened our people, our society, and our democracy.

REFERENCES

Bennis, Warren. (1994). *On Becoming a Leader.* New York: Perseus Books, p. 172.

Collins, Jim. (2001). *Good to Great: Why Some Companies Make the Leap and Others Don't.* HarperBusiness, p. 13.

Drucker Foundation. (1997). *The Organization of the Future.* Jossey-Bass: San Francisco.

Drucker, Peter F. (1997, March). *Forbes,* vol. 159, no. 5, p. 122.

Drucker, Peter F. (2002, February). "They're Not Employees . . . ," *Harvard Business Review,* vol. 80, no. 2, pp. 70–77.

CHAPTER 40

WHEN ETHICS CALLS THE HR HELPLINE

PATRICIA J. HARNED

It's 3:30 on the Friday before a long weekend. Thinking ahead, you've carefully planned your day and have only five small things left to do before heading out for the weekend. You're looking forward to the much-deserved time off, and, because you're leaving all your work in a good place, you can go with a clear conscience. You won't have to think of work at all.

The phone rings on your desk—it's the dedicated line for employees who have HR-related questions. You take a deep breath and forcibly clear your mind, so you'll be ready for the conversation that will come and respectful of the courage it took for the person on the other end of the line to dial the helpline number. You answer the call, "Employee assistance . . ." and wait for the caller to speak. "Yes, I need some advice," you're told. "For a while now, my supervisor has been inflating our sales numbers. We're supposed to be making our targets, but I know we're not. Everybody knows it. Still, our reports are showing that we are. I don't know what to do."

"Well," you reply, "first of all, thank you for your call. I know it wasn't an easy thing to do." You ask the caller several questions, only to learn that the employee wishes to remain anonymous. When you point out that the issue being raised is actually a matter related to the Code of Conduct and, therefore, an ethics rather than an HR issue, you are met with the same old response: "Can't you just help me?" You quietly sigh to yourself, ready to dive into another matter that you need to refer to the ethics helpline, knowing that because you've received the call, you're in it for the long haul.

Frustration is a phenomenon that is common to many HR professionals. Nearly 40 percent of HR professionals indicated in a recent Society for Human Resource Management (SHRM)/Ethics Resource Center survey that they are tasked with "cleaning up [ethics-related] messes," despite the fact that they were not part of the "ethics infrastructure."[1] HR professionals are being asked to address issues that may seem far afield of their expertise and to deal with problems that they had little, if any, opportunity to prevent.

And this situation is unlikely to go away any time soon. As long as the term *human* remains a part of the "human resources" title, ethics will be part of the job for HR professionals. Ethics is integrally related to the contributions of HR because wherever two people exist in a relationship, ethical issues are present. Any decision that has implications for another person has an ethical component. Ethics has to do with what "should" be done, with knowing what "the right thing" is to do, when the outcome of a decision impacts another individual.

Because of the nature of the work environment, ethical decisions are a part of every HR professional's daily to-do list. HR professionals have long recognized their role in determining policies, providing training, and, when required, enforcing disciplinary procedures to not only protect the organization but also provide a good place to work. These are all activities that are ethical in nature. Hiring practices, equal treatment of employees, and even the provision of one benefit over another all have ethical dimensions.

At the same time, ethics issues crop up all around the HR professional, and recent scandals certainly have highlighted some good examples. Incidents of overstated earnings, undisclosed conflicts of interest, and improper use of confidential information all brought risk, and even downfall, to the organizations where these acts of misconduct took place. Some were even acts that HR should have flagged. Ethics is an aspect both in and around the HR professional's job.

Of all organizational leaders, HR professionals are most equipped to live up to the ethical demands of their jobs, allowing them to be role models to others. Additionally, however, they are uniquely positioned to rise to new heights as ethical leaders in their organizations. The very fact that employees turn to HR is an indication of HR's capacity in this area. It is no surprise to hear that in many organizations, employees who should be calling the ethics helpline are contacting their HR representatives instead—after all, HR is the dedicated function within the organization that is there to assist employees. Employees should feel comfortable going to HR, and when they do, they want competent HR professionals who can be trusted and are seen as advocates for people. For those reasons, HR should be at the forefront of the ethics discussion at the early stages and not merely charged with cleaning up the messes.

THE TIME HAS COME

If ethics is part and parcel of the HR function, why not take a leading role? The challenge for the future is to not only understand the direction the ethics field has taken but also regain a seat at the table for one of the most important discussions currently taking place in organizations: the standards that will guide business conduct and the means by which organizations will deliver and uphold the message that ethics is important.

We live in a post-Enron world. We have seen organizations essentially destroyed, careers shattered, and innocent lives ruined because of ethical lapses of those in leadership positions. Now more than ever, ethics is a part of corporate life, and it will continue to be so in the years ahead. As a result of heightened public scrutiny, new legislation, shareholder and investor interests, and revisions to regulations, many companies are either establishing or revamping their efforts to address organizational standards for employee conduct. These efforts include everything from reexamining the policies in place to the type of corporate culture that is desired. It's not just a for-profit venture either. From nonprofit hospitals to international nongovernmental organizations (NGOs), the need to define, emphasize, and perpetuate ethical conduct is on the horizon for every employer.

In some organizations, the discussion is taking place because compliance with regulation requires it. For others, a more proactive concern fuels senior-level interest in changing culture, setting standards, and addressing ethical decision making. Regardless of the impetus, as ethics rises to the top of the list of priorities for organizations, the people who are among the most qualified to participate in the ethical leadership of their organizations—the HR professionals—should be present for the discussion. The absence of HR would have substantial implications for all involved—employees impacted by standards and practices, the organization aiming to set a tone from the top, and even HR professionals themselves.

WHO ELSE IS ON THE TEAM?

Ethics is now primarily a discussion among governance, legal, compliance, finance and accounting, and audit professionals, in addition to the officers dedicated to the ethics function. Two important shifts have recently taken place to bring these professionals together. First, revisions to Federal Sentencing Guidelines for Organizations (FSGO) mandate that organizations have not only an ethics program in place but also programs that are demonstrably effective in establishing an ethical culture. Historically, FSGO regulations have served as a carrot to motivate business leaders to put into place core elements of an ethics program. To lessen judicial sanctions when a company was found guilty of a crime, many companies demonstrate due diligence by pointing to a code of conduct, some form of ethics training to raise employee awareness of organizational standards, a mechanism for anonymous reporting of misconduct, and high-level oversight of the ethics function.[2]

Additionally, FSGO now places new emphasis on culture—the prioritization of ethics within a company and employee perceptions that an organization has done its best to operate with the highest standards of ethics. In many organizations, this revision has caused corporate leaders to reexamine their ethics programs, supplement training, put measures into place to gauge trends, and emphasize employee reporting of issues that arise. Leaders today are looking to positively impact the climates of their organizations and to impact the way employees go about their jobs.

At the same time, the post-Enron Sarbanes-Oxley Act has also broadened the number of individuals who have responsibility for oversight of organizational ethics functions. Reporting of financial statements, company audits, governance, and board independence are all topics of conversation that are a part of the ethics debate. Ethics and compliance were once very different functions in an organization—they are quickly becoming one. Accountability for misconduct begins at the very top of an organization, causing senior executives heartburn that they must certify the integrity of their organizations, while it remains difficult to gauge the activities at all levels and locations in which a company operates. Pressure mounts for senior executives to critically examine their organizational operations, and many are gathering trusted professionals to advise them as they revisit their organizational ethics programs.

Legislation and compliance aren't the only motivators for organizations today—public interest, shareholder value, and lessons learned by many organizations have created a climate in which more and more companies are recognizing the importance of tending to the ethical cultures of their organizations. Businesses are demonstrating that they care about ethics because ethics is good business. Thus the discussion convenes. How will we set the standards to guide conduct? How can we best communicate our policies and resources to employees? How should we monitor the environment to prevent and detect misconduct?

Why HR Belongs at the Table—Now More Than Ever

In its present makeup, the work of an ethics team does make a difference. Where formal ethics programs are in place (regardless of their independence from HR), they do have an impact; the presence of an ethics program impacts employees' willingness to report observed misconduct, perceived pressure to commit misconduct, perceptions that peers are held accountable, and employee satisfaction with their jobs and employing organizations.[3] Ethics functions that begin with senior leadership that "set the tone" from the top and continue with reinforcement throughout the organization do meet with success. Employees have higher perceptions that their organizations' ethics programs actually mean something when senior leadership communicates a commitment to ethical standards, models ethical behavior, and keeps promises.[4]

Importantly, however, ethics extends beyond senior leaders and a few formal initiatives. Interactions between peers have substantial implications for the credibility of an ethics program. The extent to which employees believe they will be perceived as a "snitch" determines the likelihood they will report misconduct they observe. Additionally, supervisors' ability to set expectations, capably receive reports from employees, and consistently discipline wrongdoers dramatically shapes the ethical culture of an organization. Differences in culture, level of management, employee status, and organizational size all affect the extent to which employees perceive the ethics of their organizations.[5] As organizational activities increase in complexity, so, too, do the potential ethical complications for the employees within it. Organizational ethics requires a high level of commitment from a number of qualified leaders.

And that's where HR fits in. For the good of all organizations and the people they employ, HR professionals must insist on participating in the ethics steering committees of their organizations, bringing their knowledge of human behavior, their wisdom in structuring policy, and their loyalty to their organizations with them. If HR is absent, organizational standards will be incomplete. HR has a contribution to make—for the good of all.

What Do We Do Now That We're Here?

As difficult as it can be to earn the ear of the right people, that isn't the only battle. Once HR has taken its rightful place in the conversation, there's more work to be done. HR can argue that it has contributions to make, but then it's time to make them—sharing the unique insights and skills that only HR can bring. HR can do several things:

1. *Educate senior leaders on human behavior.* Ethics becomes an issue when an employee faces pressure, whether to cut corners, to interpret the rules, or to stand up to powerful influences in an organization. While organizational leaders are often well versed in discussing standards and rules, the human aspect of nurturing courage to do the right thing in employees is a very different perspective. The SHRM/Ethics Resource Center research indicates that senior executives have a "rosy" view of their organizations—few leaders recognize that pressure mounts as an individual looks down the organizational chart. Even further, in most cases, the principal pressures faced by employees were the *result* of management actions: Following the boss's directions, meeting overly aggressive objectives, helping the organization survive, meeting schedule pressures, and wanting to be a "team player" topped the list.[6] By educating senior leadership about the thoughts and concerns of employees and unattended consequences of top management interests, HR professionals have much to offer to organizational efforts to help employees feel safe in taking an ethical stand.

2. *Coach executives in ethical role modeling.* Role modeling by senior leaders is essential to any ethics initiative. As eloquent as executives may be, communication of ethical standards and modeling of ethical behavior are often taken for granted. Research shows that unless leaders intentionally and regularly go out of their way to communicate and model ethics as a part of their daily activities, employees will, at the very least, assume that ethics is not important.[7] Many executives may even need a coach to help them make ethics overt in their regular communications with employees. Also, ethics policies should go beyond offering assurances that no retribution will be taken against employee efforts to report violations. Top management must reward any initiative taken to support specific ethics standards and the general culture necessary for successful ethics programming. HR professionals are adept at communicating with employees in ways that encourage positive behavior, and they should share these insights with senior leaders.

3. *Take the pulse of the employee culture.* Organizations held accountable by FSGO and Sarbanes-Oxley legislation are especially concerned for "periodically measuring the effectiveness of their ethics/compliance programs."[8] This issue now involves assessment of corporate climate. Many HR operations already have qualitative and quantitative measures in place that can help; ethics-related questions can easily be added to employee satisfaction surveys, employee interviews and focus groups, or other assessment efforts. HR professionals are often the ones in the know about the issues taking place in an organization, which is valuable information to offer.

4. *Complement the ethics function.* While the ethics function continues to evolve as a formal function in many organizations, it will likely always run parallel to the HR function. Helpline calls, employee manuals, investigations of misconduct, and employee training are often intertwined between ethics and HR—as it should be. When employees have concerns about resources available in one function, their outreach to the other should be welcomed and applauded. HR professionals should make every effort to consider themselves the natural ally of the ethics/compliance department.

It's That Time of Week Again

Great leaders know that every challenge is really an opportunity for greatness in disguise. The frustrating phone call on Friday afternoon is a reminder of two important things. First, ethics is a part of HR work, and it could never be otherwise. Second, HR has insights to share and needs to be able to share them—it's better to help create more effective systems than just avert crises.

It's Friday afternoon again. You're walking out the door when the Helpline light starts flashing. You could just let the phone keep ringing. It's probably not urgent. You don't work in an ER; it could hardly be a life or death situation. But you are who you are. You have to answer the call. Your responsibilities demand it of you. Your integrity wouldn't let you do otherwise. Most of all, you know that someone needs you. You pick up the phone and say, "Hello," in your most open and welcoming voice. Nervously, the other party starts talking: "Yes, it's the Ethics Function calling. And I'm going to need your help."

NOTES

1. SHRM®/Ethics Resource Center. (2003). *2003 Business Ethics Survey,* USA: Society for Human Resource Management, p. 4.
2. Seven elements of an effective program are necessary for compliance to Federal Sentencing Guidelines for Organizations. These are outlined by the Federal Sentencing Commission in Chapter 8 of its Sentencing Guidelines.
3. Ethics Resource Center. (2003). *2003 National Business Ethics Survey.* Washington, DC: Ethics Resource Center.
4. See note 3.
5. See note 3.
6. See note 1.
7. Trevino, L., L. Hartman, and M. Brown. (2000). "Moral Person and Moral Manager: How Executives Develop a Reputation for Ethical Leadership," *California Management Review, 42*(4).
8. U.S. Federal Sentencing Guidelines, § 8B2.1(b)(5)(B), http://www.ussc.gov/2004guid/tabconchapt8.htm.

SECTION IX

LIVE GLOBALLY, ACT LOCALLY

Some years ago a member called the Society for Human Resource Management (SHRM) president from the United Airlines' Red Carpet lounge at New York's Kennedy Airport. The member had just been told by his president that the company had purchased a company in Hong Kong and he was to "get there ASAP." As a result of his lack of global HR knowledge and experience, a sense of urgency and concern was evident. He asked if SHRM could fax to him immediately, before his flight departed, everything they had about doing HR in Hong Kong.

Yes, globalization is inevitable. And in almost every HR career, the added requirement of global HR comes sooner or later, one way or another.

For very senior HR leaders, global HR usually becomes a priority when accountability includes multicountry organizational presence.

A relatively small percentage of HR professionals are able to express early career interests in global HR and/or gain orderly development. For instance, rarely is a U.S. HR professional sent as an expatriate to Germany, Belgium, Japan, France, Thailand, Brazil, or other nations. Unlike finance, accounting, engineering, technology, manufacturing, and even sales, global HR is much more attuned to a nation's history, language, and culture, which greatly precludes or limits the utilization of HR professionals as expatriates.[1]

The giant size of the U.S. economy also gives false comfort and has an isolative effect on many U.S. national enterprises. The U.S. market is so big that some U.S. companies need not necessarily compete globally. Some can be successful by national efforts alone. Others establish their brand, competencies, and scale domestically and then try to expand their capabilities to other countries (Wal-Mart, McDonald's, Starbucks, etc.).

As a result, the U.S. HR professional is much less likely to have opportunities to gain meaningful global experience. Therefore, as illustrated by the Hong Kong scenario, for many, the entry into global HR is immediate and unanticipated with little or no time to prepare.

The good news is that just as many nations admire the Japanese for their productivity and the Germans for their quality, the U.S. approach to HR management is respected around the world.

Also helpful in advancing the interests of global HR is the World Federation of Personnel Management Associations (WFPMA). Greater than 50 country-specific, HR professional organizations share research, knowledge, practices, and experiences.[2]

Although some professional differences exist from one country to another, there are greater similarities than differences. Thus, if a person is a good HR professional in his or her own country, that person can usually also be a good global HR professional. All the person need do is recognize and adapt to the differences in other nations.

In this concluding section, five chapters help show the way.

John Hofmeister shares his practitioner worldwide experience on the importance of maintaining global and local balance in HR in Chapter 41.

Vladimir Pucik in Chapter 42 challenges HR leaders as to whether they are ready to address the issues associated with an increasingly global environment. How will HR respond to the challenges of complex business strategies? How will HR build and sustain global organizational capability while responding with the required speed and efficiency?

Fons Trompenaars and Peter Woollimas remind us in Chapter 43 that globalization has sometimes been taken too far. Unattended consequences occur when programs and tools are applied to other countries, without modification, simply because they were used successfully in the home country. They provide a framework of recognition, respect, and reconciliation to help balance the interests of acting globally but adapting locally.

In Chapter 44, Mary Ann Von Glinow, Ellen Drost, and Mary Teagarden report on a 10-year research study on global best practices. They examine where various global HR practices are now versus where they should be in the future. Their gap analysis suggests (especially in selection, training and development, compensation, and performance appraisal) that there are some "universal" best practices. But there are also important "regional" best practices. These findings shed important light on those practices that global managers want for the future.

In the final chapter (45), Arthur Yeung shares his HR experiences from China. As this major nation continues to develop, it is also wrestling with the challenges and opportunities of growth, globalization, and intensified competition. His contribution describes how most Chinese firms are being managed now. He highlights what roles HR professionals are playing now as well as what roles they must play in the future.

Globalization is natural and will affect almost everything we do. HR professionals are not immune. These chapters help us focus on choices for making global and strategy choices.

Notes

1. This is not necessarily the case in some other nations and especially Europe, where an economic union of countries with increasingly common HR directives, intercountry freedom of travel, and work opportunities exists.
2. The World Federation of Personnel Management Associations (WFPMA). See www.wfpma.com.

CHAPTER 41

GLOBAL AND LOCAL BALANCE IN HUMAN RESOURCES LEADERSHIP

JOHN HOFMEISTER

"Would the honorable speaker please explain how HR decision makers in London, The Hague, or Houston could possibly impact talent development of young Nigerian petroleum engineering graduates working in the Niger Delta?" said the person from the back of the audience.

During the 35th Annual Conference of the Institute of Personnel Management of Nigeria (IPMN) in Abuja in October 2003, it became obvious that the relevance of maintaining global and local balance in HR leadership was paramount, yet unclear. Approximately 900 delegates were present to explore, learn, network, and share best practices from presentations about all the major HR processes that impact their work. The themes of HR excellence, business partnering, leadership, and talent management dominated the meeting. There were presentations from representatives of national enterprises, foreign multinationals, government, nongovernmental organizations (NGOs), and academia.

Theory met practice head-on. Articulate thought leaders engaged day-to-day practitioners in plenary and in breakout sessions in one of the most dynamic and diverse nations on earth. The debate about global dominance and local pragmatism was lively and invigorating. Does global or local win the HR end game? Everyone won his or her argument. And everyone lost. Why?

This meeting takes place every year. How many other such meetings of HR leaders take place in country after country, year around, across the globe? How often are presentations by global company representatives confronted by challengers who represent local realities? How many versions of international corporate HR processes are not fit for purpose and not aligned with operating unit, national, or regional priorities on both a global and local basis? And who decides whether local realities overtake global expectations? Or vice versa? In this conference, for example, there were open debates among delegates over the utility and effectiveness of global versus local programs for leadership education, variable pay, career development, and HR information systems.

The debate about the soundness of global HR leadership belongs among the top priorities of HR leaders at all levels of organizations. The cacophony of views, the pragmatics of applications, the strength of dominant international organizations, and the needs of local interests combine to present global HR leaders with an unresolved conundrum. Who's right? Who's wrong? What works? What doesn't? Business and organization success depends on getting better answers to these questions across the spectrum of what HR leaders do. The underlying, unresolved conflicts are counterproductive and inefficient.

GLOBALIZATION OR LOCALIZATION OF HR LEADERSHIP

In a world of global brands, global companies, global processes, and systems, global leaders are right to expect that their people processes and systems fit naturally into the evolution of simplicity and standardization that's expected everywhere in the world. The twin mantras of "efficiency and effectiveness," together with the rallying cry of "competitive reality," demand that one-size-fits-all solutions work for HR leadership, the same as for the underlying employee value propositions (EVPs) and other management processes and systems infrastructure that support leading global organizations.

Tens of thousands of consultants at the best service companies in the world are responding to help top companies adapt workable business models that enable commonality over difference. Even greater numbers of managers and staff, perhaps in the millions, are being engaged and trained within top companies to readily accept these common applications so that economies of scale, leverage, and synergy will deliver the value that companies promise to shareholders and other stakeholders. Will it all work? Well, it must. Business plans are predicated on execution. If current leaders cannot successfully make commonality work, we replace them with those who can.

Meanwhile, these same companies, or most of them, are concluding that diversity and inclusiveness, defined comprehensively, are potential twin towers of future strength and deserve top billing within the corporate hierarchy of priorities. Making the most of local talent and different national and local capabilities, adapted to succeed at the customer-facing or local stakeholder side of the business, is seen as the success factor of the future. HR leaders and top company officers are praised and rewarded for their willingness and ability to recognize localness and to address the talent development and employee value propositions of local people who execute the work of the organization, wherever it takes place. The continued expansion and growth of major multinationals in developing markets around the world, not the least including India and China but also throughout the entire developing world, depend on the adaptability of such firms to operate successfully in local ways. Leveraging diversity and inclusiveness for organization success competes with synergy and simplicity. Both sets of objectives conflict with organization end games, that is, globalization and/or localization. The same dichotomy touches other major HR processes, including reward, appraisal, development, communications, and so on, and, as we shall see more specifically, talent management.

What's an HR leader to do when setting his or her leadership agenda? Drive the commonality of global processes? Dismantle global processes so local operations can do what works for them? Seek balance? Or, more valuably, combine elements of all three? If the last choice, how does the HR leader manage the consequences of such complexity in the face of inevitable organization demands for productivity and cost effectiveness in HR leadership?

SOLUTIONS

To make the right choices, the HR leader needs to appreciate that there is no simple answer to any of the questions. The HR leader who answers the globalization and localization balance questions has to identify and recognize the implicit and the explicit, the obvious and the intuitive, the theoretical and practical, and the values-based and business-based parameters within which he or she operates. There are a few boundary conditions that can help with the choices that an individual needs to make. In the brevity of this chapter, it is possible to just point them out and then to offer a some-what deeper explanation for at least one major HR process that impacts all companies at every geographic level, that is, *talent management*. The boundary conditions are discussed next.

UNDERSTAND THE OPERATING FRAMEWORK

The nature of a company; its industry; its brand and reputation; the cultural and historical backdrop; the reach and scope; the structure and governance; and the public, state, or private ownership impact the basic operational framework for the HR leader. A century-old, multiproduct, multitechnol-ogy multinational that has survived wars, bubbles, depression, and genera-tions of technology and people operates with a different global/local outlook and experience than a one- or two-decades-old electronic technology com-pany that operates from a single platform. It has history, context, and ex-perience in its favor. It has learned and embedded the lessons of experience. The younger firm, however, could benefit by its newness or handicap itself by its naiveté. A fast-moving consumer goods company operates differently from a capital-intensive, natural resources firm. The challenges of technol-ogy and extensive time horizons compared to customer-facing innovation put unique demands on either industry's people processes. Industries define time, speed, and change differently. A financial services firm is substan-tively different from a utility, regardless of how international either may be. The different types of companies may have interesting stories to share with one another about their experiences. But chances that they develop the same solutions to global/local HR leadership are slim. Of particular importance is the issue of reach and scope. A multinational operating in 150 countries will see the world differently from one that operates in far fewer. Brand and reputation are also significant. Pride and trust that flow from successful longevity, coupled with brand and reputation, are powerful global equalizers embedded in organization culture, regardless of diversity and lo-calness. The HR leader requires the perspective of context and a deep knowledge of the firm and its objectives to draw the right conclusions for proper balance. Deciding against the imposition of American-style reward systems in Rhineland model or developing country markets, for example, may be anathema to results-driven business leaders. But such a decision may be the right conclusion for enlightened HR leaders.

Work within the Business Parameters

The most obvious boundary condition for global/local balance is the margin position of the company or business. High margins enable solutions different from those of low margins. High costs in low-margin worlds drive certain outcomes; low costs in high-margin environments, others. But experience also shows that margins are fickle and often aren't dependable enough to set long-term HR leadership strategy. Thus HR leaders need to consider other business parameters. The capital-to-expense ratios of the business—which vary among short-, medium-, and long-cycle businesses—indebtedness, cash flow, growth rate, profitability, and the entire range of financial measures are helpful considerations to setting HR leadership priorities. In addition, the HR leader needs to consider the "HR intensity" of his or her firm and how it operates. In other words, what are the core capabilities of the firm, how rare or difficult are they to develop in the labor markets in which the firm operates, and how much does the firm invest in people or people processes as a matter of basic business or organization commitment? The scarcer the talent, the greater is the appreciation of that talent and the more challenging it is to get the balance of global/local just right. A firm's "license to operate" in specific countries or regions also helps to determine the correct global/local balance of HR leadership. That is, if a company is dependent on a government's support to succeed, compared to a direct market position and relative lack of government involvement, the extent of global/local balance will vary. The HR leader requires deep understanding of business drivers and how money is made to draw the right conclusions for proper balance. For example, career models, that is, *job for life* or *daily contract* approaches, could vary. Higher margin companies may be more committed to career-long development of staff to help preserve margins. Low-margin companies may find it necessary to identify and develop only a small core group to enable continuity. Other staff may be locally expendable (Figure 41.1).

Figure 41.1
HR Processes

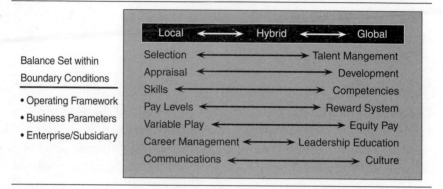

Balance Set within
Boundary Conditions
_____

• Operating Framework
• Business Parameters
• Enterprise/Subsidiary

Local ⟷ Hybrid ⟷ Global
Selection ⟷ Talent Mangement
Appraisal ⟷ Development
Skills ⟷ Competencies
Pay Levels ⟷ Reward System
Variable Play ⟷ Equity Pay
Career Management ⟷ Leadership Education
Communications ⟷ Culture

Establish the Roles and Significance of Enterprise and Subsidiary

The HR leader who understands how organizations work, where decisions are made, who makes them, what makes things happen, and how success is measured is well-positioned to combine the interests of global, local, and hybrid combinations in HR leadership. Central to such capability is an understanding of what is important for the enterprise, that is, the entire firm, and what is important for the local operation, that is, the subsidiary. There are many ways of managing companies, depending on what type of company it is. Choices must be made and agreed at multiple levels of an organization, or even the best firms in the world will be handicapped by their own internal confusion. These choices, however, are indeed variable because that is their nature, for example, the nature of the company and how it sees the long versus the short term, how tight or how loose the firm's decision making, and the extent to which it embraces local optionality or demands standardization. In addition, how a firm structures itself by product, market, geography, business, and function, and the extent to which matrices intersect the organization add to or delete from the complexity of providing HR leadership. Likewise, the centralized or decentralized use of processes and systems, along with strategy and structure, establishes levels of simplicity or complexity. The HR leader requires deep knowledge of organization and clarity of alternatives to draw the right conclusions for proper balance.

We next look deeper at one major HR process and its global/local complications.

TALENT MANAGEMENT: THE ULTIMATE CHALLENGE

Firms succeed because people enable their success. HR leaders with a passion for talent and the credibility to embed that passion in others are critical to the success of international or local companies. They help install competitive advantage across the enterprise and throughout its subsidiaries. They look after the near term and the long term. They recognize the impact of diversity and remove the barriers to its full realization.

Depending on the operating framework, the business parameters, and the roles of enterprise and subsidiary, HR leaders develop and implement well-balanced global, local, and hybrid talent management processes. For it is ultimately the demographics of the workforce, most importantly, the availability of capability at all levels and across all geographies, sustained over many years and repeated through all business cycles, that determine the talent competence that delivers the objectives of the company. The HR leader must have an appreciation for and depth of understanding of global *and* local. He or she does not see conundrum, but opportunity. The choices the HR leader makes are predicated on "both/and" solutions, not "either/or."

The following elements of the talent management processes need debate and decision about the extent to which global overrides local, local takes precedence over global, or exactly what compromises are selected between the two. The debates and decisions need to be explicit. Implicit is not good enough. HR leaders need to decide the globality or localness of the employment brand, attraction strategy, recruitment sources, assessment techniques, and diversity and inclusiveness objectives on boarding programs, development assignments, cross-business/function development, extent of expatriation, leadership education, promotion policies, potential ranking, and succession planning. Within each subprocess, the range of choices themselves needs to be decided on and practiced. It's a challenge to achieve, but HR leaders must make the decisions and ensure that they work (Figure 41.2).

Talent management is only one of the major HR leadership processes that impact the organization's global/local capability. Others, such as appraisal, reward, education, and communications, are also important and necessary and constitute their own opportunity to contribute to getting the balance right for organizations.

Figure 41.2
Talent Management

Subsystem	Local ← → Hybrid ← → Global		
Employment Brand	●	◄─────────────────►	●
Attraction Strategy	●	◄─────────────────►	●
Recruitment Sources	●	◄─────────────────►	●
Assessment System	●	◄─────────────────►	●
Diversity	●	◄─────────────────►	
Onboarding	●	◄─────────────────►	●
Development	●	◄─────────────────►	●
Cross Business/ Function Moves	●	◄─────────────────►	●
Expatriation	●	◄─────────────────►	●
Leadership Education	●	◄─────────────────►	●
Promotion System	●	◄─────────────────►	●
Potential Rating	●	◄─────────────────►	●
Succession	●	◄─────────────────►	●

	Low ●	High ●

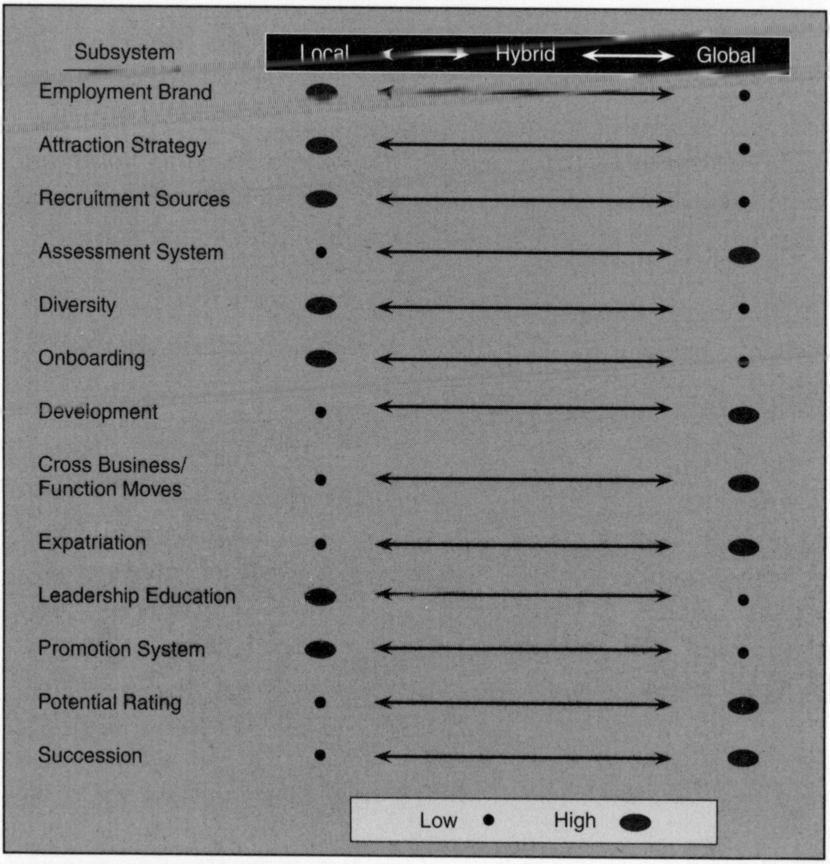

CONCLUSION

Global HR leadership is possible and doable, as well as local or a combination of the two. HR leaders are called on to make choices among all three options that work for their firm. The quality of choice is dependent on the capability of the HR leader, who is also accountable for the outcomes. Getting the balance right is the ultimate contribution the HR leader makes.

Said the speaker at the annual meeting to the challenger: "Impact is the product of many years of experience and probably lots of mistakes. But let's understand the goal of the decision makers. When Nigerian petroleum engineers are as prevalent around the world as other multinational expatriates are in Nigeria, we will know we are getting the balance right."

CHAPTER 42

GLOBAL HR AS COMPETITIVE ADVANTAGE: ARE WE READY?

VLADIMIR PUCIK

Ask any senior executive in a company that operates across national boundaries, irrespective of national origin, about the major source of tensions in his or her job, and the answer most likely will be the same—the ever-increasing *complexity* of business problems he or she needs to tackle.

Decision making involving *multiple strategic logics* is probably the major source of complexity faced—how best to structure the business model to achieve a sustainable competitive advantage. The dominant prescription for success in the world of business strategy calls for differentiation—providing local customers with unique products, services, and solutions to their needs. Yet, for most examples of successful differentiation, we can easily draw a contradictory prescription—integration, capturing the various economies of scale through global standardization of design, production, or delivery.

Second, international organizations face a business environment where economic, political, and social issues are frequently *interdependent* and *intertwined* and business decisions cannot be made in isolation from all other factors. For example, strategic decisions on foreign direct investment very much depend on the judgments companies make about the future political and social development in the target country. Sometimes the economic logic argues one way, but political considerations point the other way.

Finally, the challenge of complexity facing global firms is compounded by *uncertainty* in the environment driven by ever-increasing *speed* of change and its underlying *unpredictability*. One example is the evolution in the information processing industry. Nearly all of the dominant global

370

players of the 1970s disappeared or faded as major competitors just three decades later. During this period, the time to capitalize on new technological breakthroughs by distributing new knowledge to affiliates around the world formerly measured in years or months turned into weeks.

Old strategies, formulated during times of relative stability, certainty, independence, and simplicity cannot ensure the survival of global firms in today's environment, let alone give them a lasting competitive advantage in the marketplace. This, in turn, means that the organizational structures, processes, and systems in place must be increasingly flexible and adaptable. In other words, the complexity in the environment must be mirrored in the organization itself (the law of requisite variety). As complexity in the competitive environment drives the need for more complex business strategies, building and sustaining global organizational capability to execute with the necessary speed and efficiency become the critical challenge.

The critical building blocks for this capability are all very closely linked to people, their mind-set, and behaviors—creating an important new domain for the HR function. Can HR deliver? Where are some key opportunities and challenges for HR to make a difference?

WHY GLOBAL MIND-SET MATTERS

Several years ago, Nokia Networks, a leading provider of the infrastructure for mobile telecommunications, participated in a benchmark study at IMD on how managers perceive a company's global strategy. While corporate strategic documents carefully spelled out the need to achieve dual objectives—global efficiency as well as responsiveness to the needs of local operators—the interpretation for day-to-day activities was dramatically different. The survey showed that some parts of the organization such as product-focused business divisions had a highly global orientation, while other parts were strongly local, such as sales and service companies in rapidly growing markets. Both groups were convinced that their interpretation of corporate guidelines is correct; it is the others who "do not understand" and make it difficult to execute effectively.

Still, the reaction of most top executives to the findings was initially positive: "This is exactly the type of differentiation we need—strongly integrated product lines worrying about global economies of scale and locally oriented sales units worrying about local opportunities. We at the center then make the final decision." However, on reflection, their view changed. They realized that the consequence of this differentiation in understanding of the company strategy was that the conflicts were being pushed up to senior management for arbitration, overloading their own agendas, causing delays in decision-making, and leaving little time to focus on institutional leadership. While the product managers indeed needed to be global, they also had to understand the need to work through the conflicts with local sales units—and vice versa, the local units need to make sure that their sale initiatives were benefiting from and contributing to global synergies.

Nokia's challenge was similar to most other firms competing globally that are facing a multitude of new demands on their organization and people that are marked by tensions between opposites, perceived as contradictions and paradox. The evolving perspective is that of *duality,* the tension created by opposites. These opposites are not "either-or" choices, but "both-and" dualities that must be reconciled, replacing a continuously swinging pendulum of centralization and decentralization with an acceptance of the global organization as a fluid and dynamic differentiated network. The contradictions cannot be resolved by structure but need to be built into the way of thinking of leaders and managers by various HR tools and processes.

What has Nokia done? Engineers and managers were rotated between business divisions and the sales companies for short-term, developmental assignments. Horizontal coordination mechanisms such as task forces, account teams, and steering groups were set up with participation from around the world. Finally, a new set of measurements was introduced in the performance management process to appraise and reward global behavior. Within 18 months, a repeat survey showed that mind-set has shifted—indeed, HR did make an impact.

DEVELOPING GLOBAL CAPABILITIES

It may seem intuitively obvious that firms doing business around the world will need more and more managers with "global brains" who can balance competing business, country, and functional priorities that emerge in international management process. However, translating this idea into an operational reality is not simple. First, does every manager need to be "global"? Who really needs global mind-set? Managers are not born global. They acquire global brains through a series of experiences, many of them at a substantial cost to the organization. What is the return on investing in developing people with global brains? Making a rational business case concerning the future need and use of global managers is one of the critical strategic decisions HR has to tackle.

For example, early in its globalization efforts, Swedish/Swiss engineering giant ABB made an explicit decision that, out of a workforce of over 200,000, it would need to develop about 500 global managers, handpicked and monitored by the CEO and ready to move across countries, functions, and businesses. This number has proven to be far too small, creating severe coordination problems as the complexity facing the company increased more then anticipated. In the absence of a coherent global HR process, it took the company some time and a major crisis (and several CEOs) to recognize the severity of its management capability gap, but it requires time and resources to fix it.

While ABB might have made a mistake of underestimating the number of global managers necessary to coordinate its global operation, the other extreme—everyone should be global—could be just as problematic. It may indeed be very helpful if each employee of the firm understands the complexity of the global business at least to the degree it impacts the person's current job. However, is it realistic that any company can invest the resources necessary to develop and sustain global mind-set everywhere? Without making some difficult choices on where and how to invest, global mind-set is not much else than an empty slogan, reduced at most to an administrative measure, such as language requirements for certain kinds of management positions.

Ultimately, what kind of global mind-set is necessary depends on the competitive position of the firm. Not all companies need to become global to do business across borders. A polarized mind-set may serve a positive purpose at a particular stage of globalization. Investing in development of global mind-set when it is not necessary for the business may be a colossal waste of resources. What matters is for HR to foster the alignment and consistency in understanding the strategy of the firm across the whole organization.

Balancing Global and Local Approaches

What gets measured gets attention. This old idea is no less valid when it comes to developing global capabilities. The common mistake of many firms striving to move down the path to becoming global is to equate an understanding of the need to be global with actual practices. However, in our research with managers operating in global businesses, we have consistently seen high gaps between what was desired and what happened. The level of global coordination is often low partly because mechanisms such as teamwork and know-how sharing are missing but, even more fundamentally, because the HR practices do not encourage managers to do what they personally believe should have been done. When measurements change, so do behaviors.

Therefore, another critical component of global people strategies is performance management. Here, the commitment to implement a rigorous process is more important than the sophistication of the methodology. Such a process can start with a fairly simple template, developed with input from around the world and possibly modeled on best practice in leading subsidiaries, just as Vodafone is doing now when integrating HR practices of its numerous affiliates around the world. Based on this template, different subsidiaries then must face up to the distinctive cultural problems and undertake adaptation where necessary. One size may not fit all because, among all the aspects of performance, management appraisal and feedback are generally considered to be the most sensitive to local context.

But national culture is only one element of context. Variations in norms and values within cultures are just as important as variations across cultures. Consequently, there is tremendous variance on performance management across firms, industries, and sectors within most nations. Thus, foreign companies in China are told that because of the concept of "face," direct feedback is nearly impossible to implement, while Haier, one of the leading Chinese multinationals, posts monthly appraisals of all managers in the company cafeteria. On average, it is probably true that most Chinese employees may resent direct negative feedback, but there are always those who accept this kind of racehorse environment as superior to the traditional emphasis on educational credentials and personal connections.

What guidelines can we get from research? The evidence suggests that the design and functioning of performance management systems—from pay-for-performance to team-based pay and from stock options to executive compensation—are highly dependent on context. But, to the extent that performance management practices are an integral element of the firm's processes, a firm may choose rewards to create a unique, value-adding organizational culture by creating its own context, within limits. An American firm operating in China can pay attention to selecting and socializing people who fit with its approach to reward management (and the other elements of the performance process in which this is embedded)—just as Southwest Airlines with its distinctive culture pays great attention to selecting people who will thrive there rather than in a more "traditional" U.S. airline.

It is the internal consistency of practices and norms that is powerful. We cannot consider rewards separately from the other elements of performance management, as well as the wider context of recruitment and socialization—even though consistency creates its own constraints. For example, unless compensation is aligned to reward broader dimensions of global performance beyond an individual's job or immediate business unit, it is unlikely that we will see strong collaborative behavior or support for wider global corporate initiatives.

SUPPORTING A CULTURE OF DIVERSITY

The nature of the whole debate about the benefits and cost of doing things globally is closely tied to how open we are to the idea that we do not all necessarily share the same preferences. Enhancing global capabilities implies recognizing the benefits that can flow to the whole organization from encouraging and valuing cultural diversity in people, not just as members of distinct cultural groups, but as individuals. Success in building cross-border networks of relationships—the principal arteries of effective global organizations—depends on understanding and valuing cultural diversity. Yet, valuing diversity must go well beyond the traditional emphasis on bridging the distance between clusters of national cultures by focusing on average—and stereotypical—national characteristics.

Why is diversity critical? When development opportunities are restricted (even if not intentional) to those from the mother country or a few lead countries, local employees inevitably tend to adopt local perspectives—that is the only direction for their own future. Thus, a key task for global HR is to ensure equitable access to career opportunities for talented employees worldwide. This is not a simple challenge; it takes years of effort to ensure that selection criteria are not biased toward one cultural group and that early identification of talent works equally well in Karachi or Bogota as in New York or Paris.

Why do these barriers persist? Historically, most operational HR activities in multinational firms were decentralized into country organizations—after all, the vast majority of employees are and always will be local, embedded in the local culture, and impacted by the local legal and regulatory environment. However, when HR localization is taken too literally and everyone is treated as local, who is then global? A natural outcome of this well-intentioned, but ultimately destructive, localization bias is that nationals of the country where the corporate center is located are considered implicitly global, but all others are local with only a limited chance to advance. That's perhaps why the top HR leadership group, even among firms with extensive international experience, is generally not very representative of the employee population at large.

The acceptance of diversity should also include tolerance of people who are not global, perhaps because of lack of opportunities, personal choice, or circumstances. Anything taken to an extreme risks becoming pathological—being global is no exception. This is true for companies as well as for individuals. International management textbooks are full of examples of "dumb" multinationals and their managers that are not sensitive enough to cultural differences—which the savvy globals navigate with ease. But years of successful navigation sometimes make us forget about the rocks below the water line.

Learn Locally, Act Globally

During the past decade, a catchy paradigm, "Think globally, act locally," has often been used to capture the concept of a progressive global corporation that considers the whole world as its market but at the same time carefully nurtures and adapts to local priorities and requirements. However, for many firms, implementing this vision turned out to be a long and difficult process.

Why is this idea so difficult to implement? In a global firm that used this popular slogan on the first page of its annual report, one local HR manager commented on its application in practice: "Our firm is organized on a simple premise. When operating under stress, and that is most of the time, *they* do the thinking, and *we* do the acting." In other words, the global thinking and local acting are two separate roles. The headquarters launches the global HR initiatives, which the locals are asked to implement within local constraints.

In their passion to promote global mind-set, academics and others writing from a normative perspective sometimes tend to see global or cosmopolitan as superior to local, calling for a "universal way that transcends the particulars of places." What is "local" is seen as parochial and narrow-minded. However, global mind-set requires an approach that may be seen as the opposite to such one-dimensional universalism—it calls for a dualistic perspective, an immersion in local particulars, while at the same time retaining a wider, cross-border perspective. It requires an emphasis on local learning for the benefit of the whole organization.

Global capability is as much about learning as it is about doing. For a company to be truly global implies openness to learn from the experience of others and to understand and appreciate how others (local employees, customers, even competitors) may think. In particular, the specific needs of local customers have to be carefully assessed—hence the requirement to be able to learn and understand the local context through the *local* immersion. At the same time, there is no competitive advantage in being an "average" local firm, and the ability to satisfy those needs with a superior value proposition is dependent on the *global* mobilization of corporate resources, be it leading-edge technology, economies of scale, or global standards of performance and quality.

What, then, is the competitive advantage of a global firm? In simple terms, it is the ability to tap *global capabilities* and skills to satisfy *local customer needs*. It may be useful, therefore, to rephrase the original paradigm. Building global HR that creates a competitive advantage is really about developing people who learn locally and act globally—perhaps another contradiction, but such is the nature of globalization around us.

CHAPTER 43

A NEW PARADIGM FOR HR: DILEMMAS IN EMPLOYING AND MANAGING THE RESOURCEFUL HUMAN

FONS TROMPENAARS AND PETER WOOLLIMAS

Over recent decades, we have witnessed the development of the autonomous and reflective individual—an individual with a full set of needs, internal and external to the organization. Power is diffused and shared. "In contrast with traditional management, where structures and systems are derived from a predefined strategy, the new workplace will seek to balance what matters for the company (its strategy) and what matters for the individuals (their life strategies)."[1] In fact, management and employees decide and execute *interactively*. In this New World of the *customized workplace* in which priority for sustained personal development goes hand in hand with the employer's business performance and growth, the reconciliation of dilemmas is the new source of authority. This source is revealed even more dramatically in the process of continuing globalization.

In addition to these generic changes (especially in the Western Hemisphere), the world has recognized increasing shifts due to the internationalization of business. Yet, we still observe that the major instruments and methods used by HR professionals owe their origin to an Anglo-Saxon philosophy and are still dominated by an Anglo-Saxon signature. Typical are the instruments used for recruitment and selection. Although its original conceptual father, C. G. Jung, was a Swiss, the Myers-Briggs Type Indicator (MBTI) and Jung Type Indicator (JTI) are the most used Americanized instruments in business to assess personality type. Similarly, over 8,000 companies use the Hay System for job evaluation worldwide. Originally developed by Colonel Hay for evaluating jobs in the American army, it later became extended to the most popular evaluation instrument for international businesses. Lately, we see the enormously popular Balanced Scorecard developed by Kaplan and Norton that initially helped many North American firms to measure important perspectives of business beyond the financial.

But what have these Americanized perspectives done for (and *to*) non-American organizations? There was an era when globalization was taken literally. "It works in the United States, so let's export it to the rest of the world," was the main principle. Generally, this approach has failed. In fact, it has worked only in organizations where the corporate culture dominated the local or national cultures (e.g., the Hewlett-Packard "way" and McKinsey) and perhaps in organizations where the product was very dominant (e.g., Coca-Cola, Disney, and McDonald's).

A Proposed New Logic for HR

Our new approach to understanding HR that transcends these changes is to investigate dilemmas that derive from the tensions caused by cultural (value) differences, whether from national, ethnic, or corporate cultures. In our findings, all cultures and corporations share similar dilemmas, but their approach is usually culturally determined. For example, on the one hand, should we be directing/hands-on with staff or, on the other hand, empowering staff to be self-controlling and innovative? The success of a company depends, among other things, on both the autonomy of its people and how well the information arising from this autonomy has been centralized and coordinated. If you fail to exploit fully centralized information, your scattered but highly self-motivated personnel might as well remain totally independent. If various teams are not free to act on local information, then centralized directives are subtracting, not adding, value.

Our new framework for HR that seeks to serve this new paradigm is based on three Rs—recognize, respect, and reconciliation:

- *Recognize:* While we can more easily recognize explicit and overt cultural (value) differences, we may not be aware of more hidden, implicit differences, which explains the frequent absence of cultural due diligence from the agenda and from many of the classic HR models, frameworks, and tools. Thus, the first step is to *recognize* that there are differences in values and thus the meaning given to the same thing by different people.

- *Respect:* Different orientations about "where I am coming from" are not "right" or "wrong," they are just different. It is all too easy to be judgmental about people and societies that give different meaning to their world from ours. Thus, the next step is to *respect* these differences and accept the right of employees and customers to interpret the world (and our products and services) in the way they choose.

- *Reconciliation:* Because of these different views of the world, we have tensions deriving from these different value systems and/or current practice versus idealized behaviors. The task of the HR professional is to facilitate the *reconciliation* between these opposing differences in the area of their own function and to help build the wider reconciling organization.

Thus, for example, diversity management is not simply about compliance with legislation that demands positive discrimination to support minorities. First, we must recognize differences, whether from ethnic, gender, or age/generation origins. Next, we must respect these contrasting orientations and recognize that differing views from each group are equally valid. Then, and importantly, we must seize the opportunities that derive from these differences and integrate them so that we can benefit from the variety of new ideas, new ways of working, and new insights that a multivariate workforce can offer.

In our research at Trompenaars Hampden-Turner (THT), we have helped HR professionals elicit the dilemmas they face in their work and those that are faced by their organizations. Using face-to-face interviews as well as our Web-based systems, we have accumulated over 6,000 basic dilemmas. Applying clustering and linguistic analysis techniques, we quickly begin to see a number of fundamental and reoccurring dilemmas that are faced by HR.

When seeking to structure or categorize these dilemmas across HR, it is constructive to consider the different meanings assigned to organizational relationships. We describe four major stereotypes of different organizational logic or corporate cultures: *the Family, the Eiffel Tower, the Guided Missile, and the Incubator.* We only partly agree with Cameron and Quinn's observation that: ". . . the roles, means, ends, and competencies emphasized by the HR manager must reinforce the dominant or desired culture of the firm. Displaying different HR roles can help build or strengthen a different kind of organisational culture."[2] But the opposite holds true as well, that is, that the dominant organizational culture will breed a certain kind of HR manager.

The different roles the HR manager plays in each logic are summarized in Table 43.1 on pages 381–382.

We have observed many Western organizations that have sought to impose Western (or rather, Anglo-Saxon) HR systems on organizational cultures that were based on entirely different assumptions. The result was either "corporate rain dancing" or complete ineffectiveness of the intended outcome. What do we do with a pay-for-performance scheme in the Family? And what about a formal job evaluation session in an Incubator culture?

Similarly, our research confirms that it is too simplistic to attempt to transform an organization culture from the current mode to some idealized nirvana. Cultures act to preserve themselves, which is why so many business transformation and change programs fail. The value of our typology, however, lies in comparing the current culture with an espoused, idealized culture to elicit the tensions between them and thereby identify the important dilemmas that result and need to be addressed (Figure 43.1 on page 383).

We can illustrate the frequently reoccurring dilemmas we have found for HR with some examples.

The War for Talent: Can We Recruit the Best Person for the Job or Should We Offer Lifetime Continuity of Employment?

The process of attracting and retaining talent is one of the key tasks of HR professionals. Criteria and competencies deemed to be predictors of high and effective performance are claimed. However, hardly any attention has been given to a very much underresearched issue—the image of the organization to the job seeker. The values with which organizations entice scarce human resources are very different today.

Table 43.1
Roles of the HR Manager

Incubator	Guided Missile
A leaderless team in which people aim for personal growth. Individualization is one of the most important features. The organization exists only to serve the needs of its members. Its members are motivated by learning on the job for personal development.	"Getting the job done" with "the right person in the right place" are favorite expressions. Organizational relationships are result-oriented, based on rational and instrumental considerations, and limited to the specific functional aspects of the persons involved.

Incubator:

Person oriented

Power of the individual

Management by passion

Commitment to oneself

Professional recognition

Self-realization

Main Role of HR:

Creative business player for organizational learning

Attract, Retain, and Motivate Talent: Intuitive recruitment, self-realization, and continuous learning

Reward Staff: Learning

Evaluate Jobs: People make jobs, no formal process

Develop Staff and Leaders: On the job

Plan Staff: Where needed and short term

Main Role: Change agent by facilitating transformation

Guided Missile:

Achievement and effectiveness are weighed above the demands of authority, procedures, or people. Authority and responsibility are placed where the qualifications lie, and they may shift rapidly as the nature of the task changes. Everything is subordinate to delivering the encompassing goal(s).

Task orientation

Power of knowledge/expertise

Management-by-objectives

Commitment to tasks

Effectiveness

Pay for performance

Main Role of HR:

Strategic business partner for effectiveness

Attract, Retain, and Motivate Talent:

Quantitative measurements, high material rewards, and focused learning

Reward Staff: High material pay

Evaluate Jobs: Task makes jobs (benchmarks)

Develop Staff and Leaders: Task focused and professional

Plan Staff: Middle term where task requests

Main Role: Strategic business partner through aligning HR with business strategy

Table 43.1 *Continued*

Family	Eiffel Tower
A highly personalized organization predominantly power oriented. Employees in the family interact around the centralized power of the father or mother. The power of the organization is based on an autocratic leader who, like a spider in a web, directs the organization. There are few rules and thereby little bureaucracy.	Steep, stately, and very robust. Control is exercised through systems of rules, legalistic procedures, responsibilities, and assigned rights. Bureaucracy makes this organization inflexible. Respect for authority is based on the respect for functional position and status. The bureau or desk has depersonalized authority. Expertise and related formal titles are much appreciated.

Family:

Power orientation

Power of network

Personal relationships

Management-by-subjectives

Affinity/trust

Promotion

Main Role of HR:

Political subordinate of management for organizational loyalty

Attract, Retain, and Motivate Talent: Fit with political elite, loyalty programs

Reward Staff: Increased authority

Evaluate Jobs: By management's discretion

Develop Staff and Leaders: Knowing the power elite

Plan Staff: Lifetime across the family

Main Role: Employee champion responding to employee needs

Eiffel Tower:

Role orientation

Power of position/role

Management-by-job description/evaluation

Rules and procedures

Order and predictability

Expertise

Main Role of HR:

Administrative specialist for structural efficiency

Attract, Retain, and Motivate Talent: Fit with quantified job requirements, expertise, and lifetime learning

Reward Staff: Education

Evaluate Jobs: Formal job classification systems

Develop Staff and Leaders: Expert training

Plan Staff: Apprenticeship

Main Role: Administrative specialist facilitating reengineering processes

Mining our database generates evidence that supports the proposition that members of the younger generation—from 20 to 30 years old—have become more increasingly directed in the past few years. They dare to express their emotions more, and they feel better working in teams. Moreover, it appears that these younger, Generation X, high-potential employees have a shorter time horizon and greater self-confidence in their individual

Figure 43.1
Source of Tensions between the Current and Ideal Corporate Culture:
Typical Profile Map

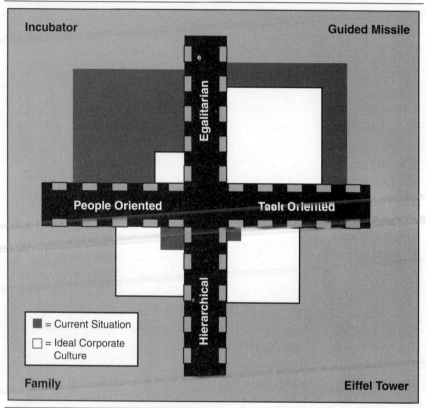

abilities. Their preference has shifted away from the task-oriented Guided Missile corporations to the person-oriented, Incubator work environment. Their rationale for career security is based on maintaining a set of personal and transferable competencies. It is their employability rating based on their contemporaneous skills profile that drives them, not the old notion of corporate security from an employer of high, long-standing regard or protection by their trade union. The old adage that working for a major corporation will ensure a job for life is no longer true or an attractor.

What might make a large organization attractive to a young, ambitious, and talented employee now? It is apparent that established organizations must make an enormous effort to catch up with the attraction of younger businesses. There is a tension between the image of these companies and the ideals that young, talented people have in their heads. The power-oriented, Family culture and the role-oriented, hierarchical structures of the so-called Eiffel Tower culture still dominate in both perception and reality.

The dilemma arises from the tension between corporate image and personal vision. Global companies such as Heineken or Shell are looking for people who are global, innovative, team players—people who think in terms of diversity, who want to learn, and who value freedom of choice (to continuously maintain their employability profile). This global corporate mind-set thinking appears to be bland ("it's all the same everywhere") and static and does not offer the freedom to develop an individual's persona. As a consequence, it is not attractive to the Generation X people. Young, talented, recently graduated candidates prefer to work locally and have fun.

Global (one-world) thinking creates tensions compared to a contrasting framework that recognizes and values diversity (many realities). Shell invites people who believe in the equal treatment of men and women and asks people from different ethnic backgrounds to develop into honorable citizens of the world. While apparently laudable, you can imagine the dilemmas that arise between being oriented toward teamwork (stability/tradition) and innovation. The Japanese experience demonstrates that this is not easy to reconcile. Apart from these dilemmas within Shell's espoused orientation, there is also the dilemma adhering to the image of a large organization and doubt whether these orientations can be put into practice.

The U.K. division of Pfizer is achieving productivity improvement through reconciling the different orientations between, for example, their researchers (who want to do brilliant research) and their committed marketers (who want to satisfy their customer base). The traditional approach based on idea productivity incentives, goal setting (productivity goals), increased automation, and quality improvement initiatives has mainly failed HR. We are helping them to create the reconciling organization in which a strong sense of core values supports an environment in which managers are better able to manage change, overcome crises, focus on corporate longevity, achieve the retention of key/effective personnel, develop motivation, and identify and thereby secure higher productivity through the alignment and integration of opposite orientations.

These are organizations that historically have a dominant Guided Missile or Eiffel Tower culture yet still seem to attract talented staff by reconciling the tensions between free choice and deep learning opportunities, between downsizing and economies of scale, and between image and reality.

Dilemmas in Selection and Recruitment: Do We Try to Recruit a Clone of the Present Outgoing Jobholder or Assess New Potential from Different Applicants?

There is the danger that recruitment is simply a sophisticated way of cloning, which is the origin of professional tools to offer objectivity to assessment. In MBTI terms, there are observable differences in personality between different countries. For example, the most predominant type in British management is ISTJ, while in American management, it is ESTJ. There is evidence from Korean MBTI research that Koreans tend to be more introverted than extroverted when the American norm is applied to interpret their score. Because introverted people are relatively pervasive in Korean society, most organizations including educational institutions and companies encourage their members to be more extroverted in public situations, and many evaluate an extroverted person more favorably. While these national differences may be more obvious, such differences also occur between functional groups including R&D, sales, accounting, and IT.

But what about these methodologies when the applications go beyond the environment in which they were developed? Suppose the culture likes the extroverted, sensing, intuitive, perceptive type? Thus, if a culture believes in judging rather than perceiving, should we just select our people accordingly? The internationalization of recruitment has clearly shown us that other types are more dominant in other cultural environments. And what about the trying to assess whether a person can survive in other cultures? The MBTI fans find solutions in the team and the complementarities of types, or they refer to the fact that the types are only preferences but that all is potentially within the person. But why were the questionnaires designed on mutually exclusive values in the first place? It is because our Western ways of thinking are based on Cartesian logic and force us to say it is "either . . . or," not to say "both . . . and." This is in contradiction to what the genius Carl Jung had in mind in the first place when he construed the underlying conceptual framework behind MBTI.[3]

Thus, in a situation where the culture in which people are being recruited has a slight preference for the sensing, what could be done when facing an environment where intuiting is the preference for making a successful career? Applying our paradigm, we can extend MBTI by slightly adjusting the instrument and the way of thinking that forms the context of its applications and thereby make it a jewel of an instrument far beyond any cultural preference.

The MBTI logic asks if you are sensing or intuiting. The more you identify yourself as sensing, the less you must be of the intuiting type. Although MBTI professionals do talk about combining the variety of preferences in teams and organizations, we cannot derive this approach from the MBTI instrument because it is based on forced choice, bimodel questions.

Let's apply our thinking to the scales of the MBTI. The following question is asked to test the preference for thinking or feeling:

- When I make a decision, I think it is most important:
  (a) To test the opinions of others.
  (b) To be decisive.

But what if in a multicultural environment you find people with different opinions? The decisive leader agonizes over the fact that many want to go for consensus. Conversely, the sensitive leader will not succeed because of an apparent lack of decisiveness. Thus, we have a dilemma between the seemingly opposing orientations of thinking and feeling.

In our extended model of MBTI, the Integrated Type Indicator (ITI),[4] the addition of two alternative options provides a means of evaluating the individual's propensity to reconcile this dilemma:

- When I make a decision, I think it is most important:
  (c) To be decisive through the continuous testing of opinions of others.
  (d) To test the opinions of others by showing decisiveness (Figure 43.2).

Those who answer "c" are starting from a thinking orientation but accounting for the feeling of others. They have successfully reconciled the

Figure 43.2
Decisiveness Option

opposites. This process involves starting from one axis and spiraling to the top right (10,10 position), and thus the individual has integrated both components (Figure 43.3).

Similarly, those who answer "d" are starting from feeling but spiraling toward thinking and again integrating the two seemingly opposite orientations.

Figure 43.3
Integrating Both Components

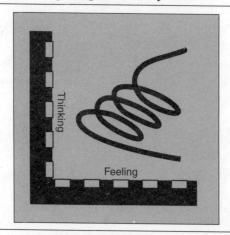

In our ITI, we use our own questions that represent the two extreme opposing values for each conjugate pair. However, we add two choices that represent the clockwise and anticlockwise reconciliation between these extremes.

By combining the answers from a series of questions in this extended format, we can compute a profile that reveals the degree to which an individual seeks to integrate the extreme dimensions (Figure 43.4).

We continually observe how high-performing individuals and effective leaders are able to reconcile opposites. For example, Richard Branson is able to switch from being David in one business situation to being Goliath in another. He reconciles the big player with the small player so that the smaller player becomes big.

Figure 43.4
Integrating Extreme Dimensions

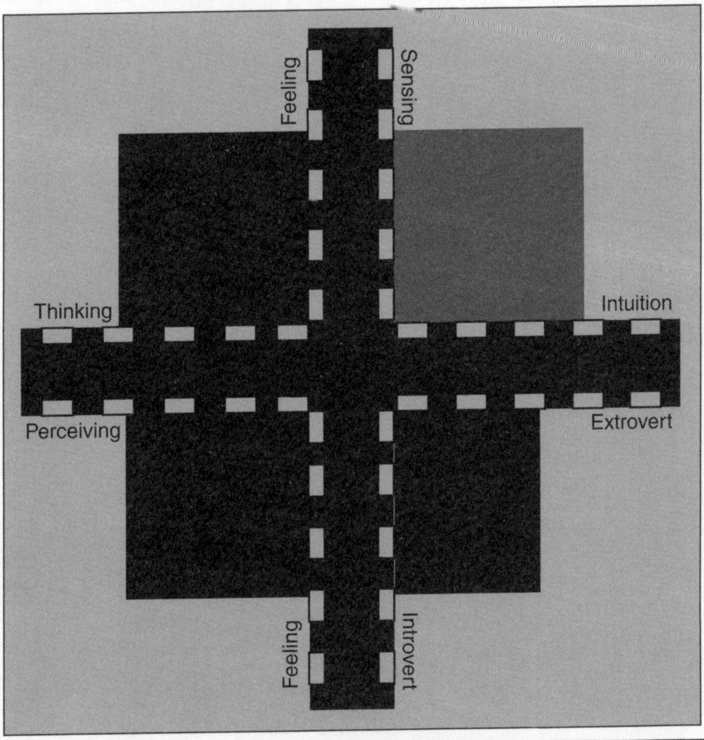

OTHER DILEMMAS OF HR

In addition to the preceding examples of dilemmas in HR, we find similar dilemmas across the spectrum of the HR function (from operational to strategic) that typically arise from:

- Individual accountability versus team responsibility
- Objective observation/evaluation versus subjective observation/ evaluation
- Evaluation of behavioral differences versus intuitive differences
- Priority for HR development versus productivity
- Balanced scorecard as a development versus evaluation tool
- Development as a specialist versus development as generalists
- Technical logic versus business logic
- Taking risks versus avoiding failure
- Task versus people orientation
- Entrepreneurship versus control/accountability
- Flexibility versus efficiency
- Exploitation versus exploration
- Mentoring versus managing

Each dilemma can be reconciled following the approach described in the earlier examples. Essentially, we ask, "How can we secure more of value A through combining with value B?" Thus, the approach to reconciling the individual versus team dilemma can be approached by making individuals responsible for how they can contribute to the development of the team and how the team can enable the development of individual members.

All organizations need stability and change, tradition and innovation, public and private interest, planning and laissez-faire, order and freedom, and growth and decay. The consequence is that the systems and processes of HR are changing to the world of dilemmas[5] created by the customized workplace and even more by globalization.

To meet the challenges of today's ever-globalizing world, HR needs to develop a new mind-set of inquiry and support centered on the reconciliation of dilemmas and thereby finally fulfilling its true identity.

NOTES

1. Hamid Bouchiki and John Kimberly, "All Change in the Customised Workplace," in Mastering People Management, *Financial Times,* October 22, 2001, pp. 4–5.

2. Kim S. Cameron and Robert E. Quinn, *Diagnosing and Changing Corporate Culture.* Cambridge, MA: Addison-Wesley, 1999, p. 46.

3. Carl G. Jung, *Psychological Types.* Boston: Routledge & Kegan Paul, 1971.

4. Fons Trompenaars and Peter Woollimas, "Just Typical: Avoiding Stereotypes in Personality Testing," *People Management,* December 2002, pp. 1–3.

5. The new concepts described here are explored further in the new books *Business Across Cultures* (Fons Trompenaars and Peter Woollimas) and *Managing People Across Cultures* (Charles Hampden-Turner and Fons Trompenaars), London: Capstone, 2004. See www.cultureforbusiness.com.

CHAPTER 44

COUNTERINTUITIVE FINDINGS IN INTERNATIONAL HRM RESEARCH AND PRACTICE: WHEN IS A BEST PRACTICE NOT BEST FOR PRACTICE?

MARY ANN VON GLINOW, ELLEN A. DROST, AND
MARY B. TEAGARDEN

Over the years, the international human resource management (IHRM) community has expressed considerable interest in what has come to be known as *best practices*. The concept of best practices suggests universally applicable HRM practices. In today's world, it is difficult to imagine that a single practice or set of practices would emerge as *best* in any sense of the word, particularly in modern, global organization forms. It is even more difficult to imagine that these best practices would be transferable with any degree of precision to other organizations or industries. Thus, the basic argument our research team struggled with was, "Are there, universal of their cultural context, best practices or purely context-specific practices that are often meaningless out of cultural context?"[1]

For more than a decade, we researched and debated this issue, eventually morphing into a multicultural, multicountry, multiresearcher team we called the Best IHRM Practices Consortium or BP Project. Our project's intent was to make *meaningful* cultural comparisons and encourage the incorporation of multiple but qualitatively different, embedded contexts—polycontextuality—into the discussion of similarities and differences in HR practices. We collected data from many countries—including Australia, Canada, China, Japan, Korea, Indonesia, Mexico, Taiwan, United States, and five additional countries that we grouped as the Latin America region, which had sufficient responses for credibility. Identification of practices that stood out as best and why they did so demanded great attention to contextual, cultural, and organizational variables. Ironically, the massive data sets caused us to reflect not just on significant differences but also on significant similarities, and therein lay our dilemma. Our learning curve was steep.

We looked at the relationships between current and future HR practices for ideological, within-culture gaps. Comparing current "is now" practices with responses to how these practices "should be" used in the future is a useful tool in determining whether current HR practices may be an effective source of added value for the firm in the long term. It also gives us a sense of how far off the bar the "is now" practices are compared to the "should be"—an ideological map. The gaps in managerial attitudes may signal practices that will be adopted in the future.

We used a standardized survey, completed by approximately 2,200 managers and engineers using personal as well as academic contacts for data collection done by mail or in person when appropriate. Admittedly, we have not analyzed the universe of all cultures, thus we cannot fully use the term *universal*. However, the same logic applies, and the following discussion focuses on what we know.

WHAT DO WE KNOW ABOUT UNIVERSAL BEST PRACTICES?

Trends that appear to have universal applicability, either now or in the future, as well as country-specific practices useful for IHRM researchers and practitioners alike, are some of our key findings. We feature the HR practices perceived as universally important *future HR practices* in Table 44.1 and discuss them in detail in the following sections.

"West Meets East" Selection

Fit matters—how well the person "fits" with the corporate and company values and how well the person gets along with others are dramatically increasing in importance everywhere. Although a common best practice in Asian countries for some time, it is much more pronounced now in the West. Traditional selection criteria are being abandoned in the West, while the list of selection criteria is growing. Job interviews, technical skill proficiency,

Table 44.1

Trends in Future International Human Resource Management Practices across Selected Countries and Regions

Practice	Universal "Best Practices"	Regional "Best Practices"
Selection	Getting along with others and fit with the corporate values signal a shift in selection to "West meets East."	Selection practices were remarkably similar among the Anglo countries. Specifically, job interview, technical skill, and work experience are the most important selection criteria. How well the person fits the company replaces work experience as one of the top selection criteria for future selection practices. Selection practices are similar in Korea, Japan, and Taiwan. Specifically, proven work experience is deemphasized as a selection practice in these countries.
Training and Development (T&D)	In all countries, T&D practices continue to be used to improve employees' technical skills. There is a growing trend toward T&D in soft management practices such as team building, understanding business practices, and corporate culture.	In the Anglo countries, T&D in soft management practices such as team building, understanding business practices, and corporate culture and the proactive T&D practices such as preparation for future assignment and cross-training are used moderately; however, a significant increase in these practices is desired. In the Latin American countries, an increase in all T&D practices is desired. In the Asian countries, T&D practices are used moderately and consistently considered satisfactory.
Compensation	Pay incentives should not comprise too much of an employee's compensation package in the future. Compensation should be based on individual job performance.	In the Asian and Latin American countries, seniority-based pay, pay based on group/team or organizational goals, and pay based on future goals are used to a larger extent now.

Note: The findings presented in this table are a synthesis of the collective publications of the Best Practices Consortium. (M. A. Von Glinow, E. A. Drost, and M. B. Teagarden, "Converging on IHRM Best Practices: Lessons Learned from a Globally Distributed Consortium on Theory and Practice," *Human Resource Management,* Special Issue 2002, Vol. 41, (1), 123–140.)

Table 44.1 *Continued*

Practice	Universal "Best Practices"	Regional "Best Practices"
	There should be a reduced emphasis on seniority. Benefits should comprise a large part of a compensation package.	
Performance Appraisal (PA)	All countries indicated that a greater emphasis be placed on *development* in future PA practices. In particular, recognizing subordinates, evaluating their goal achievement, planning their development activities, and (ways to) improving performance are considered the most important appraisal practices in the future.	In the Anglo and Latin American countries, allowing subordinates to express themselves is perceived as an important future appraisal practice. In contrast, in the Asian countries, expression is used to a low extent, particularly in Korea. In the Latin American countries, the administrative purposes of PA practices are considered important in future practice.

and work experience are all seen as the most important selection criteria today among Anglo countries. Ironically, the shift toward the more Eastern notions of "getting along with others" and "fit to company values" was seen as much more important for the future in the West.

If these best practices vary only slightly all over the world, but vary along critical contextual lines, the company could still encounter difficulties. For example, if an American manager goes to Mexico to recruit or select an employee based on "fit to the corporate values" along with their other top three criteria, they could easily miss their mark if they neglected to use personal recommendations. Similarly, it can be just as disastrous to select managerial employees in France without using a graphology test. Unfortunately, a little knowledge can be a dangerous thing. Companies that use the best practice of selecting on fit but are inattentive to important cultural and contextual elements that contribute to fit will encounter selection difficulties.

Shifts in Training and Development

Globally, the area of training and development (T&D) is moving toward soft management practices, such as team building, understanding business practices, and corporate culture, away from the usual individual training, while individual training remains much more common in Anglo and Latin American countries. Striking here is the universal alignment between these soft management T&D practices and the West meets East selection practices mentioned earlier. Although these T&D practices are common best practices, they, too, must be seen in their proper context.

Consider the Latin American example where we found a large gap between current "is now" practices and future "should be" practices. Why? In Latin America, organizations must accommodate shifts in industry requirements and the need for increased competitiveness; they are in a learning state with respect to modern management techniques. As such, T&D meets the continuous need to upgrade basic skills in labor-intensive industries—thus, the larger the gap between current and future practices, the further their current practices are from their perceived best practices. In contrast, we found no gap between current "is now" practices and future "should be" practices across our Asian sample. Why? In many Asian countries, T&D plays an important role in social mobility and social acceptance. Organizations are committed to T&D; training and development are benefits offered by the organization to reinforce employees' dependence on the organization. T&D is the glue that binds the employee to the organization in a context in which skilled employees, especially those with technical or managerial skills and talents, are a scarce resource. Here, a much smaller gap between current "is now" and future "should be" practices represents the reality that in Asia present T&D practices are closer to perceived future best practices.

Individual Compensation Matters

Despite the extraordinary need for teams in our globally distributed work context, the perception that overall compensation systems *should be* based more on individual level job performance and *not* team or organizational performance is viewed as more effective. However, in these same global firms, overreliance on seniority and pay incentives should *not* comprise much of the overall compensation package. Additionally, benefits should continue to play an important role in all company compensation packages. Thus, at a time when most Anglo countries are seeking greater sophistication in incenting high versus low performers, particularly in teamwork settings, our data suggest the opposite; indeed, from a best practices perspective, pay incentives should not play as instrumental a role as we have always thought.

While the prescription is straightforward, the application is not. In some cultures, for example, People's Republic of China or Mexico, compensation is set at the level of the "state," which also mandates working conditions. In these contexts, the company has relatively few degrees of freedom to manipulate compensation, seniority, and benefit variables. In the United States and Japan, seniority can be a bona fide occupational qualification (BFOQ), and were it to be automatically dismissed in favor of the best practice movement away from seniority-based systems, any U.S. or Japanese company could encounter relative debilitating labor relations problems despite our finding that Japanese companies wanted to get away from reliance on seniority. Thus, any of these findings must examine the contexts within which these best practices emerge as universally endorsed.

Developmental Performance Appraisal

Although ubiquitous, U.S.-based performance appraisals (PAs) have shown to be poorly executed despite their popularity. That finding is not particularly intriguing. What is counterintuitive to us is that *despite* the fact that managers often pay lip service to context, we found that context-specific issues are rarely taken into consideration when executing PAs. For example, in the West we have generally operated under the fairly old assumption of "praise in public, criticize in private." However, there are some cultural contexts, such as Japan or Thailand, where public praise presumes the employee couldn't perform the activity in the first instance, and thus praise can be seen as unintentionally demeaning—only children need public praise. Other cultures revile criticism delivered verbally—it is far more effective with line workers in Mexico to demonstrate the correct way to perform a procedure than to tell workers they did it wrong. Context matters; yet, time after time, we have discovered that company managers assert "company values" or "company PA standards" (euphemism for the corporate way) to dictate the way in which PA is executed—despite the cultural implications of this practice. Is it any wonder that PAs are as unpopular as ever?

This discussion is not to diminish the importance of the PA. Our best practice data suggest that PAs should be used to recognize subordinates, evaluate subordinate goal achievement, plan subordinate development activities, and focus on ways to improve subordinate performance—all developmental ways to change performance.

WHEN IS A BEST PRACTICE NOT BEST FOR PRACTICE?

Researchers, practitioners, HR professionals, and others managing globally must pay much greater attention to the multiple and different contexts within which international business occurs daily. These local contextual issues must not be dismissed as irrelevant to the corporate culture of the parent company. In fact, contextual issues *are critical* and can influence all HR practices that are imposed on the local enterprise, subsidiary, any indigenous peoples, or, indeed, any individual. A best practice is not *best* unless it incorporates contextual elements in its application.

Our findings highlight the critical importance of the ability to manage diversity in organizations, especially those with foreign affiliates *or that source talent globally*. If HR adopts universal best practices—with appropriate consideration of regional best practice, as we suggest—how does this intersect with considerations of managing a globally sourced, diverse workforce? Some of our findings suggest solutions to this dilemma. Selection of leaders and managers who value, espouse, and enable getting along with others and encourage fit to company values is one important step. The primary difference is that these selection practices must be extended to *all* leaders and managers, not simply those who deal with international operations. Leaders and managers holding these soft values are more likely to flex appropriately in the face of the conflicting demands for global HR standardization and local responsiveness—the incorporation of multiple but qualitatively different, embedded cultural contexts. They are the ones who can be the drivers of the polycontextualization that our findings imply.

The effective polycontextualization of HR practices in the workplace requires that leaders and managers—*all* leaders and managers—be armed with knowledge, skills, and capabilities to do so. In today's global organization, *all* leaders and managers must deal with diversity—the diversity driven by the rich cultural and contextual heritage of *all* employees. We can no longer afford to isolate the responsibility for capturing the value that this diversity brings to an isolated organizational function, for example, HR. Consequently, developing leaders and managers who can make sense of poly-contextuality of local responsiveness is key. Ultimately, it is the diffusion of diversity-supportive values and capabilities *throughout* the organization that provides the ability of an organization to balance the demands of best practice.

We believe our "is now/should be" research approach sheds light on those practices global managers want more (or less) of—compared to what they have presently—and reflects their perception of effective practices for the future including how selection, T&D, compensation, and PA should be done for an organization to grow its capabilities.

Our gap analysis reveals some universal best practices that may well contribute to sustainable competitive advantage. Although sustainability (from a resource-based view) is based on inimitable practices, understanding the polycontextuality of an IHRM practice might just provide the organization with the inimitability of such a practice, ultimately resulting in its competitive advantage. This study has contributed to our overall understanding of how context affects IHRM practices. Some of the results are counterintuitive; some reinforce our current thinking about IHRM practices. Nevertheless, best practices—or universals—do not exist independently of context.

NOTE

1. The Best International HRM Practices Consortium, a group of international scholars whose primary interest is in the field of IHRM, initiated the Best Practices Project to explore this question. See M. B. Teagarden, M. A. Von Glinow, D. Bowen, C. Frayne, S. Nason, P. Huo, J. Milliman, M. Arias, M. Butler, N. Kim, H. Scullion, K. Lowe, and E. A. Drost (1995), "Toward Building a Theory of Comparative Management Research Methodology: An Idiographic Case Study of the Best International Human Resources Management Project," *Academy of Management Journal,* 38 (5), 1261–1287, for a full description of the project; and M. A. Von Glinow, E. A. Drost, and M. B. Teagarden (2002), "Converging on IHRM Best Practices: Lessons Learned from a Globally Distributed Consortium on Theory and Practice," *Human Resource Management,* Special Issue, 41 (1), 123–140, for additional elaboration.

CHAPTER 45

BECOMING BUSINESS PARTNERS IN CHINESE FIRMS: CHALLENGES AND OPPORTUNITIES

ARTHUR YEUNG

In a recent HR management seminar, I had the opportunity to work with a group of progressive CEOs in China. Most of these CEOs were entrepreneurs who built their corporate empires from scratch due to the liberalization of the Chinese economy and rapid economic growth in the country. These CEOs, most of them in their 40s, were very bright, ambitious, and doing very well in their respective market niches. As we discussed how to align people and organizations for strategic implementation and what roles HR can contribute, most of them immediately concurred with the importance of people and organization to business success but disagreed on the roles of HR. "These are exactly the issues we are working on, not our HR functions," they argued.

I think the reaction of these CEOs reflects both good news and bad news for the HR professionals in China. The good news is these CEOs appreciate the importance of people and organizations in strategic implementation, and they are paying a lot of attention to these issues. However, the bad news is they have to address these issues based on their intuition and personal judgments. HR professionals have little to contribute to the whole process.

HR professionals in China could and should play a much more proactive and strategic role in local Chinese firms. Many CEOs desperately need help as their firms are facing tremendous challenges and opportunities of growth, globalization, and intensified competition. The following case stories illustrate some typical challenges faced by Chinese firms:

- *Rapid growth:* BenQ, one of the leading Chinese computing and communications firms, is planning to grow from US$3 billion to US$12 billion in the next six years (2002 to 2008). K. Y. Lee, chairman and CEO of BenQ, admits his biggest challenge is not related to marketing opportunities, financial capital, or manufacturing capacities, but to leadership talent to support such rapid growth.

- *Globalization:* TCL, a leading consumer electronics firm based in Southern China, acquired the TV division of Thomson in 2004. The company quickly became the largest supplier of TVs in the world, owning the brands of RCA in the United States, Thomson in Europe, and TCL in Asia. According to Tomson Li, chairman and CEO of TCL, the primary challenges of the company are not to design, manufacture, or sell the products, but to integrate the 9,000-plus Thomson employees that are located in France, the United States, and elsewhere with the 10,000-plus TCL employees that are primarily based in China.

- *Competition:* Acer, one of the top 10 PC firms in the world, faced intense competition from global giants such as Dell, HP, and IBM in the late 1990s. One of the major reasons for its eroding competitiveness during this period was its highly decentralized global operation, which generated severe internal problems in communication, coordination, and collaboration (Shih, Wang, and Yeung, 2004). To regain its competitiveness, Acer needed to overhaul its organizational design and build global teamwork.

As many Chinese firms are wrestling with the challenges and opportunities of growth, globalization, and intensified competition, there are clear opportunities for HR professionals to add value. Unfortunately, the current reality is that HR professionals are still not credible enough to play the role of business partner in most Chinese firms. HR professionals in China, similar to those in other developing countries such as Russia or Southeast Asia, tend to be more administrative and operational oriented when their companies operate in a relatively stable, less competitive, and more homogeneous business environment. However, such an era is quickly disappearing as China becomes more fully integrated into the global economy and its domestic economy rapidly takes off. In view of such economic transition, this chapter first describes how most Chinese firms are being managed and what roles HR professionals are playing. Then, we offer suggestions for what HR professionals should and should not do to add value to their organizations.

HOW MOST CHINESE FIRMS ARE MANAGED

Partly due to the impact of Chinese culture and partly due to their resource scarcity, many Chinese prefer to manage their firms based on trust, relationships, shared entrepreneurial success, and market responsiveness. This type of entrepreneurial management model is prevalent among not only privately owned firms in China but also Chinese firms in Taiwan, Hong Kong, Singapore, and Southeast Asia (Redding, 1993). The typical Chinese management approach has the following characteristics:

- *Founder/owner as the glue of integration.* The founder/owner builds the company by recruiting a group of core managers that can be trusted based on a common bond: attending the same school/university, having worked for the same company, coming from the same place of origin, or family ties. This group is managed based on a high level of trust and shared economic interests, not through formal control or monitoring systems. These managers are often entrusted with a high level of autonomy as long as they are competent and committed. The founder/owner is the reason that these managers work together. They all work closely and directly with the founder/owner. However, these managers do not owe much loyalty or commitment to each other.
- *Organizations are operated with powerful networks, not just formal structures.* The group of core managers that the founder/owner recruited in turn recruits people they can trust to work in their teams or units. As a result, networks are created within a larger network. The control and coordination mechanisms are through personal trust and loyalty rather than formal systems, processes, and policies. The line functions are very strong while staff functions such as HR are often very weak.

- *Career promotion and reward are tied to both relationship and performance.* Due to the underdeveloped management processes and systems, reward and career development opportunities are largely tied to the personal judgment of these core managers, not to transparent criteria and processes. As a result, these opportunities reinforce the culture of personal relationships and loyalty within these companies.
- *With very limited resources, the founder/owner cannot afford high base salaries for the core managers; however, they are treated as partners to create wealth through shared success.* As a result, core managers often have an ownership stake, and their performance is primarily measured by the sales and profit they generate, not their leadership styles and behaviors.
- *In terms of culture, firms operate more like* adhocracy *(things always change fast and very flexible) and* clan *(value people loyalty and harmony over systems and processes; Cameron and Quinn, 1999).* Founder/owners are often against overelaborate systems and processes because these organizational infrastructures are viewed as slowing things down and consuming profit producing business energy.
- *Strategic planning is more opportunity driven than opportunity driving.* Founder/owners outline a broad vision and key strategic goals to be achieved in the next 5 or 10 years. However, specific strategies and plans are much less clear, all depending on specific business opportunities.

In summary, this management approach is flexible, low cost, fast, and result driven because most key players have a strong stake in the firm's success. This management approach is prevalent in the start-up phase of many Chinese firms. However, in the Western context, many firms formalize their structure, systems, and processes as they grow larger. What makes Chinese firms special is that they seem to resist the formalization of the organizational operation and continue to rely on people/relationships as their primary integrating mechanism even when the organizations grow reasonably large (> 10,000 employees and billions of dollars in revenue). Working in this management context, HR professionals are often asked to take care of routine administrative tasks while CEOs and core managers maintain the power to make key decisions related to people and organization.

When the CEOs in the seminar described the HR function in their companies, they presented this exact scenario.

HOW CAN HR ADD VALUE?

As many Chinese firms face the challenges and opportunities of growth, globalization, and intensified competition, the time has arrived for HR professionals to add more value. When a Chinese firm has to grow very fast in both size and complexity, the major weaknesses of prevalent management approach are obvious, as follows:

- *Talent management and development:* The current approach relies heavily on the personal trust and subjective judgment of core managers in identifying and developing talent rather than on transparent HR criteria and processes. However, the lack of consistency and transparency in HR systems often creates a wide range of issues including the quality of talent being identified, perceived fairness of the system, movement of talent across units, and retention of key talent.

- *Diversity and assimilation of new members:* Strong reliance on informal networks makes an organization less open and receptive to new organizational members, especially people from different cultures and at senior levels. Unfortunately, as Chinese firms need to globalize in business operation and collaboration, the ability to integrate and leverage the contribution of talent from different parts of the world is not only necessary but also critical.

- *Turf and horizontal boundaries:* To encourage the strong entrepreneurial spirit of key managers and their performance accountability, Chinese firms often link the reward/career development of these managers to the results of their business units. Coupled with the strong bonding between these managers and their subordinates, organizational turf and boundary problems are often the price to bear in the traditional Chinese management approach. As the companies grow larger, more global, and more complex, the problems of cross-unit collaboration can become so serious that they may outweigh the benefits of speed, flexibility, and entrepreneurialism.

In the face of these HR/organizational challenges, how can HR add value to business success? There are both do's and don'ts. The most obvious don't is that HR professionals in Chinese firms should not blindly copy HR practices that are highly publicized in the West without fully understanding the organizational context they operate in. In the past few years, the HR practices of GE, Southwest Airlines, NUMMI, and so on have been highly publicized in the management literature because of the extraordinary results these companies deliver for shareholders, customers, and employees. When many HR professionals read and learn about these practices with great admiration, they often hope that such HR practices can be implemented in their firms. Unfortunately, this is an unrealistic aspiration for several reasons. First, the HR practices of these excellent companies are not all the same and sometimes even contradictory to each other. Second, the successful implementation of these practices very much depends on the deeply held business philosophy of their CEOs such as Jack Welch or Herb Kelleher. It is unrealistic to expect other CEOs to think like them. Third, each company has its own history and administrative heritage. If a company has been run by a group of business entrepreneurs, don't expect them to spend too much time on HR processes and forms. If the CEO or senior executives have been managing people based on personal relationships and loyalty for years, don't expect them to implement a "bottom 10% policy" and get rid of their long-term but substandard cadres easily. Like it or not, these are the cards you are dealt, and it is useless to complain about the company or CEO.

On the contrary, it is unwise to abandon the competitive strengths of Chinese firms in entrepreneurship, speed, flexibility, and low costs and impose them with complex and sophisticated systems that Chinese firms are not used to. This will only put these firms in a disadvantageous catch-up mode and lose their competitive differentiation. Instead, I suggest two possible routes for HR to add value in Chinese firms.

The first route to adding value is to work with the CEO to fully leverage the competitive strengths of the firm while avoiding the problems associated with size and complexity. For a few years, Stan Shih (chairman and CEO of Acer Group) and I have been trying to develop an organizational model called *Internet Organization*. The objective is to develop a new organizational design that further enhances the speed and flexibility of Acer through a network of highly autonomous business units that are linked together to fully enjoy and leverage the synergy of a few critical resources such as brand, intellectual properties, talent development, and procurement. To avoid the challenges of size and complexity, operating units that have grown to a certain size will be split up to maintain focus and flexibility. This is just one of the ways that HR professionals can add value to business success by developing innovative organizational models or processes that further magnify the competitive strengths of their firms while avoiding the problems associated with size and complexity.

The second possible route to add value is to pinpoint key organizational bottlenecks and develop a few highly targeted interventions. The thought process behind this approach is to build credibility through small wins while avoiding the pitfalls and unrealistic expectations of overhauling the entire organization at the same time. Some examples of focused interventions to address the common problems of leadership development, diversity, and organizational boundaries are:

- Develop a more rigorous and transparent process/system for a select, high-potential talent pool while leaving the others to follow the traditional management approach.
- Recruit senior talent from outside to supplement expertise lacking within the company. Provide strong support for assimilation based on mentoring by the CEO or other key executives.
- Introduce job rotation for key executives to avoid turf-building activities.
- Design the incentive schemes of senior executives based on a balanced mix between individual performance and team performance (e.g., 60 percent tied to their unit performance and 40 percent tied to the overall company performance).

It is too risky and ambitious for HR professionals to resolve too many problems at the same time as this process often leads to failure and disappointment.

As many Chinese firms are going through the exciting phase of growth and transformation, it is time for HR professionals to add more value to business success by working closely with CEOs to build a competitive organization that leverages the entrepreneurial strengths of Chinese firms while enhancing their organizational capacity for growth. There is no simple answer or solution to this challenge, and much more thinking and experimentation is required. However, I do look forward to the time when CEOs in many Chinese firms testify, "Our HR professionals have done a wonderful job in helping us transform our companies into highly competitive global firms."

REFERENCES

Cameron, Kim, and Robert E. Quinn. (1999). *Diagnosing and Changing Organizational Culture: Based on the Competing Values Framework*. New York: Pearson Education.

Redding, Gordon. (1993). *The Spirit of Chinese Capitalism*. Berlin: Walter de Gruyter.

Shih, Stan, J. T. Wang, and Arthur Yeung. (2004). "Building Global Competitiveness in a Turbulent Environment: Acer's Journey of Transformation." In William Mobley and Ellie Weldon (Eds.), *Advances in Global Leadership* (Vol. 4) Amsterdam: JAI Press.

CONCLUSION

REALITY, IMPACT, AND PROFESSIONALISM

MICHAEL R. LOSEY, SUSAN R. MEISINGER, AND DAVE ULRICH

In introductory statistics, we learn that we should not create averages of averages. The resulting average is not an accurate reflection of the original data. We now violate this expectation by creating a synthesis of the 45 syntheses that have been presented in this volume. Each author offered a personal perspective about the future of HR. We now try to cull common themes that emerge from these thoughtful syntheses.

We have identified eight major trends that these 64 observers believe will affect HR in the future: Three of these themes shape a new reality for HR (what it is), two define the impact of HR (what it means), and three suggest the profile of the future HR professional (who it is). The reality, impact, and professional will change as HR evolves and morphs.

THE NEW REALITY FOR HR: WHAT IT IS

The adage, "See the world as it is, not as we would like it to be," applies to HR as well as the world. At times, HR professionals declare their value without knowing why. To fully appreciate the importance of HR, we need to look outside, not inside, the profession. What we declare matters less than what we deliver. And, what we deliver can best be understood by understanding the context of our work. HR adds value because the HR work meets essential needs in any organization—corporate, not for profit, or governmental. Those who proactively use HR services do so not merely to comply but to succeed. Trends of the new reality include:

1. *The world is changing in ways that put HR in the spotlight.* Without question, change is constant. Many of the chapters highlight the changes facing leaders in the future:

   • *Demographics:* While it is debatable whether the rate of labor force growth is expanding or shrinking, it is inevitably changing. Aging employees, gender and ethnic diversity, global heterogeneity, and social and economic changes have changed the makeup of the workforce today and tomorrow.

   • *Technology:* Technology has advanced quickly, forcing organizations to change their strategy and product mix and changing the way HR is organized and delivered.

   • *Globalization:* The global village has arrived with information ubiquity and sensitivity. Just as organizations compete globally for products, so must they for talent.

   • *Competitiveness:* Customer expectations have risen dramatically, and customer flexibility forces firms to respond quickly and dramatically.

   HR must respond to each of these, and other, forces for change. Talented, increasingly mobile employees have choices. HR should take the lead in winning the hearts and minds of these employees rather then trying to capture feet and hands. HR should help organizations adapt to technological change and find ways to use technology for HR in more efficient and effective ways. Technology can free HR professionals from the historical administrative yoke they have had to carry and provide new tools for improved productivity and performance. HR needs to understand how to manage people and organization in a global economy. HR needs to build bonds with customers to ensure competitiveness.

   The spotlight now shines on HR. Organizations with effective HR systems win; those without them do not. The decision science of HR is emerging to codify the specifics of how HR matters, but inevitably HR matters. HR professionals need to go beyond accepting or responding to change and anticipate, appreciate, and master change.

2. *HR has become a profession with a body of knowledge, set of standards, and operational norms.* While relatively new, the HR profession already has a history. The names and responsibility have shifted: industrial relations, personnel, employee relations, human resource

management, and people management. Few doubt anymore that HR should "go away," and most now debate the form and shape of HR going forward. What is clear is that the body of knowledge will expand and standards will become even more explicit and demanding.

HR practitioners can enter and grow throughout their professional lives. Their work is purposeful. When HR effectively contributes to the interests of the organization as well as the people within it, enormous impact is possible. The prize is great personal satisfaction.

3. *Line managers are more accountable than ever for HR.* Collaboration grounds the HR partnership. HR professionals do not operate in a vacuum. They almost always work through line managers who bear ultimate responsibility for overall business results. They sometimes work with other staff to build stronger organizations. Examples abound:

- Collaboration with financial experts informs intangibles and builds market value.
- Collaboration with marketing and sales experts builds customer connection and share.
- Collaboration with manufacturing experts ensures productivity and operational efficiency.
- Collaboration with public relations creates consistent messages and cultural artifacts that shape a firm brand.

HR professionals who learn to collaborate impact more than those who work alone.

THE IMPACT OF HR: WHAT IT MEANS

We should not be surprised that when we ask thoughtful colleagues to talk about the future of HR, few talk about techniques or programs. Most talk about the outcomes of HR practices. In a simplistic way, we can identify two targets of HR outcomes: employees and organizations. Because of investments in HR (staffing, training, communication, performance management, communication, etc.), employees are more able to do what they need to do to help their organization succeed, and organizations are more able to compete in global markets. Both employee *ability* and organization *capability* derive from wise HR investments. Trends of the impact of HR include:

1. *HR investments increase employee abilities.* Employees represent the hidden wealth of organizations; it's the intellectual or human capital. Organizations with more talented employees will win over time; those with less talented employees will lose. We joke at times that the most strategic HR decision is to place your poorest performing employees in your competitor and hope that they stay for some time. Employees need to have energy and passion through shared goals, participation in processes, and a viable employee contract.

   When employees are properly placed, trained, and incented, they produce. It behooves HR professionals to get, keep, and grow people. Mastering the tools for enhancing employee abilities is both the heritage and future for HR professionals. HR professionals coach, architect, design, facilitate, and lead the process of developing employee ability.

2. *HR investments should increase organization capabilities.* Capabilities represent the personality or identity of the organization. An organization is known for something that shapes its culture. These capabilities are the deliverables of HR, the intangibles for investors. In this volume, we shed some light on some of the possible future capabilities:

   - *Strategy execution:* HR should help make strategy happen. HR no longer needs to ask to be at the strategy table, but is and will be a critical part of the strategy team. HR professionals ensure strategic clarity.
   - *Culture change:* HR plays an important role in defining the culture of a company. The culture represents the firm brand, norms, and values of the company. It is shaped by HR practices around hiring, training, paying, and communicating with employees. It is sustained when people make the company culture part of their personal identity and when customers and investors act on the culture.
   - *Collaboration:* HR makes sure that the whole is better than the sum of the parts by ensuring that information and people are shared across boundaries. Collaboration may be vertical between managers and employees, horizontal between business units as a network, and personal between individuals in a team. With cooperation, a new definition of power emerges where authority and accountability are shared.

- *Globalization:* HR creates practices that enable global leverage and local responsiveness. HR must shape some HR practices that ensure consistency across geographic boundaries and have some HR practices that adapt to local conditions. Emerging markets such as China and India will provide enormous opportunity for future HR challenges.
- *Social responsibility:* Increasingly, firms must deal with transparency where internal operations are exposed to external scrutiny. HR professionals can ensure that value is created by espousing and practicing values. Ethics is not abstract ideals and debates, but day-to-day behaviors that are ensured in HR practices.

THE HR PROFESSIONAL OF THE FUTURE: WHO IT IS

Trends for the future HR professional include:

1. *HR professionals will play new roles.* Roles represent what is done; competencies capture how it is done. With the inevitable business changes ahead and with the spotlight on HR, HR professionals play emerging roles, including:
   - *Chief integrative officer:* responsible for connecting disparate parts within a company
   - *Deliverer of business success:* participant in the success of the enterprise
   - *Diversity manager:* responsible for helping manage all types of employee diversity
   - *Employee champion:* responsible for human capital
   - *Productivity czar:* responsible for doing more with less
   - *Chief effectiveness officer or expert:* responsible for making the organization, not just people, effective

   As they play these roles, HR professionals will have more visibility and responsibility. We see these roles playing out even more in small- and medium-size companies where HR generalists must wear multiple hats and not rely on specialists to accomplish their work.

2. *HR professionals must have new competencies.* The competencies required to play old and new roles will grow. The body of knowledge is becoming ever more complex; thus HR professionals must become more adept at responding. We envision HR professionals becoming competent in:

- Mastering the decision science of HR
- Understanding and managing people
- Discerning, creating, and adapting culture to business conditions
- Rethinking organizations as capabilities, not structures
- Conceiving globally, acting locally
- Creating collaboration throughout the organization
- Responding to social expectations and public policy
- Learning to play new roles

  To demonstrate these competencies, HR professionals must be:
- *Competent:* knowledgeable in HR basics
- *Curious:* willing to seek and try new things
- *Courageous:* willing to take bold stands and have a point of view
- *Caring:* willing to think about and nurture people

  The HR professional of the future will pass certification tests to ensure knowledge, but also relationship equity tests to ensure impact.

3. *HR professionals must invest in themselves.* As the profession evolves, so must they. Professional development may come from:

- *Training:* HR education will be required, and certification will continue to grow as a baseline for required HR profession knowledge. This training should emphasize the decision science that is emerging in HR. This education may come from companies who invest in the next generation and/or from associations that are responsible for the development of the overall profession.
- *Development:* HR professionals will need exposure to multiple assignments to learn from experience. These assignments might be movement within the HR community (e.g., from specialist to generalist), within the organization (e.g., from staff role in HR to line manager role leading a business), or outside the organization (e.g., from a consulting firm to operating within a firm).
- *Selection:* Selection will be more demanding than ever with HR professionals selected based on their ability to play roles and

demonstrate competencies. No longer can HR professionals drop in as a casual second career.

- *Performance accountability:* HR professionals who do not measure up will be moved out. The marginal candidate will be at risk.

The real value of focusing on the future is to anticipate what might happen and commit to action today. While we don't know the future, we are optimistic about the profession's ability to respond to it. By raising the issues and encouraging dialogues that the chapters in this volume provoke, we are confident that the future will be shaped with new assumptions and challenges. These ideas challenge us to experiment with new ideas, methods, and actions. We are confident in HR professionals' ability to learn and respond.

INDEX

SELECTED TITLES FROM THE SOCIETY FOR HUMAN RESOURCE MANAGEMENT (SHRM®)

Diverse Teams at Work
By Lee Gardenswartz and Anita Rowe

HR Source Book Series

HIPAA Privacy Source Book
By William S. Hubbartt, SPHR, CCP

Hiring Source Book
By Catherine D. Fyock

Performance Appraisal Source Book
By Mike Deblieux

Trainer's Diversity Source Book
By Jonamay Lambert & Selma Myers

Human Resource Essentials: Your Guide to Starting and Running the HR Function
By Lin Grensing-Pophal, SPHR

Practical HR Series

Legal, Effective References: How to Give and Get Them
By Wendy Bliss, J.D., SPHR

Investigating Workplace Harassment: How to Be Fair, Thorough, and Legal
By Amy Oppenheimer, J.D., and Craig Pratt, MSW, SPHR

Quick! Show Me Your Value
By Theresa Seagraves

Supervisor's Guide to Labor Relations
By T.O. Collier, Jr.

Understanding the Federal Wage & Hour Laws
By Seyfarth Shaw Attorneys LLP

TO ORDER SHRM BOOKS

SHRM offers a member discount on all books that it publishes or sells. To order this or any other book published by the Society, contact the SHRMStore®.

ONLINE: www.shrm.org/shrmstore

BY PHONE: 800-444-5006 (option #1); or 770-442-8633 (ext. 362); or TDD 703-548-6999

BY FAX: 770-442-9712

BY MAIL: SHRM Distribution Center
P.O. Box 930132
Atlanta, GA 31193-0132
USA